Madmen
and the Bourgeoisie

For Renate

On the relationship between the naturalness of
resistance and the resilience of nature

Madmen
and the Bourgeoisie
A Social History of Insanity and Psychiatry

KLAUS DOERNER

Translated by Joachim Neugroschel and Jean Steinberg

BASIL BLACKWELL · OXFORD

English translation © Basil Blackwell Publisher Limited 1981

First published in German as
Bürger und Irre
© Europäische Verlagsanstalt 1969

English translation first published 1981
Basil Blackwell Publisher Limited
108 Cowley Road
Oxford OX4 1JF
England

British Library Cataloguing in Publication Data
Doerner, Klaus
Madmen and the bourgeoisie.
1. Mentally ill — Europe — History
2. Psychiatry — History
I. Title   II. Burger und Irre. *English*
362.2'042'094   RC455

ISBN 0-631-10181-0

Typesetting by Janice Buchanan, Gerrards Cross, Bucks.
Printed and bound in Great Britain by
The Camelot Press, Southampton

Contents

Introduction   1

I Great Britain

1 The Sequestration of Irrationality
  and the Public   20

2 Industrial Revolution, Romanticism,
  Psychiatric Paradigm   34

3 The Reform Movement
  and the Dialectics of Restraint   64

II France

1 Early Theoretical and Practical
  Measures for the Abolition
  of the Ancien Régime   98

2 The Revolution
  and the Emancipation of the Insane   119

3 Psychiatric-Sociological
  Positivism   139

III Germany

1 Mercantilism and the Cultured
  Bourgeoisie (Bildungsbürgertum)   164

2 Revolution from Above and
  the Obstructed Psychiatric Paradigm   193

3 From the Restoration
  to Bourgeois-Natural Scientific
  Liberalism   227

Appendix: Criteria for a Historiography
   of Psychiatry   292

Notes   301

Index   347

Introduction

A sociological view of the origin of psychiatry as a science requires an appreciation of sociology as a historical and comparative discipline and as a science of knowledge. These formal qualifications are indicated by the subtitle of this book, while the title itself, *Madmen and the Bourgeoisie* defines its contents. Its theme is the relationship between the insane and the community that made psychiatrists its professional surrogates in its dealings with the insane. If the insane represent the "object" of psychiatrists, the deranged and the psychiatrists may be called the object of this attempt to explore underlying socio-economic, political, and cultural conditions. These, together with the political and industrial-capitalist bourgeois social revolution, produced that relationship between its citizens and the insane which became the science of psychiatry. In this framework, the investigation focuses particularly on three issues that might appeal to a wider audience than would psychiatry alone. First, it traces the dialectics of modern science between its emancipatory claim in keeping with the promise of the Enlightenment and its consequent rationalization and integration of existing society. Second, the reflection that the bourgeoisie established psychiatry specifically for the *poor* insane leads to the awareness that these thematic processes were one aspect of the class struggle, as well as an early solution to the incipient "social question." This inquiry thus not only seeks to contribute to a self-examination of psychiatry, but also to shed light on a hitherto ignored root and incipient form of sociology. Third, the discussion centers on the relationship of the rational and irrational (in the form of health and disease) in the institutions of bourgeois society and in the domestic arrangements of its members.

So much for the topic and the objectives of this investigation. The unexamined or poorly studied relationship between psychiatrists and sociologists may bring the reproach that the one or the other group might find the following elaborations superfluous. Some might feel that this work might just as well have begun with the third section of this chapter. However, I feel that the two introductory sections do contribute some observations of potential interest to both psychiatrists and sociologists.

The relationship between sociology and psychiatry often takes the form of a superficial acceptance of the ideas of the one by the other, or the acceptance of the authority of the one by the other. Just as psychiatry toys with sociological "approaches" — or rather, with social statistics and social services — nearly all schools of sociology, particularly since the days of Freud, use psychiatric concepts, some of which are gradually beginning to replace economic analyses. This had led sociology into a crucial error: willy-nilly, it has equated psychoanalysis with psychiatry, thereby obscuring the fact that psychoanalysis was really a late, even though important product of scientific psychiatric thought that predated Freud by more than a hundred years. It also obscured an ongoing process: the loosening of the ties that bind psychiatry to both philosophy and medicine, not unlike the similarly problematic emancipation of sociology from philosophy and economics. This ahistorical, restrictive approach lent support to a view of psychiatrists, as widespread among sociologists who deal with its categories as it is among laymen, that puts psychiatry's two symbols — mental hospital and couch — side by side without relating one to the other, or else naively celebrates the victory of couch over hospital.

Why, we may ask, did sociology respond to psychoanalysis but not to earlier psychiatric approaches? What lent psychoanalysis its special aura was its claim of having put psychological disorders, from symptoms, etiology, pathogenesis to treatment, into the context of a continuous logical progression: starting with neuroses, it extends this model to psychoses (more resistant to diagnosis) and human behavior in general. One of the most fascinating aspects of Freudian concepts is the fact that their psychological substance cannot be divorced from anatomical, physiological, and neurological factors on the one hand,[1] and from sociological notions on the other. Methodologically, this is matched by Freud's failure to draw a sharp line between the natural sciences and the humanities, between the formulation of untested hypotheses and hermeneutics.[2] This tension, rooted in the very real problems of the subject matter of psychiatry, was not maintained by those who came after Freud. In the United States, psychoanalysis turned into behaviorism, or its biological aspect was eradicated; only then, in the more harmless form of the "cultural school" (Sullivan, Horney, Thompson, Fromm), was it able to influence the structural and functional theory of sociology; or else the "mental health" movement, in a total reversal of Freud's critical impulse, turned it into enthusiasm for various self-help techniques.[3] In Germany, following Husserl and Heidegger, psychoanalysis took a neo-ontological turn, and, robbed of its daring, found a home in schools of anthropology, existentialism, and existential analysis. This process was indirectly helped by National Socialism, which eliminated by force the threat posed by psychoanalysis.

This development corresponded to that of a sociology which, with Durkheim, Max Weber, and Mannheim, went through a process of repsychologization, ending up in a theory of interpersonal relations. In the United States it managed to combine the "subjectively intended meaning" with the existing social "system," or simply turned into a model for adjusting to the mores and attitudes of society. Methodologically, this schema either branched out into a science of hypotheses and hermeneutic humanities, or, with the aid of the continuity provided by categories of subjective meaning, ensured its historical rationality.

It would thus appear that the convergence of sociology and post-Freudian psychiatry resulted in a narrowed view, in the partial blockage of the underlying reality of both disciplines, specifically the areas offering the greatest resistance to a rational and meaningful mastery of nature. In psychiatry this applies in particular to psychotics, the core group of those who in earlier days were called the insane, who are either perceived as a species of neurotic and thus not put into proper perspective, or else assigned a separate, autonomous "world" of meaning by existential analysis. This latter process may strive for a greater understanding of the patient, but in fact it tends to obscure the seriousness of the disturbance, or rather the disease. All recent psychiatric theories, whatever their claims, are undone by the simple fact that neither the couch nor the existential encounter with the Thou could affect the harsh necessity of insane asylums, even in their euphemistic transformation into "psychiatric hospitals."[4] This troubling fact is precisely the reason for the exclusion of institutional psychiatry from the more exacting formal theory: attaching the label of "applied psychiatry" to institutional practice relegates it to a mere technical-administrative area outside the realm of theory. This narrow view also victimizes the so-called psychopaths (now also referred to as sociopaths) and the so-called sexually abnormal or perverted. They find themselves in the absurd position of being theorized about within the framework of a sociologizing model of neurosis oriented toward adjustment, while in practice they are left to the mercies of medical technology, administrative measures, and courts of law. Some even believe that the physical manifestations of psychological disorders are deterrents to theory. Likewise, the selection of promising candidates for theoretical experiments or therapy on the basis of social status, income, and intellectual achievement is by no means a thing of the past.[5] Furthermore, theoretical and therapeutic categories originate in the normative definitions of the prevailing cultural environment.

The same tendency underlies all these factors. Psychiatry seeks to dim the deeply disturbing and uncontrollable phenomena of nature and render nature itself harmless, so that what remains can be dealt with theoretically within a harmonious, humane, and scientific framework. A grandiose process of camouflage idealizes nature. Praxis is limited to hard-to-verify success in individual cases, or becomes purely administrative. This development tries to legitimize itself as a reaction to the naturalistic, materialistic nineteenth century. Yet, as in other sciences, this, if not an outright falsification, is an ideologizing simplification. For looked at from a broader viewpoint, we find that the psychiatric approaches of the nineteenth century replaced the natural-philosophical and ideal-normative frame of reference with a psychological presentation that combined the various subject areas with the constructs of the natural sciences. They did so out of an unwillingness to relinquish the claim to knowledge of their specific fields, although they were fully aware of the utopian character of every possible "not yet" explanation. Psychiatric theory after Freud, in so far as it failed to reflect or retain the claims of the eighteenth and nineteenth centuries, deprived itself of its natural-philosophic, ideal-normative, and also its utopian, expository dimension. As a result it became more deeply involved in the universal socialization process of the sciences: change can take place only through adjustment to the very social system that, according to theory, had caused the psychiatric disorder. This self-normative trend gained ascendancy when mental health, which, after all, is nothing more than a means, came to be seen as the universally aspired to objective.[6]

Precisely this dissociation of theory and practice, as well as their socialization, demonstrates psychiatry's deep involvement in the dialectic of serving both the emancipation of suffering individuals and the integration of society, i.e., the restraining of disruptive, destructive, disintegrating forces: in other words, the "dialectics of enlightenment." This same dialectics of the promise of emancipation and the quest for stability also dominates the beginning and continuing development of sociology. Another feature common to both sociology and psychiatry is their approach to phenomena the right-thinking bourgeois views as irrational, whether it be poverty or insanity or a combination of both. Our investigation is based on these critical factors common to both, for they conceal and exclude less than the previously mentioned "positive" points, and lend themselves more readily to the creation of a reflective relationship between sociology and psychiatry.

The aim of bringing psychiatry and sociology into a satisfactory dialogue via reflection on their precarious and ambivalent social situation can perhaps be made more tangible by a brief excursus into Horkheimer and Adorno's *Dialectics of Enlightenment*, a work that ranges so widely over the problems of sociology that psychiatry is bound to profit from it. The Enlightenment in their critical view is the "submission of everything natural to the autocratic subject," whereby matter was to be mastered without the "illusion of ruling or inherent powers, of hidden qualities," and recognized as chaos, hence as totally in need of synthesis to control it. If control and self-control, compulsive self-preservation, "subjugation of nature...within and without" is made "the absolute purpose of life," then everything outside that ordering and decreeing incursion must appear as an "absolute threat" to society, a source of anxiety, and thus is stigmatized and cast out as irrationality, unreason: for instance "uncomprehended, threatening nature"; "pure, natural existence"; instincts, fantasy, and theoretical imagination; "promiscuity and asceticism, excess and hunger...as powers of disintegration"; the unlinkable, the leap, pluralism, the incommensurable, cut off from "universal mediation in the relation of any one existent to any other"; "the unknown in the anticipatory identification," is marked as "the well-known"; "the very last insulating instance between individual behavior and the social norm," and authority removed by positivism; "the self-abandonment of thought and that of pleasure"; and the universal "dread of losing the self," a fear that exists so long as self-preservation, the finding of identity, remains the only governing social principle.[7]

These various expressions of so-called irrationality are merely catalogued here, not interpreted. We will come across them again as expressions of the irrationality of insanity, even though we will not be able to explore these conceptual qualities individually. In any case, they mark off the subject area of psychiatry, which encompasses those incommensurable and hence "irrational" by-products and correlates of the continuous enlightening, rationalizing, and normative process. Thus psychiatry too is inevitably caught in the same dialectics: should it, for the sake of rationalization, cover up or reveal, accommodate or clarify the unreason put into its care? For although psychiatry may owe its content and its very existence to the summarizing process of the Enlightenment as well as to its extension and countermovement — Romanticism — it has also been influenced by the irrevocable claim of the Enlightenment to be the "redemption of the hopes of the past";[8] exposing the unknown itself regardless of the rational anxiety this is sure to evoke; "to recognize the domination, even in thought itself, as unreconciled nature," and thus no longer "exchange freedom for the pursuit of self-preservation,"[9] whereby the "fractures of reason"[10] are preserved and absorbed, not cast out as irrational.

The relationship between sociology and psychiatry is thus more than a mere outward exchange of concepts and authority for the sake of the formalization of the two sciences. Nor does it consist of providing sociology with a new analytical instrument, just as social psychiatry for example — in the tradition of public health and social medicine — can be understood only in technical and administrative terms, divorced from any social or historical context or theory of science. At issue is the search for the communalities subsumed under the heading of a dialectic of emancipation and integration, as the connecting link to the answer to the "social question" and to the development of bourgeois, industrial-capitalist society in the name of reason. And the common features could reveal the content shared by both these sciences. Within this framework, an investigation like ours is necessary whenever "the social self-understanding of science...is contained as a demand in the concept of science itself."[11] Its critical criterium of truth — transcending a sociology of knowledge concerned solely with the existential condition — lies in the dialectical concept of enlightenment.

The Realm of Psychiatry and the Sociology of Knowledge

Once the goals of our inquiry have been outlined, the question

arises to what extent recent historio-theoretical accounts of psychiatry have dealt with these problems. This question is treated in
the Appendix (p. 292). The findings are paltry, yet even this poor
result helps to clarify the problem. For one thing, it tells us that
our investigation must be mainly descriptive and historical, that it
must spread the knowledge of the connection between psychiatric
ideas and action (although some readers might find the conceptual content of the inquiry unsatisfactory). Beyond that, it reveals
which aspects relevant to psychiatry have been excluded, narrowed, presented one-sidedly, or have failed ideologically to
come to terms with their own claims. This, conversely, determines
how the reader will view and think about the subject of our
investigation.

The history of psychiatry and psychiatry itself, certainly since
the 1920s, have been shaped mainly by the negation of the
nineteenth-century approach to the natural sciences. Their critique of the latter's reifying, decreeing, and atomizing tendencies
does, of course, become dubious, given the blanket indictment of
causal-analytical thought as falsifying and inadequate. The exclu-
siveness and tiresome reiteration of this critique leads one to
suspect that the new equivalents of the rejected theory also
lack persuasiveness, that the attack on the natural sciences was
detrimental to the object, practice, and self-understanding of
psychiatry, and that at the same time other — sociological —
factors that help science arrive at insights went unheeded.

However objectifying the anatomical, physiological, or sensual-
psychological hypotheses of nineteenth- (and eighteenth-) century
psychiatrists may have been, still, despite — or possibly because of
— this detachment they remained involved in their subject, the
suffering of human beings. And however controlling and officious
their conduct, they did release the insane from their chains and
moral restraints of absolutism, rationalism, and romantic philosophy. Although they may ideologically have pursued a one-sided
causal theory to the point of totalitarian absurdity, precisely in
this (inadmissible) generalization they remained interested in the
suffering human beings under their care, they did insist upon their
(utopian) postulate of an etiological explanation, and were rewarded by partial success. Their theories may not have grasped
either the wholeness of the individual or the meaning of suffering,
but they were concerned with actual treatment, and they drew
upon the available technical tools of other disciplines, acting upon
the liberal-enlightened view that human suffering was reversible.

Ever since the 1920s, and more particularly since 1945, there has been a growing tendency to pit the humanities against the natural sciences, the alleged culprit in the dark side of the Enlightenment, or alternatively to dilute them through existential analysis. Psychiatry, logically incoherent, simultaneously a natural science and a humane discipline, was in the twenties welded into a psychopathology and subsequently given a metaphysical (Spoerri) or an anthropological base (Tellenbach). Human suffering has been supplanted by the suffering human being. The individual is now seen as a whole, in his "conditional union of self and world" (Tellenbach), in the uniqueness of his existence in his world. Yet at the same time, mental illness — as in Romanticism — is given anthropological standing: it is the product of man's existential condition (Tellenbach); as a universal existential possibility, it is to be accepted as "a given totality" (Leibbrand); its manifestations become transparent for its being (Wyrsch), or respectively metaphysically identical with its essence — akin to a work of art (Spoerri). Poetically, it can then be brought back from a state of confusion to a "metaphysically ordered space" (Schöne).

This makes possible a dialogue, an encounter between existences, between "worlds." No psychiatry since the days of Romanticism has presented a closer relation to, and more immediate "application" of, a contemporary philosophy than this existential-anthropological model. Nor has any psychiatry experienced greater difficulties in mediating philosophy with its own assigned empirical area. The dialectic of the Enlightenment is obviously still with us. The asserted direct approach to the individual in his life with and among others gives rise to the suspicion that the acknowledgment of empirical reality was a mere formality.[12] The postulated continuity of ideas makes us suspect that it serves to cover up a break in this flow — a claim that cannot be countered because it cannot be verified.[13] The inroads of unlimited and ruthless understanding, of interpreting, of lending meaning to that which has no meaning, can become so pervasive as to be more totalitarian than the hypotheses of natural history.[14] The faith of the Enlightenment, no matter how utopian, in the possibility of eradicating suffering forfeits its validity when suffering is endowed with an anthropological basis and metaphysical dignity. From here it is only a short step to a romantic assumption that man is responsible for his suffering. Understanding is extended to the individual, not to the illness, which, under the guise of historicity, is biographically incorporated into man.

Psychiatric theory thus is no longer in danger — as it was in the nineteenth century — of losing its relationship to philosophy, but rather of exhausting itself in bad philosophy. It relinquishes its own traditional claim: to understand its object, mental illness, to mediate its causal explanation, and to supervise a treatment aimed at altering the person. The gulf separating metaphysical interpretation, the various disciplines engaged in etiological and therapeutic research, and the mass practice of institutions is wider today than in the nineteenth century.

These neglected conditions are the very ones that define the object of our inquiry more precisely. The question is how certain extremes in human thought and action could be viewed and thought of as mental disorders, systematically subjected to a causal analysis, and — building on this — subjected to rectification. For it was this unity of theoretical view, analysis, and practice that made possible the creation of a science in this area. Beyond this we find that psychiatric historiography in this century — in its critique of the relativizing particularization of historicism — is concerned with the continuity of intellectual history, with the inner coherence that cancels spatial, temporal, and social modes. It evokes a *Zeitgeist* which, unlike Hegel's cannot sustain social connections but only integrate them. It hopes to achieve super-temporal continuity through "archetypal problems" or through the recurrence of the same ideas; and it sees changes and conflicts in terms of external appearance. The purpose of this intellectual-historical orientation is "to raise human activity in society beyond the limits of time and place."[15]

Pre-Nazi German historicism favored the cultural-historical approach (Kirchhoff, Birnbaum). This changed after 1945, especially in the critical view of postwar social historians of cultural history as an abstract correlative to the history of authoritarianism.[16] It relied all the more on the existential foundation, the absolute mode of being, which protects man and the world against relativization, but leaves little leeway for the aware and changing individual. In theory this development parallels that of the German sociology of knowledge pioneered by Dilthey, developed by Mannheim, and now carried on by Gadamer.[17] Our reservations thus are similar to the critique of the sociology of knowledge by Lenk,[18] Plessner,[19] Wolff,[20] Lieber,[21] Hofmann,[22] and Habermas.[23] With this in mind, our inquiry, using psychiatry as its example, hopes to contribute to a critical sociology of knowledge.

The fact that psychiatric historiography rests on an existential base explains the minor critical role it has played in the self-understanding of science, the inductive interpretation of history (Mora) that grew out of its need to legitimize the present, its function as the stabilizer of the status quo, its usefulness as prefatory material in textbooks.[24] The rejection of the nominalism of natural science may heighten awareness of existence, but at the same time its detachment acts as a barrier not only to scientific analysis but also to the judgmental process of critical historical and social self-reflection. In the eighteenth century the ruling classes, or subjective prejudice, were held responsible for preventing the acquisition of knowledge (the thesis of the treason of the clergy). But in the nineteenth century that impediment was considered an objectively necessary ideology, in line with the limited sphere of scientific or social progress. In the twentieth century this has turned into the voluntary subjugation of knowledge to conditioned existence, of judgment to the continuity of meaning of the now historic prejudice, into the automatic adjustment to the events of which we are a part.[25] "Philosophy, by again questioning its point of departure, man's 'being-in-the-world,' for its existential or permanent conditions, either completely loses sight of history and society as concrete processes or else coagulates them conceptually into 'historicity' and 'sociability.'"[26] Plessner offers a similar critique of the transposition of objects into a phenomenal conceptuality or respective "world" of their own, a process that aesthetically seems to let matters rest, but in fact cedes the objects to positivist empiricism. He writes: "Corporeality as a structural factor of concrete existence, with which it must deal and which permeates it in the most divers forms of submission and resistance does not become a problem as the body per se. That is left to biology and the organic natural sciences."[27]

Yet the concept of science includes both, not only the progressive stabilization of itself, its area of relevance, and, consequently, its society (in technical mastery, system formation, as well as meaning). It furthermore includes the progressive enlightenment of itself, its area of relevance and its society, its critical questioning and venturing beyond the status quo — always measured against the claim to knowledge and change through which this science legitimizes its activity. In this way, scientific sociological analysis, even when dealing with the past, achieves a practical, not merely contemplative-affirmative significance for contemporary psychiatry. Such objective, perceptive thinking does not stop at the subjective understanding as mediated through the consciousness of the individuals in question. It "rules out the dogmatism of the experienced situation not simply by formalization, admittedly overtaking the presumably subjective meaning more or less by marching through established tradition, and thus breaking it open."[28] This type of critical sociology must perforce be historical. "Unlike the sociology of knowledge, [this sociology] derives its categories from a criticism that can demote to an ideology only that aspect of it whose ideas and goals it had taken seriously." It is objectively and not subjectively rational in so far as it "deals with fractures of reason, in Hegel's language: with the imbalance between that which is and its concept."[29]

Psychiatry's realm of relevance obviously encompasses "fractures of reason" in human thought and action. Thus, and in the historical connection with the "social question," psychiatry in a manner of speaking constituted a sociology before the emergence of sociology as a science. This is significant precisely because our inquiry is confined to the era of psychiatry's genesis. From the viewpoint of the sociology of knowledge we have to go beyond the formal question of how certain extremes of human thought and action could be seen as special and thus become the subject of a discipline. We must ask how it was possible for these extremes to turn into concrete social needs and dangers — oppressive and ominously fascinating. What was the nature of a society — its public, its economic development, its moral norms, its religious notions, its political, legal, and administrative authorities — that could see this as a preeminent problem calling for change (order and enlightenment)? And what was the nature of contemporary scientific and philosophical thought and its apostles who had to respond to this now visible need and claim, who in this transitional stage had to add a new link to the canon of existing ideas, to develop theories and causalities, and from them derive methods and institutions that promised change? All other questions derive from these.

Methods of Investigation

After defining the object of the investigation and its framework as well as the critical claim for tracing it throughout history, the question of the where and how of the material needed for the analysis remains. Because we are dealing with the genesis of psychiatry, we will as far as possible follow Thomas S. Kuhn's *Structure of Scientific Revolutions*,[30] a critical appraisal of the belief in the linear, cumulative development of sciences. In Kuhn's view a science comes into being when, in the (philosophical) discussion of a given area, there emerges a view of the world combined with an exemplary concrete achievement, i.e. a paradigm, which can accommodate most of the problems in question, end all further conflict about fundamental questions among a larger and permanent community, generate specific theories, methods, aspects, and laws, and give rise to scientific institutions (professions, places of work, journals, associations, textbooks, teaching possibilities). Scientific development occurs through revolutions not unlike political upheavals, i.e. through an exchange of world views which rethinks and casts new light not only on theories but also on facts. This presupposes a crisis: the realization that the old paradigm does not apply to crucial new problems and needs. Consequently a public discussion takes place between the old paradigm and the one that aspires to its place. The victorious paradigm must offer the promise of being better able to meet the new needs; yet personal and political authorities, power of persuasion, philosophical reflections, even feelings of aesthetic adequacy can also play a part in this. And formerly visible aspects can become obscured or relegated to another science, to metaphysics, or to a different area of social activity.

This analysis, however, based on the natural sciences, holds only partially true for psychiatry. Kuhn knows that the situation of, say, medicine, technology, or law is more complicated, since these disciplines cannot stake out their areas of research at will, but must follow the dictates of external, socially urgent needs.[31] Kuhn's formalistic, questionable schema is unsatisfactory both in content and structure; we are using it merely as a technical aid for comparisons of developmental stages in different societies. Psychiatric theory and practice have always been significantly influenced by a wide range of social pressures.[32] And this degree of socialization has continued to increase until psychiatry, as social engineering, has been assigned the task of eliminating social anxiety.[33] Critically speaking it might also be said about psychiatry that the "perception makes the objective connection being investigated a part of the research process undertaken by the subject,"[34] and that "the knowing subject [must be comprehended] in terms of the relations of social praxis."[35]

Given such complexity it is not possible to rely on the methodology of any single discipline. It might be preferable to follow Habermas' approach in his analysis of a similarly complex subject — bourgeois society: the method in the analysis of an "epochal-typical" subject is, unlike formal sociology, historical, i.e., it does not generalize in terms of ideal types and is not applicable to formally identical combinations of random historical conditions.

At the same time, this method, unlike history, is sociological, since specifics can be interpreted only as examples, as instances of social development. "This sociological procedure is distinguished from the precepts of rigid historiography by a seemingly freer discretionary treatment of historical material, yet following the equally rigid criteria of a structural analysis of the overall social connections."[36] Social history, as understood by Conze or Heinrich Mommsen,[37] and utilizing such approaches as history of ideas, biography, and statistics, today lends support to this sociological method.

It now became necessary to provide a solid foundation for the methodical framework of the historic understanding, i.e., to incorporate the greatest possible number of details of the available material into a causal or comparative explanation or, failing that, at least quantify them. The limits of such attempts were set both by the complexity of the object and availability of sources. Antecedence of scientific achievements, for instance, once a controversial issue involving national pride, again assumes relative significance in comparing the development of a society and its psychiatry. In our subsequent investigation we traced the development of psychiatric institutions, particularly hospitals, but also textbooks, associations, periodicals, the influence of scientists on each other, and the establishment of psychiatry in faculties and universities. The expansion of its sphere, i.e. its patients and jurisdiction, and thus its social role and interrelations, had to be described. The advances in the natural sciences and medicine, which had technical and theoretical consequences for psychiatry, had to be dealt with. The same holds true for the development of the literary and political scene as for the development of economic productive forces and needs in the respective societies. Related disciplines like psychology and anthropology had to be compared. The relation of psychiatry to philosophy and the process of its dissociation had to be delineated. The national and social policies of governments and bureaucracies, as well as the emergence of social movements were of significance, as were the dialectics of the emancipation and the integration of other social groups in the time of the emergent and developing bourgeois society (e.g. workers, Jews). Stress was placed on the gathering, analysis, and, where possible, quantifying evaluation of the biographies of the psychiatrist, and not only of the "great men." Due to the inaccessibility of source material, however, this effort was only partially successful, and limited largely to Germany. All these factors were worked into a comparison of three societies, Great Britain, France, and Germany, crucial to our theme.

Accordingly, our presentation adheres to this structure. It follows a very simple scheme, reporting chronologically and sequentially on the genesis of psychiatry in the above-mentioned three societies. The fact that German psychiatry was the last to arrive on the scene suggested its treatment as the "belated nation."[38] Beginning each phase of the genesis of psychiatry with England is in keeping with psychiatric historiography.

The frequent admonitions are intended to remind the reader that this is not meant to be a history of psychiatry. On the other hand, its sociological character calls for a description of an overall psychiatric reality alien to sociology. For the sociological purposes of this inquiry are manifold. Not only does it wish to portray the social conditions underlying the genesis of a science (and thus also contribute to the sociological enlightenment of psychiatry), and not only does it wish to use the origin and growth of psychiatric thinking to explain its roots and similarities with later sociological thought that in the course of sociology's self-examination have become lost or forgotten. It also wishes simply to "report" to sociology about a reality that has long remained closed to it yet ought to be of vital interest: the relationship of society to both individually and socially inner and outer unreason, as seen in the relationship of bourgeois psychiatrists to the (poor) mentally ill, and taking into account the ambivalence between identification and differentiation (distancing), between emancipation and integration, into which the "dialectics of enlightenment" has placed us. Thus, here too, we have to look for and test the promise and claim of the Enlightenment, without which no institution, no law, no theory, and no treatment could have come into being. Whoever, like Foucault,[39] unmasks and rejects them all as ideology enters into an age of post-Enlightenment. Yet precisely this abstract negation keeps one tied to the Enlightenment and limited to a merely reactive anti-Enlightenment position.

The Historical Background: The Sequestration of Unreason

The genesis of psychiatry as a modern science must be seen against the background of a movement that radically changed the social landscape of seventeenth-century Europe. The Age of Reason, mercantilism, and enlightened absolutism coincided with a new and rigorous spatial orientation. It put all forms of unreason, which in the Middle Ages had been part of a divine world and in the Renaissance a secularizing world, the civil world of commerce, morality, and work, in short — beyond the pale of the rational world — under lock and key. Beggars and vagabonds, those without property, jobs or trades, criminals, political gadflies and heretics, prostitutes, libertines, syphilitics, alcoholics, lunatics, idiots, and eccentrics, but also rejected wives, deflowered daughters, and spendthrift sons were thus rendered harmless and virtually invisible.

In 1657, the vast *hôpital général* of Paris, a special complex combining several older institutions, began the task of concentration. Lyons was the first French city to put up such a special building, in 1612. By an edict of 1676 every French city was ordered to erect a *hôpital général*; by the time of the Revolution, 32 provincial towns had complied. In Germany, the construction of prisons, penitentiaries, and workhouses began at Hamburg in 1620. However, this movement did not really get underway until the end of the Thirty Years' War — 1656 (Brieg and Osnabrück), 1667 (Basel, and 1668 (Breslau) — and continued apace until the end of the eighteenth century.

In England, the same development had begun earlier, with certain differences. Laws ordering the building of houses of correction had already been passed by 1575. But the idea did not take hold, despite threats of fines and inducements to private entrepreneurs, and despite the existing policy of enclosures (which allowed large landowners to streamline farming and send a flood of "freed" and landless peasants into the towns).[40] Scotland resisted almost completely. Generally what happened was an expansion of existing prisons. The establishment of workhouses was more successful; some 126 went up between 1697 (Bristol) and the end of the eighteenth century, mainly in newly industrialized regions.

In examining the reasons for this development throughout Europe, we must keep in mind that in urban areas the army of the poor and jobless amounted to 10—20 per cent in dioceses, and in times of economic crises 30 per cent. This previously "normal" circumstance was bound to strike all contemporary authorities as provocative and as endangering their effort to have reason control nature and unreason. It threatened absolutism's desire for civil order, capitalism's principle of regular, calculable labor; the sciences' striving for systematic mastery over nature; the churches, especially Puritanism, and the heads of families who learned to translate rational rule as sensitivity to *honnêteté* and against the corruption of the family. This epoch of the administrative sequestration of unreason (1650—1800) might be described as one in which the church could no longer, and bourgeois-capitalist society could not yet, encompass the various forms of the irrational, especially the poor and the deranged. At the same time, this epoch created the premise for the later socio-economic order: it taught people to see work as a moral duty, and later, as a generally valid social necessity. The houses of correction, prisons, and workhouses were conceived as an elastic instrument: "cheap manpower in the periods of full employment and high salaries; and in periods of unemployment, reabsorption of the idle and social protection against agitation and uprisings."[41] More important than the already questionable performance of these institutions was their function for bourgeois society: in a negative way they showed the bourgeoisie the space in which they could move without scandal, ergo "freely"; and they also showed them how to interiorize an attitude that made them into moral and working citizens. To the extent that the bourgeoisie adopted this attitude, those institutions lost their function and were either razed or rebuilt.

The insane were among the outcasts. On the average, with local differences, they probably made up ten per cent of the inmates of institutions, especially since calling an idle or eccentric person either a madman or a fool or whatever was an arbitrary matter. Yet at the same time, special forms emerged, whereby the unreason of the insane was related to social rationality. Unlike the mass of the outcasts (visible not as themselves but only as the forbidding stone walls of institutions) the insane occupied a special position — and particularly the most dangerous among them, namely the frenzied, the angry, the threatening, i.e. the maniacs. These were quite literally exhibited as caged "monsters" to a paying populace, which nowhere more concretely than here was an object of administering reason, the object of its educational and ordering intention — against the background of coercion. Contemporary accounts and travel books tell how these exhibitions in Paris, London, and various German cities vied for audiences with animal acts. These spectacles had more in common than merely the bars of cages and the skillful baiting of the keepers. They were displays of a wild and untamable nature, of "bestiality," of absolute and destructive freedom, of social danger which could be demonstrated far more dramatically behind the bars of reason, just as that same act showed the public reason as the necessity of the control over nature, as a limitation of freedom, and as a guarantee of authority. If in earlier days, insanity was a symbol of the fall of man and — in its connection with saints and demons — held the promise of a Christian afterlife, it now testified to a political afterlife, to a chaotic natural state of the world and mankind, to the frailty of human passions, i.e., to a condition such as Hobbes described in *Leviathan* and from which he could find no way out except by subjugating man to the state, to his second, social, nature: "For in the differences of private men, to declare what is Equity, what is Justice, and what is morall Virtue, and to make them binding, there is need of...Civill Law. The Law of Nature therefore is a part of the Civill Law in all Commonwealths of the World."

The arrangement that presented the insane as wild and dangerous beasts[42] was an appeal to the public to accept the moral yardstick of the absolute state as its own measure of reason. That the absolute animal freedom of the insane could be dealt with only by means of absolute force, that they were to be viewed as objects of a process of obedience training, that their aberrations had to be countered by rational truth, their violence by corporal punishment, and, finally, that the threat they posed to society was transformed into demonstrable powerlessness, gave exemplary and clear emphasis to the goals and sanctions of this moral and political appeal. The emergence of psychiatry as a science was contingent on the specific metamorphosis of the institutions of enlightened absolutism that had merely isolated unreason. The social conditions, the direction, and the effects of this change form the subject of our discussion.

PART I

GREAT BRITAIN

1

The Sequestration of Irrationality and the Public

Public Concepts

As mentioned earlier, the social impetus toward the sequestration of unreason manifested itself in England as well, and quite early at that, but it did not take on the same dimensions as either in France or Germany. By the early eighteenth century, the social institution of the spatial separation of reason and unreason had become the subject of a discussion that presaged its end. England rather early on developed a more thoughtful approach that did not concern itself so much with the moral and educational goal of such institutions as with their utility for both society and the inmates themselves, for the very existence of such institutions lent visibility to the distinctiveness of their inmates. Factories protested against the cheap competition of the workhouses; Daniel Defoe voiced the criticism that the use of inmate labor merely shifted unemployment and poverty from one area to another. At the same time, of course, the English economy was not strong enough to absorb the mass of mendicant or vagrant paupers. On the other hand, a growing number of merchants showed an interest in workhouses as well as in the separate, private insane asylums. The latter mainly cared for the well-to-do; but they also entered into contracts with parishes to share the expenses for "pauper lunatics."[1] In 1714, an Act of Parliament for the first time took up the subject of "the more effectual punishing [of] such rogues, vagabonds, sturdy beggars, and vagrants," calling for their confinement insofar as they were "furiously mad," but also, for the first time, treated these pauper lunatics as a group apart from any others subject to these laws. Thus, for example, they were not subject to the penalty of flogging.[2] Even Bedlam, the largest institution of confinement in London, differentiated among its inmates, and despite its fearsome reputation its atmosphere was far more hospital-like than that of its Paris counterpart, the *hôpital général*. Nonetheless, Bedlam was still putting its inmates on display at a time when such public shows had become unthinkable in post-Revolutionary France. Yet that very fact helped focus attention on Bedlam after it moved into its new quarters (1676), and made it a critical starting point for attempts at social reform.

What, in a society in which the movement for the sequestration of unreason had barely got under way, sparked these impulses toward differentiation and discussion, toward the consideration of utilitarian factors, toward a contemporaneity of the non-contemporaneous conducive to criticism? It was not to be found in the France of that time, and certainly not in Germany. These conceptual factors, which are also constitutive for the medical practice of the early nineteenth century, can only be explained within a larger historical framework. According to Koselleck the classical absolutist state on the Continent was a product of the religious civil wars, and it came to an end with another civil war — the French Revolution. In contrast, he reduces "England's special position" to the terse comment that "on the Island both events virtually coincided. Here the nascent absolutist state had already been destroyed in the religious civil wars; the religious struggles were in fact the bourgeois revolution."[3]

This thesis proves its validity when it also explains the persistent side-by-side existence of old and new structures, though in a new, postrevolutionary "milieu" that institutionalized their conflict. Thus the rule of the aristocracy in Britain did not end with the revolution. Instead, a taxed gentry that anyway was land- rather than blood-based adjusted to the new forms of divided power (party and Parliament), began to engage in trade, and found a common ground with the bourgeoisie even in literature. Steele's *Tatler* (1709) and Addison's *Spectator* (1711), Arnold Hauser points out, bridged the gap between the aristocracy and bourgeoisie.[4] Likewise, the old religious struggles continued in modified form in new virulent social conflicts between established religions and dissident sects. A growing aristocratic upper-middle-class skeptical intellectualism soon found its counterpart in the overflowing emotionalism of the middle classes.

The situation was no different with the institutions of confinement for the irrational. They were the absolutist instrument in a process of education and coercion, geared to a public that was regarded as nothing more than the object of this didactic process of enlightenment. And although this structure also lasted throughout the eighteenth century, another public emerged. This group, seeing itself as the subject, discussed and dissected that structure like all other earlier structures, questioned its usefulness for the individual and the nation, and sought to make necessary changes. This thinking public was to dismantle the didactic instrument to the degree that, on the one hand, deeming itself informed, it internalized the lessons taught (the duty to work, bourgeois morality) and on the other, became convinced that the sequestered unreason could by various routes be brought to a more appropriate and more useful reason.

The unity of the public as subject, and a "milieu" in which this subject exposes its own self to others in discussion, constituted that which Habermas sees as the emergent "political public" of that era. He poses Koselleck's question more concretely and tries to "clarify why, in England so much earlier than in other countries, conflicts ripened, which were fought out with the participation of the public. A literate, informed public also existed on the continent. But there it became politically virulent only when, under the aegis of mercantilism, the capitalist mode of production had reached the level of England's soon after the Glorious Revolution."[5] According to Habermas, three events of 1694—95 ushered in this development, which was marked by the awareness of a new conflict of interests between restrictive trading and expansive manufacturing capital: the establishment of the Bank of England, which made England the world's financial center, stimulated the introduction of new production methods; the first cabinet government, a decisive step toward the parliamentarization of state power; and the Licensing Act which abolished press censorship and helped turn a belleletristic aristocratic literary public into a political one, with a diversified press disseminating political information among a wide, thinking audience.[6]

Coffee- and teahouses, clubs and streets, became as much the institutions of this new "public spirit" as the political pamphlets and journalists championing the cause of the respective parties and governments, men like Defoe and Swift, Pope, Bolingbroke, and Gay. Overt opposition against a government as a reasoning "permanent controversy" instead of the violence of earlier centuries was first invoked by the Tories (Bolingbroke, Swift, Pope, Gay) against Walpole's Whig government (1721—42). Their critical and satirical commentaries about the stock speculations and subsequent collapse of the South Sea Company (1720) lent support to the opposition's successful appeal to the moral power of the "sense of the people," the "public spirit," "common voice," and "common sense." The public clamor ultimately forced the Parliamentary Whig majority to yield.[7] The Whig Defoe and the Tory Swift became representative voices of the great public debate that ranged from politics to philosophy: the rational optimist Robinson Crusoe (1719), who, appropriating nature, made the most out of nothing, confronted the pessimistic world of Gulliver (1726), who sarcastically exposed the reverse side of the Enlightenment.

Bolingbroke based his faith in the infallibility of public opinion and common sense on the adage that "if all men cannot reason, all men can feel." It contained the same element of immediacy in which Locke had shown faith when he put the opinion of private individuals, the "law of Opinion," on the same level with divine and state law, arrived at "by a secret and tacit consent." And insofar as it is a "measure of virtue and vice," Locke even calls it the "law of Private Censure."[8] On the one hand Locke, with the same self-confidence and certainty, sees the property structure of bourgeois society, the proprietary rights of the individual with regard to the products of nature as "the natural basis of a contractual state power."[9] On the other hand, with this edict on private property he establishes the autonomy of man as man, an autonomy that "seeks to assert itself in the sphere of the bourgeois family, in love, liberty, and education, in short: realize itself as humanity."[10] This implicit equation of "proprietors" and "individuals" proved useful in the fight against the absolutist demands of the state. It proved fictitious, of course, when the "natural order" was understood in terms of categories of the mobility of bourgeois society itself.[11]

Thus, diverging developments were influenced by Locke. On the one hand, Mandeville's liberal, mechanistic *Fable of the Bees* (1714) made the natural right to property for self-preservation the motor of the Commonwealth: "Private vices made publick benefits." On the other hand, Shaftesbury linked up with Locke's direct human element and with the reflective, inner-directed formative role of subjectivity. The aspects of common sense Shaftesbury emphasized were tacit consent, humanity, obligingness, and a sympathetic awareness of the relationship of objects that discursive reason had sundered "It is not so much a feature given to all men, part of natural law, as a social virtue, a virtue of the heart more than of the head, that Shaftesbury has in mind,"[12] and which Scottish philosophy was to call a "moral sense." Idealistically transcending this social dimension, Meinecke begins his "birth of historicism" with Shaftesbury, seeing in him "an early acceptance of the principle of individuality," according to which all special forms have their "peculiar spontaneity," their "inherent genius." Thus Shaftesbury was able to see rational objects in an inner harmonious coherence, in their "inward constitution": pleasure and pain, selfish and social inclinations, the repulsiveness and the beauty of savage beasts. He was similarly fascinated by the closeness between the liberator and the oppressor, or, respectively between the fool and the true prophet, since both of them feed on enthusiasm and resemble each other, and since the dividing line between health and hubris is faint."[13]

Insanity in that era must unquestionably be seen as a political issue in the broadest sense of the word, and contemporary medical approaches and practitioners were strongly influenced by the concepts of the emergent bourgeoisie. "Madness" and the "English malady" were favorite topics in the coffeehouses. Locke and Mandeville were themselves physicians, who dealt with the insane, as did the natural scientists Boyle and Hooke and the pamphleteers Defoe and Swift. This, as well as the interest in the problem of content, was predicated on the closeness of political and scientific-medical terminology and ideas and their material-physical, though not necessarily analogous relationship. This relationship appeared to be especially close just as it was beginning to disintegrate. Notably, concepts dating back to the beginning of the Royal Society of London exuded an aura of physical and socio-moral substantiality. In the subsequent century they were to become a source of great confusion in their various subjective, objectively neutralizing, and metaphysical manifestations, before assuming their divers places in the scheme of modern science. Thus, the view of the invisible public spirit as a politically tangible, a feeling and activating force was doubtlessly connected with the medical doctrine of the spirit, especially as formulated by Thomas Willis (1667) in the first coherent anatomical neurology. According to him, the *spiritus animales* within the organs was stimulated by the outer object and driven inward, thereby creating sensations. The switchboard of these movements that pass through the nerves in waves, to and fro, as though mechanically driven — and this was the basis of another seminal concept of bourgeois society — was the *sensus communis*, the common sense of the mid brain. This *sensus communis* not only was said to affect the perception of experience, but was also the seat of fantasy, imagination, and memory. Conversely, common sense drives the nerve *spiritus* from the inside to the outside. Thus it arouses desire or a corresponding motor response, as well as, in cases of frequent repetition, an automatic, independent causal relationship of sensation and motion, i.e., habits.

Willis, however, was not only the first inventor of the nervous system. He also presented this activity of the nerve spirit as being inspired by the "Corporeal (vital and sensitive) Soul," it, too, a delicate and active matter of the mid brain, and covered over by the rational soul. By subsuming the processes of the nervous system under the label "psycheology" he introduced the term into medicine.

Willis' neurological-psychological system superseded the traditional humoral-chemical explanations and put its stamp on the eighteenth century. Disease was the result of mechanical disturbances by external factors. The various forms of insanity sprung up without any apparent bodily injury, for the only visible damage was that of the nervous spirit. Thus, even after the end of an era accustomed to thinking in terms of body and soul, we entered into a realm in which almost any mental, moral, social, and political phenomena could be called "sick" or "abnormal" — precisely because of the invisibility of the postulated (or contested) bodily injury. The factor of the power of the invisible, intrinsic to the doctrine of the "spirit" and "common sense," allowed both the physician and the politician to determine, by reasoning, whether a controversial matter was sound or unsound, beneficial or dangerous, was a part of bourgeois society or was to be cast out from it.

Hysteria and Bourgeois Identity

Interestingly enough, the only disorders Willis took over into his nerve theory almost in toto were hysteria and related complaints, removing them from their venerable site in the uterus, and turning them into "nervous" diseases. But the seat of melancholia, on the other hand, remained partly traditionally chemical, partly nervous (empty babble), and partly in the heart (sad feelings). The theoretical explanation (low spirits) is linked more to the nervous model, and the therapy (replacing sad passions with pleasant ones) more to the heart — the first hint of the subsequent division of labor between a theoretical-scientific and a practical-romantic approach. Even more peripheral and merely derived from other forms is Willis' treatment of mania and madness, the major forms of insanity.

This accurately reflects the fact that hysteria was openly accepted or played a crucial role in public discussion, whereas the insane were largely still under sentence of the actual and therefore also of the scientific sequestration of unreason, and therefore we cannot speak of a theoretical-practical psychiatric science before the middle of the century. Nothing describes the situation better than the rationalistic training, the punitive and harsh treatment that Willis considered appropriate for the insane:

For the curing of Mad people, there is nothing more effectual or necessary than their reverence or standing in awe of such as they think their Tormentors. ...Furious Mad-men are sooner, and more certainly cured by punishments, and hard usage, in a strait room, than by Physick or Medicines....Let the diet be slender and not delicate, their cloathing coarse, their beds hard, and their handling severe and rigid.[14]

Thomas Sydenham, likewise a fellow of the Royal Society and a friend of Locke and Boyle, published an account of hysteria in 1682, which, going beyond either Willis' or Glisson's[15] was a sort of underhanded moral description of England's bourgeoisie at the turn of the seventeenth century. Clinically, he identifies the hysteria found in women with hypochondria, its equivalent disorder among men, and with melancholia. He thus supplements the approach of Willis. Little mention is made of actual insanity. Practically only those women "such as work and fare hardly" are free of hysteria. Conversely, the main male victims of this disorder are those "who lead a sedentary life and study hard,"[16] or in other words, men in commerce or similar offices or in academic or literary professions. This notion of hysteria thus encompasses the economic and literary-humanistic community, i.e., that segment visible to an academic: the typical bourgeois suffers from hysteria or hypochondria. The rest remain more or less in the dark — a social myopia that again and again will lead psychiatrists and others to false conclusions.

Hysteria is initially explained as a disorder, ataxia of the *spiritus animales*. However, Sydenham's differentiation interiorizes Willis' principle — also methodologically:

As the body is composed of parts which are manifest to the senses, so doubtless the mind consists in a regular frame or make up of the spirits, which is only the object of reason. And this being so intimately united with the temperament of the body, is more or less disordered, according as the constituent parts thereof, given us by nature, are more or less firm.[17]

We can probably go along with Foucault's interpretation that here Willis' neutralizing natural-scientific observation is replaced by an inner vision, which, by relating the spirit to the corporeal constitution, links the psycho-physical dimension to the moral dimension, the weakness of the constitution to the weakness of the heart.[18] For it is precisely this connection that Sydenham uses to substantiate the greater predisposition of the weaker women to hysteria, and thus, the feeble, inconstant, feminine character of the new bourgeois society:

Hence women are more frequently affected with this disease than men, because they have receiv'd from nature a finer and more delicate constitution of body, being designed for an easier life and the pleasure of men, who were made robust, that they might be able to cultivate the earth, hunt and kill wild beasts for food, and undergo violent exercises.[19]

Sydenham's recommended therapy is, first of all, the thorough purgative voiding of the body, then fortifying the spirits with iron tonics, and regulating them naturally with daily horseback rides.[20] The last of these recommendations may be the first instance of the trend to make the patient's total behavior part of the treatment plan. For, since the symptoms of hysteria are seen as a motor defect of both the nervous spirit and social behavior, the therapy must aim at realigning this sociosomatic movement. A story told of Sydenham, though possibly apocryphal, is rather instructive. Having come to the end of his rope in his treatment of an aristocrat who stubbornly resisted his best efforts, Sydenham finally sent him to a fictitious, allegedly renowned colleague in Scotland. By the time the patient returned to London after a long and futile journey, full of reproaches, he was cured. Explanation: the arduous trip (travel as an end in itself, "traveling without arriving") and the subsequent reaction to the mythical doctor had given the patient "a motive of sufficient interest to divert the current of his ideas from the cherished theme" and thereby restored him to health.[21]

Thus the disorder manifested by the bourgeoisie — hysteria — became the medical model for nervous or mental diseases.[22] Until the mid-eighteenth-century doctors were guided by Willis' and Sydenham's theories about this representative complaint. Just as the insane by and large remained outside the public realm — and thus outside what the community construed as society — and, indeed, outside the interests of the state — hysteria dominated the public interest. It became an instrument by which the bourgeois could bring his personal and social-national self into harmony. One condition for this was that doctors, amid the enthusiasm of the wide-ranging public discussion, lost their traditional authority, especially since they saw themselves as merely another group of discussants. Of the four most important hospitals in London, two considered themselves Whig and two Tory. This gave rise to the image of the physician as a man who is concerned with politics, economics, and literature, but who knows little more about medicine than how to turn it into a profitable business. Consultations were frequently held in the coffeehouse, and even that aspect of medical activity which later became psychiatry was limited to office hours — for hysterical patients: hence "office-hour psychiatry."[23]

The interlocking relationship of society and physician not only explains why everyone, physician and layman alike, was writing about hysteria, but also why most of these books and articles were biographical, and why, aimed as they were at the general public, they did not refer to any medical authority. Instead, they offered detailed plans for self-treatment. The core of all public debate, whether on a political level as in Locke,[24] or an individual level, was the effort to find the way out from the threat posed by "instability" and to find a stable order, an identity, a self, that comes into being and functions spontaneously rather than being imposed by external authority.

Mandeville, both in his life and medical writings, might be viewed as the model of the contemporary physician. He was casual about his practice, and in fact drew a pension from a number of Dutch merchants. His interests were literary, political, and economic rather than medical. A frequenter of literary circles, he knew both Addison and Benjamin Franklin. In 1711, he wrote a *Treatise of the Hypochondriack and Hysterick Passion*, together with an account of the "real art of physick itself...writ by way of information to patients" based on a "method entirily new" in the form of a dialogue between the doctor and the patient. Here, too, the author's own disorder — his fear of syphilis — is worked in. What is of therapeutic importance to him is not any personal theory, but the reassuring and enlightening discussion that satirizes the foibles of the patient and of his colleagues. Mindful of his own preference for the function of the "selfishness of man," he allows the patient to work out his aggressions against him — and is paid for this according to the time spent. Also, citing the example of a patient's hysterical daughter, Mandeville prescribes a "course of Exercise" which carefully divides up and fills out the day. This schedule includes early rising, horseback riding, a good scrub-down by a servant, and walking. This set the hygienic ideal for daughters of the upper-middle-class.

Beyond this, it became fashionable during the first half of the century to use hysteria for identifying individual and social self-consciousness as though utilizing an individual shortcoming to explain the uniqueness and greatness of bourgeois society and the nation; however, Sydenham still saw it as an undesirable instability. In 1725, Blackmore, a medical journalist, wrote a *Treatise of the Spleen and Vapours: or, Hypocondriacal and Hysterical Affections.* He, too, regarded the complaints of men and women as forms of the same disorder. The spleen determines the degree of lasciviousness or indolence of a person in his sexual or any other activity. Furthermore, Blackmore sees the "English Spleen" as a kind of individuation principle affecting the diversity of individual genius and the uniqueness of the nation. In contrast to other nations,

the temper of the Natives of Britain is most various, which proceeds from the Spleen, an Ingredient of their Constitution, which is almost peculiar, at least in the Degree of it, to this Island. Hence arises the Diversity of Genius and Disposition, of which this soul is so fertile. Our Neighbours have greater Poverty of Humour and Scarcity of Originals than we....An Englishman need not go abroad to learn the Humours of these different Neighbours; let him but travel from Temple-Bar to Ludgate, and he will meet...in four and twenty hours, the Dispositions and Humours of all the Nations of Europe.[25]

The English Malady: or, a Treatise of Nervous Diseases of all Kinds...with the Author's Own Case at Large, by G. Cheyne, was published in 1733. Here the designation of the national disease is turned into proud acceptance of foreign sneering use of that term. For Cheyne, the reasons for the greater frequency of this illness in England include "the Richness and Heaviness of our Food, the Wealth and Abundance of the Inhabitants (from their universal Trade) the Inactivity and sedentary Occupations of the better Sort (among whom this Evil mostly rages) and the Humour of living in great, populous and consequently unhealthy Towns." Moreover, the victims are not "Fools, weak or stupid Persons, heavy and dull Souls" but those "of the liveliest and quickest natural Parts...whose Genius is most keen and penetrating, and particularly where there is the most delicate Sensation and Taste, both of Pleasure and Pain." And this results from "the animal Oeconomy and the present Laws of Nature."[26] Cheyne, too, sees this illness only as physical, manifesting itself by a feebleness or tonic disorder of the nerves, although here, too, the basic

"Character and Temper of the Patient" is decisive, so that the "English Malady" must be called a "Nervous Distemper." That is why its symptoms vary depending on what part of the body is affected; every organ has its own "sentiment."

With the establishment of this thesis of hysteria, one element of sequestered unreason — specifically the passions — became accepted as a vital component of bourgeois society, not simply as a dangerous evil crying out for rational control, but as a recognizable, physical, autonomous social, and moral force. After the revolution (Sydenham, Shaftesbury), the romantic and the rational aspects of the English Enlightenment formed a single entity. The hysterical passions were a physical sign of individual genius and originality as well as of the commercial-capitalist wealth — and soon also of the freedom — of society, but also of the instability and physical and moral suffering, the price that had to be paid. Speculations and the collapse of the South Sea Company of 1720, the so-called South Sea Bubble, became a paradigmatic event. One of the consequences was, strangely enough, a greater increase in patients "whose heads were turned by the immense riches which fortune had suddenly thrown in their way, than of those, who had been completely ruined by that abominable bubble. Such is the force of insatiable avarice in destroying the rational faculties."[27] Thus Montesquieu expressed amazement that compared with the Romans, the English commit suicide for no apparent reason, even at the height of happiness. The sociosomatic conditions responsible for the hysterical disorders demanded appropriate therapeutic measures. For gone were the days (even if not for ever) when these ills were seen as atonement for transgressions. Yet neither were hysteria and spleen looked on as "imaginary Whims or Fancies" unrelated to the body or society. It is practically impossible to clarify an error through rational explanation, "to counsel a Man..., tho' never so eloquently apply'd."[28] Hysteria showed both the individual and society that it had become possible and also necessary to treat oneself reflexively to achieve stability through one's own efforts. Stability *must* perforce be relative since it was not granted by an external authority, and *can* only be relative, because individual originality on the one hand, and the interrelation of the public, commerce, and wealth on the other hand, depend on the degree of guaranteed stability. Only this can assure the satisfactory strength and vitality of both the animal spirits and the public spirit.

The Attack on Unreason

Once the irrationality of hysteria was not only integrated into but almost identified with the bourgeoisie, the sequestration of unreason — of poverty and insanity — could no longer remain absolute. Nor would the general public continue to accept the existing demarcation as an objective guideline. This process was a gradual one. The "pauper lunatics" remained outside the purview of medical science; they stood at its theoretical and practical periphery. Yet even here a movement of simultaneous differentiation and identification was beginning to develop. In his *Essay Concerning Human Understanding* (1690), Locke inclined toward that view. Characteristically, he created a free field for his inquiry by ignoring the role of physical conditions (animal spirits and the like) in the genesis of sensations and ideas. In this way he was able to arrive at a representative definition of insanity as distinct from idiocy. "Madmen, having joined together some Ideas very wrongly,...mistake them for Truth. [And,] the difference between Idiots and mad Men [is] that mad Men put wrong Ideas together, and so make wrong Propositions, but argue and reason right from them: But Idiots make very few or no Propositions, but argue and reason scarce at all."[29] Without developing any somatic explanation Locke nevertheless arrived at the identifying assumption that his notion of madness, as the faulty association of ideas occasionally applies to all human beings. They are then, in this respect, no different from the inmates of Bedlam. Such faulty associations are chiefly caused by fixed habits, leading to antipathies and sympathies. This is the only process for which Locke allows an explanation in terms of the *spiritus animales*, of "something unreasonable" affecting human reason. "When this combination is settled," reason becomes powerless, since ideas now develop a life of their own; only time can bring a cure.[30]

Defoe's (1697) distinction between madmen and idiots is based on whether they had lost their reason or had been born without it. The objective, however, is a practical one. Both "Fools" and "Naturals," i.e., the abstract opposite of reason, are closer to his pure faith in reason than are madmen. Thus, in an age which made no provision for the care of the insane, he demanded a "Fool-House." It took exactly one hundred and fifty years before this became a reality. His proposal that the costs be borne by those whom nature or God had endowed with more reason than other men is another example of utopian Enlightenment. Such persons, because of their advantages (and their high standing and income)

should take care of those without reason, as of younger, disin-
herited brothers, "tho' they are useless to the Commonwealth."
By an Act of Parliament, the necessary funds could "be very easily
rais'd, by a Tax upon Learning, to be paid by the Authors of
Books."[31] And Defoe was among the first to protest against the
"private Mad-Houses," against the lack of controls that subjected
inmates, paying guests and laborers, to exploitation and abuse.
And he criticized the practice of citizens "among the better sort"
who used these houses to rid themselves, temporarily or permanently of wives they had tired of. Defoe therefore demanded of
the "Civil Authority" in 1707 and 1728 that "all private Mad-
Houses should be suppress'd at once....For the cure of those who
are really Lunatick, licens'd Mad-Houses should be constituted in
convenient parts of the Town, which Houses should be subject to
proper Visitation and Inspection, nor should any Person be sent
to a Mad-House without due Reason, Inquiry, and Authority."[32]
Swift's contribution was a virtual anti-utopia. The Laputa of
Gulliver's Travels might well have been intended as the rebuttal
against all-too-abstract projects like Defoe's Fool-House. Laputa:
the kingdom of planners, project-makers, and overly demanding
rationalists who let reality fall by the wayside.[33] On the other
hand, Swift's approach was in fact more practical than Defoe's
plan for the support of idiots. Not only did he arrange to have
himself elected as a "Governor of Bethlem" in 1714, but his will
also provided for the erection of the first madhouse in Ireland.
Work began in 1746, one year after his death. In an allusion to
Blackmore and Cheyne, he wrote his own epitaph.

> He gave the little Wealth he had,
> To build a House for Fools and Mad;
> And shew'd by one satyric Touch,
> No Nation wanted it so much.

Swift's anti-utopia went still further. He stood contemporary
attitudes on mental illness on their head. One of the Yahoos in
Gulliver's Travels suffers from spleen. He is cured by hard physical
work, not by the pleasant activities (travel, swimming, riding, etc.)
typically prescribed in Swift's day. "To this I was silent out of
partiality to my own kind; yet here I could plainly discover the
true seeds of *spleen*, which only seizeth on the *lazy*, the *luxurious*,
and the *rich*; who, if they were forced to undergo the *same
regimen*, I would undertake for the cure." Conversely, Swift
makes a utopian identification with the insane who were forced

to perform hard labor. In *A Tale of a Tub* (1697) there is a section on "The Use, and Improvement of Madness in a Commonwealth." Here, the "peculiar talents" of kings, conquerors, ministers, philosophers, and religious fanatics are related to the contemporary notions of madness. Then: "... this *Madness* has been the Parent of all these mighty Revolutions that have happened in *Empire*, in *Philosophy*, and in *Religion.*" Swift then applies this ironically to himself:

Even I myself, the Author of these momentous Truths, am a Person, whose Imaginations are hard-mouthed, and exceedingly disposed to run away with his *Reason*, which I have observed from long experience to be a very light Rider, and easily shook off; upon which account, my Friends will never trust me alone, without a solemn Promise, to vent my Speculations in this, or the like manner for the universal Benefit of Human kind."[34]

These lines were written at the same time that Defoe with equal justification, was calling for the most careful and responsible public control of the precise differentiation between madmen and idiots and between madmen and sane people. And when a new system of differentiation was introduced in 1733 — Bedlam opened a special section for incurables[35] — Swift bridged even this extremely problematic distinction with the help of an identification. In *A Serious and Useful Scheme to Make a Hospital for Incurables*, he regards himself, along with the most disparate collection of other people, as a proper candidate for admission — as an "incurable scribbler." The self-enlightenment of psychiatry can do without neither Defoe nor Swift.

2

Industrial Revolution, Romanticism, Psychiatric Paradigm

The Socio-Economic Constellation

This section covers the years from 1750 to 1785: the time of the birth of industrial capitalism, the first surge of Romanticism, the first step toward sociology in Scottish moral philosophy, and the beginning of psychiatry — for England and thus for the whole of Europe. We cannot do justice to the full range of these overlapping developments, yet we also do not know of any discipline that has ever succeeded in this endeavor. Our task, instead, is to demonstrate that in this era something first came into being that may rightly be called psychiatry, and that this can be understood only in connection with other movements.

By mid-century, England had already developed some crucial prerequisites for industrialization. On the one hand, expanded trade, through colonialism and the mercantile policies of the Crown or the governments, had led to a significant accumulation of capital; on the other hand, the early expansionist tendencies of the landed gentry and the scientific streamlining of agriculture (crop rotation, stall feeding) had increased the size and productivity of farms, while driving a sizeable number of peasants off the land and into the towns.[36] Furthermore, by 1750 the freedom to engage in a trade of one's choice had become established, the upshot being that countless tradesmen were "free" to be out of work. The direct impulse for the subsequent development was probably also due to the wars against France and her allies throughout most of the colonized world between 1744 and 1763. The Peace of Paris (1763) underscored England's political and colonial pre-eminence.

The concomitant expansion of foreign and domestic trade demanded a like expansion in production. This brought to light a contradiction: "the old production methods and tools were

turning into obstacles to the expanding market and the corresponding expansion of output."[37] This situation laid the groundwork
for the Industrial Revolution. Three interlocking processes contributed to this:
1. The inadequate tools of workshops had to be replaced with
more productive machines. In the 1760s, England became the land
of technological inventions. e.g., the steam engine, the spinning
jenny, the power loom, as well as the technological advance in
the construction of the first economically important canal.
2. The building and operation of the new machines and means
of transportation required vast investments (mostly stemming
from trade) as "permanent fixed assets." This is what distinguished
the industrial enterprises from the workshops. The capitalist
industrial revolution began with the age of the first mass investments of such permanent fixed capital — in conjunction with free
competition. In England, the preparation and mobilization for
this industrialization began in the 1750s and lasted until the
early 1780s.
3. On the one hand, this change to new and more efficient
methods of production destroyed the subsistence base of many
of the workers in the old shops, creating want and insecurity.
On the other hand, the need for workers was greater than ever
before. The new situation brought mass investments not only of
fixed, but of variable capital as well, i.e., the mass mobilization
of human labor and its involvement in the capitalist economy.[38]

These processes, particularly the last, were accompanied by
profound social changes. In the face of the leadership claim of
the aristocracy and the haute bourgeoisie — "the better people" —
a sense of self-consciousness, albeit contradictory, developed
among a broad stratum of the middle class and petty bourgeoisie.
This was shown, on the one hand, in the economic sphere. While
a portion of the middle stratum became impoverished, another
segment, through the expansion of trade and industrialization —
i.e., entrepreneurs, engineers, colonial officials — prospered and
gained social standing that had little in common with that of the
old-style trader or the landed gentry. On the other hand, the
"revolution of feelings," the romantic stylization of the private
and personal realm, gave the middle class the self-consciousness
of ultimate victory over aristocratic rationalism and skepticism,
at the very moment when society's "darker side" was becoming
visible. We will come back to this in connection with hysteria.

At the same time, however, a process of dissociation of bourgeois society was set in motion. Once this sector no longer felt

compelled to take a defensive position against the external coercion of absolutist authorities, and after its victorious emergence as a "society," it so to speak came to grips with itself, and in doing so laid bare the fictitiousness of the Lockean identity of the social individual as proprietor and human being. The political and literary communities came into conflict. On the one hand, the right to the protection of property, the right of the systematic utilization of the ownership of economic goods was combined with the concept of property as the right of acquisition of the small property owner working for himself.[39] The second half of the eighteenth century saw the transition to "political economy," which made the laws of bourgeois society and its state formulated by Locke in terms of Natural Law the natural laws of society itself.[40] Adam Smith assumed his professorship in Glasgow in 1751. Immanent in this movement was the contradiction between economic and political liberalism. The movement stressing the primacy of the "purely human" took root in the literary community. Romanticism was its literary expression, and the clamor for human rights, its political expression. In a separate development, yet one paralleling their increasing objectification and neutralization, the natural sciences took on a humanitarian, philanthropic dimension. This demarcated the functional area within medicine that gave rise to psychiatry. Inherent in these three developmental directions was the danger of the contradiction of relating man as an abstract subjective entity to an abstract, objectively conceived state — while short-circuiting his social and economic existence. In this context moral philosophy, by seeking to establish a critical harmony between the utility of a bourgeois economy and the authority of the state, played the role of intermediary on behalf of the "natural history of civil society," according to which mankind naturally inclined toward the improvement of its condition.[41]

Germane to all these processes was a condition that, although touched on only peripherally, contributed substantially to the radical change of the resultant social structure, and bore out their cohesion. The sequestration of unreason, that reasonable measure promoted by absolutism and the old social norms of natural law, collapsed. Now, in a dual expansion, the irrational — in effect the poor and the mad — entered into civil society, and conversely, society extended its liberating, integrating thrust to include the irrational, although this ambivalent dynamic was not free of contradiction. Unreason manifested itself in different ways in the different sectors of society, yet everywhere feelings were quite literally mixed. In the economic sector on the one hand there was industry's growing need for manpower — specifically for individuals who, insofar as they were poor, i.e., needy and unfettered, not bound by traditional social ties, and thus completely available — while on the other, farmers and the lower middle-class were haunted by the specter of ruin. In political thought, this obliteration of the dividing line appeared under the dual aspect of the extension of the right to freedom of all men and of the claim to an equally comprehensive integration and the prevention of political unrest. Romanticism experienced this development — threatening and fascinating — as the power of unreason over man. And the experience of the churches was no different. They saw it both as a threat to their jurisdiction over morality and as a call to broaden their welfare and pastoral activities. Medicine in particular was caught in the web of these disparate and conflicting economic needs, political demands, social and scientific objectifications, and humanitarian promises, from which it could perhaps disengage itself ideologically but not in fact. It achieved social standing as a science, quite independent of its level of knowledge and technology. This applies to medicine as a whole, e.g., with regard to its role in fighting epidemics, in increasing life expectancy and general hygiene (with regard to food, clothing, shelter), and raising the level of work performance. But equally important was the division of labor it instituted by making psychiatry into a separate branch. This made possible the differentiation and demythologizing of classic unreason, i.e., to assign to the "hard core" of irrationality, to madness as a sickness, a rational institution. It helped to assuage the fears of the vast majority of those who lacked reason — the poor — and allowed their smoother incorporation into the new rationality, that of the economy. For conversely, what led to psychiatry was not so much the philosophical deduction of irrationality, not its bourgeois form, hysteria, nor even the existence of private madhouses or Defoe's concern about making them into repositories of unwanted wives, but rather the social visibility of unreason, i.e. of madmen as "pauper lunatics."

The social interest in the "pauper lunatics" had already manifested itself in various ways, although not medically, to be sure. These preparatory and revealing processes included, an Act of Parliament in 1736 abrogating all laws "against Conjurations, Inchantments, and Witchcraft," which had formed the basis for the prosecution of the insane as possessed beings, witches, or sorcerers.[42] In 1744, a revision of the law of 1714 not only required parishes to keep their "pauper lunatics" in a secure place in the interest of public safety, but also to offer treatment: "curing such Person during such Restraint."[43] The scientific community of physicians at first remained fairly uninvolved in this matter.[44]

Like the legislators, the churches also took early notice. As though to compensate for their loss of political power some of them became extremely active in the social sphere, particularly the Methodists under the leadership of John Wesley. The state may have served the goal of legality but not of morality. This was first brought into the state through the activity of the citizens or the churches. Wesley and his co-workers and followers succeeded in bringing the new masses created by the Industrial Revolution closer to Christianity. It has been said, and rightly so, that Wesley's enthusiastic and popular approach to the conversion of the poor helped stave off major political and social upheaval in England.[45] The immediate effectiveness of Wesley's visits to the poor, of his preaching "in the open...in the fields," which he began in 1738, brought fear to the bourgeoisie.[46] Sorrow and suffering, the very topical, albeit depoliticizing themes of his sermons to the workers, were the very emotions that the bourgeoisie was about to enjoy in sublimated form in Romanticism. Wesley's concern, however, extended beyond the spiritual realm to physical salvation. In 1747 he set forth his instructions for self-treatment. His view on the spiritualization of the physical accorded with the medical notions of his time, particularly with regard to the phenomenon of electricity. Immediately after Benjamin Franklin's first experimental use of an "electric treatment machine," Wesley adopted the method — more than ten years before any hospital. He gradually acquired several such gadgets for treating the poor without charge. In 1760 he set down his experiences under the significant title *The Desideratum: or Electricity Made Plain and Useful. By a Lover of Mankind, and of Common Sense.* He saw it as the cheapest and "rarely failing Remedy, in nervous Cases of every Kind."[47] Hysteria or spleen thus ceased to be the privileged ailment of the well-to-do, physical quality was more and more becoming a psychiatric-moral factor, proof of the extent to which these matters were indicative of social problems to which medical science adjusted half-heartedly. Writing in his journal (1759) Wesley reflected: "Why, then, do not all physicians consider how far bodily disorders are caused or influenced by the mind?"[48] This hints at the peculiar relationship between depoliticization and the tendency to abandon the view of disease as a somatic phenomenon. Since then, we have been given ample proof of how easily the purely psychological view of illness can ensnarl medicine in the integrating movements of a society.

William Battie

The clerics of the various denominations who after the Revolution became such aggressive watchdogs of the moralization of the expanded society, and later expounded the new Romantic literature from their pulpits, while at the same time fighting one another, were — so it would appear — often the progenitors of the first wave of psychiatrists. This also holds true for William Battie (1704—76), who until recently was the forgotten man of psychiatric history. Yet Battie, it seems to us, supplied psychiatry as a science with its first "paradigmatic" approach to its subject matter, encompassing the institution, the practice, and the theory. The doubled-edged concept "Mad Business" now turned into a scientific medical discipline, and the "pauper lunatics" into patients. This must, of course, be understood as anticipatory: Battie merely represented — though for a long time exemplarily — the beginning of the long trek of the insane, as one component of sequestered unreason, toward social integration. We have already mentioned that social developments had made this need visible. Battie was able to respond to it. Left without means after his father's death, he studied medicine, and soon began to lecture on anatomy. He published editions of Aristotle and Isocrates, and so successful was his practice near Cambridge that in 1738 he was able to move to London. He became a Fellow of the Royal College of Physicians, lectured and published on physiology and clinical medicine, received various honorific commissions, and ultimately became president of the College in 1764 — evidently the first and apparently the only psychiatrist ever to be so honored. If it is crucial for the establishment of a new science that the prospective founder enjoy standing in another discipline and that influential people be interested, then Battie was eminently well qualified: he was one of the most renowned physicians in London and enjoyed social prestige. In addition, he was an active and versatile man — he enjoyed building houses as much as litigation — and his reformist zeal, which began with his own person, aroused the indignation of the bourgeoisie. Thus, in the country, he pretended to be one of his own workmen and dressed accordingly. He was the first to have his boats towed along the Thames by horses rather than men, which earned him the enmity of rich and poor alike. Battie can best be likened to those entrepreneurs of later times who, upon becoming aware of social injustice, instituted reforms without neglecting their own profits. At his death, Battie left a fortune of between 100,000 and 200,000 pounds; among his enterprises was a madhouse he had opened in 1754.

His psychiatric activity began with his election to the board of governors of Bedlam Hospital in 1742. Here, in addition to his medical and other duties, he spent eight years observing the inmates and seeing at first hand the abuses they were subjected to. This was the time that brought the Romantic writers to Bedlam; Hogarth used it as the setting for some of his drawings; cartoonists made caricatures of politicians in chains in asylum cells. In 1750, probably at Battie's suggestion, six prominent Londoners (including two businessmen, a druggist, an apothecary, and a physician) issued an appeal for funds for a new and better institution for "pauper lunatics." That document by Battie represented a revolutionary departure. Not only did it speak of "cure" rather than "care," and not only did it point out that there existed no institution for pauper madmen, and that the treatment was long and expensive; but it is also the first document to demand that the attendants of insane asylums receive special training. And finally it dared to suggest that this new institution should serve as a psychiatric training center for medical students: "For more Gentlemen of the faculty, making this Branch of Physick, their particular Care & Study, it may from thence reasonably be expected that the Cure of this dreadful Disease will hereafter be rendered more certain and expeditious, as well as less expensive."[49] The revolutionary nature of this unprecedented demand becomes obvious when we learn that as late as 1843 Bedlam still refused to admit medical students for clinical training. The next year, 1751, saw the opening of the new institution, St. Luke's Hospital. Battie was the first physician appointed to it by its board of governors, and in 1753 they gave him the first teaching position, as it were. Although restraints were used there, for instance handcuffs, there were none of the abuses or scandals of Bedlam. Nor were any public mad shows held. Battie replaced that practice, in which the sequestered inmates were made to serve a moralizing purpose, with one in which the insane — drawn into social activity — yet screened off from the general public — were assigned to a neutralized sector, that of medical science, which, through the admission of students, had become an immanently medical public realm.

Battie's theoretical *Treatise on Madness* did not appear until

1758. It was the first text to rely on extensive personal experience instead of resting on the traditional theoretical base; yet at the same time it was thorough and admirably brief (99 pages). In the introduction the author presents himself in a pragmatic context: when the citizens of London planned St. Luke's, he writes, they did so with an eye toward the future and with the insane of all nations in mind, seeing it as an opportunity and challenge to physicians to familiarize themselves with the problems and treatment of lunatics. It was for these and other students that he was now recording his ideas. Thus was born the first psychiatric textbook and also the canon of formal components and institutions that make psychiatry into a combination of research, teaching, and practice.

The theoretical content of Battie's book is also exemplary and programmatic, if for no other reason than that in it he links ideas into a concept that held together for a fairly long time, and in part has continued to feed the controversy about certain underlying principles of psychiatry. In a kind of negative-dialectical pragmatic manner he distinguishes between what we know and what we do not know, between a "positive" and a "negative" science, yet acknowledging the importance of both in the search for "practical Truth."[50] The seat of "natural sensation" according to his anatomic explanation is in the nerves and the brain, and nowhere else. He draws a distinction between the more remote causes of external and internal objects or stimuli and their essential, inner cause, which we do not know but which must inhere in the composition of the nerve substance itself. The final link, whose effect we know from objects, is the pressure on the nerve substance. For objects cannot be the immediate cause, if only because madmen can have perception even without seeing the corresponding objects. Taking the perceptions of the insane seriously, Battie arrives at his definition of madness:

Deluded imagination, which is not only an indisputable but an essential character of Madness ... precisely discriminates this from all other animal disorders: or that man and that man alone is properly mad, who is fully and unalterably persuaded of the existence or of the appearance of any thing, which either does not exist or does not actually appear to him, and who behaves according to such erroneous persuasion....Madness, or false perception, being then a praeternatural state or disorder of Sensation.[51]

This spells out one of the differences with Locke: Madness is no longer purely a disorder of the mind, a false association of ideas;

now sensation itself — outer as well as inner, sensation as well as imagination — can be disordered, false, deluded. With this approach, the madman is no longer seen in enlightened-absolutist terms, according to the model of a rational refutation of error or a coercive sequestration of unreason. Instead, the disorder is recognized as more profound and more real, as a new, autonomous reality — precisely in its fictitiousness. Because the sensation itself is seen as a disorder, it is placed in a larger framework, in which its "interior," on the one hand, is anchored in the concrete corporeality of the nerve substance and, on the other, is thereby guaranteed an autonomous psychic space. Some years later, this combination made possible the psychological analysis of delusion, hallucination, and paranoia, as Leibbrand and Wettley point out;[52] but for the time being, Locke's disorder of reason remained the model. Yet beyond that, the formula of the "deluded imagination" showed that Battie, too, was touched by the Romantic movement. Yet the same conception that led to the enthusiastic invocation of "imagination" to eradicate the dividing line between health and disease, as Samuel Johnson was wont to do,[53] also put madness at arm's length by localizing it anatomically and making it the province of material nature and her laws.

Battie also criticized those who professed to see a rational plan of salutary objectives, i.e., the rule of a prevailing reason, as governing the phenomena of life. In explanation of these Willis had introduced the metaphorical designations "Nature" and "Anima," and Stahl had mistakenly "deifyed" them. However, they are nothing more than useful abbreviations for medical facts, and the young practitioners should take care, Battie warned, not to confuse them with a real "intellectual agency" of "animal oeconomy," of "vital action"; that would be as absurd as the "Faculties of the Ancients."[54] In other words, the earliest conception of madness is tied to the assumption of an autonomous, self-regulating economy, with no governing reason "from above."

Two quantitative-mechanical disorders of the sensation are to be distinguished from madness as qualitatively new: anxiety or overexcitement produced by "too great or too long continued force of external objects," and, on the other hand, the obverse, "defect or total loss of sensation," the result of various factors, from insensibility to idiocy. Battie's perception of anxiety as a possible trigger of madness, and insensibility (or idiocy) as its terminal stage, was the first time that madness was conceived as a historical process, in which the qualitative-irrational disorder is understood as an intermediary, but not fully reducible stage of a rationally tangible, quantitative-mechanical process. Out of this, too, competing alternatives later develop — depending on which aspect is emphasized — the quantitative or the qualitative.[55]

Battie draws an etiological distinction between (1) "original madness," the result of an "internal disorder" of the nervous or medullary substance," and (2) "consequential madness," in which the disorder arises *ab extra* and passes through a stage of medium pressure to produce that intermediary stage of madness. The possible mechanical and psycho-moral (more remote) causes are catalogued with exemplary, still valid detail: injuries, cranial exostoses, inflammation of the cerebral membrane, concussions, sun stroke, muscular spasms (fever, epilepsy, childbirth, passions like joy and anger), poisons (including alcohol and opium), venereal disease, protracted concentration of the mind on a specific object, inactivity, indolence, and gluttony.[56] With "original madness," Battie not only anticipated the modern problem of endogeny; he also, in a negative, clinical way, defined the "idiopathic madness" philosophically deduced by G. E. Stahl in Halle: madness is likely to be original if its causes are not readily discernible, the nervous system shows congenital damage, and the illness comes and goes spontaneously, "without any assignable causes," which is why this form does not respond to medical treatment, but might disappear spontaneously. In contrast, "consequential madness" may be cured by removing the determining causes — but only if intervention is prompt. Otherwise, with the habituation of the mechanical or moral causative factors, the disorder, like a second nature, becomes as intractable as the naturally determined original madness.[57] This emphasis on the power of habit formation shifts an essential part of the unreason of madness — as also of hysteria — with regard to possible medical practice, into the realm of moral philosophy.

This influence was responsible for Battie's later sponsorship of the "moral management" movement for the total socialization of all madmen. His lapidary pronouncement that "management did much more than medicine" meant that the emergent medical field of psychiatry dismissed the resort to countless drugs as senseless and also that this new speciality was moving in the direction of a moral science. For those madmen who were entering civil society through the medium of St. Luke's or similar institutions, Battie's statement was significant. It meant that their previous exclusion, their unspoiled "freedom," their exposure to arbitrary treatment and exploitation, random violence and general lack of rights, was being replaced by something new: an all-encompassing, allegedly philanthropic, yet universal moral order, so long as this illness was "inexplicable by general science and the common law of Nature." This qualification shows that Battie's moral management was merely a surrogate for the admitted failure of control over nature. Later eras, however, crossed this "negative science," the recalcitrance of nature, off their books of knowledge and looked on moral management itself as a specific device. A further factor distinguishes moral management from the era of rationalist sequestration: measured by the yardstick of objective truth, madness ceased to be seen as an error curable by correction. Instead, it is now seen as a deviation of the sensations or behavior from the golden mean of "animal oeconomy." The cure is the reduction of the extremes to this mean of practical truth. The rules of this management are as follows: complete separation from social relations (home, family), whereby scientific authority overrides social authority, even in the case of the wealthy, who are to be deprived of their familiar servants; shielding the nerves from all stimulating objects; checking all unruly appetites; diverting the fixed imagination; exercise with or without the consent of the patient. Within the framework of this regimen, an attempt must be made to remove the discernible causes, whereby the passions are to be lowered to a less tempestuous state either by narcotics or by stimulating the opposite emotion (anxiety as opposed to anger, worry as opposed to joy). With gluttony and indolence, the doctor is permitted to use force, e.g. irritating medicaments, in order to lead the patient to a more restrained and more active way of life.[58]

Turning to a "vulgar" apprehension of things, Battie does not confine himself to wresting madmen and their unreason from the controversies of the schools of philosophy.[59] He polemicizes, above all against his powerful competitor and spokesman for the traditional notion of madness, John Monro, the physician of Bedlam. And he also polemicizes against the private owners of lunatic asylums. He holds their silence, the "defect of proper communication," responsible for the defective knowledge in this area, knowledge which can only be gained through an exchange of experiences of physicians. Battie's publication of his own experiences was a frontal attack on this private and silent exploitation both of madmen and the knowledge about them.[60]

His experience led Battie to this humanitarian, emphatic conclusion:

We have therefore, as Men, the pleasure to find that Madness is, contrary to the opinion of some unthinking persons, as manageable as many other distempers, which are equally dreadful and obstinate, and yet are not looked upon as incurable: and that such unhappy objects ought by no means to be abandoned, much less shut up in loathsome prisons as criminals or nuisances to the society.[61]

However, he warned the young practitioner in particular, against therapeutic activism, which can also prevent a cure, for one never knows what puts the greater strain on the nerves, the madness or the therapy: the nerves must be given the "liberty to recover natural firmness." Also, the physician must always strive to mitigate the suffering of his fellow creatures, albeit if only for a brief spell.[62]

Monro understood this polemic very well. And nothing points up Battie's epochal significance more than Monro's immediate response to this challenge, which ended the two-hundred-year-old silence of Bedlam physicians about madness. That very same year, 1758, Monro published his *Remarks on Dr. Battie's Treatise on Madness*,[63] which attempts to prove the pointlessness of making madness a topic of medical discussion:

Madness is a distemper of such a nature, that very little of real use can be said concerning it; the immediate causes will for ever [!] disappoint our search, and the care of that disorder depends on management as much as medicine. My own inclination would never have led me to appear in print, but it was thought necessary for me, in my situation, to say something in answer to the undeserved censures which Dr. Battie has thrown upon my predecessors[64]

Yet these words reveal the dialectics of the conservative stance: once it engages in verbal exchanges it becomes, even against its will, subject to the laws of reasoning. Just to criticize Battie, Monro had to offer his own definition against Battie's "deluded imagination": madness, for him, is "vitiated judgment" — in line with rationalist tradition. Now we may say that Battie's more comprehensive formula turned out to be more fruitful for nineteenth-century psychopathology, yet we must also admit that Monro put out a warning signal at the very start of the new movement. For, whereas the definition "vitiated judgment" implies a restrictive use of the concept of madness, inherent in the idea of madness as a disorder of the imagination is the danger of losing sight of its limits and applying it to any social behavior that deviates from any arbitrary norm. Though Battie avoided this danger, many of his successors evolved a theory from the practical socialization of madness that turned psychiatry into an instrument for the preservation of moral order and social integration. Nonethe less, Monro rightly finds fault with this expansive tendency in Battie: "It is certain that the imagination may be deluded where there is not the least suspicion of madness, as by drunkenness, or by hypochondriacal and hysterial affections."[65]

The Battie Monro controversy stirred up public debate. Both books were thoroughly analyzed in *The Critical Review*, and Smollett, in *Sir Launcelot Greaves*,[66] borrowed entire passages from them.

In the wake of this discussion both the medical and governmental authorities became sufficiently aroused about the "Mad Business" for the College of Physicians to change its position and agree to collaborate — it had refused to do so in 1754 — on a bill for the control of private madhouses. In 1763, Parliament set up a commission to deal with this issue. On it served such luminaries as Henry Fox and William Pitt. Battie and Monro gave expert testimony before it, both agreed on the necessity of official supervision of private enterprises of this type. But on two separate occasions, in 1772 and 1773, the bill went down to defeat in the House of Lords. Not until 1774 was the first Act of Parliament for regulating madhouses passed. The limited jurisdiction of that law reflected the conflicting interests involved. It assured the rights and welfare only of the well-to-do, paying inmates of the private houses, and excluded the "pauper lunatics" — whether in workhouses, alms houses, etc., as well as those in publicly supported private institutions. Under the provision of that law anyone wishing to keep more than one madman in a house had to obtain a license from five "Commissionars" appointed by the College of Physicians who, among other duties, had to inspect these houses once a year — although only in daytime. All new inmates — except for the "pauper lunatics" — had to be registered officially by the owners, in London within three days of admission, in the provinces within fourteen days. The same exception applied to a regulation that commitment required written statement of a doctor. The enforcement of this imperfect law was correspondingly lax; for some houses no report was ever filed. Even though the "pauper lunatics" — like the "labouring poor" — were known to exist, it took another half century for them to be judged worthy of legal protection.[67]

Their theoretical disagreement did not prevent Battie and Monro from cooperating in practice. Frequent mutual consultations as well as various court appearances bear witness to that. When Monro, sued by a former patient for illegal confinement, appeared to be losing the case, Battie was called in as an expert witness. Through skillful questioning he led the plaintiff to reveal his particular delusion, which had not been uncovered during the cross-examination, and Monro was acquitted. Thus, not only did Battie prove in practice the superiority of his approach over Monro's concept of vitiated judgment, but the case became an oft-cited example in English legal history of the need for expert psychiatric opinion. Furthermore, precisely this forensic aspect makes Battie's "paradigm" complete; for ever since, psychiatric practice has been intertwined with law in a most ambivalent fashion.

The development of psychiatry thus received its impetus not from theory but rather from the social visibility of the "poor lunatics" and from the creation of a special institution for them. Battie's theory may not have had much direct response, but his institution was promptly emulated, first, not coincidentally in industrialized Manchester. In this economically developed town, the proposed care of the "poor lunatics" mixed economic and philanthropic motives with the explicit need for a comprehensive social order in which both rich and poor — although properly separated from each other — occupied an assigned place. Manchester made plain that capitalist economic liberalism, dependent on the "labouring poor," also had to take the "poor lunatics," though segregated, into the civil structure. In the first planning for a "Publick Infirmary" in 1752, the authorities found it extremely inconvenient to admit "poor lunatics" — because of the expense of building and staffing.

In 1763, however, they revised the plan and agreed also to include those who met Battie's definition in the program. The reasons given were: (1) care of, and the protection of society from, the insane, for even these least fortunate of human beings, for whom no one felt responsible, needed a place, order, and protection; (2) families had to be relieved of the burden of paying the owners of private madhouses. In line with these principles, The Infirmary, Dispensary and Lunatic Asylum, Manchester, was opened in 1766, and expanded in 1773. Manchester was even more pace-setting and far more restrained in its use of physical force than St. Luke's — precisely because of the clearcut motives of economics and order. Battie's example was also followed in Newcastle-upon-Tyne in 1767, York in 1777, and Liverpool in 1790.[68]

In this situation the theoretical contribution of that sector of medicine that lacked the opportunity for firsthand observation, i.e. special madhouses, in keeping with the new approach to madness, represented a comparative step backwards: Because the treatment of the insane had already progressed so substantially and become so interwoven with socio-economic needs, the traditional view of it as a subdivision of a universal pathology was regressive. This held true especially for Scotland, which, by dint of special laws, could successfully oppose all English demands for a new order for the insane — both in the traditional and the new form. Consequently, until the late nineteenth century the majority of Scotland's deranged population was "free," and the possibility of first-hand medical observation was hence limited.

Yet it was the Scottish school that produced some of the leading figures in medicine after 1750, among them not only Robert Whytt (1714—66), but above all his successor, William Cullen (1710—90), who linked philosophical empiricism to the theory of nerves and thus based almost all of medicine on neurophysiology and neuropathology. He did this by combining the findings of the German physiologists Friedrich Hoffman (spontaneous activity of the muscle fibers) and Albrecht von Haller (distinction between the sensitivity of the nerves and the irritability of the muscles) to arrive at an identity of nerves and muscles (nerves have only sentient and moving extremities) and therefore at a uniform "nervous energy," which is identical with physical life itself, though, to be sure, in interplay with an immaterial, rational soul. All diseases, as unnatural movements of nervous energy, are therefore nervous diseases, "*morbi neurosi*," "neuroses." The neurological theory developed by Willis, Sydenham, and Whytt through the middle-class disorder of hysteria now became the pathogenetic basis of all pathology. The latter was expanded by Cullen as a complete, "natural" system, structured after the botanical method of Linnaeus' *Genera morborum* (1763). Cullen's system of (nervous) disease distinguishes four classes, one of which being the class of neuroses in a narrower sense because it bears almost exclusively on the nervous system, the others the feverish, cachectic, and local diseases.[69]

The concept of nervous energy dynamically changed previous mechanical nerve theories, especially since the varying level of nerve fluid ceased to be the criterion for a healthy or defective life, but rather its mobility, the alternation between activity, excitement, tension and relaxation, collapse, brain atony, both temporal and spatial. Man was now seen, so to speak, as something more than a physically operating entity. Psychiatry owes to Cullen above all its thinking in terms of polarities of forces and drives (strength and weakness) and of feelings (exaltation and depression), as well as the notion of disease as intensified processes of health.

Cullen's class of neuroses comprises four orders: comas (e.g., apoplectic stroke), adynamiae (e.g., hypochondria), spasms (e.g., hysteria), vesaniae (insanity). The last was traditionally defined as "judgement impaired, without pyrexia or coma." In line with this theoretical derivation of insanity, which belongs to a now obsolete phase of social development, Cullen's therapeutic concept still followed along lines of physical restraint, although one of its functions — the protection of society against madmen — was not stressed; however, the other — a means of steering the mind onto the right track — emerged all the more distinctly: "Restraint is also to be considered as a remedy…is usefull, and ought to be complete…and the strait waistcoat answers every purpose better than any other that has yet been thought of."[70] Instilling fear is also useful since fear calms the mind and counteracts overexcitement. Hence, the people in contact with madmen should always seek to create "awe and fear". "Sometimes it may be necessary to acquire [it] even by stripes and blows. The former, although having the appearance of more severity, are much safer than strokes or blows about the head."[71]

Notwithstanding Cullen's eminence, his only impact on psychiatry was made where some of his disciples were able to deal with practical problems of insanity (especially Thomas Arnold, A. Crichton, J. Ferriar, and W. S. Hallaran). Moreover, Cullen's theory became the most influential model for the founders of psychiatry in other countries, who either followed it, or critically elaborated it. For instance, Philippe Pinel in France, Benjamin Rush in the United States, Chiarugi in Italy, and a number of German doctors. The existence of a seemingly complete outline by one of the most famous physicians of his day must have been of enormous help to these men in their pioneering work with the insane, however theoretical that model and however different their results based on their own experiences. Against this backdrop, it may be easier to understand why John Brown (1735—88), a pupil of Cullen who was far ahead of his mentor with regard to the speculative simplification of neurophysiological findings, met with little response in England, whereas in Germany his influence greatly overshadowed Cullen's and led to virtually a philosophical controversy over *"Brownianism."* The ex-theologian Brown, in his *Elementa medicinae* (Edinburgh, 1780), generalized

Cullen's speculative nervous energy into a total vital energy, excitability, i.e., the faculty of being aroused by stimuli; and everything that affects the organism is a stimulus. Life is essentially (innate) excitability, just as iron is magnetic; and at the same time it is forced, being dependent on the stimuli and their intensity, and the stimulation of a part affects the whole. These ideas burst through the limits of a mechanistic medicine; it was replaced by the principles of totality and energy-polarity of Romantic medicine, which explains the impact on Germany (especially on Schelling).[72] Disease, too, follows these principles of life and health. Disease is merely a sthenic or asthenic departure from the normal, average intensity of excitability to which health corresponds. With regard to the various forms of madness, this means that mania is overexcitement, hence a sthenic disease, caused by a cerebral defect or excessive stimuli (passions). The last-named, however, can increase so greatly as to destroy excitability and thereby bring on an asthenic state in the form of weakness (epilepsy or apoplexy). In contrast, melancholia signifies underexcitement, i.e., a diminution of the exciting passions; in this way, a real weakness has produced an asthenic state. The therapeutic principle derives from that theory. It consists of a system of diverse counteractive remedies or a balance of stimuli, methods involving diet as well as punishment and/or the stimulation of the passions, which are to counteract the pathological extreme until a mean is reached.

Brown's theory was basically no longer part of that era (his extreme formulation of Cullen resulting in something qualitatively different alienated his former champion) and was applied to psychiatry only because of its claim to universality. Coevally with Cullen's and Brown's chief works, another Cullen disciple published the second specifically psychiatric textbook (after Battie), which contains some aspects highly characteristic of this transitional era of the social integration of the insane and the establishment of institutions for and theories about them. As its author, Thomas Arnold (1742–1816), makes clear, the view of madmen as the subject of special public interest had already reached the private madhouses, for Arnold owned the third biggest madhouse "in the country," at Leicester. One reason this had come about was that since 1774, the private houses had become subject to legislation demanding that they shoulder their national responsibility. Thus more and more, the private entrepreneurs in the "Mad Business" placed notices in newspapers informing the public that they also accepted "pauper lunatics." Arnold, too, perceived his own insane asylum as a "generous and patriotic institution": Eight of its inmates did not pay the full rate, and "two others [were] free of all expence whatsoever." Beyond this, he himself worked to abolish the pre-eminence of private enterprise in the "Mad Business": at his instigation plans for a public asylum were launched in 1781, and the house was opened in 1794, with Arnold as the first physician of the Leicester Lunatic Asylum. His two-volume work, published in 1782 and 1786 respectively, propagated these objectives. After Battie's, his was the first book by an actual psychiatrist, deeply concerned about scientific standards, systematic, and carefully annotated. The introduction contains a vehement denunciation of private houses for making the insane the objects of private exploitation while ignoring the scientific and public interest "of the few whose situations have afforded ample room for observations in this way, how small a number have seen it proper to throw what is so conducive to their private emolument into the public stock!...This essay will...sufficiently attain its end...by acquainting the less informed part of the public ...with these disorders."[73] Furthermore, the epigraph on the title-page is a quotation from Epictetes in the original and in its translation into English: "Men are not disturbed by things themselves, but by the opinions which they form concerning them." All this clarifies something that Battie had first touched on: like paupers, the insane were not to be left solely to the mercy of nature. Instead, society viewed itself increasingly as an autonomous sphere obligated to integrate those individuals as well, and as being in need of them as instruments of its dual expansionary drive. It needed the poor for its outward expansion — as workers in the economic domain, and as soldiers in the colonial-military expansion. But it also needed the deranged for its internal expansion, for the establishment of an internal circulation essential to its self-understanding, its identity. For in the bourgeois revolution, in the emancipation from external, physical authority, society, self-reliant and at the same time following the market principle, was forced to orient itself in terms of itself. It did so via the sensations, passions (no longer integrated in *ratio* and *physis*), and opinions. Society learned how to suffer from them as though of something subjective, self-posited, while simultaneously making them the transmission belts of the social movement and of self-understanding. Hysteria and spleen had already established themselves in this circular motion by about 1750. Only now the insane also became a part, and their autonomous aspect made them even more suitable executors of this function.

"Industrial and animal oeconomy" ceased to be separable, however great the contradiction between the proprietor and the human being. Since bourgeois society derived its claim to public authority not from the outside but from within itself, and therefore was constantly forced to legitimize itself, both the poor and the insane were being functionalized in that respect as well. They were the outstanding examples for justifying the duty of the civil state to vouchsafe internal order and protect the public — by means of social welfare and social coercion — precisely in the area beyond the reach of the criminal court.

Arnold touched on these themes, even if his practice and theory do not figure among the reform attempts of the subsequent epoch. His book makes the frequency of insanity in England a function of freedom and opulence. This not only extends Blackmore's and Cheyne's ideas to England's status as an industrial society, but also, and for the first time, it extends the functionalization of hysteria and spleen to forms of actual insanity: while the French have the lowest incidence of insanity of all civilized nations because of their diminished predisposition for deep, strong, tender, lasting passions (cf. Addison and Hume) England is well-endowed with these feelings, especially with regard to religion, love, and commerce; and these very emotions are the crucial causes of insanity. Thus, love, in France is a casual gallantry, not a serious affair of the heart as in England (see Sterne). Nor can religion in France arouse genuine passions (e.g., guilt feelings), since its dominant religious institution, the Catholic Church, can calm the troubled by its power of absolution. Finally, the French are barely affected by a desire for wealth or profit, since they still dwell in a land of slaves under an absolute monarch where commerce and agriculture are held in check. England, in contrast, "this happy land of liberty," has created conditions in which a "sound philosophy and genuine christianity [taught] the proper use and intrinsic value of the blessings they enjoy." In France, where "the character of a trader and a gentleman are supposed to be incompatible," and where official restraint suppresses all passion, the yearning for property thus cannot become so great as to cause insanity. Hence, luxury in France exists only among the upper classes, whereas in England it is for all classes. Insanity is thus functionally bound, above all to the spread of property, riches, and luxury and hence more prevalent than anywhere else in the world "as in this rich, free, and commercial [English] nation."[74]

Arnold's theory cannot be divorced from such views. It was

influenced not only by his teacher Cullen, but, given his extensive practical experience, by Battie as well. The obligatory sensualistic position is arrived at not merely via Locke, but also via David Hartley,[75] a physician with an interest in psychiatry. Arnold continues in Battie's direction when he accepts disorders of the sensations, i.e. hallucinations, as "ideal insanity" as opposed to "notional insanity" — conceptual delusion, i.e. the rambling speech, the associational disorders of the Lockean tradition.

Various peculiarities and emphases would seem to indicate that Arnold was beginning to lean toward the internalization of the Romantic experience. He stresses not only the affective (melancholy or manic) character of insanity, but also the possibility of insanity due to a passion that has gained ascendancy and become a habit. The "empire of passions" and thus the basis of "pathetic insanity" comprises love, superstition, avarice, misanthropy as well as nostalgia, "and all inordinate desires and affections which manifest themselves...in fondness for scheming and traffic of the most romantic, extravagant, childish, or absurd kind."[76]

Moreover, he sees a fluid line dividing the follies common to all men from actual insanity. That is to say, all men, because of their inherent passions and disposition for derangement, are drawn into the natural, moral sphere of madness with the ever-present possibility of the unnatural-medical form of madness: "moral insanity" is the natural, universal basis of "medical insanity." The fool and the genius are, in this respect, endangered socio-moral borderline cases, vide Shakespeare. Arnold's individual accounts show that he bases his concept of insanity on the experiences of man's self-importance and his disorders (alienation, deprivation).

The ambivalent position that Arnold assigns to the passions reveals the contradictions in the structure of civil society. On the one, the economic side, the intensity of the passions is an indicator of an enterprising spirit, of the pursuit of risk-taking, wealth, and luxury, and thus of the greatness and freedom of the nation; in addition, the passions are legitimized by a "sound philosophy" and Christianity. The other, the private, inward side, has to foot the bill for this. Here, the passions, the desires, not only carry a much greater risk of insanity, but they also spur moralizing about human behavior. Arnold delivers an indictment of extremes, an adjuration to uphold moral norms, the truth which is found in the mean, the average. Deviant behavior — whether of the fool, the eccentric, or the genius — apparently invites the threat of punishment in the form of disease, of "medical insanity." However, since the tendency to moral deviation is an inherent human trait, the concept of "moral insanity" (in contrast to "medical insanity," from which it differs only in degree) poses a universal threat that no member of society, as a human being, can escape. This is exemplified by "appetitive insanity," in which a person is intent upon satisfying a desire even when the conditions do not warrant it. "It usually attacks those who, though in a single state, and under the outward restraint of an artificial modesty, have imprudently indulged in the wantonness of lascivious thoughts, and amorous desires, of which they had neither the sanction of law, nor of custom, nor of religion."[77]

In 1809, Arnold published a third volume, *On the Management of the Insane*. By now, he could already look back on forty-two years of treating the insane, and the ratio of successful cures in his private institution and the public asylum was, $3:2$ and $2:1$ respectively. The social distinction expressed by this becomes even more obvious when Arnold pleads for humaneness and "mild and indulgent treatment," yet openly states: "Chains should never be used but in the case of poor patients, whose pecuniary circumstances will not admit of such attendance as is necessary to procure safety without them."[78]

The Functionalization of Hysteria

Let us trace the course of hysteria or spleen, since 1750, i.e., of those less serious nervous ailments that had already won public acceptance. 1746 saw the publication of the first book on epilepsy, by John Andree. As the founding physician of the London Infirmary, he had gained firsthand experience with this disorder. Thus, here too, practical experience brought scientific advances. At any rate, it led to a sharper distinction between hysteria and epilepsy, a graver and apparently organic disorder, even though that distinction ultimately took a hundred years. In 1796, Giovanni Battista Morgagni, the greatest anatomist of his day, published the results of some seven hundred dissections. While undeniably furthering anatomical research, the work made it clear that assumptions about the physical basis of cerebral and nervous diseases should be approached with critical reserve.

Even more important was the dissociation of medical concepts that emerged in the middle of the century. The spirits that hitherto had symbolized the almost metaphysical unity of the physical and nonphysical, of the external and internal phenomena, were now being gradually replaced by models of nervous activity that, together with the advances in physiological experiments, leaned more heavily on physics: on the motion of solid and liquid matter, the tonicity and tension of elastic fibers, the fibrations of taut strings. On the one hand, this created the premise for welding the various medical fields into a unified science of the laws and functions of the human body, while on the other, this physical orientation took on symbolic significance at odds with its function of explaining bodily processes. The "nature" of man became ambiguous, dissolving into an internal and external self. The "inner view of the somatic-psychosocial spirits of Sydenham now excluded the body, whose functions were being seen as merely external phenomena; there developed an increasingly psychological approach with a vision of a direct and subjective truth. For "soul," "feeling," "sympathy," "sensus communis," "passion," the external-visible became purely a means or analogy for understanding the internal-invisible. And the concept of "constitution" likewise became an instrument for learning about the inner, the mental disposition, from external signs. The extent to which the passions followed moral norms rather than natural laws was a theme in Arnold. And Wesley, we know, found electricity a useful model for the investigation of the inner life of man and related practical matters. The extreme example of Brown showed how von Haller's concepts of sensibility and irritability that grew out of his physiological experiments were altered to meet medical and philosophical requirements. And these conceptual internalizations became a subject of literary romanticism in England.

Robert Whytt, Cullen's predecessor who made Scottish medicine a factor to be reckoned with, was a major figure in this movement. In 1751 Whytt created a somatic neurological medicine largely free of spirits, and in 1765, he wrote the only significant book on hysteria of the late eighteenth century. As a "neurologist" he not only discovered such highly important reflexes as the reaction of the pupils to light, the rigidity of the pupils after the destruction of the corpora quadrigemina, sneezing, choking, coughing, voiding of the bladder, erection and ejaculation.[79] His reflex experiments brought him a clearer understanding of the relationship between muscle activity and feeling. This connection led him to the assumption that movement may be triggered by a nerve impulse even in the absence of a higher will or external stimulus; i.e., there exist "vital" or "involuntary motions" without "express consciousness," that is, without any directing authority such as Stahl's "soul." In that case there is no anima, no "vital or

sentient soul" that we have in common with animals and no
separate, purely human animus, "the seat of reason and intelligence." Instead, "there seems to be in man one sentient and
intelligent PRINCIPLE, which is equally the source of life, sense
and motion, as of reason."[80] It is this "principle," abstract in
Whytt, that permitted him to replace the traditional demarcation
line between conscious human and unconscious animal functions
by another, which according to Hunter and Macalpine, differentiated between a neurophysiological and psychological approach,
whereby both — the one external, the other internal — are able to
describe the same totality of human functions as an autonomous,
virtually closed circuit.

This also holds true for Whytt's analysis of hysteria and hypochondria, the "nervous disorders" of women and men, respectively.
Their cause is "an uncommon weakness, or a depraved or unnatural
feeling, in some of the organes of the body." The characteristic
multiplicity of afflicted organs and their remoteness from one
another, which can only be explained by the greater mobility
of the somatic relations (especially in the case of women, who
therefore are more frequent victims of disease), i.e., by excessive
"sympathy" or "consensus." The last two exist in the organs, yet
at the same time they are a form of sensibility disseminated by the
nervous system. The other cause of nervous disorders is thus "a
too great delicacy and sensibility of the whole nervous system."[81]
These qualities are mental, even moral categories, and Foucault
rightly remarks: "From now on one fell ill from too much feeling;
one suffered from an excessive solidarity with all the beings
around one. One was no longer compelled by one's secret nature;
one was the victim of everything which, on the surface of the
world, solicited the body and the soul. And as a result, one was
both more innocent and more guilty."[82] On the one hand, nerve
irritation, a feeble and delicate constitution, drove the afflicted
persons to physical and unconscious reactions, including loss of
consciousness. On the other hand, in a much more profound
sense the disease could be regarded as the natural punishment for
a wrong, precisely because reason no longer was an independent
authority whose error had to be perceived and corrected. Where
the stored-up feelings exceed the absorptive capacity of the
irritated nerves, a mere error becomes a moral failing, a person's
personal behavior a sin against nature, here posited first as the
bourgeois norm of naturalness,[83] and second, as physical nature
and as predisposition toward abnormal reaction becomes the
agent for moral punishment. Such a secularized-bourgeois crime-

and-punishment relation, serving a self-regulating social order can encompass all possible claims to needs, passions, and conceptions, but especially all abuses, all "unnatural" extremes: a sedentary urban existence, reading novels, going to the theater, faulty diet, thirst for knowledge, sexual passion, and the practice which because of its criminal nature could only be alluded to: masturbation. Obviously, in contrast to Arnold's moral insanity with its threat of madness, this conception of hysteria had a far more immediate effect, since even at the most tentative attempt at self-observation and self-understanding, it served as a fascinating and compelling interpretative schema.

The moralization of sensibility and the "revolution of the feelings," the new conception of nervous disorders and literary romanticism were not only simultaneous, they not only interacted both on the theoretical and practical plane, but they also corresponded in their social functions. For just as the economic revolution began in the middle of the century, so did the restructuring of the bourgeois personal realm, the outward and inward expansion. The concept of "capital" established itself, and the Sternean adjectives "interesting" and "sentimental" gained currency.[84] With industrialization, writers lost political and economic influence as well as their political patrons, and so they turned their attention on man, his nature and inwardness, his personal life and self-perception. The road of bourgeois man as proprietor and as individual diverged; both entrepreneur and genius were free individuals, and though apparently living in two inherently contradictory worlds, they were in fact mutually compensatory. Along with others, the petty bourgeoisie was swept up in a veritable reading craze, which soon became the instrument that led via passion to nervous disorder or "mania." Smollett was the first to operate a "literary factory." Around 1780, a growing publishing industry helped make book production more efficient. Demand had grown so large that the manufacturer looked at books solely as a commodity for an anonymous market whose requirements had to be weighed and met competitively. A literary device used in this competition involved the cultivation of originality: In 1759, the cleric Edward Young wrote his *Conjectures on Original Composition.*

But just what did this burgeoning middle-class readership want? By the middle of the century, the sequestration of the overtly irrational had become a visible fact, and man's hidden unreason a literary theme. Not only had reason been dethroned medically by Whytt and included as just another instance in the circuit of mental laws, or furnished by Arnold with the compass of civil laws, habits, and religion, it had also earned the profound distrust of writers, as for instance the melancholy Samuel Johnson in *Rasselas* (1759): "Of the uncertainties of our present state, the most dreadful and alarming is the uncertain continuance of reason. ...No man will be found in whose mind airy notions do not sometimes tyrannise, and force him to hope or fear beyond the limits of sober probability. All power of fancy over reason is a degree of insanity." The reverse of this mourned relativization was the apology offered on behalf of the right to emotion, which unquestionably fulfilled a demand of the middle class.

In its origin, Romanticism is an English movement, just as the modern middle class, which here speaks for itself for the first time in literature independently of the aristocracy, is a result of English conditions. Thomson's nature poetry, Young's "Night Thoughts", and Macpherson's Ossianic laments as well as the sentimental novel of manners of Richardson, Fielding and Sterne are all only the literary form of the individualism which also finds expression in *laissez-faire* and the Industrial Revolution.[85]

Once popular opinion became convinced that man was not completely rational, the growing visibility of sequestered unreason became more tolerable, and even the insane ceased to be looked upon as completely irrational. On the contrary, the madman's visible irrationality and one's own hidden internal irrationality were seen to share certain qualities, such as intoxicating emotions, especially of a painful sort, passion, sensibility, irresistible desires, fancies and dreams and other aspects of the dark side of the soul. The identification of this communality, in which the nervous disorders constituted the model of a randomly calibrated connecting bridge, did not have the same provocative impact as in Swift's time, when madness was still sequestered. In fact, it was something that many authors and readers were able to share with pain or observe with pleasure. Yet this identification could be provocative when, say, Sterne's Tristram Shandy, the "knight of the hobby-horse," borrows the freedom of the individual from the world of the mad, who as an oddity, an eccentric, accepts the limitation of man, thereby proclaiming the renunciation of the rational personality and the perception of the absolute and of worldly accomplishment: "I triumph'd over him as I always do, like a fool."

On the one hand, individualism as the demand for the untrammeled development of all faculties was indeed a protest against the aristocracy, and here the writer and the entrepreneur were comrades in arms. On the other hand, it was also a protest against that which had replaced the aristocracy, and here the writer stood against the entrepreneur, against the leveling, mechanization, and depersonalization of bourgeois economic society. In this framework, the attack against the calculating rationality of the economy arose out of an irrational emotional depth, and in the face of a society that exploited nature man's nature took on moral attributes. Thus the suggestion and exaggeration of one's own feelings, the self-contemplation and the absorption with every mood and emotion were now not only directed against aristocratic aloofness, but "a compensation for lack of success in practical life."[86] By reducing these various needs to a literary formula, Richardson became one of the most successful writers ever. He made the personal life, the emotional problems of simple but virtuous ordinary people a spiritual drama of sentimental intimacy, nervous tenderheartedness, and edifying self-revelation. His world is one of temptations, to be overcome by inner steadfastness after a profound moral struggle. *Pamela* (1740), the endangered yet virtuous heroine who is rewarded by marrying her nobleman, is the prototype of all later romantic fantasies and moralizing novels in which virtue is the petty-bourgeois means to an end: the immoral success morality of the unsuccessful. The hero gives meaning to the reader's unfulfilled life. The moral justification for the bourgeois social order as the "natural" structure and the ideology for the battle with life come together in this psychology. And virtually every writer held nervous disease responsible for his hero's or his own sorrows: society, the civilized, urban world, became one big spectrum of stimuli which held the sentimental and hence moral citizen in their sway, while those who remained unaffected, who had no stomach for it, who simply went about their business, showed themselves to be insensitive, unemotional, "un-sympathetic,"[87] and thus, in the civil sense, immoral — non-citizens. Now, idiocy and imbecility all the more appeared as not just the consequence and irreversible final stage of madness, but also as a moral causal relationship: the dreadful punishment for the crime of not tightening the moral reins on the pleasurable instrument of sentimentality, of giving in to the temptations of artificial urban life, of allowing the passions to become immoderate, and overstepping the boundaries of the bourgeois norm and of naturalness. Restraint and renunciation could solve the moral problem posed by sentimentalism, the privilege of the bourgeois, and success was the reward. If no solution was found, sentimentalism was likely to increase to the point of unnatural immoderation, with illness one of the possible punishments. The transitional stages were flexible: nervous disorders — madness — insensibility. Arnold's presentations used other concepts: moral insanity and medical insanity. The awareness of moral guilt and the notion of mental disease as a punishment combined to sanction the moral order and threaten the good citizen. Johnson's words in *Rasselas* that "No disease of the imagination...is so difficult of cure, as that which is complicated with the dread of guilt" should be seen in this context. While the economy followed rationality, utility, and self-preservation, James Vere, a merchant and a governor of Bedlam, in 1778 invoked the nervous disorders to develop a compensating bourgeois morality: when the "moral instincts" lose their authority over the "lower order of instincts" (i.e., "self-preservation," "self-love"), the result is "a sort of internal war, which divides the man against himself: and hence a large share of disquiet and restlessness will be the unavoidable consequences."[88]

But how do the middle-class protagonists of novels, their romantic authors, and the physicians of nervous disorders carry the day in this inner mental and also sociomoral struggle? By resorting to the guaranteed device of unsurpassable effectiveness and popularity: escape, retreat from the workaday world of achievement, from the turmoil of the cities, the stresses and failures of their professions, and the nerveracking pleasures — in short, from the flood of stimuli, from the responsibility, guilt, and sickness, to which the sensitive soul is exposed.[89] The direction of this flight from civilization is laid out. The individual gets in touch with this essential "humanity," his inner "nature," the subjective truth about himself, via the harmony and innocence of virgin external nature, and the result corresponds to moral "naturalness" which tempers the behavior toward the norm. What began with Cheyne became a fashion with Richardson (who was reputed to have symptoms of "bibliomania"), a physical-moral therapeutic institution. Pastoral life, outings, hunting, fishing, riding, gymnastics, took on an aura of wholesome moderation, as did the English Garden, milk cures and other natural diets. Since the nerves were seen as vibrating, taut strings, music also was said to possess ideal sympathetic-regulative healing powers (while romantic literature made for overexcitement).[90] The cathartic effect of water, linked since time immemorial to the myth of inner rebirth, became institutionalized: in the eighteenth century Bath became a center of social life.

While these measures often involved short trips — and thus were

used mainly in the treatment of minor disorders of the petty bourgeoisie) travel in general, the grand tour became the prestigious
cure for the more serious distresses of the upper middle class.
While a mere hundred years earlier travel was still considered the
cause of illness (homesickness) and while Sydenham still believed
that travel did nothing more than bring symptomatic relief, by
the middle of the century it had become the primary remedy as
well as the fashion. The young in particular were sent on the grand
tour, to France and Italy: education, enjoyment, and the cure of
Weltschmerz, of moral scruples and unacceptable habits, before
entering the real world or recuperation from its demands — were
part and parcel of this. Escape into nature and into the past were
one and the same. Horace Walpole, Smollett, Matthew Green,
Boswell, Beckford, Goldsmith, and Sterne all took Sterne's
Sentimental Journey (1768).[91]

The poor, needless to say, did not share in these cultural products, neither in the more sublime forms of the nervous disorders
or in the costly, truly liberating instrument of their cure. The only
methods — if any — available to them were the traditional purga-
tives and similar coercive measures, Wesley's discovery of the
cheapest remedy, the electrical machine, and its use for the poor,
represented a step toward integration, putting the poor on the
same level with some better-off citizens. However, this was also a
medical device for their integration into the industrial world,
as the story of Dr. W. St. Clare's successful therapy demonstrates.
In February 1787, a wave of hysteria accompanied by convulsions
and anxiety attacks, swept through the female workforce of a
textile mill, and even spread to another plant at some distance.
The factory, which employed some three hundred workers had to
halt production. A physician was called in, and he succeeded in
curing all the patients with his "portable electrical machine...by
electric shocks" within a short time, and the factory was able to
reopen.[92]

Scottish moral philosophy played as large a part as Romanticism
in the genesis of a medicine of the human mind, of psychiatry.
This holds both for the theoretical justification of this area of
inquiry as well as for the evolution of a pragmatic, humane attitude of physicians toward the object of their science, the insane,
and for the definition of the social function of psychiatry. Like
Romanticism, Scottish philosophy was rooted in an immanent
dual protest. It was skeptical of metaphysics and sensualism alike.
It opposed the absoluteness of external authority, yet wished to
preserve it — with utility as the criterion. That is to say, it did not

trust an authority bending with the changes in civil society, but
rather it held to tradition as the basis of a continuous process, a
natural progress. "Its criticism is in harmony with the conservatism of natural history itself."[93] In assigning the heart primacy
over the head, in making sympathy a social virtue, the Scots went
along with Shaftesbury, and with common sense, which made
possible original and natural judgments, and hence social existence:
"They serve to direct us in the common affairs of life, where our
reasoning faculty would leave us in the dark."[94] To be sure, they
made common sense subjective. It no longer had a medically
definable site in the organism, as in Willis, and now related to
nature only by analogy. Relatively detached from it, common
sense constituted a realm of subjective evidence. Scottish philosophy "replaced knowledge in its real sense with a pragmatically
determined reliance on the validity of 'common sense' and on
the fact that truth was always central....Common sense was a
statistical mean of all the beliefs found in the world."[95] It was an
attempt to arrive at a statement about mental and social conditions, with only indirect reference to the mind and the body, to
rational knowledge and nature.

Thus we find Hutcheson trying to prove the same thing as
Battie, Arnold, and Whytt: that in the human subject there is a
realm in which the rationally obvious and morally judicable
become autonomous, virtually acting with the force of a second
nature, against which any effort at rational correction is impotent,
and merely serves rationalization:

"...and commonly beget some secret Opinions to justify
the Passions."[96] For Thomas Reid this was so self-evident that in
his eyes introspection into one's own mind was the only means
toward his objective — an "anatomy of the mind," an "analysis
of the human faculties." But even such introspection, in the
form of reflection, always comes too late to reduce the level of
inculcated biases to the "simple and original principles of the
constitution."[97] This was the starting point for enrolling this
type of psychology in the service of medicine. J. Gregory, professor of philosophy and later of medicine in Aberdeen, believed
this could be achieved via a "comparative Animal Oeconomy of
Mankind and other Animals." For — concurring with Whytt — he
saw instinct rather than reason as an infallible principle for human
beings and as a sound basis for psychological understanding. The
good, natural instincts of animals and savages persuaded him that
in man those instincts should be distinguished from the "depraved
and natural State, into which mankind are plunged." Thus not

only Richardson, but also Scotland led the way toward Rousseau's critique of civilization. The practical application of such a "comparative observation" makes psychiatry into a "progressive art," since "intimate knowledge of the Human Heart" and "employing one Passion against another" can be taught only by life, not by books.[98] Indeed, the functional view of hysteria made psychiatry from the very beginning part of that movement which ascribed the origin of evil to what civilization, and specifically bourgeois society, had superimposed and inflicted on nature, and which conversely could claim, not so much through the exact sciences but through science as art, to be able to restore the natural sound condition, which the normative realm of common sense transformed into bourgeois-moral naturalness. Scottish philosophy's most important contribution to psychiatry is the notion that the (mental) laws of the heart and its disorders represent a distinct reality, which nevertheless is as real as physical nature: "Although the fears of these patients are generally groundless, yet their sufferings are real....Disorders in the imagination may be as properly the object of a physician's attention as a disorder of the body." Gregory also realized that psychiatric medicine from the very outset distinguished between two socio-economic groups — the "pauper lunatics" and the "nervous disorders" of bourgeois society:

It is not unusual to find physicians treating these complaints with the most barbarous neglect, or mortifying ridicule, when the patients can ill afford to fee them; while at the same time, among patients of higher rank, they foster them with the utmost care and apparent sympathy: there being no disease, in the stile of the trade, so lucrative as these of the nervous kind.[99]

3

The Reform Movement
and the Dialectics of Restraint

Crisis — the Liberal and the Conservative Responses

Generally, psychiatry in both England and France is said to have
begun with the French Revolution, in particular with the opening
of Samuel Tuke's "Retreat" near York, in 1796. Yet what took
place between the establishment of this new type of institution
and Conolly's No Restraint Movement of the 1840s was nothing
but the development, execution, and realization of an idea given
impetus in and after the middle of the eighteenth century, particularly by Battie, but also by Whytt, Cullen, and Arnold. This
development can be understood essentially in the context of the
economic revolution, Romanticism, and the psycho-sociological
philosophy of Scotland. That is to say, we are not dealing with a
new approach nor with a new paradigm, but more precisely, a
reform movement paralleling England's social Reform Movement
that had its basis in the existing civil society and out of which,
subsequent to the Revolution, bourgeois society — and psychiatry
— constituted themselves in France.

After the political reversal following the American War of
Independence, a general discussion began under the Younger Pitt
(1783) about securing the peace and the economy, about programs of thrift, political freedom and rights, and a variety of social
reforms. In particular, a continuing controversy was set off concerning the potential usefulness or harm and legitimacy or necessity
of state interference in the social and the economic order. This
debate gave birth to the concept of the "social problem," which
was to question the very content of civil society. And just as the
"laboring poor" and the "poor lunatics" had become visible,
they now also figured within that same social question which the
public was programmatically asking itself. Understandably, the
labour question was of greater general interest than that of the

insane, yet the two were closely connected. In some respects, the solutions to the latter were trailblazing for the former — notably with regard to the role of the state. Once their claims had seemingly been met, the controversy surrounding both issues died down around the middle of the nineteenth century, only to resurface with renewed vigor at the turn of the century.

Toward the end of the eighteenth century and the beginning of the nineteenth, industrialization had become so widespread that farsighted politicians and writers could no longer fail to recognize that the workers had become a part of civil society — albeit distinct from the middle class — and that their situation of constraint and their poverty were of a social nature. Constraint and poverty could no longer be minimized as the criteria of an irrationality beyond the realm of an enlightened and humane civil society. They were no longer part of an unquestioned natural order. Rather, they were products of the industrial economy, were among the means of producing its goods, and thus the products of a rational society and of the Enlightenment. The rationality of society, the claim of the Enlightenment, had become dubious. The workday became longer, wages fell, female and child labor became more widespread, penalties for breaking factory rules, and the truck system added to the coercion. Housing was poor, the family was disintegrating, schooling was a myth. Malnutrition, fatigue, and work accidents sent disease and mortality rates sky-high. Alcoholism added its share in stunting lives. Classical economics offered no hope. According to Ricardo, wages could not go much beyond a civilized minimum subsistence. Malthus, in 1798, advised workers to add self-restraint to moral restraint, and not procreate, so as to keep wage pressure down. Ricardo and Malthus for the same reason opposed both the poor laws and all public welfare assistance. "And so all in all, the very consolidation of the new, industrial conditions worked to undermine the humanitarian hope of the Enlightenment."[100] The scope of these problems even increased with the cyclical overproduction crises, the first of which occurred in 1792—93.[101] It became obvious that even a consolidated, capitalist production could not function smoothly and without crises. And, likewise in 1793, the course of the French Revolution showed that the most sublime struggle for human rights could end in terror — an experience that turned the majority of the English people against social change through revolution. Among the other external signs were the strikes of 1815, the Peterloo Massacre near Manchester (1819), the struggle surrounding the establishment of trade unions beginning in 1824, and the Chartist movement of the thirties and forties. The defeat of the Chartists in 1848 marked the relative integration of the "labor question" and "social question" amidst rising prosperity.

The unease that began to spread throughout England around 1750 could still be understood as a conflict between town and country, as the power of passions versus rationality, and as the quest for a moral social order in accordance with, or at least analogous to, a direct relationship between nature and reason. These issues were found in the early Romantic novels about human inwardness, in moral-philosophical psychology, and in the practice and theory of early psychiatry. All these forms could still be seen as models for the quest for self-understanding of civil society in its struggle for emancipation from the constraints imposed by absolutist, rationalist authorities. But by the end of the eighteenth century this justification was no longer valid: poverty, restraint, unfreedom, and other forms of irrationality had become part, and indeed the products of, society itself. If society was the author of its own ills[102] — as evidenced by the still marginal workers as well as the endangered petty bourgeoisie, ruined farmers and leaseholders, and bankrupt entrepreneurs — and if according to medicine from Whytt to J. Brown, sensibility, the nervous and vital energy, i.e. man's innate tendencies and self-induced stimuli, were the producers of disease, then the unease about society becomes a crisis of its self-perception. Its history was no longer natural history, no longer unquestionably reasonable, no longer identical with natural progress toward the freedom and prosperity for all. The thinking sparked by this crisis had to choose between two alternatives, depending on the diagnosis of the situation.

If the thinking that reflected the crisis sees it primarily as a stage in the emancipation of a society whose ills could be cured provided that society continued along that road, and the assumption is made that the claims of the Enlightenment are yet to be realized, then this thinking is bound to arrive at a consistent theoretical analysis that builds on the dynamics inherent in society or in man and seeks to understand the natural laws governing these dynamics. It would draw up a technological plan for a future society in which authority virtually merges into the rationality of organization. The problem with this approach, however, lies in its impractibility: man in general is not sufficiently rational, nor does there exist a social class as a subjective bearer to make this *liberal model* a reality. Practice determines that this model, under the given conditions, on the one hand must lead to social utopias, while its theoretical strength assists in the birth of the sociology of knowledge, psychology, and psychiatry. The champions of this approach include Jeremy Bentham and John Stuart Mill as well as most advocates of the early Social Movement (e.g. the Agrarian Socialists, the radical-individualist religious dissenters, and the philanthropist William Godwin),[103] and phrenological-scientific psychiatry, and the youthful literary humanist-atheistic Romantics (Coleridge, Shelley, Byron) who protested exploitation and industrial towns; and perhaps even more so, the unsentimental Tory Walter Scott, whose naturalistic-sociological approach turned the early Romantic psychological novel into a portrayal of class differences and the social factors in character development.[104] Although contemporary liberal ideology assured industrialism great scope for development, it proved unable to work any practical change in its side effects. Because liberal thought did not yet have misgivings about social restraints, it directed its main thrust against the vestiges of the "old" constraints of the state, which explains its success in such areas as prison reform.

According to another school of thought the crisis, though chaotic and anarchic, was not the fault of the state and other traditional authorities, but of the boundless and rampant liberalism of the social movements, and thus of the ideas of the Enlightenment itself. This diagnosis led either to a romantic quest for a return to pre-Enlightenment, pre-industrial traditional social structures, or to the acceptance in essence of the achievements of civil society, to stabilize them by incorporating them into expanded, unquestioningly accepted authority structures. Here there was no trust in a rationality that would assert itself through the dynamics of social and human drives and needs. Instead, a newly won social autonomy was to be imbedded in irrational authorities: grounded in the family, an authority borrowed from nature; surrounded by moral norms, trimmed to a standard, and intensified by the established institutions of state and church.

This *conservative model*, like others of its kind, was theoretically weak, since it is difficult to use rational arguments in defense of an order pledged to unquestioned authority and articles of faith. Hence, this model found acceptance in the sciences not so much through theory as through practical application, and more readily in the normative disciplines than in the causal natural sciences. For the theoretical weakness of the conservative model was matched by its practical strength: while the ideas of the Enlightenment and the rights of man as well as the mechanisms of a capitalist economy constitute abstract authorities, and the

natural sciences and social planning depend on formalization, the
institutions that conservative thought sees as the ideal vehicles of
an integrated society are eminently concrete. They either can
control vehicles of education on their terms (family, state, church),
or else they are the immediate recipients of such education (socio-
moral behavior norms). In any case, this thinking relied on the
media of direct, practical influence; it appealed to the autonomy
of the inner man, to his need for normative ties. And it aimed at
orderly groupings in which man's faculty for moral guilt — even
beyond penal justice — was functionalized, as we have attempted
to show, e.g., within the context of the development of the
notions about hysteria. Of course, the conservative model turned
ideological at the very point that the liberal model turned utopian,
namely when it proved incapable of altering social conditions.
Instead, it left them to the development of capitalism and justified
them by adjusting man to them and only offers them irrational-
authoritarian compensatory possibilities beyond the economic
sphere: the economically unsuccessful citizen as authoritarian
head of the family, patriotic subject, puritanical and virtuous, a
victim of society, who will reap his reward in the hereafter.

Obviously this conservative model was able to link up to the
traditionalist and simultaneously utilitarian elements of Scottish
moral philosophy, and to the early romantic apotheosis of bourgeois inwardness, of the escape to the country and the heroic
past, and no less to the depoliticizing spiritualization and philanthropic practices of the Methodists and similar movements. These
causes included social and welfare reforms, the developments in
practical psychiatry (to be discussed), various economic regulations such as the family-oriented restrictions on female and child
labor (1819 and 1833), laws on industrial hygiene, factory inspection (1829), and the regulation of the work day (1847). All these
measures entailed the considerable expansion of the government
bureaucracy. Early Romanticism played no less a part in this than
machine-wrecking anticapitalism or the aesthetic myth built around
tangible exploitation (Shelley, Coleridge), and Wordsworth's
celebration of the purity of nature and childhood and the uncon-
ditionality of moral duty — this, for the first time, consciously
didactic and in simple language. The conservative trend — in
functional relationship to the simultaneous economic expansion —
reached its apogee in the Victorian age, especially around the
middle of the century. "The theoretical reaction against economic
liberalism therefore proves to be an internal affair, a kind of
self-deliverance, of the bourgeoisie. It is supported by the same

stratum as in practice represents the principle of economic freedom and it merely serves to counterbalance the materialism and
egoism in the Victorian compromise."[105]

After the defeat of the English working class, "the aristocracy
and the common people thus became, to a certain extent, fellow-
sufferers and fellow victims." Their motives were not those of Lord
Ashley, but those of emotionally inclined thinkers like Carlyle:
anti-liberal, state-authoritarian, and Romantically philanthropic.
"Disraeli's feudalism is political romanticism, the 'Oxford Movement' religious romanticism, Carlyle's attacks on comtemporary
culture social romanticism, Ruskin's philosophy of art, aesthetic
romanticism; all these theories repudiate liberalism and rationalism
and take refuge from the complicated problems of the present in a
higher, superpersonal and supernatural order, in an enduring state
beyond the anarchy of liberal and individualistic society."[106]
Even though the utilitarians, capitalists, and materialists may have
been more deeply bound to the ideas of the Enlightenment than
their romantic-conservative opponents with their yearning for
irrational authority, there is no doubt that the latter left their
mark on the noneconomic realm of "enlightened" society: both
through the social reforms and the establishment of a moral
order that translated external constraint into inner moral order.

The "pauper lunatics" were literally the embodiment of the
ills and incipient crisis of the mid-eighteenth century. When that
crisis became obvious at the end of the century, they became a
major topic of public debate: the number of publications increased by leaps and bounds;[107] insanity figured in the themes
of the innate unreason of mankind and society; and the deliberate
inducement of healing crises played an ever greater role in
therapy.[108] And then — as if designed by the cunning of reason
in history — the supreme ruler, King George III, lost his mind in
1788, proving that insanity was a universal human possibility
and therefore demanded universal regulation. Because psychiatry
granted the psyche a varying degree of autonomy it was admitted
into that circle of sciences confronting the crisis, commingling
and differentiating, liberal and conservative, enlightened and
stabilizing elements.

In psychiatry, too, the reform debate began not with the new
paradigmatic approaches of theory, but in response to social
needs and to the question about the concrete possibilities of
psychiatric practice. 1771 saw the publication of the first book
on hospitals and other institutions for the poor (*Thoughts on
Hospitals*, by Dr. J. Aikin) which gave currency to the term

"asylums" for pauper lunatics. Aikin used the Manchester institution as his model. To be sure, what Aikin calls the humane and "generous and disinterested zeal of individuals" might in the social context also be construed differently. Perhaps it represented a humane advance, yet it was based on unmistakable economic interests. Indeed, once industry compelled society to absorb the reservoir of previously segregated irrationality, it became indispensable that this area also be policed, that an external social order be vouchsafed, and that a minimum of humanitarian and life-preserving institutions be provided. Distinctions and accommodations had to be created, permitting the entrepreneur an overview of the potential manpower available to him in this realm, and guaranteeing an indisturbed functioning of his business — and of public commerce. For this reason, special and separate institutions had to be created for the "pauper lunatics," and also to relieve families (women and children) of the burden of caring for a mentally ill member so that they could be brought into the labor process.

Aikin was the first openly to delineate the economic motivation for asylums. For, in addition to their own suffering, lunatics were

a nuisance and terror to others; and are not only themselves lost to society, but take up the whole time and attention of others. By placing a number of them in a common receptacle, they may be taken care of by a much smaller number of attendants; at the same time they are removed from the public eye to which they were multiplied objects of alarm, and the mischiefs they are liable to do to themselves and others, are with much greater certainty prevented. [Public institutions] instead of being a burthen...would be a saving to the community, not only from the relief of private families, but that of parishes.[109]

Bourgeois society as an economic unit integrated the formerly sequestered unreason by setting it apart and placing it in special institutions. Although it gathered them up more systematically and localized them in a more "orderly" fashion, it would be wrong to say, as Foucault does, that this approach silenced the insane more effectively and made them disappear. The reality is more complicated. Because the insane were admitted into the social sphere, brought closer to the rest of mankind, and also became part of the debate about civil rights, society became more efficient. more dynamic, but also more irritable, more unstable, and more in need of norms. The very inclusion of the insane in society with all its attendant dangers mandated the protective, distinguishing, and ordering measures instituted. Indeed, in a special sense, the insane remained visible and functionally related to the social structure because the socio-economic and moral order of bourgeois society defined itself by their uniqueness. And, conversely, the framework created for meeting the economic needs offered the possibility of cure for at least some of these sufferers. Interestingly enough, Aikin's argument that the asylum would relieve families of a burden and make them available for work predated the formal sociological argument that after the transition from the agrarian extended family to the bourgeois small family, the latter could not possibly take care of an insane (retarded, ill, old) member, and therefore special institutions proliferated.

The reform of the treatment of the insane was given a significant and effective impetus by one of the exponents of the Reform Movement, John Howard, an exponent of prison reform whose work on prisons, hospitals, and lunatic asylums (*An Account of the Principal Lazarettos in Europe*, 1789) affected thinking throughout Europe. A friend of Aikin's, Howard not only catalogued the dreadful situation of the "pauper lunatics," he also set up guidelines, similar to Aikin's, for building asylums, helped to give visibility to the insane by differentiating between them and the inmates of jails, prisons, work- and poorhouses, and helped plan and finance the lunatic asylum in Liverpool. Several aspects of this institution, located in an industrial center, demonstrate that it was the product of combined utilitarian and enlightened interests. In 1789, its first physician, J. Currie, in an outline for its establishment, wrote: "In the institution of a Lunatic Asylum there is this singularity, that the interests of the rich and poor are equally and immediately united. Under other diseases the rich may have every assistance at their own homes, but under insanity, relief can seldom be obtained but from an establishment for the treatment of this particular disease." This view of the democratizing function of madness has an economic as well as humanitarian purpose: "It is the policy of an asylum to make these two classes connect with each other, so that the increased payments made by the rich, may serve to diminish in some degree, the demands on the poor."[110] On the other hand, Currie's notion of the neutral character of madness as a physical illness led him to build his asylum as part of a hospital, whereas most institutions in the early nineteenth century, because of the romantic-psychological view of the nature of this disorder, were built far from the cities, in rural surroundings.

Nowhere does the autonomy of the social structure of society and the psychic structure of man as a utilitarian and rational being emerge more clearly than in the works of that other great reformer, Jeremy Bentham (1748—1832). His blueprint for organizing society deals both with capitalist industrialization and the sectors of previously segregated unreason. Both realms were to be socially integrated, objectified, and utilized to the fullest. In 1791, he put forth his plan under the revealing title *Panopticon; or, the Inspection-House: Containing the Idea of a New Principle of Construction Applicable to Any Sort of Establishment, in which Persons of Any Description Are To Be Kept under Inspection.* He conceived of a cobweblike design for prisons, houses of correction, poorhouses, workhouses, insane asylums, and industrial installations. From a central room permitting an overview, corridors running along rows of workrooms or cells are to radiate out as from a star to facilitate surveillance by a single person, or two or three at most — i.e., maximum efficiency at minimum cost. In insane asylums and other institutions this principle even paid lip service to the most important hygienic tenet (predating the age of bacteriology), namely that fresh air prevents the spread of contagious diseases.[111] Every cell was to have a barred window to the outside. Bentham saw his plan as a gesture of liberalization for the insane: chains and other such physical restraints were supplanted by a more efficient architectonic-organization restraint. Until 1851, numerous institutions based on Bentham's star-shaped, H-shaped, or semicircular model were built throughout England — huge domed structures of unparalleled dimensions. The fact that on the Continent this pattern was adopted for prisons, but only rarely for insane asylums, is related to the later start there of reform and with the more pronounced Romantic influence.

Bentham's contribution was not confined to the efficient organization of the external economy of the expanding industrial society; he was also concerned with the internal, mental state of the individual. Taking off from Thomas Reid's analytical explanation of the natural history of man, Bentham, in 1817, sought to objectify "the springs of action," i.e., the operations affecting the will "in the way of immediate contact." These "psychological entities," whose conception includes Robert Whytt's involuntary reflexes and the habit formation of the Scots, are not the factors that affect the will through the sentient state but rather the natural basis of those factors. To lend scientific validity to these connections, Bentham, in *A Table of the Springs of Action*, introduced two concepts that only won acceptance more than fifty years later (with the increase of scientific-neurological knowledge), and still later became psychiatric core concepts; psychodynamics and psychopathology: "Psychological dynamics (by this name may be called the science, which has for its subject these same springs of action, considered as such) has for its basis psychological pathology." Pathology, here, is not yet a theory of disease. Rather, it comprises the ends/means relationship of pleasure and pain, and, being the basis of the doctrine of human action, proves to Bentham's satisfaction that self-involvement and self-interest are the motive force of human behavior. "For there exists not... any motive, which has not for its accompaniment a corresponding interest, real or imagined." Bentham also recognized that unacceptable "desires and motives" in us or others (with regard to such elemental drives as hunger, sexuality, the quest for wealth, love and power, feelings of friendship and dislikes) are covered over by "fig-leaves," regarded as "unseeming parts of the human mind," and ascribed to some other motive — the first reference to the concept of projection and repression.

Nevertheless, psychiatric practice of that era tended to follow the romantic-conservative model. It is no accident that this facet of the Reform movement had its origin in various church-related groups. The Retreat near York had been founded by Quakers, the Methodists' fight against psychic disorders was still in full swing, and many renowned personages working in psychiatry were both clerics and physicians (or simply clerics), e.g., B. Fawcett, William Pargeter, W. Moore, S. Walker, and Francis Willis. Their devotion to psychiatry was in direct proportion to its emphasis on the mental (and self-induced) origin of psychic disorders. The same trend is evidenced by the fact that in this era, the late eighteenth and early nineteenth century, psychiatrists often were not only "men of letters" or "medical journalists" but creative writers as well, and thus with links to the Romantics. Among these writers were William Perfect (a prominent Freemason), Thomas Bakewell, Erasmus Darwin (the grandfather of Charles), J. Ferriar, Thomas Beddoes, Thomas Brown, P. Earle, and Thomas Trotter. Crichton's *An Inquiry into the Nature and Origin of Mental Derangements*, the first English psychiatric work to draw on German research, used a product of early German Romanticism, the *Magazin für Erfahrungsseelenkunde* as one of its sources. Finally, the psychiatric practitioners mentioned here were mostly the very ones who stressed the mental origin of disorders, who established or elaborated on the method of moral management, who championed the importance of education, and who were the first to use case histories as a literary device. Their approach thus coincided with the Romantic-historical component of Scottish moral philosophy and

Battie's psychiatry.

At the very outset of their work, history came to their aid. The event that won them the support of English public opinion and also exerted considerable influence on the direction of the emergent psychiatry on the Continent was the mental breakdown of George III in 1788—89 and the spectacularly successful cure effected by Dr. Francis Willis (1717—1807), a clergyman, physician, and owner of a private madhouse. The public response was all the stronger because of the publication of the testimony of the consulting physicians before a parliamentary commission of inquiry. Circumstances did indeed favor Willis: he was called over the objections of the leading specialists only after their failure had become obvious, and thus also some time after the first manifestations of the disorder and after the acute phase had probably run its course. Willis promised a cure if his "moral management" were followed. He attributed the illness to excessive strain and "little rest," and ordered the isolation of the king from his family and his ministers. Medication was kept to a minimum (in accord with Battie's generalization that "management did more than medicine"). The king was put in a straitjacket from time to time, and according to some reports he was also flogged to break his resistance. But Willis' decisive and epochal method was to arouse "a wholesome sense of fear," for crushing the will, winning complete control over the patient, was essential to a successful cure. The physician was to be an object of respect and fear. Only on the basis of this sort of subservient relationship did moral management permit compassion and liberality. Yet the threat of physical restraint was always present to discourage the possibility of rebelliousness. And how does the doctor win control over the patient? Solely by the power of his personality, particularly the steadfastness of his gaze.[112] The fact that Willis kept no written records only added to his reputation as possessing magic healing powers. The curious public, medical and lay, had to make do with mystifying, secondhand accounts. Thus in 1795—96, a visitor wrote: "His usually friendly and smiling expression changed its character when he first met a patient. He suddenly became a different figure commanding the respect even of maniacs. His piercing eye seemed to read their hearts and divine their thoughts as they formed. In this way he gained control over them which he used as a means of cure."[113] When Edmund Burke, a member of the Parliamentary commission, voiced doubts about Willis' competence, the latter demonstrated his special talent by fixing his gaze on the philosopher, who, reportedly, was as overwhelmed as his colleague, the dramatist Richard Brinsley Sheridan.[114] Willis, who claimed that nine out of ten of his patients were cured, was awarded one of the highest pensions in medical history for his successful treatment of the king. And he practically doubled this income a few years later when he was called in as consultant for the Queen of Portugal.

Willis' nationwide renown raised public interest in the reform of the treatment of madness in general and the approach to its mental causes and of moral management in particular. Almost every psychiatric publication made reference to the royal cure. Nearly all these physicians now wrote in terms of their practical work in private or public institutions, i.e. they were compelled to indicate criteria of active, changing practice. Under the circumstances, that could be done only by locating the causes of the illness in the mental realm. Accordingly, that realm — the emotions of the patient — took on overwhelming importance as a sphere of possible effect among the more remote causes, until the abstract difference between immediate and indirect causes became blurred. The victory of moral management eradicated Battie's critical distinction between autochthonic and secondary diseases.

The pathogenic and, at the same time, curative effect of the passions now became the dominant theme. The methods of moral management involved consideration of the patient's individual make-up. The largest collection of case histories was furnished by William Perfect, the owner of a private madhouse and author of a popular work that went through five printings between 1778 and 1809.[115] The doctor's personality, his magnetic power over the patient, his ability "to catch his eye," took on major importance.[116] Pargeter's description of one particular case is most informative. His emphasis on the magic power of eye contact makes clear its vital role in the control over the will of the individual:

I took two men with me, and learning that he had no offensive weapons, I planted them at the door, with directions to be silent, and to keep out of sight, unless I should want their assistance. I then suddenly unlocked the door, rushed into the room and caught his eye in an instant. *The business was then done* — he became peaceable in a moment — trembled with fear, and was as governable as it was possible for a furious madman to be.[117]

The somatic aspect of the illness had become insignificant. While discarding physical restraint, doctors nevertheless demanded that the patient surrender, voluntarily as it were, to an inner moral restraint — a fictitious situation in which external coercion hovers outside the door, ready for action should the patient refuse to obey.

The theory of the mental source of madness which, closely related to the Reform Movement's need for action, sought to stand on its own feet, independent of earlier theories, superimposed a new, psychological interpretation on many traditional therapeutic methods. Thus J. Ferriar, physician at the Manchester asylum, wanted to employ vomits, not only because they rid the body of noxious matter, but also because of the "uneasy sensations which they excite." This tested method retained its place in Ferriar's concept of moral management, which he saw primarily as "a system of discipline," to make the patient "sensible of restraint." Other punishments were also meted out for recalcitrance, for instance isolation on a starvation diet in a dark cell "till he shews tokens of repentance." Likewise, progress in the cure is identified with "regular behaviour," the "reward" being a better room; for the goal of medical-moral therapy is "a habit of self-restraint."[118]

The "rotatory machine" was also given a mental interpretation — and by the inventor himself. In 1804 J. M. Cox, a physician and owner of a madhouse, based his description on technical data by J. C. Smith (1790) and Erasmus Darwin (1796). To be sure, the principle had already been applied by Mandeville. Originally, Cox had been somatically oriented. He saw insanity as a physical ailment that permeated the entire system and so shielded it against any other illness. Hence, he hypothesized, an externally forced "introduction of some new disease into the system" would so shake the "animal oeconomy" as to heal or attenuate the insanity. This new, curative sickness was to be artificially induced by a device that would rotate a patient attached to it at an individually regulated speed, and cause vertigo, vomiting, circulatory disturbance with occasional loss of consciousness and even convulsions. Cox was convinced of the efficacy of this therapy, and so were psychiatrists throughout Europe.[119] W. S. Hallaran so improved the rotatory machine in his Irish asylum that by 1810 four patients could be treated simultaneously with up to 100 revolutions per minute.

His somatic theory notwithstanding, Cox also gave his method a moral twist. He called it "both a moral and medical mean in the treatment of maniacs," a "Herculean remedy" that calms not only the body, but also the mind. In particular it evokes the wholesome "passion of fear," which can be heightened by conducting the procedure in darkness, accompanied by fearsome noises or smells. In this way, false notions can be corrected, pathological associations destroyed, and "the force and effects of vicious mental habits" broken.

The Retreat, or the Internalization of Restraint

The institutions or therapeutic models whose romantic-conservative, yet active and practical character was described in the previous section already existed. By and large, they were operating and part of the expansion of a development that had begun in the mid-eighteenth century when the Retreat near York was founded. Hence, to claim that English psychiatry originated with the Retreat is plainly wrong. However, because the Retreat perfected the characteristics under discussion it became a suitable model for discussion or imitation. Its founding exemplified an administrative drive on the part of the English middle class and a degree of sociopolitical activism of England's religious communities unrivalled by continental psychiatry. In 1791, a female member of the York Society of Friends fell victim to insanity and was brought to that city's madhouse, in existence since 1777. The patient was not allowed to have visitors, and she died a few weeks after being admitted, under mysterious circumstances. Thereupon the Quakers of York in 1792, decided to open a less restrictive institution for their community. One of their members, William Tuke, took charge of the project. He gathered information by visiting the asylums of Manchester and St. Luke's, raised funds and built the house. In 1796 it was ready to receive its first patients. The house had a "matron" for female patients, and a "superintendent" for males. Tuke remained involved, its virtual "manager in chief." When a physician was supposed to be engaged, A. Hunter, the doctor at the old institution of York, applied, but he was turned down. It was feared that he was too authoritarian and not well enough qualified. The post went to Thomas Fowler, an apothecary who in 1786 had introduced arsenic into medical therapy. Unlike most contemporary institutions the new house was open to visitors. Prospective superintendents of other asylums were granted permission to stay there for purposes of observation. As a result of this voluntary opening up to public view, the Swiss physician G. C. de la Rive was the first to publish an appreciative account of the Retreat entitled *Letter to the Editors of the Bibliothèque Britannique*

(1798). An internal appraisal entitled *Description of the Retreat* was published in 1813. Its author was Samuel Tuke, "Quaker philanthropist and merchant of York, treasurer of the Retreat," and the grandson of its founder.

In his lay book about this lay institution, Tuke stated that aside from warm baths, all the traditional methods of somatic medicine had been tried and found to be ineffective. His first conclusion, therefore, was: "The experience of the Retreat…will not add much to the honour or extent of medical science." But he was quick to mention that doctors were not useless: "The physician, from his office, sometimes possesses more influence over the patients' minds, than the other attendants." He thus operates not as a medical practitioner, but "from his office," i.e. through the authority of his professional and social position. The therapy itself is based almost solely on the principle of "moral treatment," here given its widest application since Battie. The goal was to teach the inmates the "salutary habit of self-restraint." This virtue could be forced upon them in two ways: one, a practice current since Willis, was to arouse a wholesome feeling of fear, with punitive isolation for disorderly and violent conduct. The other was to appeal to their "self-esteem." This involved the help of visitors who importuned the patients to be on their best behavior. It also took the form of an informal friendly talk between the superintendent and the patient, and of teaparties. At these the patients had to dress and carry on formal conversation, i.e., overcome the last vestiges of their "deviations" by mobilizing their highest "moral feeling," "to strengthen the power of self-Restraint."

In the process of the interiorization of restraint, the principle of self-esteem went beyond that of fear, although both principles were celebrated as freeing the patient from (external, physical) restraint. In the latter the patient is seen as an individual capable of doing wrong and being punished, who, by making an effort, is able to suppress his violent tendencies, or else is led to do so by punishment or the threat of punishment. Self-esteem, however, presupposes a social personality, normal social behavior, on the part of the patient, a subject engaged in dialogue with another subject. For here, in contrast to the fear principle, the partner in the conversation administering the treatment is expressly forbidden to converse "in a childish, or…domineering manner"; he must accept the other as a "rational being." A perfect fictive situation. If, until the mid-century, medical texts based on rational Enlightenment had encouraged individuals to treat their nervous disorders themselves, now the insane were pushed into circumstances that created the illusion of self-therapy — a fictive emancipation to a subjective dialogue and to an internal self-restraint of one's deviations, passions, and violent eruptions through proper social and moral conduct. This was a process not covered by reality of turning the insane into subjects rather than objects, as Foucault maintains.[120] For it ignored the objective hampering of subjectivity and the self-restraint of the patients by the actual and generally untreatable process of the disorder,[121] or at best excluded it as a secret and surmounted it ideologically.

Of course, the undertakings of the Quakers and of the above-mentioned physicians were praiseworthy efforts to solve the problem of insanity through understanding. And Samuel Tuke was justified in formulating his task as "carrying out the noble experiment, as to how far the insane might be influenced through the medium of the understanding and the affections, and how far they may be beneficially admitted to the liberty, comfort, and general habits of the sane."[122] However, this humane protest against the age of chains and blows did not succeed. By seeing the insane as individuals only at the cost of abstracting from the objective nature of their disorder, thereby basing the comparison of their subjective behavior and that of the healthy person on moral failure, it replaced the cruelty of external restraint with the greater cruelty of inner restraint. Understanding turns into control and into an instrument of integration if it occupies the realm of the merely explicable. It becomes more controlling than objectification of natural science could ever be. The same holds, now as then, for the construction of a general intersubjective encounter structure in a conversation if that structure does not protect itself against becoming an ideological camouflage for a onesidedness growing out of objective obstacles.

To gain a better understanding of the Retreat and similar places, we must uncover the authority structures that could move the insane toward self-restraint through fear and self-respect. These same principles guided the romantic-conservative reform program for overcoming the crisis of bourgeois society. At the same time that bourgeois society emerged in France with the Revolution, England faced the problem of the utilitarian organization or romantic integration of the forces that appeared with the industrial expansion of bourgeois society. From the point of view of the Romantics, insanity as a form of unintegrated irrationality was a product of the anarchy of subjective behavior, the corrupt state of human nature (thus Gregory), which had to be restored to the natural-moral norm. Moderation, order, and lawfulness — that is how M. Jacobi, Tuke's German translator, summed up the method of the Retreat.[123]

Equally significant were the references to the natural authority of the family. Tuke never tired of reiterating that the Retreat was structured like a family. The patients had to be taught that their deviant behavior harmed the family, and the resort to fear also drew on the experience of the family, to be used in the degree "which naturally arises from the necessary regulations of the family." Like children, the insane must be punished or rewarded promptly for their actions. They must first be intimidated, then encouraged and asked to participate in a dialogue. The family represented an island of healthy, natural authority in an anarchic society. Foucault quite rightly says about the Retreat: "Madness is childhood.... Apparently this 'family' placed the patient in a milieu both normal and natural; in reality, it alienated him still more."[124] Long after the poor, like the mad, had become charges of the state, the insane asylums still retained the aura of a simulated family — psychologically real, institutionally fictitious — and for the insane rationality converged with the patriarchal figure of the father.

Furthermore, the Retreat was religious, not just as a Quaker establishment, but also as a therapeutic principle. Like the family, religion too could be presented as natural and orderly. Since, for a believer, the religious element was impervious to disease, the insane might be reached through their religious faculty. Religion as a way out even for the insane justified the use of fear and self-restraint as pressure on their consciences to win a quasi-spontaneous, moral victory over their disorderly desires. Reason would go hand in hand with the wholesome world of religion. This, of course, turned the institution into a milieu for the patient "where far from being protected, he will be kept in a perpetual anxiety, ceaselessly threatened by Law and Transgression."[125]

Finally, the curative power of pure, romantic nature itself, untainted by urban life or civilization, was called into service. After the Retreat, nineteenth-century asylums were for a long time situated in the countryside. "This house is situated a mile from York," de la Rive tells us, "in the midst of a fertile and smiling countryside; it is not at all the idea of a prison that it suggests, but rather that of a large farm; it is surrounded by a great, walled garden." Nature was to heal insanity like all the other problems caused by chaotic social progress. Work, too, in the form of farm labor, was part of this salutary, pristine order, albeit merely as beneficial exercise and occupation, an end in itself or a means of moral self-restraint.

The Retreat literally was just that, an escape from the anarchy of industrial society. The blame, however, was laid not so much on society but on the individuals, who with their unnatural inclinations, irrational passions, boundless license, and immoral desire were both guilty and sick, and through a grandiose pedagogical arrangement were now to be purified, absolved, and cured. Tuke constantly emphasized the pedagogical character of his healing method, which, to be sure, was hardly an education of the head, of the mind, by persuasion, for this had proved as untenable as the chain and somatic-medical therapy. Rather, it was an education of the heart, the sentiments, through the normative device of integration into the moral order. Reason was to become a replica of moral practice rather than its guide. The ends/means span of this education was in line with the perspectives of Romantic escapism: family, nature, religion, and moral introspection. It was a social movement conscious of the uniqueness of human individuality, but at the cost of the passive acceptance of the objective advance and social consequences of the economic process, leaving it intact, merely intensifying it ideologically and compensating for it morally. Likewise, the Retreat was concerned simply with the moral integration and self-restraint of individuals while accepting the objective natural history of the illness itself, the very factor that prevented these individuals from acting independently. That is to say, Romantic practice was contemplative, not incisive, so long as it held the individual responsible for deviant behavior and sought to induce the return to the norm through an elaborately staged moral appeal without searching for the objective causes of, or differences between, the disorders or illness, or for the chances of radically altering or eradicating them. It was not a crucial matter, as far as the Retreat was concerned, whether the acute and violent phase of a patient eventuated in a cure or ebbed into mere tranquillity and tractability. In either case, the disturbing and dangerous aspect of the madness had been overcome and peace and order restored. Although the Retreat saw itself as a training ground for superintendents of other institutions, it did not entertain the idea of offering clinical instruction for medical students and physicians. The development that reached its apogee in the Retreat is responsible for the fate that befell Battie's paradigm, even though his model did contain the germ of that development. Nevertheless, this non- or downright antimedical aspect of reform bears as importantly on the evolution of psychiatry and the concretization of its social function as does the other aspect, i.e. somatic psychiatry and Bentham's utilitarian model. In every country, psychiatry grew out of the struggle between those two positions and their determining social movements.

The Retreat, although the model of a voluntary institution was indirectly responsible for handing over the mentally ill, the products of social anarchy, into the protective custody and authority of the state. Tuke's account of 1813 was, to a considerable extent, responsible for bringing the situation of the insane to attention. This in turn led to exposure of the deplorable conditions at York and Bedlam, and ultimately to the inquiry into madhouses by the House of Commons in 1815—16.

The liberal tenor of three recommendations of this committee set them apart from the reports of previous investigations: 1. The demand for greater scientific and therapeutic involvement of physicians. 2. Whereas heretofore, the emphasis was on protecting the public against the violent behavior of the insane, the state was now asked to protect the latter against the violence and coercion of institutions, i.e. to protect the individual against unwarranted interference. 3. The criterion applied in the classification of conditions was delay in recovery. That is to say, Parliament's concern now focused on minimizing the loss of manpower and the cost to the public. The new reasoning that restraint was inhumane, insofar as it delayed reincorporation into the labor process, constituted a demand on psychiatry to make the insane socially functional.

It took a while, until 1828, for the passage of a new law that superseded the inefficient regulation of 1774 and allowed for greater control over madhouses. Now, for instance, every certificate for admission to an institution had to be signed by two physicians — except for "pauper lunatics": their commitment required only one signature. On the judicial level the old discriminatory affinity of poverty and insanity apparently persisted. And it was furthermore extended to criminality, as demonstrated by the Insane Offender's Bill of 1800. Hadfield, a regicide, was found not guilty in 1800 because his counsel, Lord Chancellor Thomas Erskine, convincingly made out a case for his client's insanity. But since no legal basis existed for the institutionalization of Hadfield, a law was promptly promulgated committing "criminal lunatics" to Bedlam or any County asylum. Thus, for instance, a plaque at the entrance of the asylum near Bedford, opened in 1812, proclaimed that it was a Madhouse of the County of Bedford for criminals and pauper lunatics.[126] However, scarcely anything testifies more impressively to the lasting distinction between "poor lunatics" and other mentally ill than the testimony of Thomas Monro, physician at Bedlam, before the Parliamentary commission of 1815. Asked about his rather free use of restraint by chains and fetters in Bedlam, but not in his house, Monroe replied: "There is such a number of servants, there is no sort of occasion; I have forty odd patients, and as many servants." When pressed as to his opinion of such restraints, he said: "They are fit only for pauper Lunatics; if a gentleman was put into irons, he would not like it....I am not at all accustomed to gentlemen in irons; I never saw any thing of the kind: it is a thing so totally abhorrent to my feelings, that I never considered it necessary to put a gentleman into irons." The state of insanity of a gentleman of superior rank was more likely to be irritated by such a mode of confinement than that of a pauper lunatic.[127]

Just as Tuke's report had mobilized public interest in exposing abuses in 1813—14, and set off the Parliamentary inquiry of 1815—16, this phase also ended with a victory of the Retreat. The entire staff of the York asylum was dismissed and its reorganization entrusted to the Retreat. And at Bedlam, both Thomas Monro as well as the apothecary John Haslam were dismissed. Incredibly overbearing, Haslam had nothing but disdain for modern psychiatrists who claimed to be able to manage without all restraints and to control patients merely with the "strong impression and strange powers which lie within the magic circle of the eye," but who in fact would not come close to a violent inmate unless that patient was in a straitjacket, and then only in the presence of several attendants: "I have never been able to persuade them to practice this rare talent (such pantomime) tête-à-tête with a furious lunatic."[128] Haslam, though the only well-known critic of the Romantic Reform psychiatrists, was also the only one to add to the theoretical knowledge of contemporary psychiatric theory (see below).

Once the question of the protective and supervisory role of the state was raised by Tuke and the report of the Parliamentary commission of 1815—16, it was never again laid to rest. Even Thomas Bakewell, whose private madhouses had been run as a "family business" for generations, in testifying before the commission, supported the creation of "National Hospitals, for the cure of Insanity alone," and of a "sweeping legislative measure, that should recognize every Lunatic as a Child of the State"[129]:

Turning the insane into wards of the state to protect their rights and for the good of society. This formula sums up the continuing distrust of psychiatrists toward society, which prevents them from espousing an unproblematic liberalism, and has made them the spokesmen for a policy of state intervention in a society unable to resolve its problems. George M. Burrows, physician and madhouse proprietor, took pride in the English people for having given rise to philanthropy and learning whereas in other countries, the initiative tended to come from the government. But in the case of the insane, he believed in state intervention in the legal regulation of matters concerning society and the individual. Lunatics and idiots, he felt, had to be placed under state control, as the only way to protect freedom and property. Likewise, the state had to regulate the organization and operation of madhouses, for that was the only way of effectively counteracting the widespread belief that insanity was incurable, a belief that deprived society of many potentially useful members. Overall, the "ratio of cures" in private madhouses was greater because that ratio "is always commensurate with the means, and the judgment in administering them." Hence the public asylums had to be improved, for that would benefit the economy. However, their administration had to be supervised, its power over inmates and staff was enormous, and man being a week vessel, the temptation to abuse that power was great. In this connection, Burrows was among the first to stress the importance of qualified attendants. Since they must have high moral qualifications — a premise for moral treatment — they ought to be well paid, and suitable provisions made for the support of superannuated or disabled keepers. Finally, Burrows was probably the first to deal with the moral approach of Romantic psychiatry, as practiced in the Retreat and by Tuke, and to push its claim of theoretical absoluteness to the point of absurdity. the Retreat shows that even Quakers, i.e. people who lead well-nigh perfect moral lives, can become insane. And that fact confounds those who believe that "insanity consisted in a 'mind disease'"; some physical illness must be involved. "Yet be the precepts and practice ever so perfect, no community of persons can be exempt from the infirmities of mortality. All that can be conceded to superior morality, and of this truth I am fully persuaded, is, that the fewest lunatics will be found among the members of the Society of Friends." [130]

Accommodation in the System, or The Invisible Restraint

The inquiries and the report of the committee of inquiry in 1815—16 and Burrows' argumentation in 1820 mark the period — to be sure, one that cannot be defined precisely either in terms of individuals or time — in which the romantic and utilitarian traditions came together and entered the complex relationship that constitutes nineteenth-century psychiatry. The preceding thirty years had been molded by romantic reform psychiatry. Because the irrational passions and unnatural tendencies it had referred to could be related to all behavioral deviations, the insane had become the model of an instrument of social stabilization that — utilized patriarchally and sentimentally by clerics and assorted laymen within the framework of a fictitious family — took the individual seriously and released him from his chains. But in the process the cause of the evil, the disease itself, was forgotten. In regarding the insane as the children of a didactic familial authority, they were excluded from the free interchange of the economic order, protected against its *laissez-faire*, and, conversely, did not interfere with its smooth operation. From here it was only a short step to handing over the paternal authority to the state, for the state could take care of these two reciprocal functions far more efficiently. Here too, the old relationship between poor lunatics and poor workers remained the same. Let us not forget that this age saw the first serious workers' uprisings and also the first moves to regulate female and child labor (1819). These controls can also be interpreted in two ways: as intercession of the state in the economic order to protect the workers, or, conversely, to protect the smooth operation of the economy against disturbances by the workers. And just as the patriarchal integration of the insane grew out of the idea of education, so too the labor regulations of 1819 were initiated by Robert Owen and his system of universal education and social amelioration.[131] But for Burrows and later psychiatric schools, the utilitarian and scientific approach again took precedence, while the conservative reform model, above all in the Victorian era, continued to serve merely as a kind of stabilizing superstructure of institutional practice. Not until later, with the emergence of a somatologic, independent psychopathology, did it regain importance. For Burrows, the institution fulfilled its social function by returning more inmates in less time to civic usefulness. He even proposed a competition among institutions, by having them publicize their annual ratio of cures. He himself was one of the first to employ statistics on a larger scale, both to analyze the success of an institution and to prove his thesis that insanity was not incurable; like any other physical disability, it could be treated, and its incidence was not linked to modern life. Against this last pessimistic assertion, he claimed that the importance of "that peculiarity of organization, denominated hereditary predisposition" was exaggerated and led to resignation. The role of heredity had been stressed particularly by the Romantics. In contrast, Burrows evolved a kind of milieu-theory of crises: only in times of sudden economic, religious, or political "changes" (e.g. poor harvests, scarcity, an ailing monarch) does the incidence of insanity increase, and gradually return to the old level when the crisis has passed. The statistical comparison also did away with the long-held belief that England had the largest number of insane, splenetics, and suicides. Instead Burrows advanced the pragmatic and doubtless objectively more valid idea that the English had simply paid earlier and greater attention to madness and had greater understanding of it.[132] Apparently it would seem that now that insanity had attained the rank of illness, this sort of positive national identification had become impossible.

For Burrows, in the last analysis insanity was not the product of man's inner nature — his disposition, propensities, passions, or morality — but a physical disorder unrelated to his inner nature. In support of his assertion he referred to (a) etiology: the possibility of differentiating between the causes of physical illness and the results of dissection, cited by Burrows as well as Haslam and the anatomist A. D. Marshal (1815),[133] (b) therapy: the cures effected by medication for somatic disorders. By now the idea of the dissociation of the inner and outer man, of soul and body, of reaction and stimulus, had become accepted. It had not been part of Thomas Willis' common sense and anima, yet it did persist throughout the eighteenth century, even if artfully covered over by the concept of nervous or vital energy. It now was possible to draw distinctions and choose among alternatives. The psychiatrists committed to the idea of a somatic disorder experienced a sense of relief and release. Their problem was simplified by a sort of division of labor. The inner man and morality were relegated to institutions run along the Romantic principle. And the psychiatrists were free to follow a scheme that allowed them to look for unambiguous physical causes, to explain insanity etiologically and divide it up into various illnesses, and, following the road mapped out by the established natural sciences, arrive at the appropriate therapeutic methods. It also offered them the utopian hope of some day discovering all causes, or *the* cause, of insanity and thereby extirpating it as a manifestation of unreason. This scheme and this utopia — more or less in contrast to or intertwined with the Romantic counterpart or superstructure — marked psychiatry throughout the nineteenth century. They formed the basis for establishing new and more direct ties to medicine, ties that had disintegrated during the Romantic reform yet which Battie had still taken for granted. And this also led to the acceptance of psychiatry as a medical specialty and to its elevation to a profession. Thus, in 1823, Sir Alexander Morison began his course of regular psychiatric lectures in London and Edinburgh. In 1842, John Conolly introduced the first clinical course in the provinces (at the Hanwell asylum). Nothing shows the decline of the medical aspect of psychiatry in the days of the Romantic reform movement as clearly as the fact that the clinical instruction at St. Luke's Hospital, introduced by Battie in 1753, was halted in the early nineteenth century and not resumed until 1843. 1841 saw the founding of the Association of Medical Officers of Asylums and Hospitals for the Insane, and in 1853, this group launched its first periodical, the *Asylum Journal of Mental Science.* Meanwhile, in 1848, Forbes B. Winslow launched the more analytical and theoretical *Journal of Psychological Medicine and Mental Pathology.*

Beginning in 1820, this phase of the development and institutionalization of a somatically natural-science-oriented psychiatry largely under French influence, was marked by changed assumptions about the social roots of insanity. Analagous to the tendency of looking for the cause and the cure in extraneous phenomena, psychiatry also supplanted the Romantic villainous role of the inner man and passions with the social environment, the "milieu." That related not only to Burrows' political, economic, and religious crises or Charles T. Thackrah's medical attack — the first of its kind — on the misery of the industrial environment (1831),[134] but also led to the criticism of the existing institutions, which John Reid described as "nurseries for and manufactories of madness,"[135] and which were to be improved by changing the external conditions of the asylums.

The theoretical and practical optimism of these psychiatrists who, in contrast to Battie, were unequivocally somatologic, found support in various early-nineteenth-century discoveries, which seemed to justify the assumption that mental disorders were invariably the symptoms of organic brain diseases: (1) The explanation of pellagra and its mental symptoms;[136] (2) The difference between alcoholic *delirium tremens* and other kinds of deliriums;[137] (3) The connection between insanity and cerebral factors in progressive paralysis (later recognized as syphilitic), which Burrows publicized in 1828 based on French sources.[138] (4) The proof of the difference between the motor and sensory nervous systems by Charles Bell in 1811, which led to the advancement of neurological theory and the reformulation of associative psychology that marked the nineteenth century. The same direction was taken by the evolutionism of the ethnologist W. Lawrence, denounced as atheistic and dangerous. In his comparative anatomy and physiology, he developed the thesis that the mind was merely an expression of the "functions of the brain."[139]

In connection with ethnology another social issue aroused public interest: the protection of indigenous populations. Here too, from the very outset psychiatrists were involved for either theoretical or practical reasons (evolutionism or reform movement). In deference to the moralism of the times another outstanding contemporary ethnologist, James C. Prichard, a practitioner of psychiatric medicine, gave a religious cast to the third edition (1836–47) of the evolutionary theses of his *Physical History of Mankind*. (The second edition had appeared in 1826.)[140] The first anthropological association, the Society for the Protection of Aborigines (London, 1838), was still primarily impelled by and committed to reform. However, the concept and institution of "science" had already become so formalized and professionalized that a mere five years later a scientifically more neutral counter-organization, the Ethnological Society of London, came into being.

During those years, psychiatrists took part in at least five socio-political movements: for paupers and workers; for prison reform; for the protection of aborigines; for the education of children; and for the reform of mental institutions. All these movements were vociferous champions of emancipation; all of them, of course, also had their — mostly unnoticed — integrative implications, on both a scientific and institutional level, as exemplified in the drive for reform in the treatment of insanity. All of them had romantic and liberal, moralizing and natural-scientific components, intertwined with historistic, naturalistic, and evolutionistic concepts of history. And there also existed all sorts of inter-relationships in the perception of the various targets of these reform movements. The image of the child, for instance, was made to apply to the poor workers, prisoners, aborigines, and insane. And "poor" was not just an economic appellation, but began to be invested with sentimental overtones, and "child" could mean either an admirable purity and independence or a lamentable backwardness that had to be overcome. The expanding society — economically into the colonies, and scientifically into its origins — added the idea of the primitive and the child to the forms of unreason awaiting integration or emancipation. Thus G. Rosen rightly asserts, though without differentiating between the romantic and liberal models:

> Irrationality and madness were now the consequence of historic development and a changing social environment. As civilization developed and spread through the inexorable march of progress, irrationality and insanity were conceived as due to man's separation from nature, to a deranged sensibility arising from a loss of immediacy in his relationship with nature. Madness was the obverse of progress.[141]

Gall's and Spurzheim's phrenology bore importantly on the somatic theoretical foundation of psychiatric and related (anthropological, psychological, sociological) research and social behavior. Andrew Combe (1797–1847), a Scottish physician who had become acquainted with it in Paris during 1818, brought it to England in 1831.[142] This doctrine sought to locate human characteristics, above all, the instincts, in the various regions of the human brain. It lent a physiological, brain-pathological "materialist" basis to insanity, yet at the same time admitted a physical and a — functionally related but otherwise autonomous — mental and social etiology and symptomatology. Given Combe's definition of insanity as a "functional derangement of the brain" the adjective "functional" has continued to this day to oscillate between the meanings of "psychogenic disorder" or "result of organic injury." Based on this and other French foundations, Prichard in 1835 formulated a concept that was to play a significant forensic role: "moral insanity" vs. "intellectual insanity." With this, contemporary psychiatry assumed the greatest and most problematical expansion of its jurisdiction for mental illness. For under this designation any deviant social behavior could potentially be labeled as sick. What Arnold with his "moral insanity" vs. "medical insanity" still saw as healthy could now psychiatrically be called abnormal. Prichard, in his *Treatise on Insanity*, defined moral insanity thus:

> A morbid perversion of the feelings, affections, and active powers, without any illusion or erroneous conviction impressed upon the understanding: it sometimes co-exists with an apparently unimpaired state of the intellectual faculties. There are many individuals living at large...of a singular, wayward, and eccentric character.

The determination of what constitutes natural behavior became practically unassailable by dint of scientific authority, since even here we are dealing with an organic brain disease. Fifty years later, this contradictory combination gave rise to the psychiatric and forensic problem of psychopathy. At any rate, the conviction that insanity had physical causes led Prichard to conclude that in England only the general public — laymen not qualified to comprehend the special knowledge of scientists — believed that such a thing as mental illness existed — and beyond them only such strange minds as the German Romanticist Heinroth.[143]

Another expansion of psychiatric interest, likewise the product of the somatic orientation, was less problematic. Now, at last, both psychiatric science and society began to distinguish between idiots, morons, and epileptics with regard to their protection and integration. Up to that time they had been isolated from society, just as the insane prior to 1750, since even most asylums refused to admit them. Around 1820, with the increasing industrialization of society, this in the abstract purest form of unreason seemed to represent the comparatively smallest social threat and disturbance, but also the least economic advantage, became visible as both a disturbing element and one in need of protection. Psychiatry found that these people were curable and thus were potentially of greater economic utility and more reliable than the insane. Here too, Burrows in 1820 rendered another great service. Lamenting the fact that institutions did not admit epileptics, morons, and idiots, and that presumably no pauper had ever been cured of epilepsy in England, he demanded special institutions for them. Various psychiatrists joined with him by differentiating among specific disorders; they called for the establishment of separate institutions and their pedagogical fervor found these patients more suitable, i.e. more malleable objects than the insane. In 1847, with the help of pedagogically interested philanthropists and of John Conolly, the first home for idiots was opened in London — exactly one hundred and fifty years after Defoe's proposal. Shortly thereafter, in 1855, the Asylum for Idiots at Earlswood was opened, and Conolly volunteered his services to that home during the first few years of its existence.

We can thus see how psychiatry developed into, in nineteenth-century terms, an independent science, intertwined with various sociopolitical movements and borrowing from other disciplines, both medical and nonmedical. The first phase of psychiatry in England came to a close with the Non-Restraint system, which is identified with John Conolly. The Romantically oriented asylums, most of them private, which survived throughout the Victorian era, had as little to do with this as with the expansion of re-search in the natural sciences. In fact, the distinctive form of moral management — as recently demonstrated at least for the early-nineteenth-century United States — considerably widened the gap between the poor and rich insane, who heretofore had been treated equally badly.[144] The Non-Restraint system, on the other hand, was primarily a product of public institutions, their natural science orientation and milieu theory, and their utilitarian faith in the superiority of external organization.[145] This move-ment began with Bentham, whose influence on institutional architecture lasted until 1850, and his principle of combining freedom and unrestricted movement with effective supervision. This framework (according to Jetter) explains the logic of the development of the mechanical therapeutic devices: straitjackets replaced chains. Then came Cox's rotary machine and swing. However, after 1820, the instruments that allowed manic patients greater freedom to express their restlessness and urge for actvity, to let off steam and calm down — the classic liberal approach — were being replaced by the padded cell, which was of no help in calming down agitated patients.

One consequence of this was the substitution of real work for the occupational therapy of the Romantic movement as a moral end in itself. This not only kept the patients busy and served a social utilitarian purpose, but the profit from the sale of their products helped defray the operational costs and overheads of the asylums. According to Hallaran, the County Asylum of Hanwell, under the medical directorship of William Ellis, was a prime example of this policy. Ellis' phrenologic concepts ruled out all punishment, given the fact that the patients were suffering from a disorder of the brain. Once a patient's unique qualities had been ascertained he could be assigned work appropriate to them. Ellis hired instructors to teach unskilled patients a trade. The products of their labor were sold in the asylum or on the outside. For Ellis, the relationship of poverty and insanity was clear-cut: Poverty and unemployment lead to insanity, and insanity exacer-bates poverty. This first systematic advocate of a social or work psychiatry also saw the risk in the transition from the institutional environment to the outside world. He introduced the idea of trial release and set up a fund to reintegrate ex-inmates into the labor structure. Thus, Ellis in 1834 was also the only psychiatrist to testify before Parliament about the situation of the "labour-ing classes." Never before had the insane met the utilitarian requirements of the economic order so well, and hence no other psychiatric achievement proved so convincing as this one. Ellis was the first psychiatrist to be knighted.[146]

In connection with these trends, the abolition of restraints in fact predated Conolly. The Lincoln Asylum had anticipated him. Its head physician, Edward P. Charlesworth, in 1823 systematically began to restrict the use of restraint. This gradual reform turned into a revolution in 1835, when Robert Gardiner Hill (1811—78) became the house physician. He launched an investigation of the institutional milieu; his report reads like a scientific sociological experiment:

Finding that good effects invariably followed a milder treatment, I made statistical tables with great labour; I tabulated the results of different modes of treatment; I considered the several cases individually; I lived amongst the patients; I watched their habits....At length I announced my confident belief that under a proper system of surveillance, with a suitable building, instrumental restraint was in every case unnecessary and injurious. I mentioned this opinion to Dr. Charlesworth and the Governors; I adopted it as a principle; I acted upon it; and I verified my theory by carrying it into effect.[147]

This experiment based on observation, case histories, and statistical analysis yielded this result: after the incidents in which restraint was used between 1834 and 1838 dropped from 647 annually to 0, the ratio of cures increased, there were no suicides or undesirable incidents, peace and harmony reigned in the home, violent outbursts became rare, feelings of resentment of and vengefulness toward the attendants diminished, personal cleanliness improved even among the morons, and all the inmates were "much more happy."

Hill published these first results in 1839. He compiled a list of organizational measures which were to be substituted for unacceptable methods of "personal restraint": "Improved Construction of the Building...classification — watchfulness — vigilant and unceasing attendance by day and by night — kindness, occupation, and attention to health, cleanliness, and comfort, and the total absence of every description of other occupation of the attendants."[148] This was a register of tested principles, with one crucial addition: the omnipresence of attendants. External and inner restraint was replaced by men who neither flogged nor punished nor educated morally, but simply were there. The vigilance of attendants day and night was as novel as the regulation barring them from holding other jobs and from showing hostility toward obstreperous or malicious inmates. In addition to holding poorly paid, socially denigrated, hazardous jobs, the attendants now also had to deal with the liberation of inmates, with the new system. No wonder that Hill was ultimately doomed to fail. Denounced as a utopian, visionary, speculator, and quack, he was accused of embezzlement and of cavalierly endangering the lives of others. Despite his successes and Dr. Charlesworth's support, an indignant public turned on him, in the belief that the insane were to be set free again — which shows the sort of threat the very idea of free-roaming mental patients posed to industrial society, and what anxieties they (philanthropic) institutions were supposed to allay. Finally, the attendants were encouraged to disobey Hill. In 1840, forced to give up his position, he withdrew to private practice — embittered, repudiated professionally, and unappreciated by the public.[149]

But in 1839 he had a visitor: Professor John Conolly, a sophisticated, socially aware man with connections in the highest reaches of society, and enough of a Romantic to add a familial touch to Hill's and Ellis' puritanical organizational plan. Conolly paid Hill a visit at the Lincoln asylum before taking up his duties at Hanwell to see at first hand how the Non-Restraint system worked. He subsequently introduced it in Hanwell, and with it won worldwide renown.

Conolly came of a poor family, married, had a family, and led a bohemian life in France. After returning to England, he studied medicine. A lover of Shakespeare, he set up practice in Stratford-on-Avon; there he stayed for five years, became an alderman, was elected mayor twice, and for the rest of his days contributed to liberal, progressive medical journals and remained committed to bettering the lot of the working class. He joined the Society for the Diffusion of Useful Knowledge, started an organization to assist the poor, and wrote popular articles about health as well as a book on cholera and a series of articles geared specifically to workers. He was among the founding members of the British Medical Association (1832), the *Medico-Chirurgical Review*, the phrenological society of Warwick, the Ethnological Society, the Medico-Psychological Association, the National Association for the Promotion of Social Sciences, the first institution for idiots in Earlswood. In addition, he was professor of medicine in London for five years, taught the first course in clinical psychiatry in Hanwell beginning in 1842, promoted the training of attendants, was one of the most sought-after therapeutic, consulting, and forensic psychiatrists, was instrumental in the acceptance of free psychiatric experts, became president of the two competing psychiatric societies, and was responsible for at least the continued use of non-restraint. Thus on the one hand Conolly obviously personified the involvement of psychiatry in most of the social problems brought to the fore by industrialization in the middle of the eighteenth century which the Reform movement allayed temporarily in the mid-nineteenth century. On the other hand, he also mirrored the relative halt of the development of psychiatry into a science and its professionalization, i.e. the evolution launched by Battie's paradigm. And he did all this without making a single major theoretical contribution, yet addressing all the social problems with which psychiatry became involved from the very outset.[150]

What was Conolly's system of Non-Restraint based on? He saw insanity as a phrenologic disorder of the brain brought on by external physiological or social factors, the most important of these — for pathogenesis as well as for institutional organization *qua* therapy — being nutrition, physical health, and education, now once again understood as the training of the mind. Conolly conceived this in terms of the society as a whole. The neglect of these factors would result not only in insanity (particularly among women, since they were excluded from intellectual training), but also in ill-bred children, and so, he warned politicians, would spread poverty and immorality among the masses.

The psycho- and socio-hygienic organization of the asylum according to these three factors would guarantee therapeutic success. Restraint (600 mechanical devices were thrown away at Hanwell) was replaced by external reorganization; proper nourishment (less for the rich, more for the poor was the rule), good ventilation, baths, more and better-paid attendants. Rules were established for everything, records were kept and statistics compiled. Cleanliness became an obsession. Together with mechanical restraint, inner moral restraint went out the window. The director no longer instilled that "wholesome fear" but became first of all a physician, benevolent and always ready to lend an ear. Conolly won recognition because he had learned from Hill's mistakes. He augmented his system with a superstructure attuned to Victorianism, lending therapeutic weight to such established authorities as family, school, and church. Thus the physician also became the father of his "crazy children." Since Conolly believed that well-bred citizens rarely fell victim to insanity, the "pauper lunatics" became his "poor illiterate patients." Education was to adjust the aberrant needs of the insane to the social norm. Reconciling the liberal-utilitarian with the conservative-romantic model in the system of Non-Restraint, Ellis' rigorous work therapy was toned down — only half the patients now qualified for it — and replaced by "social activity" (outdoor entertainments, concerts, even dances). Finally, the public was invited: the traditional isolation was to be breached, prejudices eradicated, and the insane no longer made to feel like outsiders.

The newly visible "pauper lunatics," having shed their physical shackles since Battie's days were now to shed their inner restraints as well. Restraint was nowhere to be found. Its place was taken by the system of Non-Restraint, by hygiene, by the social organization of the environment — analogous to the legally regulated factories for the "labouring poor." At the same time, the insane were integrated, first in the Romantic fiction of the family unit, and now that notion was expanded to include the public institution as the social and self-contained fiction of society itself, akin to the integration of the "labouring poor," whose attempt at emancipation failed around this time. Along with greater wealth, the mid-nineteenth century brought English society a relative invisibility of social tensions, a — seeming — social peace, both in the labor question and the problem of insanity. At this juncture, 1847, the year of the factory laws, Conolly completed his first book on Non-Restraint with a vision of social peace that his system brought to Hanwell, the artificial society for the insane;

Calmness will come; hope will revive; satisfaction will prevail....Almost all the disposition to mediate mischievous or fatal revenge, or self-destruction, will disappear....Cleanliness and decency will be maintained or restored; and despair itself will sometimes be found to give place to cheerfulness or secure tranquility. [This is the place] where humanity, if anywhere on earth, shall reign supreme.[151]

Only in the late nineteenth century did it become apparent how many problems relating to insanity and labor had earlier been artificially harmonized, covered over, or repressed, how far the balance between social emancipation and integration had achieved nothing more than a more or less perfect simulation of attainable freedom.

PART II

FRANCE

1

Early Theoretical and Practical
Measures for the Abolition
of the Ancien Régime

If in bourgeois England, the institutionalized sequestration of
unreason was never fully implemented, absolutist France knew no
such deterrent. The time span of that exclusion can be fixed
precisely. It began in 1656 with the royal decree for establishing
the Hôpital Général in Paris, and, like absolutism itself, it ended
with the Revolution. Since the hôpitaux généraux were institutions of absolutism, their objective, to train the paupers they
housed to work, met with little success, given the low level of
economic development. Only Colbert made a major effort to
overhaul the hôpitaux into work places — without appreciable
results. The other functions of these institutions emerged all the
more distinctly: they served absolutism in the exercise of power
and in its determination to teach its subjects morality. That was
why paupers and the insane found themselves in the company of
political or simply immoral prisoners, possibly a disobedient
son or someone like the Marquis De Sade. The *lettre de cachet*,
easy to procure and almost impossible to challenge, was enough
to send an unpopular individual — for whatever reason — to an
hôpital.[1] That institution, virtually autonomous and untouchable,
stood between the power of the police and the power of the
courts. It was a third internal instrument of absolutist power in
the service both of control and welfare, punishment and education
for order, work, morality, and reason. In line with the universal
functions of these institutions, the directors, as representatives
of the monarch, enjoyed absolute authority: "They had power
of authority, of direction, of administration, of commerce, of
police, of jurisdiction, of correction, and punishment."[2] All the
classical means of restraint were at their disposal.

The Hôpital Général, as the model of absolutist rule, furnished exemplary justifications for Montesquieu's call for a division of powers. And the critical voices raised in the latter part of the eighteenth century made it the symbol of the fight against tyranny. Since the absolute state with the help of these institutions sought to isolate all major social problems to support its claim that the existing social order was rational and moral, the social significance of the actual "social issues" remained largely hidden. Until the late eighteenth century they were merely discussed as forms of the "political question," the change of the state form, and the liberation of the individual. They became visible only at the moment of crisis, immediately before and during the Revolution. This holds true for the paupers and insane alike. Even when the literary community turned into political critics, they did not deal with the situation of the insane for a long time. Nor did medical science discover them as a special subject. Although the hôpitaux généraux also carried out administrative welfare functions and employed physicians, the insane did not arouse their particular interest. Because the situation in England was different the French developed their notion about the incidence of madness and melancholia, of spleen and suicide among the English, and coined the term *Morbus Anglicus.* Stirrings of interest in the insane began only around the mid-eighteenth century, with the start of a process that had been going on in England for decades — i.e., when a first sensible, then sensitive reflective citizenry created a space for public reason, and the more genteel forms of unreason (*hystérie, vapeurs, maladies nerveuses, hypochondrie, mélancolie*) became first visible and acceptable, and then fascinating.

Within this framework, beginning in 1750, developed all the elements that had led to the practice and science of psychiatry in England, and subsequently in France. Yet, in a peculiar way, they remained hidden and separate from one another. Apparently, they could not form a practical and theoretical paradigm so long as the hôpitaux généraux, the heart of absolutism, kept the insane from becoming socially visible — i.e. so long as bourgeois society could develop self-consciousness yet fail to achieve political power. Or so long as the bourgeois critics continued to link unreason to the authority structures of absolutism, it was inconceivable and, above all, unnecessary to entertain the possibility of unreason as a problem or product of bourgeois society. The constituent elements of preconditions of the paradigm are: society under absolutism, medical vitalism, sensibility, Rousseau's romanticism, and the medicine of nervous disorders, physiocratism, and the futile attempts at reform in the field of insanity.

Vitalism and the Enlightenment

"In France, too, a politically reasoning public emerged, though only after the middle of the eighteenth century....During the early part of the century, despite Montesquieu, the criticism of the *'philosophers'* focused mainly on religion, literature, and art. Not until their encyclopedic publication did the moral intention of the *philosophers* develop, at least indirectly, into a political one."[3] In the last thirty years of the century, the clubs first formed by Bolingbroke and other English emigrés and visitors turned into institutions of public criticism. There, literary discussions turned into a materialistic, moral, or economic debate on the state of society and nature. From here, the physiocrats Turgot and Malesherbes were appointed to the government in 1774–76 – "virtually the first exponents of public opinion."[4] And here, as in the fraternal orders, another English import (more than 600 by 1789) and coffeehouses (around 1,800 in Paris by 1788), congregated the groups to whom Necker in 1781 and Calonne after him addressed their presentation of the state budget, the *compte rendu*. This made the haute bourgeoisie a vital political force, just as it gradually began to lay its hands on the economic levers. And with this development the power of the king and his bureaucracy, the nobility and the clergy, became increasingly a formality.

Of chief interest to us is how this bourgeoisie felt about another aspect – the internal one – of the political and economic power it had acquired: its soul, its nature, and its disorders. Since 1750, the crucial impulses in medicine had come from Théophile Bordeu and his vitalist school of Montpellier. He and his successors Barthez and Bichat had arrived at their position from a dual rejection. They could no longer accept Cartesian rationalism, which dualistically separated the dead matter of the body from the soul on the basis of physiological experimentation (Glisson, Von Haller, Whytt). Yet Stahl's animism also would not do; Stahl considered all research – for example the investigation of conscious as well as automatic reflexes – pointless, and he covered it over metaphysically by linking these problems to the rational soul. While countless German men of medicine continued to philosophize about the matrix of all life, Bordeu and Barthez replaced Stahl's *anima* with the more neutral concept of *la nature* or *principe vital*. The assumption of such a basic force – a kind of regulative idea – eliminated all metaphysical problems, and opened up the field of living matter, of the organic, to empirical investigation.

This possibility, however, was not realized until the Revolution:

François-Xavier Bichat, in his *Anatomie générale* (1801), starts off with the structural uniqueness and innate vitality of all organs and tissues. In making Von Haller's concepts more precise by differentiating animal and organic sensitivity and contracture, he laid the histologic and chemico-physical basis for the nineteenth-century dominance of French medicine.[5] The school of Montpellier deprived the body of its mechanical explanation since the laws governing lifeless matter could not explain the phenomena of life; instead the body acquired an autonomy which science had to acknowledge. The soul, on the other hand, lost its Cartesian special position and became an axiomatic dynamic explanatory principle for animate nature, the *principe vital*. The physiology based on this followed not a mechanical, but a "vitalist materialism."[6] It did not need a rationally deduced natural system — as last developed by Sauvages in 1763. Rather, it began with describing the facts created by external and inner sensations and their unique qualities imparted by the *principe vital*, by nature, that had to be analyzed. That held for the analysis of organs and tissues[7] whose special structure determined the nature of an illness no less than for the analysis of passions, instincts, thoughts, and other subjects of a psychology that even though dependent on the laws of life, within the framework of this physiology has been given free scope for empirical research.

The analytical method which henceforward, and especially after the Revolution, was adopted by the vitalist physicians as well as by the ideologues and psychiatrists, was spelled out by Condillac's adaptation of Lockean sense perception.[8] Contrary to Descartes, science must begin not with a definition, but with "established facts." It must dissect a fact into its components, and guided by experience reassemble them. This is the analytical or historical method, or the origin of ideas. The life of the soul, essentially the product of the sensations, Helvétius' *sensibilité*, unfolds in line with outer circumstances and education. At most, hunger or self-interest are innate drives. Despite their psychology of self-interest, these men of the Enlightenment had little insight into psychic disease. They, like Locke looked on them as mental aberrations. Soul, i.e. *sensibilité*, grew directly out of the organization of animate matter. It may, as for example in the case of mental disturbance, lose some of its potency, but it can be snuffed out only with life itself. De Lamettrie, a medical man, was actually content with Galen's explanation of insanity as a corruption of the humors.

This was symptomatic of the difference between the structure of the bourgeoisie of France and say, England. While Arnold could link the theme of the passions to the suffering of established bourgeois society and use this to explain insanity, France still needed this theme as a political argument in the struggle for such a society against the external authorities of the monarchy and the church, against the *trahison des clercs*, a fight that touched the lives of most proponents of the Enlightenment — through imprisonment, emigration, book burnings. Thus, in 1770, Holbach wrote about responsibility for wrecking "public opinion": "The royal courts are the true breeding grounds of the corruption of nations....Those responsible for leading us are either deceivers or else caught in their prejudices, and they forbid us to lend an ear to reason....Thus the passions that are innate to us and essential to our preservation have become the instruments of our destruction and that of the society whose preservation they ought to serve." Not only did men not dare "to demand happiness from kings, whose task should have been to make them happy," but they also allowed the deceitful clergy to keep them away from reason through "religion, whose basis has ever been ignorance and whose guideline has ever been the power of imagination....It is not nature that has made mankind unhappy, nor did an affronted God desire that they live in sorrow, and certainly no congenital corruption has made mortals evil and unhappy. Rather, these regrettable manifestations are simply the result of error....If there is a panacea for mankind for its most diverse and most complicated diseases, then it can doubtless be only one, namely truth, which must be sought in nature."[9]

The Encyclopedia also put *folie* into this still rationalist framework of error and truth of nature, in which the movements of the body and of the passions correspond to morality: insanity is the error that one no longer is aware of, the departure from reason, "in the reliance and in the solid conviction of following it....Veritable madness, then, are all the derangements of the mind, all the illusions of self-love, and all our passions when they are carried to the point of blindness; for blindness is the distinctive characteristic of madness."[10] Hence, self-love or passions do not in themselves produce madness, but rather their illusion or delusion. Madness is error, or at any rate, mental disorder, whose causes are to be sought in the illusory, physical and moral, external circumstances, or in man's failure to recognize reasonable and moral nature.

Error, bias, deception, dogmatism. For the Enlightenment in absolutist France this was more than the subjective opinion that could easily be resolved analytically.

The error which the Enlightenment endeavored to deal with was the false consciousness of an epoch, anchored in the institutions of a false society which in turn secured the dominant interests. The massive objectivity of the prejudice, for which the metaphor of prison walls would be more appropriate than that of figments of fantasy, became tangible in the repressions and denials of an adult autonomy withheld.[11]

In the face of such irrationality, the Enlightenment could survive only by incorporating the courage, the will for reason, into its own sphere of interest. "Reason is equated unquestioningly with the talent for adult autonomy and with sensibility to the evils of the world. It has always made its decision in favor of justice, general welfare, and peace."[12] Therefore, insight into the laws of nature also had to offer instructions for the morally proper life. Of course, the adult autonomy demanded was for the bourgeoisie, which is why the "prison walls" of the hôpitaux généraux were seen solely through the prism of that claim. They were to fall to the extent that they impeded the freedom of the bourgeoisie. The insane and the poor, who could not partake of adult autonomy or, if workers, only to a limited degree, did not become visible as themselves. Since they aroused little interest, the insane were incorporated into the rationally deduced scheme of mental derangement, without even the benefit of Condillac's analytical method, observation, and fact gathering. This interest arose only when, with the Revolution, bourgeois society gained power over itself, and with that had to face the problem of the limits of the newly won freedom, and the possibility that society can inflict harm on itself. This is also the period that questioned the validity of the belief of vitalist medicine and of the Enlightenment in nature as the physical and moral binding force, in which the sciences of animate nature began to objectify themselves in a division of labor and positivistically, and in which it is no longer the same reason that distilled the laws of moral life from that nature. Conversely, the weakness of the sensible Enlightenment became obvious when all it could pit against the objectivity of absolutist power and irrationality was the faith in a similarly objective rationality and a static-unhistorical nature. This put its psychology of sensation in danger of turning into a passive receptacle for impressions of objects and circumstances, one of no use in altering the behavior of the subject, similar to Marx's later critique of Feuerbach's materialism, "that the subject, reality, sense perception, is grasped only in the guise of the object or the view, but not as a sensuous human activity, praxis; not subjectively."[13]

Rousseau and Mesmer

Rousseau did not offer this criticism, but not only did he show the reverse side of the Enlightenment, as has often been said, he also broadened it substantially, bringing it closer to practice. If Diderot, in *Rameau's Nephew* (c. 1760), had showed the reader someone who actually belonged outside the walls of the Hôpital Général, who described himself as ignorant, lazy, impertinent, and mad, Rousseau actually led such an asocial, rambling, painful life, or at least demonstrated his individualism.[14] The men of the Enlightenment championed the common people, took their part, but they led upper-class, even aristocratic lives. "Rousseau is the first to speak as one of the common people, and to speak for himself, when he is speaking for the people." He does not call for reform, "he is the first real revolutionary" who all his life remains the same petty bourgeois, declassé, plebeian.[15] Inspired by Richardson's moral-sentimental novels, Rousseau irreversibly expanded the reading public, and with it the political public, far beyond the confines of high society. This was a factor in making the lower classes, more so than in England, the bearers of the Revolution and, at times, raising the Revolution out of its bourgeois frame-work. Rousseau both expanded and reversed the criticism of the Enlightenment, directing it from the outside to the inside. He showed that coercion and suppression were not so much the fault of the absolutist state, but the product of man and society — and of the learned, enlightened sector in particular. This led him via the negation of theory to the primacy of direct practice, and to seeing the Revolution not as a smooth, unproblematic step for-ward, but as an upheaval, a crisis, with unpredictable consequences. "Rousseau, the first to criticize not only the existing state, but with equal vigor, also the society critical of the state, was likewise the first to place their interrelationship under the rubric of crisis."[16] Finally, it was Rousseau who arrived at the conclusion that absolutism and aristocratic rationalism could not be fought with the tools of the Enlightenment. He even nursed the suspicion that the weapon of enlightening reason came from the arsenal of the enemy. "He turned against reason, because he saw in the process of intellectualization also that of social segregation."[17] He was therefore able to articulate his misgivings about rational culture, which he saw as degeneration, not progress, more radically and effectively than the early English Romantics. His *ordre naturel* was not immanent in existing society, like that of the physiocrats, but transcended it. From it the revolutionaries would derive the innocence and clear conscience of their actions, since Rousseau made "the powers of the heart and of the feelings and of the *volonté générale* available for the political conflict."[18] To be sure, Rousseau's nature would also be immanent in established bourgeois society, a society fighting bourgeois nature that would be dominated, exploited, and transformed into an inequitable distribution of property by rational law only partially through cultural-anticapitalist criticism; and would then become its justifying superstructure. That is to say, Rousseau's nature would deprive objectified, alienated nature of its moral aspect and oppose it with an internalized, subjective, bourgeois naturalness, stylized morally-aesthetically into a yearning for the "simple life," into "nature as mood," into a historical celebration of living individuality. It would transcend the process of reification, alienation, and disintegration of nature and man — that is how it interprets the capitalist mode of production and its consequences — subjectively through the idea of the "beautiful soul," of spontaneity and originality, objectively in the autonomous totality of the work of art.[19]

Rousseau's program, insofar as it affected psychiatry, was already contained in his first major work, an essay submitted to the Academy of Dijon, which posed the question whether the sciences and the arts promoted morality. His answer in his *Discours sur les sciences et les arts* (1750) was emphatically negative. Science and philosophy, he held, promote indolence and hence are the source of most ills, destroy faith and virtue, and are thus "the foes of public opinion," by which he understood the traditional customs and opinions of the simple good, common people and not the reasoning of the enlightened sector.[20] Furthermore, science and literature stimulate an interest in commerce, money, and luxury, and thereby create greater inequality; they undermine true morality and the well-being of the nation; they corrupt taste, the simplicity of earlier times; being sedentary occupations, they weaken the body, deprive the mind of its flexibility, and affect the attention span; they make citizens unfit for military service. Finally, they ruin the education of children, whose minds are filled with absurdities, while the education of the heart, doing one's duty, innocence, ignorance, poverty, and the direct, spontaneous good deed are castigated.[21] Nothing so deeply influenced the course of psychiatry in France than Rousseau and the mania for self-observation and self-reflection[22] that began with him.

These ideas of Rousseau's were to become part of psychiatric theory and practice. He directed attention away from the outside to the inner person, to the individual suffering from his own self, who himself had brought on his lack of freedom, his psychomoral alienation from moral nature, his mental suffering, through indolence, the sedentary life of the city-dweller and the student, through rational education, luxury, economic selfishness, passions, estrangement from nature, a turning away from religion, from patriotism, from taste, and from the education of the heart, through revolution, or rather through the consequent moral decline. All these factors and their countless variations will, according to psychiatric etiology, trigger mental disorders always in conflict with the positivistic, scientific countertendency, which denies this and which in individual cases has indeed proved to be morally liberating. Rousseau has had a corresponding influence on basic therapeutic ideas. The stages of mental recovery lead via romantic escapism into the inwardness of feeling, into restrained happiness, into moral naturalness, back to the rustic life and physical activity. The road of the education of the heart will ward off or cure the ills inflicted by society and an overburdened mind, and make for the rebirth of original, "natural man." Rousseau himself went to Montpellier in 1737 to treat his complaints and passed himself off as an Englishman. He believed in a *morale sensitive* and hoped that he would be able to guide the actions and hearts of people imperceptibly by harmonizing sensory stimuli — colors, sounds, landscapes. Music, which he so loved, seemed to him as "the most suitable means for reaching the affective region without being filtered through the sieve of rational ideas: music operates directly upon the soul."[23]

The "office-hour" psychiatric treatment of nervous disorders, of hypochondrias, vapors, and melancholias, which, in response to public demand, expanded after 1750, and which was increasingly Rousseauian, based itself on the physiologists' new models of the nervous system: on the vital quality of sensibility or on the hypothesis of the nerves as taut and slack fibers that transmit vibrations. This last notion in particular facilitated analogies to mental processes. On the one hand, the mental state or its disorders can be seen as tension, resilience, attention, or relaxation and distraction. In this way, mania, as a steady vibration of the sensibility through the overly tense nervous fibers, could be put into a polar, antithetical relationship to melancholia, in which the relationship with the outside world is impeded by the slackening or paralyzing tautening of the fibers. This led Pierre Pomme (*Traité des Affections Vaporeuse*, 1763) to the conclusion that hysteria and hypochondria were caused by a too close — sympathetic — proximity of the organism to itself due to the shrinking of the nervous system. Moreover, the tension theory — whether mechanical or as the manifestation of a nervous or vital force — offered the concrete possibility of letting the most diverse therapeutic devices operate on the model of music: as a direct-aggressive and regulatory force, independent of reason which restores the harmony and the optimal medium tonicity of the nerve-fiber tension or the average of moral naturalness. In 1769, P.-J. Buchoz developed a precisely graduated theory for treating the various states of melancholy with corresponding counteracting musical qualities. This was the same time that musicians, for their part, constructed a doctrine of affects, according to which every affective emotion was to find its parallel musical expression.[24]

Anne-Charles Lorry's (1726—83) work on melancholia, *De melancholia et morbis melancholicis* (1765), stood on the threshold between the new theories. He therefore compromised by positing two forms of melancholia: the traditional *melancholia humoralis*, caused by bile secretions, and the modern *melancholia nervosa*. His theoretical interest, however, focused on the second form, which is a disorder of the firm, solidary parts and at the same time, unlike the humoral condition, also immaterial (*"sans matière"*). He based his assumption that melancholia often turns into mania on the theory of nerves — a theoretical bridge of major practical significance because it made it possible to extend the interest in that fashionable disorder to the truly insane inside the prison walls of the hôpitaux généraux. The texture of one's nerve fibers (this too is Rousseauian) defines one's personality, whether one tends to be aggressive or poetic. The extent to which melancholia was henceforth seen as the product of the individual organism was demonstrated by the fact that Lorry discarded the long-held notion of noxious matter that had to be expelled, rendering blood-letting and purgation useless.

"Even tension" (*homotonie*) had become the health ideal. happiness and well-being were linked to a balanced tonicity of the nerve fibers, in a medium able to adjust elastically to the demands of life. Most of the therapies he recommended — travel, baths, conversation, games — were connected with the vogue of watering-places, whose curative properties — including the little "gallant escapades" — had already been extolled by Bordeu.

After 1750, Spa became the French Bath.

Simon-André Tissot and his major work, *Traité des nerfs et de leurs maladies* convincingly linked melancholia and nervous disorders to the nervous system or to the sensibilities, which were now conceived of in a Rousseauian moral sense. Tissot and other practicing psychiatrists acknowledged Rousseau's influence. It was Tissot's belief that the impulse for sensation and movement was conducted by the same nerve. In explanation of the first function he developed the theory that the nerve stimulus was transmitted by a series of small bodies, one pushing the other, and for the latter, the theory of a continuous wavy movement of the nerve sap. The sensibility of the physiologists is thus now transferred to mental-moral qualities. People with nervous disorders are said to have an oversensitive nervous system and also an overly sensitive soul, a too emotional heart; compassionate and sympathetic, they are quick to take on the burdens of the world. This extreme responsiveness may even lead to a diminution of feeling when the nervous system reaches such a peak of irritation and reaction that it is no longer able to work through or interpret impressions. This too is a theoretical bridge that allows the coupling of nervous disorders and insanity. With this notion of sensibility, the individual can be made responsible for his nervous complaint, for it is the moral punishment for his preference of the unnatural stimuli of social life over a wholesome, natural life. These ideas validated Rousseau's critique of cultural degeneration as well as his naturopathic methods. The physician was no longer an enlightened guide to maturity and stability but a moralist thundering against a deviation from nature brought on by the patient himself. "A clear and pure conscience is an excellent prophylactic" against insanity according to Tissot. Ideal health and moral perfection converge. The belief that nervous disorders were continuing to increase — also used as a prophetic warning — and that they contained the threat of moral and national collapse, became part and parcel of contemporary cultural criticism, including Tissot's. Thus one aspect of insanity that emerged into at least theoretical view was the price to be paid for the progress of civilization. And Matthey, another physician influenced by Rousseau, reminded men of the feebleness of their reason, since chance or a vehement emotion of their souls could transform them into raving maniacs.[25] The recommended therapy for both social degeneration and individual suffering was a return to the harmonizing rhythms of natural life and physical work — a liberation from social restraints, a return not to animalist license but to the law and truth of moral naturalness. That was how Tissot depicted it, and that was how the Romantic exotic Saint-Pierre described how he cured himself of the illness of his mind, a recovery he owed to Rousseau, not to the physicians.[26] Nor was it a coincidence that during this period, the late eighteenth century, the Belgian village of Gheel was rediscovered. It seems that ever since the Middle Ages, more than half of Gheel's inhabitants had been insane, yet they lived and worked among the peasant population without either restraints or treatment. If in earlier days such an arrangement may have been construed as a method of isolating the insane, after Rousseau it was reinterpreted and praised as an idyl, in which the insane were exposed to the whole spectrum of nature's curative powers and where the majority regained their sanity within a year's time. This also recognized the beneficial effects of the natural-moral element of the family, even before the French and English institutions saw themselves as families.

The fact that theory began to see the insane was not so much due to the Enlightenment as to Rousseau's sense of crisis. Insanity was the ultimate symbol of man's rejection of his earlier simple existence, of contemporary social compulsions and the threatening degeneration of culture. The irrationality of insanity now existed theoretically within society — internalized and more comprehensive: declared a product of society or of the socialized individual, insanity now seemed a form of man's alienation from his beginnings, his self, his nature, from the laws of the heart, from his historical destiny. Alienation was the term under which Pinel subsumed the first paradigm of psychiatry in France. As a form of alienation, insanity symbolized the consequences of the break with the immediacy of nature, and it symbolized man, insofar as he had become alienated and sold himself to the artificial and degenerate state of society. Given this reasoning — and the fact that the equation of the nervous system with sensibility, the vital force of the human organism, allowed everything to be related to every other thing regardless of the barriers of "class" — even the most minor medical recommendation was seen as possessing grave moral and political consequences for society. Thus cold water was found effective for toning up and harmonizing the nervous system and the entire organism and hence, unlike hot beverages, was recommended for nervous disorders. This led J. B. Pressavin, the author of *Nouveau Traité des Vapeurs* (1770), to some far-reaching conclusions: "Most men are justly criticized for being degenerate in having taken on the slackness, the habits and tendencies of women; all that is wanting is the similarity of their bodily constitutions." Excessive enjoyment of hot drinks — an attack on the coffeehouses that were gaining in popularity — "accelerates the metamorphosis and makes the two sexes almost alike, both physically and morally. Woe unto the human race if this practice spreads to the common people; there shall then be no more peasants, laborers, and soldiers, for they will soon be deprived of the strength and resilience required in such vocations." Effeminacy, nervous complaints, and enlightenment were considered signs of the times. Still, the higher reaches of society might perhaps be allowed to indulge in them, so long as the ordinary people were shielded from them and so long as their simplicity and labor continued to be available as the moral-economic counterpart.

The France of that period offered the only appropriate setting for the spectacular and scandalous epitome of office-hour psychiatry: mesmerism, the movement of animalist magnetism. Franz Anton Mesmer (1734—1815), the son of a royal gamekeeper of Constance, had studied theology, philosophy, and law before turning to medicine.[27] After completing his dissertation, *De planetarum influxu* (1766), and his marriage to a wealthy widow, he opened his practice in Vienna in 1768 in a luxurious, large baroque villa. A passionate lover of music, Mesmer staged the first performance of a Mozart opera, *Bastien und Bastienne*, in his home in 1768. In 1774 he scored his first professional success, attracting public attention through his use of a magnet to cure a girl suffering from hysteria. After 1775 he repeatedly demonstrated the success of his therapeutic method and the philosophy underlying it. In Germany, however, he met with almost unanimous rejection. Both the medical societies and the public were still too rationalist for his magic, materialist Romanticism. In 1777, after rumors of a false cure, the hostility against him became so pronounced that he was forced to leave the country. After the Revolution he returned to Vienna, but accused of Jacobinism he was forced to leave.[28] In 1778 he had become the subject of a heated scientific and public controversy in Paris. Lafayette and George Washington were among his champions, and his enormously successful private practice did not suffer even after a royal commission ruled against him in 1784. The commission included some of the foremost scientists of the day — Franklin, Bailly, and Lavoisier — as well as the physician and humanitarian J. I. Guillotin (to whose famous contraption the two last-named owed their painless execution during the Revolution). This commission concluded that the fluid of which Mesmer spoke did not exist and that his sensational results were due to imagination, touch, imitation, and delusion. Of course, these men had so much difficulty accepting a purely mental reality, i.e. suggestion, as did Mesmer himself.

Mesmer's new science was a patchwork of a series of accepted notions. But in the age of electricity, and especially of Galvani's reflexive frogs' legs, the old healing power of the magnet cried out for speculative, dynamic reinterpretation.[29] And the humoral theory about crisis in the disease process, of the critical days and the influence of the moon and the tides, had already been introduced into modern medical thinking by Bordeu in connection with the vital energy of the nerves.

Since Mesmer believed man and the universe to be made of the same substances, influenced by gravity, climate, and the moon, he could reasonably assume that a "fluid" — both matter and energy — could explain the movement of the heavenly bodies and the nerves as well as their influence on one another. Something that used to be ascribed to the work of spirits, gods, and demons, was now, thanks to this "vital magnetism," found to be due to natural forces, thus effectively putting an end to the old superstitions. The irritability of the nerves allowed man to share in the "toning" vibrations of the humors and of nature, the epitome of harmonious movement. Disease was the obstruction brought on by irritability, hence disharmony, a case of out-of-tune, slack nerve fibers. Only nature could heal, and the only method available to man for strengthening her curative powers was the magnet, which was simply a counterpart of nature, endowed with the same qualities (e.g. polarity) as the human body. The magnet was the transmitter of vitalist magnetism, conveying it through music, concentrating it, mirroring and storing it, stirring up "salutary crises" — driving the insane, epileptics, and hysterics to violence, since only a thorough upheaval can effect a cure. By drawing an analogy to gravitation, electricity, and magnetism, Mesmer merely tried to bring the ideas of his age — sensibility, irritability, the nerve-fiber theory, assumptions about remote "sympathetic" effects, vitalist life energy, the immediacy of Rousseau's and Tissot's nature — into a single rational and natural scheme of explanation. He therefore thought of himself as belonging to the Enlightenment, and in his final work, *Mesmerism or The System of Reciprocal Effects*, 1814, he came out for a democratic state and a religion somewhat like the rationalism of the Revolution.

The vague universality of those ideas with their moral-practical implications was merely the obverse of the precision of the empirically rigid natural sciences. Both were by-products of the dissolution of the classical union of the natural and moral sciences, the same movement in which bourgeois society freed itself from the constraints of the absolutist state, and in which a relationship not consistent with the division of labor, particularly in incipient psychiatry, was established between theory and practice. When translated into practice, Mesmer's intention, born of the enlightenment goal to incorporate the irrational forces of life and nature into a rational supertheory, turned into spiritualism and magic.[30] Enlightenment, as his contemporaries came to understand, was not a linear-rationalizing movement, but one of conflict and opposition of the rational and irrational.[31] As Mesmer's practice developed, his original approach became increasingly internalized and technological. At first, in keeping with his theory, he did in fact use a magnet. But by 1776, he had shifted the therapeutic emphasis from the magnet to the person of the practitioner, who, by touching and stroking, diverts the fluid to the patient. Finally, concentration of the will replaced the contact by touch. Consequently one of the movements sparked by Mesmer dubbed itself "voluntarism." The specific method involved interaction, the encounter between two individuals, of whom one was endowed with the power of radiation, the other with receptivity. This in turn gave rise to any number of variations of spiritism as well as to one aspect of the state of nineteenth- and twentieth-century psychotherapy. The other line of development was the mechanization of the arrangement, which, in the opinion of behaviorists, was solely responsible for the cures achieved.[32] Mesmer's success, i.e. the demand for him, inevitably turned his practice into big business, including a chain of homes, hotels, and hospitals for the growing number of patients. The treatment rooms contained the so-called *baquet* — a Mesmer invention — a tub filled with water, iron shavings, and crushed glass, with protruding iron rods connected to the patients by bands — an imitation of an electric battery. In addition to the treatment rooms, there was the padded "crisis room," where the patients could recover from their crisis symptoms (fits of laughter, weeping, screaming, rage, hiccups, convulsions, and fainting). An assistant physician and attendants ("handsome youths" — for the mostly female clientele) were hired, and they too were allowed to magnetize. Orchestral and vocal music, with perhaps a painting of a rustic scene as a backdrop, the lilac-colored garment and the gilded rod of the master, who made his entrance only after a long, suspenseful pause — all these added to the spell that produced both the crisis symptoms and their contagious spread: the realization of Rousseau's *morale sensitive*. Thus, in the commission report of 1784, Bailly made reference to the inherent moral danger, since the close, confidential relationship between the mesmerizer and his sensitive female clients had clearly sexual overtones.

In keeping with the commercialization of the enterprise, a kind of publicity department headed by a banker and a lawyer was set up. One hundred shares at 100 louis d'or were issued in a subscription drive. The stockholders formed a secret society, the Order of Harmony: they were sworn to secrecy about the doctrine that Mesmer was about to confide to them. A gesture toward the poor showed the difference between Mesmer and Wesley's proletarian-moral electricity movement. In a suburb of Paris, Mesmer blessed a tree with his vital magnetism to give the stricken poor free access to his cure, which earned him the reputation of a humanitarian. A symbol for Rousseau's moral polarization of society: While the propertied class — aristocratic ladies and *nouveau-riche*, haute-bourgeois capitalists — subscribed to stocks for subsidiary companies as far off as America, the natural, simple people transplanted cuttings from the tree of life into the provinces. Only the Revolution put an end to this business. Whereas high society artificially produced its private crises and worked them off mechanically in padded rooms, the political crisis of real society intensified until it finally exploded. The mechanical handling of this crisis took the form of a bourgeois-rational overthrow of the social order, tied to the crisis symptoms of emigration on the one side and of guillotining on the other.

With these very real movements, the nervous complaints, the swoons and hypochondrias and fashionable sentimental melancholias disappeared for a time, a not unusual phenomenon in times of political upheaval and war. The dwindling clientele also spelled the end of this era of private psychiatric practice. Mesmer's facilities no longer met a need. But in the meantime, Germany had become receptive to their underlying ideas, and eventually they were also revived in France, though in different form.

The Failure of the Physiocratic Reforms

As in England, the appearance of nervous disorders, this milder form of irrationality, their identification with the aristocracy and haute bourgeoisie, and their social functionalization — as a symbol of either status or social degeneracy — were a clear indication that the most profound class division, the exclusion of irrationality, was no longer unquestioningly accepted. After all, the concept of nervous complaints was based on the turn of science to less rational, more dynamic-subjective notions such as sensibility, dictates of the heart, vitalism. Or, to put it more generally: "The often still abstract aspect of the vegetable, animal, and human kingdoms, systematic and classifying, rooted in the class consciousness of the prerevolutionary eighteenth century, was shaken by the rising third estate....With this, the classificatory approach, concerned with absolute ties and separations, with timeless contingencies, gave way to historical explanation. Things lost their rootedness in reason and entered a more flexible, deceptive, dangerous, earthbound aspect of life."[33] Even more patently, the nervous disorders broke through class barriers when they confronted the leveling category of bourgeois work and were seen as punishment for the privilege of not working. L. S. Mercier, in *Tableau de Paris* (1783), formulated it even more succinctly than Rousseau: "This is the torture of all effeminate souls, whom idleness has driven to dangerous sensual delights and who, to evade the hardships imposed by nature, have willingly embraced every deceptive doctrine....Thus are the rich punished for the puny rewards they reap from their fortunes."

But if idleness violated the natural order and led to moral and physical ills — and this seems much more likely than the reverse — then, so the physiocrats maintained, it was more important to cast doubt upon, and perhaps even remove, the barriers against the negatively privileged, the sequestration of the irrational. Here as elsewhere, the policy of restraint of mercantilism foundered. In defiance of all work training, idleness, breeding corruption and a host of other ills, reigned at the hôpitaux généraux and state prisons. Physiocratic rationality recognized the error of the mercantilist premise: immorality was not the product of idleness. Experience had shown that economic crises brought on greater unemployment, beggary, and vagabondage, as well as a lackluster attitude toward work. Idleness and poverty were now seen as economic rather than moral problems.[34]

With this new approach, the hôpitaux and their inmates once again gained visibility, became the subject of a public debate which the physiocrats had made a critical instrument of an autonomous independent *public éclairé* (enlightened public).[35] The vision of reason that acknowledged the laws of the natural order played a greater role than Rousseau's indictment in the public airing and finally to the tearing down or at least reshaping of the "prison walls" of the hôpitaux, state prisons, correctional

institutions and workhouses, of which, according to the revolutionaries, there were 2,185.[36] This came about in four ways:
(1) the exposure of corruption, (2) differentiation, (3) economic
utilization, (4) the politicalization of the social question.
1.   As a result of the discovery of idleness in the hôpitaux and of
the true economic causes of poverty and beggary, these institutions ceased to be looked at in terms of their original purpose – as
instilling moral work habits and as a deterrent public display of
coercion – but were seen as through and through corrupt. Mercier
saw them as the concentration of the violence, humiliation, and
unhappiness of society, polluting the very air around them, as the
object of both disgust and pity. This situation gave rise to the
public perception that to this day commingles valid views (the
institutional milieu can exacerbate the condition of inmates and
erroneous ideas that contact with mental patients can cause
insanity). In 1788, Mirabeau criticized: "I knew, as did everyone,
that Bicêtre was both a hospital and a prison; but I did not know
that the hospital had been opened to breed disease, and the prison
to breed crime."[37]

This was the swamp that bred the poisonous flowers with
which, so they said, a man like De Sade schemed to introduce
naked violence into society.[38] Under these circumstances, it was
not surprising that, in 1780, when an epidemic spread through
Paris its origin was attributed to the infection at Bicêtre and its
inmates. A commission of inquiry concluded that Bicêtre was
subject to a "putrid fever" which was linked to the bad quality of
the air, but denied that this was the source of the disease.[39] Still,
events such as these spurred the hygiene-oriented institutional
medical reform movement of the late eighteenth century. In the
absence of all knowledge about the true causes and behavior of
infectious diseases, the quality of the air, the weather and climate,
took on great importance. The hypotheses of natural and moral
philosophy on the effect of the atmosphere, of air, etc., led to
moves to neutralize the institutions as a protection against their
possible corrupting, contagious influence. In line with the ideas of
Romanticism, the institutions were moved into healthy, moral rural
areas or else surrounded with a *cordon sanitaire*, i e a garden or
park. And great emphasis was laid on well-ventilated, dry quarters.
However, the humanitarian impulse behind these hygienic measures obscured the original purpose – the protection of society.[40]
2.   One of the results of the commission formed in 1776, when
Turgot and Necker were in office, to investigate the conditions in
the hôpitaux was the construction of the Sâlpetrière in 1789.[41]

Moreover, Malesherbes, the Minister of the Interior, personally visited the state prisons, and ordered inmates who appeared to be mentally ill moved to other houses, and he himself gave instructions for their treatment. The interest in the segregated unreason led to an awareness of the necessity of differentiation since the undifferentiated mixing of inmates prevented the identification of potentially functioning members, and also ruled out the establishment of any kind of order and the possibility of improvement or recovery. However, this utilitarian-rational approach turned the insane into the least visible objects of public concern. In his *Lettres de Cachet* (1778), Mirabeau, contrary to his protest and his commitment to the emancipation of other excluded groups, said: "It is only too true that we must separate from society those who have lost the use of reason."[42] The insane posed the greatest problem to the theorists of the Enlightenment; this situation changed only with the coming of the Revolution.

3.　For the physiocrats and their economic laws of the natural order, the segregation of unreason only proved the irrationality of the mercantilistic and moral policy of coercion, of absolutism itself. The paupers, beggars and vagbonds, prisoners, rascals and blackguards, libertines, debauchés, and intractables, instead of being sequestered and allowed to lie "fallow" in the hôpitaux, should be integrated as potential labor in an expanding bourgeois society and made subject to Quesnay's economic law of laissez-faire, i.e., as free persons placed under the more humane restraint of low wages, so as to stimulate their rational interest in work. Since human beings constitute a nation's primary product, Mirabeau's father, the *Ami des Hommes*, had already back in 1758 proposed that the hôpitaux be emptied and that the "filles de joie" be sent into factories to become "filles de travail." In the competition among nations, the utilization of the poor guarantees cheap production, and hence victory. "The poor are the necessary agents of those great powers [means of production] that establish the true strength of a people."[43] As a consequence of this movement the mentally sick poor gained visibility along with the poor in general (the wealthy, as in England, were cared for in private institutions, *petites maisons*). Released from physical restraints, they could now, as "free" men, share in the economic restraints imposed on the rest of the poor.

4.　The social reforms, however, were still blocked by the power of the state. The compromise of the physiocrats lay in the differentiation between their insight and the actions of the king, between science and administration, theory and practice.[44] "At a time

when English classical national economy already preached industrial and mercantile liberalism, the French physiocrats had to be
satisfied with the demand for agrarian liberalism....Here the social
question appeared above all as a question of political power."[45]
Thus, in France, more clearly than elsewhere, the *hôpitaux* were
instruments of power, and the internment of political prisoners
and people of rebellious or otherwise conspicuous behavior made
obvious the polarization between the individual's human rights
and the oppressive state. Thus, the English physician Robert
Jones was horrified by what he saw on his visit to Bicêtre in 1785:
"I could not forbear exhibiting my sensibilities, and my feelings,
at seeing such a number of unfortunate persons chained down to
their solitary abodes, without any other Cause, from what I can
learn, than the peculiarity of their conduct, or eccentricity of their
behavior."[46] In most countries, the formal natural-law interest in
the situation of prisoners and the improvement of prisons preceded the concern with the insane: Howard came before Tuke,
Malesherbes before Pinel, and, in Germany, Wagnitz before Reil.
But in France, it went beyond this: the political struggle gave rise
to a movement against the mad. There were vigorous protests
from both prisoners and institutional directors who saw the
forced coexistence with the insane as an additional, and hence
illegitimate, punishment. The insane were thus not only victims
of the *hôpitaux*, they were also looked upon as a symbol and
device of absolutist despotism. That was why, as other groups
gradually became integrated into society, they remained outsiders,
taking over more and more hôpitaux, until the Revolution abolished these institutions, the *lettres de cachet*, and with them the
absolutist practice of sequestering unreason.

We mentioned the compromise of the physiocrats. Koselleck,
citing Tocqueville, maintains that the lasting innovations of the
Revolution — a centralized administration, its control over the
people, the leveling of privileges, the transferability of property
and real estate — had their origin in the ancien régime, and that
the Revolution simply completed what the old administration
aspired to but had been unable to carry out. "The administration
of the old state fostered the Revolution as much as the Revolution
itself set off a continuous increase of administrative power. Two
seemingly contradictory trends — social revolution and state
administration — thus proved to be the mutually determining and
promoting factors of one and the same process."[47] Within this
framework, it is not so surprising that, in contrast to England,
the medical researchers and practitioners alike paid so little heed

to the situation of the insane, and that two physicians involved in the administration and inspection of the hôpitaux were just about the only ones to offer any concrete proposals for the necessary institutional reforms. In 1785, Colombier and Doublet published their *Instructions sur la manière de gouverner les insensés and travailler à leur guérison*, a guide for institutional administrators. They arrived at the conclusion that France had practically no institution that met the needs of the patients and provided adequate treatment. The reform ideas of the authors start with the architecture and the principle of differentiation. Every institution — and every province should have one — should comprise four buildings, each with its own garden. The treatment of the inmates requires three categories of rooms: the patients must be classified according to their individual condition — whether agitated, calm, or recovering. In dealing with agitated patients, restraints are indicated. Each patient must have a well-ventilated, fireproofed room of his own. Baths must be easily accessible. Great emphasis is placed on the careful selection of attendants. The description of what constitutes desirable qualities is pragmatic, not romantic: physical strength, compassion, patience, alertness, and agility. Tenon, a physician assigned by the Paris Academy of Science to write a report on the Paris hôpitaux arrived at similar conclusions. He worked with Colombier and also went to England to study the superior English asylums. In 1788, he published his findings, which voiced the same urgent demand for official attention to the condition of the insane as those of his two colleagues.

But this government was no longer in a position to carry out the reforms urgently requested by its own administration. After the Revolution, however, not only would Pinel's, and even more so Esquirol's practical reform plan explicitly refer to Colombier and Doublet, but the administration of the French institutions would become the most tightly controlled and centralized in Europe.

2

The Revolution
and the Emancipation of the Insane

No psychiatrist has had so much and so much that is contradictory, written about him as Philippe Pinel, the so-called father of psychiatry. He is generally looked on as the liberator of the insane, even though chains had already been discarded by Joly in Geneva in 1787 and by Chiarugi in Pisa in 1789, and the Retreat had been opened in 1792. That is the reason that B. Panse believes (*Das psychiatrische Krankenhauswesen*) that Pinel owes his reputation to the Revolution, while J. Wyrsch (*Zur Geschichte und Deutung der endogenen Psychosen*) sees him as having at best practical significance. Foucault even makes Pinel's liberation into the polar opposite, and claims that he actually subjected the insane to far more stringent restraints. And Pinel's theoretical approach is even more controversial. In psychiatry's long-standing controversy whether insanity is psychic or somatic, Pinel is counted among both the "somatists" (thus Kraepelin, Gruhle,[48] and Wyrsch) and the "psychists" (e.g., Ackerknecht, Leibbrand and Wettley, and Ey[49]). Finally, much of the data of Pinel's biography was unclear until recently,[50] quite aside from the myths surrounding his act of liberation. These uncertainties only make us all the more interested in examining the social and political situation of the insane during the Revolution, as well as specific aspects of medical development and contemporary philosophy before venturing into Pinel's paradigm.

The Poor and the Insane in the Revolutionary Era: Medical Reform

In August 1789 a special commission of the Revolutionary Constituent Assembly launched an investigation of the problem of beggary and poverty. In this context the Duke De la Rochefoucauld, in December 1789 issued a report on the state of the hôpitaux généraux. These inquiries were the direct consequence of the Declaration of Human and Civil Rights of August 26 of that year, which held that no person could be deprived of his freedom arbitrarily without legal cause. All the hôpitaux were to be abolished, or rather examined for their utility within the context of the new laws. The newly won civic freedom meant not only an end to restraint, but the transformation of arbitrary into legal restraint, and it demanded a new definition of the limits to freedom dictated by the need for security. Here lay one of the roots for the *fait psychiatrique*.[51] Rochefoucauld's report, like those of his prerevolutionary forerunners, sees the promiscuity of those devoid of reason as the source of all ills, and this ruled out any possibility of a more humane approach. That explains the demand for special institutions for the insane. To differentiate those who had lost their reason, Rochefoucauld proposed a general hospital reform, and with this gave the impetus for medical reform.[52]

In March 1790, in implementation of the Declaration of Human Rights, the Constituent Assembly ordered the release of all those being held through a lettre de cachet or any similar instrument — except for sentenced or accused criminals and the insane. In the latter case, however, each instance was to be checked both administratively and medically within three months, and the inmate was then to be either released or cared for in special hospitals.[53] And so on March 29, 1790, the bourgeoisie, having won control, and represented by men like the mayor and astronomer Bailly, went to Salpêtrière and Bicêtre to put an end to the sequestration of the insane, and simultaneously grant them civil liberty and integrate them into the civil legal order. But the difficulty lay in that "simultaneously." The formal release of those excluded as irrational or otherwise oppressed by the *ancien régime* — the poor, the insane, the criminals, as well as women, children, and Jews — was merely the utopian anticipation of a particular goal. At first there was the hope that the attainment of this objective would come about automatically; later the goal was pursued along moral-pedagogic lines, and finally to various degrees it became the lifelong struggle of bourgeois society itself. The situation of the insane was an exemplary illustration of the problem: there existed neither "appropriate hospitals" nor was there any such thing as psychiatry, either in actual practice or as an adequate theory or in the form of an appropriate practical idea. What developed was the social vacuum of a merely formal liberation. Just as the realization of the right to engage in trade fought for by Turgot ruined many artisans, and just as the abolition of feudal tenancy impoverished many small farmers, and just as the poor became the industrial tools in the hands of the haute bourgeoisie, the real victors of the Revolution, the situation of the insane also deteriorated. Since numerous hôpitaux and the Church's comparatively humane shelters[54] were closed, the administration could think of no better solution than to concentrate the "liberated" mentally ill paupers at the Salpêtrière and Bicêtre. In the provinces, prisons often became the only places open to them. It is thus not surprising, and in fact sheds light on the fast-moving character of the French Revolution, to find that simultaneous with the well-meaning but unworkable resolution of March 1790 to free or provide special help for the insane, a new law was promulgated for the protection of the population which regarded the insane as harmful, dangerous, and bestial. Here we find the coexistence of two opposing views, whereas in England the transition from one to the other spanned almost the entire eighteenth century. The law in question was Article 3 of the ordinances issued between August 16 and 24, 1790, making the communal administrations responsible for the prevention or amelioration of scandalous or harmful incidents that might be caused by released mental patients. The same provision applied to stray, destructive, and dangerous animals.[55] This point was reiterated in the law of July 22, 1791, and extended to the families of the insane. This provision, plus a penalty clause, was to reappear in the Napoleonic Code.

On the other hand, these two decrees pertaining to insanity have a common feature. Both show insight that revolutionary liberation cannot be realized through the free play of forces alone. Instead, the natural order attained with liberation requires official organization and control as well as administrative reform. Unlike the English (and American) Revolution, the French Revolution knew from Rousseau that one cannot automatically count on the self-discipline of selfish interests, for human nature has been corrupted by society. And it was also known that the poor and prospective workers had already become important props of the Revolution. Consequently, the political revolution had to aim at social reform and at the same time reach out politically through administrative control, social integration, and the mobilization of moral impulses.

Medical reform was one expression of this quest for social reform, and Pinel personified merely one aspect of it. It is not surprising that this reform — radically empirical in its theoretical point of departure and closely oriented toward administrative requirements — was launched at the very inception of the Revolution. However, one distinctive contradiction emerged: the Jacobinic revolutionaries were extremely distrustful of the positivist natural scientists, and some continued to voice their misgivings all the way to the guillotine. The medical reformers, on the other hand, initially were good revolutionaries, but come the National Convention, they retreated — to their reform. The intellectual roots of the medical reformers, who also saw themselves as educational reformers, go back to the salon of Helvétius' widow, which was frequented by at least four of them: Cabanis, Pinel, Thouret, and Roussel. Here they became acquainted with both the Encyclopedist (through Diderot, d'Alembert, Condorcet, Condillac, Holbach) as well as physiocratic tradition (through Turgot); and here, too, they met the chemist Lavoisier, as well as Franklin and Jefferson, who contributed to the anglophile orientation of the circle.[56] Mirabeau's physician, the ideologue Cabanis, played a crucial role in the issue of medical reform. As early as 1791, Guillotin had proposed to the National Assembly that medical schools be connected with hospitals. That same year, Pinel entered an estate contest with a paper on the treatment of insanity. Although his entry did not win a prize, it proved of help nonetheless. On September 13, 1793, with the support of his friends Cabanis, Thouret, and Cousin, he was made "médecin chef de l'hospice de Bicêtre," where he launched his psychiatric reform, and continued it at the Salpêtrière in 1795. Broader possibilities of reform opened up when, in 1793, the National Convention disbanded the medical faculties along with various other institutions from the time of absolutism, and, after Robespierre's death in late 1794, the reform-oriented upper middle class regained a measure of power. Now the ideologue Garat became Minister of Education. *Écoles de sante* were set up throughout France. The Paris school was connected to three hospitals: for surgery, for internal medicine, and for rare and complex diseases. The last-named, which was also intended as a research institute, was not completed until 1815. Medical education henceforth followed the ideas of Cabanis and Fourcroy: Teaching took place at the bedside of patients, so that the only thing students had to develop along with the ability to think logically was a faculty for clinical observation. This has remained the basic formula of medical training ever since. Garat commissioned Cabanis to write a comprehensive book about medical reform, which was published in 1804. The extent to which their reform involved a division of labor went unnoticed by the pioneers, since mastering and teaching several areas was something they took for granted. Thus, beginning in 1794, Pinel taught hygiene and physics, and later internal pathology, and Cabanis taught internal-medicine, and later forensic medicine and history of medicine at the Paris medical school, under Thouret as the first director. And to complete the framework of the institutions that made French medicine preeminent in the nineteenth century: in 1796, a number of physicians, including the ones mentioned above, formed the *Société médicale d'émulation.*

The Medicine of the Ideologues

Pierre J. G. Cabanis (1757—1808) was not only a driving force in medical and educational reform; he also formulated the medical theory that formed the basis of the school of the ideologues and their positivist successors, as well as of medicine per se. With him, the reformist-administrative element was maintained politically as well, and did not yet exhaust itself in "applied" science. After the Reign of Terror he returned to politics to become Minister of Education and administrator of the Paris hospitals. He sat in the Council of the Five Hundred, became senator, and supported Napoleon's *coup d'état*, for which the latter showed faint gratitude when he called the activity of the ideologues seditious and outlawed them. Cabanis had come under the influence of Madame Helvétius' salon through his father, a lawyer, landowner, and friend of Turgot. He was subsequently adopted by Madame Helvétius and took over her salon, to which the ideologues retreated when their activities lost political support in the Institut National.

The starting point of the ideologues was Condillac's method of gathering facts and the analytic approach to phenomena, as well as the vitalists' instrument of "clinical" observation and description.[57] In this context, Condillac's sense perception and the speculative life force of the vitalists take second place. The first important result of the medical application of this approach was Pinel's *Nosographie philosophique ou la méthode de l'analyse appliquée à la médecine* (Paris, 1798). This compendium became the program of France's "clinical school." For here Pinel "with the utmost certainty was the first to state unequivocally that the 'Analytical Method' [Condillac] was conclusive also for pathological research thus making Pinel the forerunner of the renowned Bichat."[58] And in his *Traité des membranes* (Paris, 1800) Bichat did indeed refer to Pinel when explaining that human organs can be traced back to their simpler tissues, and that pathological changes depend on the type of tissues, not on the organ. These initial steps toward a positivist medicine (and Pinel's psychiatry) had already been taken when Cabanis issued his *Rapports du physique et du moral de l'homme* (Paris, 1802).[59] This represented an attempt to encompass and complete the Revolution by reform, to use the accumulated information to offer the liberated society guidelines for virtue, happiness, and perfection — while opposing Cartesian dualism, sense perceptive *tabula rasa* and vitalist life force. And at the same time it was both deterministic and voluntaristic, materialistic and idealistic. Established bourgeois society was no longer concerned with the explanation of the false ideas spread by the treason of the clergy but with the holistic analysis of consciousness. The three branches of the science of man, of anthropology, are physiology, the analysis of ideas, and morality.[60] Physiology forms the basis of psychology and moral philosophy, for, according to Cabanis, just as the stomach digests, so the brain produces ideas. That is why physicians create the basis for the rational construction of society, for all social reforms, and that is why their medical reform is of primary national importance.

On the one hand this physiologism liberated medicine from innumerable systems and theories and for years to come expanded the area in which facts could be successfully investigated. On the other hand, however, as a basis for the analysis of ideas and for practical political goals, it was by no means able to fulfill its progressive optimistic expectations. The activity of medical fact-gathering and dislocation of regulatory practice — when applied to society — developed into a tendency to look at that society as requiring the continuous perfection of its condition. Unlike the prerevolutionary Enlightenment, bourgeois society no longer had to struggle to free itself from external despotic power and a delusive idealism; it now seemed to have been realized. But in that case nature ceases to be a reference point transcending society that guarantees the right to action, and it either becomes immanent, synchronized with itself or turns into an available physio-logical basis, to be protected or preventively organized only against disturbances originating primarily within themselves. Here society began to measure itself solely by itself, whatever its actual condition, and no longer by an allegedly speculative objective truth and the binding nature of ideas, of reason. Bourgeois society as such was nature, reason, order, identity, morality, and where it deviated, where it was still unnatural, unreasonable, disorderly, alienated, immoral, it merely required its own political perfection — attained by means of administrative techniques, hygiene, education, the mobilization of moral drives and the socialization of destructive impulses.[61] The expounders of ideas — the ideo-logues — traced them back to the consciousness of the individual and of society, to that which was already physiologically active and operative among and before them,[62] to their origins, and objectified in terms of these origins, which were not made by, but make, man.

Cabanis was successful in his quest for such active and desired origins, the physiology of ideas and consciousness: that is how man acts before becoming conscious of acting, he thinks before reflecting upon it. A vast series of individual differences were posited: sex, age, diseases, temperaments, climate and diet, character and working methods, as the sum total of physical habits. Every human being comes equipped with either strong or weak organs. These organs shape the configuration of ideas, and the needs depend on the type of organs. Before acquiring the ability to speak, children have their own sign language. Like these codes, physiognomy, pantomime, and above all sympathy are socially binding, represent a vast socializing potential, which modifies the harshness of the destructive physical needs, and on which depends the degree of perfection and irritability of the individual. However much Cabanis regarded the distinction between sensitivity and irritability as a semantic exercise, and however severely he may have criticized Condillac for denying the instincts for the sake of the *tabula rasa*, he still could not grasp the problem posed by Abbé Sieyès' separation of the first principles of social relation — *faculté* and *besoin* — in the Declaration of Human Rights: for Cabanis, they may have been distinct in morality, but physiology unites them at their source.

Education is merely the continuance of creative physiology by other means: through impressions and habit formation, it creates new organs, makes necessary corrections.

The physical interior of man is conceived as energetically creative. The brain itself is a second being within man. Sleep is as much an active accomplishment of the brain as the excess of motor energy in a manic or epileptic fit, since in them the senses do not receive more impressions than usual. In contrast to sense perception, which he considers overly passive, Cabanis regards the nervous system primarily as an "active agent because of its energy," and only secondarily as a "receiver of impressions." Beyond that, he traces the nervous system itself back to deeper, actively material sources: the activity of the nerves is dependent on the surrounding tissues and vessels, on certain activating fluids, by which Cabanis — e.g., with respect to male sexual activity — anticipates the hormones; and on phosphorus and galvanic electricity,[63] by which a chemical and physical reduction grid is drawn in. And finally, Cabanis relates the absolutism of the nervous system of rationalist psychology to the old idea of the constitution, whereby, modifying Hallé's morphological typology (1797), he retains the four Hippocratic types, complementing them with a nervous and a muscular type. These were alleged to be the roots of many habits and of hereditary, hence therapy-resistent, illnesses.[64]

In this framework it becomes understandable that according to Cabanis nervous disorders, irrationality, and delirium could be caused not only by confused external impressions but also by inner sensations, by diseases of the internal organs, making prompt recovery impossible. As in the days before the nerve era, the particularly susceptible parts were found to be the region of the diaphragm (with the upper stomach), the hypochondrias (with the liver and spleen), and the genital region.[65] Insanity is manifested by way of dynamic-sympathetic relations between sensory centers in the internal organs and the common sense, or brain. In any case, not only is the order of ideas altered, but its deeper foundations are denatured and degraded: taste, propensities, affections, habits, and aspirations. When the origin is more unconscious, "automatic," by way of the internal organs, therapy depends on manipulations that do not involve the patient's consciousness but affect and alter him unconsciously. Compare Cabanis' characteristic description of the effect of music:

The in some respects universal power of music over animate nature proves that the stimulation attributed to the ear can by no means be reduced solely to perceptions grasped and compared by the brain organ: there is something much more direct in this stimulation....There are special tone associations and even very simple tones that take control of all the sensory faculties at the same time and by way of the most immediate effect arouse certain feelings in the soul — feelings that seemed ascribed to them by primal, unconscious laws of the organism. Tenderness, melancholia, somber grief, joyous animation, pleasure bordering on madness, martial enthusiasm, can now be stirred up and now soothed by songs of remarkable simplicity: this effect is all the more certain, the plainer the songs and the briefer and simpler the lyrics. All these impressions evidently fall into the area of sympathy, and the brain takes a real part in it only insofar as it is the center of sensibility.[66]

Cabanis' naturalization of speculative factors, for instance vital energy, made possible the triumphal march of positivist medicine. On the other hand, the naturalization of the utopian anticipation of a rational society posed a threat to existing bourgeois society, in that the indiscriminate ideological justification of a temporary condition might work to perpetuate that condition.[67] When Napoleon saw the activity of the ideologues, i.e. all analysis of consciousness, as a threat to a positivity that he would rather have left to the dictates of the heart, he failed to recognize "that the *idéologues'* analysis of consciousness was not all that incompatible with ruling interests. It already contained a technical-manipulative element. Positivist society has never relinquished that element and has always kept its findings in readiness for mutually opposed purposes."[68]

Pinel: The Historical Paradigm and the Road to Administered Morality

Pinel's background and life can add to our understanding of how psychiatry came into being in France.[69] Philippe Pinel (1745—1826) was born in a village in Languedoc. His father was a surgeon (a profession practiced by barbers until 1743 and which for some time to come did not enjoy respectability) and local politician. In 1762, Pinel matriculated in theology at the Collège Lavour of the Jansenist-Encyclopedist Doctrinaires; he studied philosophy — including Rousseau's — and took holy orders. In 1767, he transferred to a similar college in Toulouse, and there in 1770 he began to study medicine and mathematics. In 1773, after submitting a dissertation entitled *De la certitude que l'étude des mathématiques imprime au jugement dans son application aux sciences*, he was granted a license to practice medicine. Yet he continued his studies for another five years under Sauvages, Bordeu, and Barthez in Montpellier. The vitalist influence was a permanent one. In 1778, he continued his studies in Paris with the same enthusiasm, stubborness, and unwillingness to shoulder social responsibilities. As before, he earned his livelihood though private tutoring, notably in mathematics. He also went on a sort of pilgrimage to Rousseau's grave, attended lectures by D'Eslon, a student of Mesmer's, joined the Society of Encyclopedists, and frequented the illustrious circle of the Helvétius salon. So impressed was he by Benjamin Franklin that he almost emigrated to America. He translated books from the English, among them Cullen.

Finally, at the age of thirty-nine, after twenty-two years of studying, he began to show signs of bourgeois socialization. From 1784 to 1798, he published the *Gazette de Santé*, writing articles on hygiene, a medical specialty that had acquired great political importance since the physiocrats' interest in human productivity.[70] In 1784, he also became the house doctor in a Petite Maison, a private institution for wealthy mental patients. In this house, owned by the carpenter J. Belhomme, Pinel had his first direct contact with the mentally ill, and he plotted the progress of their illness with daily systematic records. Needless to say, the outbreak of the Revolution found him an enthusiastic champion of the Third Estate. He became a municipal administrative official. His revolutionary fervor was checked by the Convention, the Reign of Terror, and the execution of the King. Together with his close friend Cabanis, he tried to find a haven for the fugitive Condorcet. It was at this time that Pinel withdrew from political life and, as mentioned earlier, became involved in medical and educational reform, as a professor of hygiene and medical director at Bicêtre, where he launched his "liberation of the insane." During the Empire, his prestige grew. He became a consulting physician to Napoleon and, in 1804, was inducted into the Legion of Honor. He bought a country house with a small farm and became mayor of the town. His practice prospered, he was popular with his students, until forced to retire in 1822, when the Liberals purged the medical school.

The book that made Pinel the starting-point of French — and German—psychiatry appeared in 1801:*Traité médico-philosophique sur l'aliénation mentale ou la manie*. Even more distinctly than Cabanis' *Rapports*, this was an attempt at integrating the bourgeois-liberal achievements of the Revolution by way of social reform and securing them against any attempt to restore feudal institutions and rationalist thought, but even more so against all the more extreme elements of the Revolution, which, Pinel felt, were releasing the perverse instincts of the lower classes, the poor. Based on the example of the insane, Pinel saw the bourgeois category of individual and social identity and of the treatment and prevention of its forms of alienation as the central problem. Practice took precedence over theory: observation, description, the gathering of "practical facts," living with the insane, the internal policing of institutions and the moral treatment, all these took precedence over natural systems or theories and laws arrived at solely by reason. There was no doubt in Pinel's mind that these procedures had been made possible by the Revolution, which had liberated science from religious institutions, private greed (the change from private to public institutions), and public prejudice. The Revolution had established the principles of free inquiry as well as free education, including education through observation in the hospital, and the recognition of the importance of socio-moral therapy as opposed to traditional medications.[71] On the other hand, it was also the Revolution that had enlightened men about the effect of the instincts, passions, and social needs on the animal nature of the individual and society and on the origin of insanity. Finally, for Pinel, the Revolution had not only produced mental alienation by unleashing extreme passions, but it had also brought awareness of the necessity of order and education, i.e. recognition by the administration and government that institutions had to be built — in those terms — purely out of humane motives, both disinterestedly and in the interest of order. Thus Pinel put psychiatry into the area between medicine and the science of guiding the state and society. All hope was to rest on a stable government concerned with public welfare, and in this context Pinel's book was to furnish the requisite premises and suggestions.[72]

The only place Pinel's practical and theoretical goals had been realized was in bourgeois England. Hence in his documentation he relied almost exclusively on the English experience, on Crichton, Cullen, Haslam, on Ferriar's work in Manchester, on Fowler's in the Retreat, and on Francis Willis'. As with all writers of the Revolutionary period, the heroic age of Antiquity formed the background of Pinel's work: Hippocrates, too, had proceeded along individualizing-descriptive lines and had found a close connection between his medicine and all other things. If we had to decide what was the one most telling effect of the Revolution on Pinel we would have to say it was amazement — amazement over the forces released by man since the beginning of time, forces not dreamed of by sense perception: the power of the mind, of the will, of man's instinctual drives. This amazement left Pinel with feelings of great ambivalence. His successors, however, following in his footsteps, were no longer amazed.

Out of this experience of the Revolution, out of elements of vitalism and of Encyclopedic sense perception, out of the physiocratic faith in government, of Rousseau's belief in nature and moral education, out of aspects of English Romantic reform psychiatry, out of hygiene's aspiration to order and cleanliness in the service of social and economic interests, and out of the perennial medical and philosophical debates of the ideologues, among whom Pinel ultimately must be counted,[73] there emerged the first French psychiatric paradigm, Pinel's historic variant of the clinical condition, method, and practice — even though he himself did not acknowledge these sources. Still, the crucial prerequisite for the expansion of psychiatry was the closing down of the absolutistic institutions of sequestration after the Revolution, for it was this act that brought on the call for and necessity of the social integration of liberated unreason, of the poor and the mad, for their maximum economic utilization. At the same time, only society's *public* institutions for the poor could open up the opportunity for the establishment of an "exact" science. For only the relationship between the bourgeoisie and the poor could guarantee an objectifying social distance to the research object, as well as a sufficient number of objects, i.e. "cases," which in turn made possible the establishment of empirically arrived at laws or typologies. The fact that these conditions were also essential to the specialization of the other medical disciplines has been pointed out by Lesky: "In the eighteenth and frequently also in the nineteenth century, a practice for the poor was the road to specialization."[74]

Pinel created the latitude for his scientific approach by rejecting all contemporary systems (Cullen, Sauvages) as well as the generous reductions of the ideologues, that had made the insane, the allegedly incurable *séquestrés de la societé*, the victims of medical indifference or segregation. The alienist, as "conscientious historian," was supposed to look and *observe* the unstructured chaos of the strange manifestations of derangement, whereas the psychological analysis of ideas of the ideologues was to be complemented by the analysis of the moral disorders. Pinel's scientific motive for internal institutional reform was born of the belief that methodologically controlled and comparable observation was possible only if "cases" could move "freely," without chains, although within the framework of a strict, unchanging institutional order free of outside interference, but under the watchful eyes of observers to chart the course of the manifestations. Only such a historical depiction of symptoms and their relationship to the patient's background could lead the doctor to the "facts," i.e. the individual history of the origin and development of the symptoms. These, not the subject of a particular obsession (e.g., love), but rather formal genetic concepts, are to serve as guidelines in the diagnosis of the disorder. Just as Pinel saw insanity as part of the history and philosophy of the human mind, so the philosophy of the disease was a combination of the history of its symptoms, its progress, its varieties, and its treatment.[75]

Pinel conceived insanity not only as case history but also as mainly erupting from within man, a disturbance of his self-command, self-control, self-preservation, identity, which is why "alienation" — partly synonymous with "mania"[76] — was chosen as the generic term for the various forms of madness. This was reflected in the concepts used by Pinel in his innumerable case histories, and demonstrated once again that insanity had become an accepted form of unreason in a bourgeois society based on self-control and identity. Just as even in the nineteenth century the bourgeois notion of the rational had a largely voluntaristic note, so after Pinel, the unreason of insanity increasingly came to be seen as derangement of the will rather than as a derangement of reason, as an inexplicable, uncontrollable force, uninhibitable, destructive, automatic instinctual energies, erupting from the inside, from the constitution, from the depth of the individual being and manifesting itself in rage or passivity, in the destruction of others or of oneself. Here, too, Pinel drew on the experiences of the Revolution and developed the concept of *manie raisonnante*: the excess of physical strength and willpower in undisturbed functions of the mind, an observation — akin to the idealogues' prerational linkage of voluntary action and outside resistance (Destutt) — that prompted Pinel to cast doubt on the idealistic unity of the mind, as in J. J. Winkelmann, and on Condillac's statue model,. i.e. the relatedness of all ideas to sensations. The historistic, voluntaristic, constitutional, and psychological nature of the descriptions allowed German physicians and philosophers to find in Pinel the connection they could not find in sensualism.

However, the somatic school in Germany also found support in Pinel. For although Pinel believed that the only approach to alienation was via the description and analysis of the mental symptoms of each specific case, he nevertheless regarded it as a physical disorder whose primary seat was not so much in the nervous system or the brain, the transmission belts of external impressions, as in the sensations and hence in the disposition of the internal organs, notably the gastric region and its nerve ganglia, which also produce the "corresponding" vegetative symptoms — from loss of appetite and constipation to insomnia. Therefore, as far as Pinel was concerned, the ideal-typical form of alienation was an ordinary mania that grew out of an inner disposition and — as self-alienation — continued along an autonomous course and was most resistant to (outside) therapy. External causes, on the other hand, could only trigger something going beyond their own effect and actually played a role only in manias following an irregular pattern, although these made up the majority of cases. Therefore, heredity, disposition, and constitution rank first in Pinel's catalogue of causes. The second through seventh places are held by mental causes (from unrequited love to religious fanaticism and superstition). Only after that does he mention physical causes, often of a mechanical nature. An investigation of the professions as to their susceptibility to insanity showed that "science" evaluated itself as positive because of its realistic approach to life: Rousseau's polarization of poets as opposed to peasants and soldiers was replaced by the notion that priests, monks, and artists were the most likely, and the natural scientists and mathematicians the least likely to fall victim to the unreason of alienation.[77]

To be sure, Pinel's order of the five forms of disease followed traditional patterns. His own clinical description notwithstanding, his hierarchy was based on the principle of mental derangement. Melancholia, as the first form, is the domination by monomania of the faculties of sound reason, hence a partial derangement of the mind, usually in the form of megalomania or micromania. The second form, with the provocative name of *manie sans délire*, epitomizes Pinel's practice and his experiences in the Revolution: a pure disorder of the will and an undisturbed mind, i.e. a bodily tension with no external causes, manifesting itself merely in a spontaneous, blind drive, in an (abnormal, affectively perverse, criminal, forbidden) action, but nevertheless a disease. This construction, under various labels to this day continues to inject a political note into the debate of psychiatrists and legal scholars, especially with regard to personal freedom.[78] The most impressive aspect of Pinel's paradigm was this: with the admission of sequestered unreason into established bourgeois society, this irrationality itself was extended beyond the rationally and comparatively easily delimitable mental disorder to the entire realm of human activity, its abnormalities, deviations, alienations, and its tendency to transcend order in a disorderly fashion. Here, however, only norms can be established, not unequivocal, objectively rational limits or laws. In this realm open to both individual and political interpretation something new arose. The liberation and integration of the unreason of insanity gave rise to an unexpected complication in connection with the integration of this voluntaristically expanded irrationality into bourgeois society.[79]

Pinel's third disease form is the "normal," the most frequent form of alienation, manic frenzy, a periodic phenomenon, that affects one or more mental functions. Whereas mania produces errors in judgment, the fourth form, dementia, robs the patient of all judgment. It offers a picture of anarchic, chaotic coming and going of ideas and feelings, unrelated to outside stimuli, of aimless activity, an automatic existence, a "moral disorganization." The fifth form, finally, is idiotism, innate or acquired, a more or less complete atrophy of the faculties of reason and free will. Pinel's historical method allowed him to see a progression from the first to the fifth type of disorder, an idea which was later advanced by the proponents of the concept of "unitary psychosis" (*Einheitspsychose*) — i.e., the idea that the various manifestations of mental disorder are not separate sicknesses but various forms of a single process.

Because Pinel's "liberation of the insane" was a practical necessity for the scientific objectification as well as for the administrative integration of sequestered unreason, the claim that his motives were purely humanitarian seems rather questionable. Although the Declaration of Human Rights had made the insane "free" and "equal," they were nonetheless the victims of social chaos. What happened to the poor happened to an even greater degree to the insane. Political liberation in bourgeois society did not yet mean social liberation. Legally speaking, the insane enjoyed the status of animals. The decreed new "suitable institutions" failed to materialize and the old ones were shut down. The insane were hard hit by the spreading famine of the revolutionary era. Mentally ill males in Paris and surroundings were concentrated in Bicêtre, which also served as a prison until 1836 (and was also the scene of the first experimental use of the guillotine), while females were in the Salpêtrière. Chains may have been the "symbol of the coercive rule of some over others,"[80] but in this context their removal was not simply a political, revolutionary liberation, but also a necessity of the social, reforming integration of the liberated — with the means available to the new society in the process of organizing itself. According to Pinel, when the chains were removed rebelliousness subsided. With one stroke the conditions for the establishment of order, inner policing, moral treatment and scientific observation were brought into being. The myth of this liberation has been told again and again in singing the praises of kindhearted Pinel.[81] In 1793, the Jacobinic scourge Couthon inspected Bicêtre in search of enemies of the people suspected of hiding among the insane. The insults and obscenities of the chained inmates disgusted him. When Pinel requested his permission to release them, Couthon retorted: "Citizen, you must be mad yourself to want to free these animals." Pinel insisted: "Citizen, I am convinced that these madmen are so unbearable only because they are deprived of fresh air and freedom." Couthon capitulated, saying: "Do whatever you like with them, but I fear that you yourself will become the victim of your bias!" That same day, Pinel took the chains off forty inmates, and the horse-whips from the attendants. Instead of chains they were given straitjackets or similar restraints, and sixty years were to pass before Conolly's system reached France.

But now the road was cleared for Pinel's *traitement moral.* However, it involved downright draconian rules and morality. Like the authors of the Revolutionary constitution, Pinel believed that freedom had to be administratively organized and had to mobilize the moral impulses in bourgeois society.[82] The administrative character of Pinel's practical methods emerged not only from that reflection of current conditions, and not only because Pinel was himself an official. The actual executor of the new treatment seemed to be not so much Pinel as J. B. Pussin, the *Directeur de police intérieure*, and his wife. Their positions in France soon became more powerful than those of superintendent and matron in England. Pinel often stressed the great psychological and therapeutic gifts of the Pussins; and Ideler, a contemporary, even believed that Pinel's role was actually more that of an interested observer."[83]

Nevertheless, in his book, Pinel discussed the treatment methods in connection with his theory in detail. In contrast to the contemporaneous English Romantic reform psychiatry practiced in the Retreat, the anticlerical Pinel did not want to create a religious "milieu" in his institution, out of fear that the superstitious tenor of the pious books might stimulate the incipient insanity. On the other hand, the moralizing substance of religion was certainly used and adapted to teach the values of the bourgeois order, social morality, work, and family. There was an important connection between Pinel's theoretical and practical approach: on the one hand, the disease, the moral alienation, was innate to the patient, and on the other hand, a primordial moral structure within the same individual had to be stabilized from outside. Hence the institution of marriage and harmonious family as well as hard physical labor and sexual morality were capable not only of healing, but also of preventing mental illnesses. This led Pinel to conclude that the two classes that did not accord with these moral ideas of the Third Estate were particularly endangered: the aristocrats, too proud to obey the law of physical work, were especially resistant to treatment, and so their cure took longest. On the other side, there were the lower-class families, rent by immorality, fighting, and poverty, the breeding ground of mental illness. It would thus appear that it is the education toward the norms of the Third Estate that guarantees a mental identity to all members of bourgeois society, including the other classes, and protects them against alienation. Yet even if the aristocrats — the rich, powerful, and wicked — are difficult to heal, lowness remains the greatest potential for the genesis of mental disease: the lowness of the individual, whose instincts break through rational inhibitions, and the lowness of society, whose lower class with its aggressive drives has not yet been integrated by bourgeois institutions. The correspondence between the insane and the poor was thus restored on the new social and scientific level.

Therapy had to take all those factors into account. There was a direct connection between treatment and inner policing, a connection linking England's liberal and Romantic reform models. The institution was intent upon the rigorous differentiation of the types of the disease. It set forth a strict minute-by-minute daily schedule. A large number of attendants moved among the patients to let them know without saying a word, that their ranting, violence, and resistance had little chance of success. Every aspect of the institution had to be so organized as to create the compelling impression of the sovereign power of the administration — with possible punishments looming in the background, though under medical supervision. In this "humanely controlled" framework, freedom for the insane was possible in so far as it was compatible with their own safety and that of others. The unified order in itself had a soothing and salutary effect on the patients. And the system of regular physical work was highly effective both therapeutically and pedagogically. This induced Pinel to propose this approach for all the large national institutions of this kind — the insane asylums, prisons, and old-age homes — that still operated after the closing of the hôpitaux, as the only assurance of health, morality, and order. Work, understood as methodically regulated movement went to the heart of the problem of alienation: the outbursts of activity and their counterpart, the retreat into idleness and stupor. Hence, all the institutions — in physiocratic Rousseauian fashion — were to be converted into something like farms.

This system enabled Pinel to bring the patients in line with all the norms of the bourgeois economic order: the value of property, since the land belonged to the institution and the patients learned how to nourish themselves and the institution with the products of their own labor; the division of labor, since the patients were divided according to various kinds of work, including handicrafts; competition, since their performance was a gauge of their recovery. And finally, this regimen was meant to arouse the instinct of self-preservation and the natural inclination to make the earth fruitful.[84]

Nature was also the issue in therapy itself, not, of course, as rationally deduced reason, nor for her romantic potential of inducing moral feelings, but rather for her alleged power of socialization. Consequently Pinel's first therapeutic commandment read: Wait and be patient. Nature must be given time to unfold her effectiveness. The outbursts will gradually diminish and the social instincts, and hence reason, regain the upper hand. However, nothing must be left to the countless disruptive external influences; nature's purpose must be given a helping hand if the desire for the good and socially valuable is to win out over the destructive instinct. This can often be done only by bringing the entire institutional administration into a manipulative constellation which — by indirect influence on the consciousness — forces the alienated behavior back to the social-moral identity and so once again coordinates the individual who is beside himself with the desired, acceptable self. This scheme is adhered to by an infinitely rich store of methodic pedagogic lies: i.e., one pretends to go along with a patient's delusion, creating a fictitious complicity, to shatter the delusion through staged events. For example, a patient who thinks he has no head is made to wear a heavy leaden cap until he capitulates. One who believes that there is a snake in his stomach is given an emetic, and a snake is surreptitiously introduced into the vomit. The guilt-ridden melancholic is put on trial, and is absolved of guilt. A megalomaniac believes that he is Christ: no one is allowed to speak to him; left to his own devices the patient feels deeply humiliated in his social isolation and soon gives up his idea in order to be taken back into the community. The man who claims to be king is told that his neighbor also claims to be king yet is powerless and the butt of jokes. This gives the patient a mirror to help in his demystification. Finally, the theater is enlisted in this effort. Not only is the spectacle supposed to rid the melancholic of his fixed ideas or forcefully counteract a depressive indifference, but there is also the attempt to present a perfect illusion of the delusionary world of an individual patient, and through this objectification demonstrate its absurdity, a game in which the physicians and all

employees of the institutions join in. Thus, as we know, the director of the asylum of Charenton allowed the inmates to stage plays
under the direction of the Marquis de Sade, in part for the public,
until the head physician, Royer-Collard, informed the chief
of police in 1808 about the scandalous decline of morals and
authority.[85]

What all these techniques had in common was a surface acceptance of the patients' madness in order to confront them directly
with themselves. This confrontation was considered necessary, and
no patient was exempted. Pinel's *traitement moral* paralleled the
"moral incorruptibility" of his contemporary Robespierre. In the
rise of French bourgeois society, where it is a commonplace —
more political, hence more radical than in England — that it
produced its own disorders, Pinel anchored mental disorders
deeper within man than did his English colleagues. But if man
produces his destructive impulses and fixed ideas himself while at
the same time being their victim, the cure also rests with him.
Thus he arrives at the realization that he is his own prisoner. By
thus shouldering the blame for the social alienation of his own
self, he has achieved the goal of the *traitement moral*: the patient
has regained moral responsibility, his social drives have been
mobilized, he can master his destructive impulses and return to
his own and to social identity.

The extent to which the physician, in Pinel's system — as a
punishing judge and gentle father — derives his therapeutic power
from the striving to replicate the norms of the bourgeois order
within the institution can also be demonstrated from the negative
side.[86] Those patients who had transgressed bourgeois norms
at their most sensitive points were excluded from the humane
benefits of Pinel's institution. And those who were recalcitrant
out of religious fanaticism, i.e. who made the other patients
rebellious out of the belief that obedience to God transcended
obedience to man were not admitted at all. Inside the institution
patients who refused to accept the universal law of work, and
thereby incited other patients, were punished with solitary confinement, as were those who committed crimes against property.
Esquirol was to add a fourth idiosyncratic social transgression:
since Pinel, the old method of submerging patients to the point
of drowning was generally rejected as barbaric and sadistic, but
Esquirol permitted it if the cause of the derangement was thought
to be the unnatural and dissolute practice of masturbation.[87]

Foucault has drawn a parallel between Pinel and Tuke. But
this is too much of a generalization. Tuke's Romantic reform

stands outside the context of any analytic-scientific goal, and moreover represents only a single phase within the development of British psychiatry, a discipline which in France only began with Pinel. Pinel is hence comparable at best to what took place in England between Battie's "revolution" and Tuke's reform, for he tried to accomplish both things at once. Despite their historio-social and scientific differences, Battie's and Pinel's functional similarities make them the fitting founders of a psychiatric paradigm. Each had already made a name for himself in another medical area; each had published a significant work on internal medicine and enjoyed social prestige. And then, when for economic and/or political reasons the social segregation of the insane had become untenable, each was the first in his country to give them social visibility. They did this through years of observation, then by radically changing the social conditions of the insane through practical activity and the introduction of a psycho-moral treatment. And only afterward did they undertake to publish their respective works on their approach and therapeutic method. Furthermore, each, contrary to theoretical tradition, sought to relocate the site of madness in the innate mental (and physical) being of man. Finally, despite their long-range importance, both had few direct disciples, and the practical-reformist aspect of their paradigms did not find wide application until decades later.

3

Psychiatric-Sociological
Positivism

Since the Revolution, and especially since Cabanis' medical functionalization of the mind and Pinel's historical-comparative method, it was more or less self-evident for medical investigations of disorders and their treatment to encompass society as well as individuals. The perilously utopian metaphysics of the eighteenth-century philosophers no longer seemed to fill a need, and there was mistrust about its potential to transcend the status quo. Instead, there was a longing for control of the social anarchy unleashed by the Revolution, while securing its achievements. And the methods of the natural sciences seemed to have achieved both control and security and precisely to the extent that they had turned their back on philosophy and had focused on positive facts. Why, it was asked, could this model not also be applied to the political, social, and moral phenomena to furnish them with theoretical underpinnings and make them controllable. Here, medicine offered itself as the life science and especially the recent advances made therein: physiology with its reduction of phenomena, not so much to the outer as to the inner predisposition; hygiene in its orientation toward preemptive and preventive organization and education; obviously, the doctrine of mental-moral alienation and, before long, the anatomically derived innate drives of phrenology. This medicine had not been shy about its invasion of the social realm, and so it hardly needed Comte's Encyclopedic law, in which the logical and genetic sequence of the sciences is so arranged that nascent sociology is preceded by physiology and its subdivisions, the physiology of the brain and the nerves.

Pinel's immediate and more remote successors were thus faced with the necessity of producing scientific testimony about political and social facts and, as *chefs scientifiques* of the people, take their place alongside the *chefs industriels*, as Comte formulated it in 1820.[88] And the essential premise in the case of both *chefs* was that they were dealing with the "people," with the mass of the poor and their integration. For just as scientific medicine was dependent on an available pool of people, on "treating the poor," and — as we have seen in Pinel — on their tractability for its undisturbed, controlled, and comparative studies, so the poor, the people, not only became visible in the Revolution, but also expressed their own "instincts" and willpower. And increasingly, because their labor was needed, they became the key problem of the capitalist economy and of industry, which had begun to expand by leaps and bounds in 1820, above all after the July Revolution, and was striving to follow the political recapitulation of the "English" eighteenth century with its economic recapitulation. Hence, the general awareness of crises repeatedly manifested itself as social awareness, as the question of the situation of the poor and the workers and their integration in bourgeois society. This holds true for the traditionalism of conservatives like De Bonald as for the industrialism of Saint-Simon and his disciples up to Comte. In connection with the problems of the crisis — reconciliation of revolution and reform, progress and order, society and state — the latter were not so much concerned with changing the objective conditions, the economic or state order, but with changing the subjects and their attitude, with ending spiritual and moral anarchy, with perfection in history, with the advance of (scientific) ideas and the dominance of scholars, with the — at times romantic — organic harmonization of the active soul of society. And above all, they were concerned with a comprehensive education, served by a functionalized immanent (neo-catholic-socialist) religion.

The psychiatrically oriented physicians became inextricably involved in these ideas and goals once they were persuaded of the positive-autonomous nature of mental phenomena. Psychiatry and sociology began to influence each other in various ways, and this gave rise to the comparatively active political role of French psychiatrists in the nineteenth century.[89] Thus we find P. P. Royer-Collard, a doctor at Charenton, as Liberal President of the Chamber of Deputies (1828), leading the fight against the clerical stamp of education. Close ties existed between Comte, Gall, and the physiologist Broussais. A wide circle came under the influence of Saint-Simon and his liberal-romantic blend of progress, heredity, hygiene, Catholicism, and socialism. This held true for P. J. B. Buchez, the president of the National Assembly of 1848 and theorist of cooperatives; and for the psychiatrists U. Trelat,

L. Cerise, and A. Morel, the author of the psychiatric paradigm of degeneration, and a friend of R. Lamennais. In the 1880s, the psychiatric reformer P. Brousse also became the head of a Socialist wing named after him; and finally, a director of an institution (L. Lucipia) who even joined the Commune of 1871 and subsequently was exiled. The fact that the first generation of psychiatrists had served as doctors with the Revolutionary or Napoleonic armies in their march through Europe, e.g., G. Ferrus, J. Esquirol, and F. Broussais, probably played a part in their political activization. Finally, the social background of many psychiatrists was indicative of the change in the social structure sparked by the Revolution. In contrast to other countries, a substantial number came of poor families and had to support themselves while pursuing their studies. Some were "children of the people" (E. Georget, F. Leuret, E. Foderé) some the children of men who had died in, or been impoverished by, the Revolution (Broussais, Ferrus), while others came from families in commerce and business (Esquirol, Gall, Morel).[90]

For these reasons, the psychiatrists in the era of the Bourbons and the citizen king, to the degree that they tried to implement the psychiatric paradigm, were also drawn into the efforts to solve the social and political crisis, and this involvement was of constitutive significance for the emergent disciplines of psychiatry and sociology. Pinel, still under the immediate influence of the Revolution, had only wanted to prepare patients for entry into bourgeois society. With his successors the social critique of the new existing bourgeois society was of primary concern. Society was to be reformed by scientific analysis, an undertaking in which the restorative-stabilizing intentions often became intertwined with liberal-emancipatory objectives.

Restoration and Psychiatric Reform

Between 1805, when he submitted his dissertation, and 1838, when the laws on insanity initiated by him were promulgated, Jean-Etienne Dominique Esquirol (1772–1840) carried out Pinel's paradigm both theoretically and practically. He no longer felt himself to be, like Pinel, a participant, albeit a skeptical one in the Revolution. And he took its achievement, the freedom of scientific thought, for granted. He was aware that the Revolution had compelled him to interrupt his studies, that he was defending suspects before the Revolutionary Tribunal, and, above all, that the great social crisis which he tried to resolve through organizational measures was a product of the Revolution. Thus Esquirol was one of the Royalist and moderate conservatives of the Restoration. As a result, he was dismissed from his position as Inspecteur de l'Université (to which he had been appointed in 1823) during the July Revolution. Like Pinel, he began as a theologian, and studied in Toulouse and Montpellier, where he devoted himself to mathematics. In 1796, he came to Paris, studied with Pinel, and in 1810 succeeded him as head doctor of Salpêtrière. And in 1826 he was appointed to the same position in Charenton. For a time, he also headed a private asylum at Ivry — a refuge for romantically distraught writers, and for Comte as well — but ultimately he was forced to vacate this second job.[91]

Esquirol's single-handed organization of nearly all sectors of the scientific-administrative portion of psychiatry brought Pinel's model to fruition. In 1814, he offered the first clinical instruction in mental disorders, and up to the middle of the century he numbered just about every French psychiatrist among his students. In 1818 the Ministry of the Interior delegated him to inspect the asylums of thirteen cities. His public report made clear that the vaunted liberation of the insane was — except for the Paris area — confined to the paper on which the Declaration of Human Rights and the legal code were written. Esquirol pointed out that the insane were not even granted the status accorded to wild beasts in the Code Napoléon:

These unfortunates are treated more wretchedly than convicts, and they are worse off than beasts. Almost everywhere the mentally ill are being housed in damp and unsanitary quarters. I saw them covered with rags, with only a handful of straw to protect them against the clammy coldness of the ground on which they lie. I saw them given coarse fodder, deprived of air to breathe, water to quench their thirst, without the most basic nourishment, and at the mercy of the violence and maltreatment of veritable jailers. I saw them in narrow, stinking holes without air or light, chained in caves in which one would hesitate to lock up those wild beasts that a profligate administration maintains at great expense in the capitals.[92]

As a result of Esquirol's report, an official bulletin issued in 1819 for the first time contained protective provisions not against but for the insane.[93] The infamous subterranean cells were prohibited; rooms for the inmates had to have flooring and windows; the insane were not to be confined with other inmates of hospitals or prisons; food had to be served several times a day; chains were to be supplanted by straitjackets; bullwhips were forbidden; and even therapy was indirectly alluded to — a daily visit by a physician was ordered.

Esquirol also developed an architectural model for insane asylums. Following Cabanis' inspiration, dormitories were to be replaced by smaller and more hygienic dwelling units better suited to therapeutic purposes. A great many asylums in France and elsewhere were built according to this model. The internal order he introduced in Charenton realized Pinel's approach but somewhat attentuated its revolutionary rigor. This regimen served as a model for the Continent until the introduction of the English Non-Restraint movement; for prior to that no one, not even Esquirol, had rejected coercion.

During the 1830s, Esquirol also worked on official measures to promote public health and hygiene. His last two major achievements on behalf of the institutionalization of psychiatry came in the year 1838. One was his textbook, the first major work of this kind since Pinel. The other was the law on insanity framed by the citizen king, which bore the unmistakable mark of Esquirol's influence. The ambivalences of the law were characteristic of the political situation as well as the problematic position of the insane in bourgeois society. The goals of the law were undoubtedly libertarian, based on the ideas of the Revolution. Thus it did away with the mandatory declaration of incompetence prior to commitment, and this guaranteed the retention of the patient's rights as a free citizen. But as we saw with the spiritual fathers of the Revolution: the only freedom is a politically administered freedom. So in the case of this law as well, the administration emerged as the victor. The only deranged persons eligible for commitment were those who threatened public order or the safety of other persons. Admissions, aside from those based on medical certification, could take place only through the police prefect in Paris and the prefects in the Departments. Finally, all releases, even those opposed by the physician, had to be approved by the prefect. The law paid no heed to the concepts of treatment and healing. Thus, civil law still looked on the irrationality of the insane as a disturbance of order and safety, that had to be kept in check by the state. Furthermore, the physicians felt that this administrative centralism constrained their freedom of movement and jurisdiction, particularly since as psychiatrists they had only just come to believe in the curability of insanity and thought the early, non-dangerous stages of the disease held the greatest promise of a cure. It goes without saying that these laws worked mainly against the poor insane; the well-to-do could afford the

private asylums. Under these circumstances the stated equality of
the economic-administrative and medical directors of the institution, both appointed by the Minister of the Interior, corresponding
to the positivist model of a dual rule of economists and scholars,
was somewhat of a formality. By way of comparison, we might
add that the United States, whose constitution followed a more
liberal tack, also solved this problem at the very outset by putting
only doctors in charge of its asylums.

After the mid-century, this French legislation became political
dynamite when public voices began to be raised, charging the
government with using the law to turn the institutions into a
political tool, an obvious allusion to the hôpitaux généraux.[94]
The very title of Esquirol's 1838 textbook — *Des maladies mentales, considérées sous les rapports médicaux, hygiéniques, et
medico-légaux* — indicates that ambivalent features of the law did
in fact show that the position of the insane in society was part of
the social question between medicine and the state administration,
or the place of psychiatry between the natural sciences and the
sciences of moral and political phenomena. But it also makes
something else clear. The concept of alienation, which Esquirol
himself had still used in his dissertation, was now replaced by the
term "mental diseases." This not only emphasized the pathology
character of insanity, as opposed to Pinel, but, even more important, the historistically joined elements of Pinel's paradigm had
now moved apart even more, gaining a relative and, if you like,
positivistic autonomy. On the one hand, insanity had more obviously become a physical ailment, and its site shifted from the
gastric region to the brain, which at the same time lent greater
significance to the mind and its disorders. This shift was almost unavoidable after the successes of Bayle's anatomical psychiatry and
of phrenology. On the other hand, this made the actual substratum
of psychiatry even less physiologic, for clinical observation was
now concerned primarily with mental or moral factors. The
question as to the ultimate causes is overshadowed by the analysis
of the internal and external mental and social conditions of the
nonetheless essentially somatic or cerebral malady. In this development, begun by Pinel himself, not only the body but also the
subjectivity of the stricken individual attains greater autonomy.
This is not entirely unrelated to the establishment of the new
scientific method. Clinicians, ideologues, and positivists all agreed
that metaphysical speculation about causes and sheer empiricism
could be avoided and the laws governing the relations between
phenomena found only if the faculty for observation were

elevated to the reigning scientific principle and imagination in particular deprived of its traditional intellectual ruling position. Comte's formula for the "positive or real stage" was: *"Principal caractère:* La Loi ou Subordination constante de l'imagination à l'observation,"* a revolution through which, in the maturity of our mind, "a completely normal mental state can be brought about."[95] This faculty for observation or its constitutive power of attention was now also applied by Esquirol to his patients, as the yardstick of a normal state of mind. Feeble attentive energy meant mania; too intense concentration, monomania. This held true not only for the mind, but also for the affective realm, for sympathy. Indifference of the heart, or the passions that exceed the morally natural middle range under the artificial stimulus of civilization are abnormal, pathological conditions. Attention and observation, moral respect for existing relationships, morality and religion, all these must rule the mind, for the development of moral strength is as important as the power of the mind.[96] More than Pinel, Esquirol saw insanity as an immoral change in the passions, a disorder of the will, and he therefore believed that a deranged ego-consciousness in the sense of a "homo duplex" was entirely possible. The fact that these ideas were based on the model of the nerve fiber strung at medium tension ("at-tention") served their intended anthropological holistic purpose and made them more convincing.[97]

Esquirol incorporated this approach into his general societal analysis, for which he thought himself exceptionally well qualified. For he saw the asylum as the coarsened image of bourgeois society. Here its instinctual structure and physiology can be studied at first hand, since the insane present all possible variants of the passions in all their nakedness, whereas in normal society, those passions lie hidden, covered over by rationalizations. Thus, in Esquirol's view, the insane are "the most interesting members of society." For in them the scientist can discover the true state of society. Esquirol's diagnosis about the state of civilization is pessimistic: in France intellectual and moral anarchy has reigned since the Revolution. Notably the political form of the republic is destructive since it gives free rein to the passions corresponding to artificial rather than natural instincts (ambition, greed, egoism, indolence, speculation, lust for power), which leads to more insanity. A similar effect is brought on by all "public movements," for they mean an exaggerated (artificial) mobilization of the energies. Despotism and property, on the other hand, are wholesome, and to prevent suicide Esquirol recommends the curbing of the free expression of opinion by banning the discussion of the subject in newspapers and books, and on the stage.[98] But unlike his predecessors, Esquirol arrives at "more sociological" opinions. Revolution and similar "political aberrations" arouse the people only briefly. Far more dangerous, because it is irreversible, was the disruption of morality, of the moral order of the past thirty years. The social question is incomparably more alarming to him than the political question; their relationship is like that of a fatal chronic disease to a (potentially curable) acute illness. The interpretation follows the traditionalists. The ideas of freedom and reform create "dangerous innovations" and make for unrest. In the cities, passions and disease flower to the degree that intelligence is trained too one-sidedly and too many stimuli are made available. Therefore England is paying for its excesses of civilization with the greatest number of insane. Speculation in both its forms is condemned — the material speculation of the businessman and the speculation of the theoretician, through which reason escapes the rule of morals and religion — for it bursts through the boundary lines of the status quo. The decline of education is crucial; it is either too intellectual or too emotional. Due to faulty education young men moving up into a higher social class become subject to mental diseases.[99] And likewise, Esquirol holds the loose education of girls responsible for the fact that women who are supposed to be the guardians of morals, pay for their looseness, their indulgence in reading novels, fashion and frivolity, with a greater incidence of mental illness than men.[100]

Whereas among the poor insanity is likely to be caused by external factors (e.g. physical ailments), among the rich the causes are more generally due to internal factors, i.e. hereditary and moral. This is one of the documentations of the reality of the social distance between bourgeois physicians and the mentally sick poor. In regard to the poor, scientific experience was gathered primarily through observation at a distance. For the wealthy or for members of the observer's own class, in addition to the economic link of private payment there was the link of the shared social language of patient and psychiatrist. Esquirol is therefore able to give much more precise evidence about the pathogenesis in his own class: businessmen lose their reason because of speculations and "extravagant projects"; public officials because of their professional dependence; poets and actors because of the onesided training of the imagination; officers because of their dependence on chance; court dignitaries and the rich in general because of idleness. But as though wanting to compensate for his scanty information about the poor, Esquirol warns against exalting the contrasting virtue of the common people as some philosophers are wont to do. Upper-class education may have its shortcomings, but lower-class education is nonexistent, and so corruption is widespread, and most of the vice, crime, and mental illness of the society is to be found here. This is demonstrated by the continued affinity between the classical forms of irrationality — immorality, crime, poverty, insanity — even in emancipated bourgeois society.[101] Whereas Pinel still sought to trace the inner conditions and evolution of phenomena along historical lines, to substantiate their changeability and individuality casuistically, and separate them from his naturalistic hypotheses, Esquirol's era is one in which — since the expanding industrialization and the success of natural-science medicine at around 1820 — historical and practical facts turned into positive facts. It was a period in which internal conditions were also seen in terms of natural science, and similar events became statistically determined regular "processes." Comte formulated the universality of method, and at the same time the modern-positivist limitation of its task, and of its subject matter: "Whether we are dealing with the least or highest effects, with impact and gravity or with thought and morality, we can really know only the reciprocal connections peculiar to their courses without ever fathoming the secret of their creation."[102] This unity of man's scientific knowledge is, for Comte, "based with irresistible rationality immediately on the immutability of the human organism, whose manifold characteristic physical, moral, and intellectual faculties are essentially the same on all rungs of the social ladder and must remain harmoniously arranged among themselves, since the more or less protracted development granted them by the social condition can never alter their nature."[103]

Similarly, for Esquirol, the immediate cause of insanity remains a secret of nature, and he notes a plethora of "events" in the phenomena he observed, which represent not so much history (as in Pinel) as naturalistic, regular "processes." Thus began the secular process of the "clinification" of the irrationality of the insane. Esquirol demonstrated Comte's law of three stages via the example of suicide, which was subject first to religious law, then civil law, but now as an illness, had become a medical concern. The same holds true for demonomania, the religious form of melancholia. Initially those suffering from that disorder were persecuted as witches; then the Enlightenment revealed that the erroneous religious notions underlying it were the work of the treason of the clergy, and now these manifestations were seen as an illness, although in view of "universal education" they had become rare. If they occur at all, it is mostly among the lower classes and in Germany. But his simultaneously somatic and social analysis led Esquirol to the critical conclusion that the fear of demons had been replaced by the fear of the police and official persecution.[104] In general, Esquirol, like Comte, regards wars as obsolete and psychologically detrimental.

For Esquirol, history itself, having added to man's intellectual growth and diminished his moral stance, becomes a process. In this connection the social hierarchy is conceived as a process of accumulation of intellectual and moral energy. That is why the moral and intellectual etiology of insanity (excessive passion or attention) is most often found among the wealthy, the possessors of maximum energy. And they are the most easily curable because they not only have the requisite economic means but also the greatest willpower — evidence that the naturalistic awe of economic success in a France dedicated to the pursuit of wealth was not limited to the social utopians, even if Esquirol sought to compensate for that reverence with his moral cultural criticism.

Esquirol also sees insanity as a continuing process, whether in the sequence of the types of disorder (melancholia — monomania — mania — dementia), or in the progressive deterioration from functional-mental to structural-physical impairment, unless the process is interrupted by a "salutary crisis" induced either by nature (the incidence of a new physical illness or passion) or by the physician (creation of a disease, e.g. inoculation with scabies, or through education, e.g. the manipulation of passion). Finally, aging is also seen as a process. Here Esquirol accepts the start of the illness as the inevitable consequence of the sociosomatic condition, i.e. of education, whereby the determinism is traced back to the earliest possible age, to the triad heredity constitution early childhood experiences, a tendency which to this day has supported contradictory but accepted theories, if for no other reason than they are not easily falsified. If by the time the individual has reached puberty, the educational institutions — family, church, state — have failed in their assigned role, then, according to Esquirol the nascent passions are at the mercy of the chaotic condition of society. They become speculative and overwrought or indifferent and unenergetic, giving rise not only to insanity, vice, and crime, but also to the decline of civilization.

Within this framework Esquirol established three new conceptual differentiations — (1) idiocy, (2) hallucination, (3) monomania.
1. Pinel's differentiation of dementia and idiocy was inadequate.

If dementia represents the terminal phase of the disease process, then idiocy, despite the similarity of symptoms, constitutes a theoretically important, formal contrast. Idiocy is not a developmental stage, but the absence, or premature absolute arrest of, development, not a becoming, but a being, not a disease, but a condition. The demented man is an impoverished rich man; the idiot has always been poor.[105]

2. While in the case of illusion the senses have a real object before them and only the mind is mistaken about it because of a disorder, hallucination, according to Esquirol, is a "sensation without the senses"; that is to say, the brain operates so energetically that ideas are realized or personified without the intercession of the senses or the outer world, and so convincingly that the hallucinating man is compelled to act in accordance with his perception.[106] As distinct from delirium, this is conceived as an autonomous phenomenon and constitutes an important step within the tendency to discover autonomous mechanisms, not linked to the senses or the outer world, in the mental realm. Esquirol sees this as the "devitalizing" fall of psychiatry to a soulless, undynamic mechanism and atomism, to vivisection.[107]

3. Monomania, finally, is the epitome of Esquirol's sociological diagnosis of his era, and along with phrenology, brought psychiatry to public attention. Yet Esquirol here merely took off from Arnold's and Prichard's moral insanity and Pinel's *manie sans délire*. While melancholia is the sad, inner-directed variant (the will to nonvolition) of partial insanity,[108] monomania is the outer-directed variant, the expansive projection of the disorder into behavior. In keeping with tradition, Esquirol recognizes three subforms: (a) *monomanie intellectuelle* (determination by *one* false principle); (b) *monomanie affective* or *manie raisonnante* (emotional disorder as unsuitable behavior with rationalizing); (c) *monomanie instinctive* (disorder of the will as a compulsive act against one's own reason). In their other capacities, these patients are healthy, "normal." For Esquirol, monomania is the disease of his era, the disorder of going to extremes, of singularization, and onesidedness, the disease of progress, of the too violent turn to the outside, of expansion, of the alienation of human nature. It is "the mental disease of civilization" — and thus a striking example of the fact that a "disease" can be conceived and hence also "originate" more easily through social than through medical observation. Monomaniacs are one-sidedly intelligent, egotistical, overwrought, expansive, driven by passions and imagination, by speculation and illusions about the future. A crucial

factor is that the education of the heart has not kept pace with intellectual progress: irrationality was now viewed within the framework of an early psychiatric cultural-lag theory.[109]

More rigidly than with Pinel, monomania also served as a political tool, used to label all alien and strange actions, every departure from the social norm, as a form of insanity, as a disease. Conversely, this concept could also serve the interests of an individual. It enabled the psychiatrists to exculpate defendants on trial. In particular, the phenomenon of (instinctive) homicidal monomania — i.e., the totally incomprehensible homicide without an apparent motive, completely out of character of the otherwise seemingly normal, healthy perpetrator — brought the Cassandra-like prediction from the legal profession that Charenton would in future replace the Bastille, and according to the politicians, wreck the foundations of the state, while the philosophers feared for the spirit. Esquirol defended himself by saying that monomania was not a matter of theory but a "fact," which finally makes it possible to sort out the sick from the criminals. He saw himself as the successor of those fifteenth-century doctors who first defended "witches" against the Inquisition with the words "*nihil a daemone, multa ficta, a morbo pauca*," adapting this slogan for his own time to read "*nihil a crimine, nulla ficta, a morbo omnia.*" The provocative nature of Esquirol's accomplishment must be seen against the background of a legal system that up to that time was not likely to exculpate a defendant on the grounds of insanity, except perhaps in the case of advanced age or idiocy.[110]

The creation of monomania is also connected with the establishment of psychiatry and sociology as separate scientific disciplines. While Comte had separated his sociology from physiology by monopolizing the historical method, a similar dissociation took place in psychiatry. On the one side, the somaticizing, natural science tendency fought to free the insane from the stigma of irrationality by demythologizing and neutralizing insanity into a somatic ailment, which at the time was also the most powerful motive for humanizing the treatment of the insane. However, the other side of the same process made another area of insanity all the more clearly visible, one in which, conversely, disease was practically identified with the person, an area in which the disease was no longer the subject to be described, but rather the human being, his development, his "fate"; the disease was no longer a pathological process so much as an abnormal condition. This state was in any event to be defined as a weakness, on the intellectual plane as idiocy, and on the moral plane as monomania, both of which were first brought to public attention by Esquirol. Thus, implicit from the very beginning was something Campagne had said in 1869 in the course of the endless discussion: "Il y a des idiots et des imbéciles par le coeur, comme il y a des idiots et des imbéciles par l'intelligence."[111]

The insane (today's endogenous psychotics) never really took the emancipatory step from irrationality to mere disease, and never succeeded in becoming separated from the monomaniacs, the weak of heart, the morally defective.[112] And this development was in fact regressive, since psychoanalysis and existential analysis again saw the insane "as persons" — and in acknowledging factors like "behavioral guilt," not without ambivalence. Nevertheless, it is the monomaniacs who represent those forms of irrationality which, in their respective onesidedness, correspond to the social and moral norms of bourgeois society. For the concept of mono-mania supplies the formulas that make possible the identification of the "transgressors" of the norms psychologically as well as morally, politically, and legally. Monomania is the framework for the "excessive," hence offensive extent of, say, self-confidence, arrogance (megalomania), need for love (erotomania), demand for legal rights (querulousness), craving for alcohol (dipsomania), impulse to steal (kleptomania), incendiarism (pyromania), etc., but also for all kinds of compulsives, homosexuals and sexual "perverts," recidivists or habitual criminals, and finally the many other abnormal individuals, those later called psychopaths. For the political dimension, it may suffice to point out that since the mid-nineteenth-century the leaders of abortive — but not those of successful — revolutions have generally been called or certified as psychopaths.[113]

This conceptual scheme was also applied to those who "super-seded" the norms. Thus the gifted were likely to be called one-sided, morally defective, egotistical, and, to use another of Esquirol's concepts — speculative.

In sum, in Esquirol's eyes monomaniacs were the products of the one-sided intellectual evolution of mankind, of the dialectic of civilization and progress, and they show this progress to be immoral. Therefore, in his examples, megalomania, a disorder marked by man's alienation from himself and from the morality of the heart, is always incurable. Here, too, Esquirol is a political traditionalist. His diagnosis of Comte, a patient in his private clinic in 1826, as a megalomaniac is not unrelated to his unease about the state of civilization. Comte avenged himself by writing about the "infamous Esquirol" and his sickness-producing "absurd treatment," stating triumphantly that the inner strength of his organism helped him overcome both the ailment and the cure.[114] But Esquirol's diagnosis of incurability did not prevent him from attending the lectures of the positivists a year later together with Broussais and Alexander von Humboldt, which as we have seen, did influence his thinking. By the time Comte, in his old age, postulated the preeminence of the heart, the emotions, and love, over the rational mind, Esquirol, who would have welcomed this, was already dead.

Esquirol's idea of contraction, deriving from an ability to encompass the totality, leads to one-sidedness and isolation, brought him and monomania the approbation of a romantic public dismayed by the growing specialization in the sciences and economy. This dismay found literary expression in the individualism of Chateaubriand's incurable despair and, soon thereafter, in the antibourgeois doctrine of art for art's sake. Monomania became a model for Daumier's political caricatures, and above all for Balzac's novels: Balzac's characters too are monomaniacal, their actions controlled and compelled by a single specific passion; and this very one-sidedness makes them unique. For Esquirol as well as Balzac, the monomanias represent an attempt to base previously psychic phenomena on an irreducible and — physically or socially — material reality. Thus in Balzac, monomanias are at once incomparable natural phenomena and mere agents of a social group, since "for him a character in itself...only becomes interesting and significant as the agent of a social group."[115] It is therefore not surprising that he nursed the idea of depicting capitalism medically as a social disease in a "pathology of social life." "He diagnoses it as a hypertrophy of the striving for profit and power and attributes the evil to the egotism and irreligiousity of the age. He sees it all as the consequence of the Revolution and traces back the dissolution of the old hierarchies, especially that of the monarchy, the Church, and the family, to individualism, free competition and inordinate, unrestrained ambition."[116] This was in complete accord with Esquirol's diagnosis of the era. Both of them saw the past, the family, love, religion, and monarchy, in imbuing people with those values as the road to salvation, even though this ominous, inexorable progress was not without fascination.

Accordingly, Esquirol's therapy places greater emphasis on moral training than did Pinel's. Thus it would almost seem as though he wanted to avenge himself for his dismay over the state of civilization and bourgeois society when he recommended:

"ingeniously conceived unpleasantness" as one of the methods in the treatment of monomania.[117]

Somatism and Progress

The somatic basis of psychiatry, which marked its development during the nineteenth century, was laid by a number of physicians in Esquirol's time, most of whom were neither psychiatrists nor weighed down by Esquirol's retrogressive pessimistic outlook. Instead, they viewed the unreason of insanity as a disease which they would come to terms with in the near or more remote future. And practically speaking, the question of insanity and society was one of rational organization rather than of the education of the heart. In part they were materialists, and in part were only called that by their opponents because they were positivists in the field of natural science. Some were atheists, others neo-Catholics or liberals, or Saint-Simonean socialists. And most greeted emancipation enthusiastically; they were not skeptical about progress, and they were producers of facts — especially for Comte.

Franz Joseph Gall[118] (1758–1828), the son of a merchant, was born near Pforzheim, Germany. After studying medicine, he opened a practice in Vienna in 1785. At the same time, he began his neurological and cerebral-anatomical research. As early as 1791, he wrote a Romantic, natural-philosophical treatise on instinct, which he regarded as "characteristic of all organic nature," and which, being "a universal law, a single force," governs all living beings.[119] Soon thereafter Gall began to present his findings in a series of private lectures. Under church pressure, the government proscribed these lectures because of their atheistic and materialistic orientation. And in 1805, Gall and his pupil J. G. Spurzheim were forced to leave Vienna. After a lecture tour of Europe, Gall settled in Paris, while in 1813 Spurzheim carried the new doctrine into the English-speaking world. If the Romantics had made Paris receptive toward Mesmer, the natural sciences did the same for Gall, especially his comparative-historical method. Even though Napoleon sensed a materialistic threat in Gall, he was reassured by his personal physicians Corvisart and Larrey. Scattered published accounts of Gall's theory, which came to be known as phrenology, had begun to appear, and he finally summed it up in a comprehensive six-volume work, *Sur les fonctions du cerveau et sur celles de chacune de ses parties.* Gall's cerebro-anatomy represents the extent to which technique depends on socially acceptable ideas. Unlike his predecessors he did not present his brain sections purely mechanically, but sought to trace an evolutionary path from the oldest to the most recent layers of the cerebrum and the cerebellum. In this way, he managed to discover delimitable structures, fiber systems, and the course of various nerve tracts to the cerebrum. This furnished the premise for Gall's basic assumption: to wit, that the brain was not a single unit but was composed of a large number of independent but functionally connected organs. Gall arrived at a more detailed definition of the relation between structure and function by systematically comparing the brains of adults and children, invalids, of insane and deaf persons, of idiots, criminals, and highly gifted individuals, as well as diverse animals.

Combining comparative anatomy and psychology, Gall saw the development of intelligence as running parallel to the increasing expansion and complexity of the surface of the cerebral cortex, which thus is no longer merely a covering or secreting organ but the seat and organ of the soul. The unity of structure and function replaces the unity of the brain. The number of special brain organs corresponds to the number of innate mental faculties, powers, whereby the instincts and the reasoning powers (as already explained in his work of 1791) are based on the same power of understanding which alone distinguishes man from the animals. Gall listed twenty-seven organs or basic faculties. Every phrenologist had of course his own catalogue. According to Gall, the faculties, despite their innate organic base, are not determined, but constitute levels of potency practically begging for educative-developmental intervention. Insanity is a fixation, the loss of control over an organ because of its heightened activity or irritation. Craniology enabled Gall to turn phrenology from theory into practice. In his craniology he followed the principles of aesthetics, more precisely of physiology, which sees the shape of the bodily parts (face, hand, foot, or the body as a whole) as the key to the understanding of the spiritual inner being. Since in Gall's opinion the soul shapes the brain, and hence the skull (even allowing for individual differences), the quality of the individual mental powers can be determined by analyzing and measuring the cranium and its protrusions.

Phrenology is one of the most exciting demonstrations that a theory made up of socially acceptable ideas and a technique derived from them can have an uncommonly productive effect, even though the individual assumptions may be false and even grotesque. The belief that the human spirit is dependent on material conditions, and that individual faculties can be localized — the first opportunity for scientific verification of this did not arise until fifty years later with Broca's discovery of the center of speech — has continued to be part of a utopian or justified liberal faith in progress, and at the same time has been opposed by justified skepticism or by the ideological argument of the social danger.

Gall's doctrine was bound to boost all evolutionary, comparative, and differentiating ideas. In it psychiatrists found both a mental and somatic basis for all manifestations of the obvious deterioration of mental soundness, i.e. for dreams, somnambulism, hallucinations, and for the partial irrationality of monomania. With the help of these theories, they were able to separate functional from structure-altering diseases. It was Gall who gave neurology its start. For the first time, psychologists saw a chance to arrive at material statements about actual conditions instead of settling for the formal definition of faculties through the theory of associations.[120] Moreover, Gall's character diagnosis involved the study of the peculiarities of an individual for comparison with the craniological findings. His was an important contribution to the individualization and thus more humane treatment of the insane. This procedure could also be used in the education of children and the moral improvement of criminals as an alternative to punishment. Finally, Gall proposed an (official) state-sponsored psychiatry based on his principles, to improve social conditions, and especially the situation of the poorer classes.

Gall and Comte were friendly with Broussais, who had developed the first physiological therapeutics for the French clinical school. Based on Brown's theory of irritation he made fever and the irritative inflammatory process, especially of the gastro-intestinal tract, the basis from which all diseases derive. Broussais also saw insanity as a functional-inflammatory irritation of the organ of instinct and intelligence, i.e. the phrenologically conceived brain, that subsequently turned into a structural lesion.[121] In the face of contemporary doctrinal philosophers, the somatist Broussais insisted that concepts like ego, consciousness, rationality, and mental disease had to be deontologized, since they were actions of the nervous and constantly changing brain matter. On this basis, he opposed the criminal accountability of the insane, and his functional and dynamic concept of matter likewise promoted the belief that physical, moral, and intellectual measures can be useful therapeutic tools in the treatment of insanity, including its hereditary predisposition.[122]

The development of the somatic basis of nineteenth-century psychiatry came to an end only with the first psychiatrically relevant, purely natural-scientific, cognitionally irreversible discovery. A. L. J. Bayle, in his dissertation of 1822, which was based on only six observations, demonstrated that the mental manifestations of certain types of insanity (megalomania and intellectual debility) as well as progressive paralysis could be causally traced to a pathologically ascertainable chronic inflammation of the brain membrane, "arachnoiditis." Bayle also mentioned syphilis as a possible cause of this inflammation, but it took another forty years before this found acceptance, and a hundred before the discovery of the pathogenic agent that caused what we today call progressive paralysis.[123]

One reason Bayle's discovery was so exciting was that the long-awaited "direct cause" — and an anatomical cause at that — had been found for at least one form of the unreason of insanity.[124] Moreover, now dementia was no longer merely feebleness of mental energy but also anatomically visible destruction. This however threatened at least the uniformity of Pinel's and Esquirol's mentally conceived pathology. Progressive paralysis became the model of a psychiatry that more and more saw itself exclusively as a natural science, marked, particularly in the latter part of the century, by a continuing utopian demand, one drawing sustenance from triumphs like the above, to neutralize all psychopathologic phenomena according to Bayleian precepts and make them amenable to somatic-rational explanation.

Comte's encyclopedic scheme does not even allot psychology a place among the sciences, since to him its method seemed speculative and introspective, that is, not verifiable. It was the somatically oriented physicians — Gall, Broussais, and to some extent Cabanis and Bichat — toward whom he looked for the physiologic basis of his sociology. Just as Comte was among the earliest members of the Société phrènologique formed in Paris in 1831, in his positive philosophy phrenology was to form the bridge between the two organic sciences — biology and sociology. He saw Gall as the first one to make possible the positive study of the "transcendental portion of biology," the intellectual and moral, i.e. the cerebral functions,[125] for Gall succeeded in overcoming the Cartesian dualism of mind and matter in the theoretical identification of intellect and instinct. Gall's malleable powers of instinctual drives substantiated Comte's doctrine of the dialectic of drives: according to this, the natural preponderance of lustful-egotistic instincts over psycho-social instincts, which can be established by a reading of the cranium, motivates human conduct and prevents speculation and self-destructive love of one's neighbor, whereas only the channeling of the psycho-social drives can moderate the instinctual pressure of their antipodes, and so — and this fifty years before Freud — culture and morality are born. That is how social dynamics operate within the social equilibrium; social progress is locked into the framework of the social order — analogous to physiology and anatomy. Despite the phrenological foundation of sociology, Comte postulates sociology's independence of physiology. Gall and especially Cabanis are criticized for making sociology a "mere appendage to biology" and confusing historico-social changes with human nature — as in the case of Gall's postulate of the unalterability of mankind's martial propensities, even though history teaches us that they are obviously declining. Physiological thought, so Comte tells us; is comparative, while sociological thought is historical.[126]

Now what were the consequences for the practical situation of the insane in a time that saw progress as the task of organizing the positive industrial-scientific social order, that localized the means of scientific progress, the mind, as well as its disorders, insanity, somatically and specifically in the brain ("cerebrally")? These very intentions would seem to indicate that scientific activity in France since the 1820s had been developing into a significant and accepted social institution, which believed that its theoretical work justified its existence by contributing to the organization of bourgeois society through its establishment of a structured order of facts. It was only on this basis that one could pose the question about the practical applicability of the results. The preeminence of factual research and its theorization became patent in psychiatry after Pinel, in contrast to the English psychiatrists, who, from Battie to Conolly, tended to base their theories on practical experience. We need merely recall Hill's empirical investigation with its purely therapeutic aim.

In France this scientism resulted in a theoretical objectification and differentiation of the victims of insanity based primarily on these two models: insanity as a disease of the brain (Gall, Bayle, Georget)[127] or as an instance of arrested development (Gall, Esquirol, Voisin).[128] But Gall was not the only one to coordinate the cerebral and evolutionist theses. In 1833, Pinel's son Scipion had written a book that reflected the ideas of Comte: *Physiologie de l'homme aliéné appliquée à l'analyse de l'homme social*. In it he classifies man along a scale of one to nine, from primitive to rational, and determines the mental qualities of

each category along a parallel scale of possible disorders, from
the complete absence of all mental faculties to the various forms
of insanity up to the dominance of the rational free will, with
corresponding anatomical brain damages. The passions form an
independent, social scale: the little man knows only minor emotions, whereas the grand passions are reserved for the great minds.
This elitist trait leads to an apotheosis of the will: "Free will
is the only point of contact between God and man....The will
beyond any doubt is the most unfathomable intellectual function:
it resists all analysis: like life itself, it is or is not; it is the
destiny of man, yet he is the master of willing his destiny.
Fatalism is merely ignorance of one's own being....The insane
cannot will; they are worse than non-being, they are living non-
being."[129] And hovering above this system of Pinel's, a synthesis
of nearly all contemporary trends, is Christianity, which, in
that anarchic time, seemed to the author the sole means of
integration.

In addition to objectification, the positivist approach brought
a further differentiation of insanity: for instance, according to
disease types (following Bayle's model), individual peculiarities
(in line with monomania), degreees of destructiveness (e.g., Scipion,
Pinel), or disease stages (acute vs. chronic). To the degree that
psychiatry became a medical specialty among others and accepted by sociology as the theoretical basis for the organization of
society, it was also becoming a tool in the practical integration
of the insane, for they never completely achieved the status
of patients: they are seen as sick people among other sick people.
Their differentiation was not merely theoretical; the institutions
also carried it out in the organization of their physical accommodations. New facilities were added. The interest in both idiocy
and the mental disorders of children was in accord with the
evolutionist Voisin who installed a corresponding section at
Bicêtre in 1833.[130] G. Ferrus called for special facilities for
the criminally insane to get them out of the prisons and rid
the institutions of them. The insanity law of 1838 extended
the Napoleonic principle of regional social and health care for
the population to the insane: the jurisdiction of the institutions
extended over all of the respective *départements*, i.e. the insane
as well as the protection of the public against any problem caused
by the insane became their responsibility. Positivist, somatically
oriented criticism also raised the emancipation of the insane
another notch: moral activism in therapy receded somewhat.
The somatic neutralization to disease severed the moral linking

of insanity and classical irrationality. No longer were fear and arcane punishments used to force patients to accept moral guilt to make them accessible to treatment. In 1840, when F. Leuret recommended intimidation and painful showers for breaking patient resistance and making them malleable,[131] he was generally regarded as regressive.

This, however, is only one side of the coin. As mentioned earlier, the unreason of madness, on the one hand, was shifted to something outside of man, a physical disorder, while on the other hand, as in the case of monomania and its products, it was anchored all the more deeply within man, as heredity, disposition, constitution, or traumatization in early childhood. That which on the one side was seen as an illness, on the other was identified as an abnormality within man. What was excused there, became innate guilt here, and not only in the legal sense. There arose an abstract contrast in the latter part of the century, and this very abstractness made possible that dichotomy of class vs. race which contributed so greatly to the theory of degeneracy.

Lastly, the receding moral activism had still another facet. It gave rise to the question whether, based on somatic findings, moral activism was to be replaced by therapeutic nihilism. In coming to terms with this growing problem, two approaches were followed, both motivated by the sociological-positivist idea of progress. Hygienic measures were strengthened and systematized. In 1833 Ferrus realized Pinel's dream by opening an agricultural adjunct to the Institution of St. Anne, a frequently imitated model. The insane were now given regular, scheduled work, a minutely organized daily plan, common meals, planned diets, rest schedules, bedside care, exercises, outdoor activities, cleanliness, etc. The purpose of all this was no longer the moralizing of patients, but the creation of a general and comprehensive orderly milieu that would ultimately have a soothing effect on their disturbed organism.

The other approach involved education. Influential here were, above all, Buchez, Trélat, and Cerise, disciples of Saint-Simon, who extended their religiously tinged socio-emancipatory fervor for the proletariat and women to the insane. Buchez, whom Karl Marx compared to Lasalle,[132] had published a work on hygiene in 1825 with Esquirol's disciple Trélat. He also developed an evolutionist theory of progress and was the author of *Studien zur Entwicklung des Irreseins*. Following in the footsteps of Gall and Bichat, he sees ideas within the framework of a twofold objective order: the nervous matter and the spiritualist order of speech symbols. Thus he considers the brain the organ of the symbols, and hence of human productivity. Insanity arises gradually through the loss of the self-determination of the soul due to organic damage. Psychiatric therapy, for Buchez, consists of hygienic measures and re-education: one must focus on still sound ideas to influence the unsound ones. False concepts must be confronted with correct ones, and the comparative faculty must be activated — a technique of reorganization that can turn into obedience training.

Others departed even more from the earlier notion of getting the insane to accept moral guilt. At the same time, they relied more heavily on the intellectual power of language and the institutions that are able to transform the body and even modify hereditary predisposition.[133] Teaching a patient an activity involves making a verbal connection between him and social reality and ultimately changing his body. L. Cerise, a champion of workers' associations and production cooperatives, stresses both the individually and socially therapeutic value of communal labor:

One goal of activity is a source of ideas and sentiments that determine the production of numerous phenomena of innervation....The doctor should not only take into account the physiological influence of a special and individual goal of activity, but also the influence of a general social goal, the basis and preserver of nations. It is the common goal of activity that contains the ·explanation for the general characteristics that distinguish nations, tribes, and classes.[134]

Positivist factual research created a vacuum which was now occupied by a simultaneously liberal—Progressive and Catholic—socialist faith that man is able to transform scientifically proven determinism through the realization of the *oeuvre sociale*, into self-liberation. Thus, at the end of the formative phase of French psychiatry, which began with the Revolution, the belief that science had the power to change society equated the emancipation and integration of the unreason of the insane with the emancipation and integration of society, though this had less effect on practice than it did in England.

The formative phase of French psychiatry can be regarded as coming to an end in the 1840s with the publication of the first national psychiatric journal, the *Annales médico-psychologiques* (1843), on which Cerise collaborated, and the founding of the equally important psychiatric society, the Société médico-psychologique (1847), by Ferrus and others.

PART III

GERMANY

1

Mercantilism and the Cultured Bourgeoisie (Bildungsbürgertum)

In Germany, as in England and France, the end of the sequestration of unreason and the social visibility of the insane was part of the process in which the bourgeoisie's demand for economic and political freedom brought with it the relative liberation of the broad masses. At the same time an educated class was gaining a foothold which, both in the wake of and opposition to the Enlightenment, turned romantically toward their own inwardness and its concomitant irrationality. The historical conditions of Germany, or rather the multiplicity of German states, modified that development, delayed the emergence of a psychiatric paradigm, and created a kind of moratorium that created the conditions for a unique, highly ambivalent "deepening" of the relationship between scientists, the state, and the indigent insane—a deepening that ultimately led to such events as the physical extermination of the unreason of the insane.

Population Politics and the Differentiation of the Outcasts

The German states too were swept up in the European wave of the sequestration of the poor, beggars, vagabonds, of the asocial, immoral, and syphilitic, of orphans, the insane, and others at odds with reason. In contrast to the Western countries, the isolating facilities were uncommonly diverse because of the differences in the individual states. There existed prisons, correctional and custodial institutions, and alms-, work- and poorhouses, orphanages, foundling homes, insane asylums. The speed with which the system spread was contingent on the ability of the enlightened absolutist princes to make the army and the officialdom the backbone of their states on how they as sovereigns, and with the help of the bureaucracy sought to regiment the public and the private and familial order according to rational maxims, and how they, as the "first entrepreneurs" of their state and again with the help of officialdom, sought to instill in their subjects a belief in the moral value of hard work to help them extract every last ounce of wealth from the land and people under their sway.

The internment measures promulgated in Germany must be looked at in the light of population politics, because the catastrophic legacy of the Thirty Years' War with regard to both the population and the economy continued into the eighteenth century, and because the German states could compensate for their comparatively limited space only through the size of their population if they wished to have any say in the European policy. For this reason, and for the creation of an autarkic economy, it was necessary, if at all possible — and by coercion if need be — to make their subjects into parents, workers, taxpayers, and soldiers. This involved the "policing" of the outcast, the reserve army of asocial individuals, who, particularly in the ecclesiastic lands, made up more than 25 per cent of the population.[1] Furthermore, this stratum was constantly being augmented by victims of a variety of accidents and misfortunes: people made homeless by fire, the crippled and sick, including the insane, disabled veterans, the aged, widows and orphans, demobilized soldiers and officers, lawbreakers sentenced to flogging, etc. Two other factors entered into this picture: this substratum was gaining greater visibility as the monasteries, cloisters, and other church holdings were disbanded and thus no longer in a position to neutralize a substantial portion of the beggars, and other social structures that since the Middle Ages had been dealing with misery and misfortune and helped make life for the victims more bearable were also falling apart: the cooperative supports of trade associations, guilds, and neighborhoods. These latter were among the stated objectives of the mercantilist drive for making society efficient. One of the rare instances in which the eighteenth-century Reichstag acted with dispatch was in passing the 1731 law concerning the reform of handicrafts, transferring the powers and rights of the guilds to the state. Finally, within this same framework, there developed that family feeling in which responsibility for the well-being of relatives was limited to the immediate family and the needs of distant relatives were ignored. Here too the officially tolerated or even compulsory female and child labor practiced in many parts of the country contributed to the loosening of the traditional family structure. All this was bound to affect the situation of the insane in particular. Melancholics, idiots, and

morons could no longer readily find a quiet corner or the necessary help in families. Others, the village fools or village idiots
were no longer accepted as members of the community. Hence,
incidents involving disturbed persons were bound to become more
frequently visible and a public nuisance. An administration acting
on rational principles had to feel particularly provoked by the
impregnable unreason of the insane and become aware of their
growing number and the danger they posed to the community.
Another reason for putting them under the jursidiction of an
administration proclaiming the virtues of order, reason, and work
was that the enlightened churches were no longer in need of the
insane as witches and persons possessed − neither on theological
grounds nor for asserting their secular power. The character of
the threatening outsider, the insane, in states whose policy aspired
toward autarky against all alien influences was also demonstrated
by the fact that they were not only interned in secure houses, but
also shoved across borders, or shipped to the New World or to
colonies.[2] Existing institutional regulations prohibited the release
of the insane from their chains even in the event of a fire because
of the public danger they presented.[3] The attitude toward them
was symptomatic of the spatial political orientation of the terri-
torial states: whoever overstepped the boundaries of rationality,
work, and decency was quite literally put outside the social orbit;
whoever alienated himself from order was turned into an alien;
whoever became deprived of reason, the truly human factor,
became part of the poor; whoever gave free rein to his animal
nature was grouped among the animals and like them was put on
public display in cages; those whose ideas and actions were exclusive and fixed were excluded; and those whose judgment was
out of step found themselves stepping into houses of correction.
This spatialization reached its extreme in an appliance that was
designed to keep the dangerous expansion of the insane to a
minimum and eradicate it: the *Dollkasten* − the mad-box −
movable boxes or cases designed to restrain the mobility of their
rebellious contents for as long as deemed necessary.

Although the system of mechanical restraints and the punishments meted out at the various prisons and workhouses were
public knowledge, communities and families felt relief if they
were able to snare a much sought-after place for one of their
members. It seemed the most humane and, at least on the surface,
the most orderly solution for passing on responsibility for a
mentally ill incompetent. As a rule, only violent, i.e. dangerous,
individuals were admitted to these houses, and some of them

restricted admission to local residents. A revealing commentary on the penal system is contained in the statement signed by a melancholic prior to his release from an institution in Kiel in 1760: "I, the undersigned, do hereby warrant, in lieu of an actual oath by the word of everlasting truth, as truly as the Lord is my Saviour, that after release from this confinement I shall not seek revenge against anyone."[4] It seems that in the adjacent region of Neumünster something out of the ordinary had taken place: an asylum attendant had been dismissed for mistreating inmates without provocation.[5]

The matter-of-fact response to the coercive treatment in houses of internment can be understood only if one realizes that the underprivileged community, which even late in the eighteenth century had barely attained self-consciousness and literacy, itself constituted something like an asylum whose inmates had been taught by the state and church, through a system of rewards, but mainly through coercion in support of rationality and the work ethic, that to work for the general welfare would improve their own lot. This was in keeping with Frederick the Great's adage "everything for the people, nothing by the people." In this sense, it was widely admitted — voluntarily or perhaps even critically — that many princes, with their mercantile support of aristocratic and bourgeois entrepreneurs and their fight against the economically wasteful aspects of the social hierarchical order were more progressive than the rest of the civic community. Thus with regard to the state's compulsory labor and its support of private manufacturers the inmates of prisons were not very different from other kinds of unemployed or from the wives and children of soldiers. "In response to a Complaint by the cloth-manufacturers that they lack yarn," reads a Prussian document of 1761, "it was ordered at the beginning of the year 1761, to all lords — in Silesia — that they induce all persons of both sexes, old and young, to be found in their villages, who have no other trade or earnings and are indolent...to spin wool for the cloth and other manufacturers located in their regions." And in 1763, a similar order said that "the wives and children of soldiers are compelled to spin."[6]

Even if the outcasts had to toil as hard as they could, the educational role of the workhouses for the rest of the population was held to be at least equal to their immediate economic utility. Their very existence was intended as an exhortation to the population to hard work, just as the public display of the insane served both as entertainment and moral instruction. Thus it was thought advisable, a view also shared by Viennese cameralists like Sonnenfels, that factories, both because of the obvious advantage but also as a warning, be situated near prisons, workhouses, and orphanages. In a contemporary source we find this: "A country will experience an upswing if the silk- and wool-manufactories are well equipped, and a house of correction is near-by, the fear of which will guide the dissolute riffraff in the requisite diligence and labor....It is... certain that houses of correction and orphanages are quite incomparably and most effectively linked with newly planned and opened manufactories."[7]

The economic policies of the princes, the labor training they offered, and the support of private businessmen, contained elements that led to the growing self-assertion of the capitalist economy and to the growing self-awareness of the bourgeois public. Just as mercantilism succeeded in raising the formerly private economic activity to the highest level of public interest, the same process shifted the economic orientation from the model of household economy to that of the free market into an order in which economics was no longer a part of the administrative doctrine, the police. It was an order in which the subject of the state administration, of public power, emancipated itself into the subject of a social community in which bourgeois society constituted itself vis-à-vis the state. "Society is the form in which the fact of mutual dependence for the sake of life and nothing else assumes public significance and where the activities connected with sheer survival are permitted to appear in public."[8]

But the personal freedom of the participants in the economy and the labor market, their ability and freedom to enter into legally binding contracts, as objective conditions of the economy were part of this public space oriented toward life and its preservation. This led to the economic and — closely linked to it — humanitarian critique of the expediency and morality of the mercantilist instrument of forced labor and the institutions of sequestration, as well as to the inevitable conclusion that unfree labor is inefficient.[9] As earlier in England and, partly, in France, these insights found no response in Germany until the 1780s, the beginning of industrialization, early Romanticism, and the first social reforms.[10] Mechanized factories demanded personal initiative and the willingness to take risks. Mechanical production processes raised the question of the quality of specialized workers and a readily available pool of people whose freedom of movement was impeded by mercantilist restrictions. Expensive long-term planning taught the importance of health care and preventive hygiene for the entire population.

Of course, so long as the bourgeoisie neither prepared for its political emancipation nor had the necessary capital for machinery, it was the state — unlike England — that promoted industrialization with its own factories or through the financial support of private entrepreneurs. This held true for the introduction of the first spinning jennies in the Rhineland, Saxony, and Berlin, and the first steam engines in the Ruhr, Berlin, and Upper Silesia. Whereas in England, the interval between the start of industrialization and industrial revolution, i.e. the first mass investment of fixed capital, was brief, and in France, this process was forced by the physiocrats and the political revolution, in Germany, it continued into the late 1830s/early 1840s, i.e. it took half a century. This time shift corresponds fairly closely to the establishment if not of a paradigm then of a theory of psychiatry. The tardiness of German economic development was related to the national and economic dispersal, the landed nobility's lagging mechanization of the large estates, and the restrictive trade regulations, as well as to the "autocratic organization of German Protestantism," which, unlike England, also played a part in the belated political development of bourgeois society.[11] In short, the weakness of the bourgeoisie was responsible for the fact that the enlightened-absolutist states themselves initiated the overdue economic (and later political) revolutions and — because of their increasingly inadequate planning — barely letting them gain momentum.

The same administrative ambivalence — between liberating mechanization and mercantilist protectionism — governed the reforms of the institutions of sequestration during the second part of the century. With the start of industrialization in the 1780s, public interest in work focused not so much on its moral and pedagogical aspect as on its profitability, and made obvious the need for the social liberation of the useful segment of the outcast groups. In determining their employability the question arose — in the absence of a generally accepted attitude toward the insane — whether they were extraordinarily wicked, unwilling to work, uneducable, and therefore to be harshly punished, or whether they were incapable of working.[12] The last, if true, opened up a number of approaches for handling them: as a "public" danger and public nuisance, they presented a policing problem. If simply incapable of working, their maintenance and care became the responsibility of the state and church, or a humanitarian duty. And if incapacitated, they were to be turned over to the care of physicians.

In the course of this new differentiation of rationality and irrationality according to physical fitness, the initial tendency was to separate the insane from the other inmates of prisons and workhouses within these institutions or in special madhouses, which generally worsened their situation. Thus, a physician at the Brunswick prison and madhouse since 1793 proposed that the other inmates not only had to help in the care of the insane, but also act as guards, and that thieves, because of their intelligence, cautiousness, and adroitness made particularly good keepers.[13] At the prisons in Schleswig-Holstein, the maintenance costs for the insane were higher than those of other inmates, and they were treated more harshly than the working prisoners. In Neumünster, for example, until the mid-century, the insane were often horsewhipped until they stopped their irrational chatter.[14] Occasionally the line between those deemed fit and unfit for work cut right through the insane contingent. In 1764, the city council of Hamburg decided, for economic reasons, not to transfer any able-bodied insane inmates from the prison, which was being operated as a textile mill, to the plague hospital for the sick and the helpless.[15] With the expansion of the social criterion of the freedom to enter into a labor contract and efficiency, the insane were stigmatized as socially useless; their irrational, unpredictable, and disturbing behavior came into public view as threatening and calling for protective measures as the social structure organized itself into an administratively and economically efficient, accountable entity sensitive to disturbance. Likewise, bourgeois sensibility was quite ambivalent on this matter. It not only intensified the fascination with the unreason of insanity, but also demanded greater security against disturbance and agitation. Thus, as of 1783, Lübeck committed not only violent lunatics, but also those suffering from delusions, not to cure them, but because the public was scandalized by them and their bizarre behavior and would no longer tolerate it. And Lübeck's new madhouse (1788) saw its purpose chiefly in the protection of the public.[16]

In view of the economic goal, it is not surprising that — as in England and France — the prisons rather than the insane asylums were the first target of the well-publicized reform campaign that was launched. In 1791, a Berlin cleric by name of Wagnitz catalogued the abuses in prisons and scourged compulsory labor in both state-run and private enterprises. For him, too, the poor and the mad were practically identical: "By poor we mean not only the poor in the literal sense, but epileptics, idiots, madmen, melancholics, raving lunatics, etc."[17] The possibility of cure is never even mentioned. Instead, we read of safety and tight discipline. And Wagnitz even wants to exclude the insane from divine services, for the worship of God demands reason and so the irrationality of the mad would defile the Gospel. Nevertheless, the enlightened Wagnitz praised the confining chair, in which the fettered inmate could at least sit up, as a humanitarian advance over the total restraint of the madbox.

This period, in which the insane found themselves in an even greater social vacuum than the relatively freer other outcasts also brought the first timid attempts at combining reform with cure. The new regulations of the Frankfurt Madhouse of 1785 partially replaced the earlier pedagogical pietism with medical principles and required a physician to visit the home three times weekly.[18] Würzburg's Julius Hospital, which once before, in the sixteenth century, had introduced a humanistic approach,[19] instituted a policy of differentiation between curables and incurables in 1785, and revised its policy about the therapeutic use of restraints.[20] In 1788, Ludwigsburg opened a "pension institution and madhouse" staffed by a physician separate from the prison.[21] The burning down of the old institutions of sequestration and the administrative reluctance to undertake their reconstruction brought the mental patients of Berlin and Hamburg under medical jurisdiction. In 1798 Berlin moved the mental patients from the madhouse of Friedrichstadt to the Charité Hospital, and in 1814 Hamburg moved them from the plague hospital to the municipal hospital.[22]

This trend toward medical reform was most apparent in Vienna, where the rational, enlightened Catholic approach of Joseph II, and the influence of the Dutch physician G. van Swieten made the emperor into the virtual liberator of the insane in one special area, even before Pinel. In 1781–83 the emperor abolished serfdom and issued a "patent of toleration" that gave impetus to the emancipation of the Jews. In the course of the secularization of some seven hundred monasteries, he learned of the practice of the Capucine monks of locking members who had lost their reason into subterranean cells, after attempts to drive out the devil proved unsuccessful. After ordering the release of these internees he issued a remarkable decree in 1783 to the effect that in future all mentally ill members of religous orders had to be reported to the district administration, that "every cloister for both sexes should treat its own members afflicted with madness with the selfsame care as those suffering from any other ailment."[23] Here for the first time, within a limited area, the insane were equated with other sick persons. One year later, this idea was placed on a broader basis when Joseph II built the Vienna central hospital and joined the "Mad Tower" to it. It was, so to speak, the first psychiatric department in a general hospital.[24] Although this strange five-story building with one hundred and thirty-nine single cells did contain some medical features (the circular structure was meant to promote ventilation and thus neutralize germs), the thick walls and prisonlike cells show that here, too, public safety was the foremost consideration.[25] Nor did the improvements made in the 1790s by the most eminent state physician of that time, Johann Peter Frank, bring any change. This is not surprising, considering that Frank himself, in his major work, *System einer vollständigen medicinischen Polizey* (1788), still saw the insane primarily from the vantage point of their social danger and the duty of the police to protect the public against them.[26]

In sum, this initial phase of reform meant that the new or at least more obvious economic aspects of social utility, of the effectiveness, efficiency, and unrestricted movement of labor led to differentiation; large segments of the outcast groups were gradually released into the community, and the situation of those still held in confinement gradually improved. On the other hand, the insane became the victims of that very same development. Precisely because they began to be appraised in terms of their fitness for work and hence, release, the social uselessness of the unfit and the threat they posed became more apparent, and with it the need to hold them in secure surroundings. As a result of a kind of social-contrast effect, they became even more isolated than they had been, yet this era also saw the first cautious steps toward treating insanity as a curable disorder.

Still, other previously sequestered groups now began to participate in the new types of education and integration set in motion by the changing economic needs. Thus in 1774, Pestalozzi embarked on his Rousseauian education of poor and orphaned children, which sparked the fight against placing houses of correction or factories next to orphanages and against the educational approach that spoke of "efficient" forced labor. And in 1781 began the debate about the emancipation of the Jews, which demonstrated even more clearly the formal connection between this movement and the reform in the treatment of the insane, for the social integration of the Jews in Germany had from the very outset been presented as the end result of a long-drawn-out educational process in whose course the Jews under the aegis of the state would first have to demonstrate their successful socialization. France, on the other hand, during the Revolution, granted Jews full civil rights by a single act, leaving their social integration to the interplay of social forces. This emancipatory or integrational movement was prompted not so much by Joseph II's decree of 1781, which on the whole had little effect, as by a memorandum of that same year by the Prussian statesman, C. W. Dohm on the civic improvement of the Jews. Dohm, a friend of the Jewish enlightened circle of Moses Mendelssohn, firmly believed that Jews would think of themselves primarily as individuals and citizens rather than Jews if only the oppressive conditions under which they lived were altered and consequently they would be reeducated: "I can concede," he wrote, "that the Jews may be ethically more corrupt than other nations...but I must add that this presumed greater corruption of the Jews is a necessary and natural consequence of the oppressive situation in which they have found themselves for so many centuries."[27] The state had to inaugurate and supervise their emancipation, which was only a special instance of the "timely" task of "dissolving" all class, corporative, and religious barriers within society (including the institutions of segregation "in the great harmony of the state." In this context, "love of one's fellow man and true state interest" were identical. Whereas Dohm was urging at least a partial amelioration of their legal position during the next twenty years, here as in other reform areas, aspects of political and economic utility, protection against feared dangers, outweighed everything else: i.e., "the utilization of the Jews in the state," the "neutralization" of the dangerous intentions of the Jews, defense against a "national scourge," and the "training for industry."

The situation and the perspectives matched those of the insane in every detail, except, of course, that the insane as a group were unable to speak for themselves. Like the Jews, the insane were a minority of outsiders for whom economically and politically expanding society had to find a new integrating status. Otherwise, with the dismantling of exclusionary, protective class barriers it would become politically and psychologically difficult and economically inexpedient to accept outsiders. In the case of the insane, and of the Jews, it was essentially a matter of emancipating or integrating the vast majority of their members, i.e. the poor. For despite their formal exclusion and insecurity, affluent Jews lived comfortably, just as the well-to-do mentally ill lived tolerably well in private institutions.[28]

The fact that both insanity reform and a psychiatric paradigm presupposed official and economic concern for the poor once again brings us to the connection between medical specialization and population policies.[29] In the second half of the century, Berlin, Göttingen, and Vienna, following in the footsteps of Strasbourg and London, opened obstetrical clinics, and in 1778, Vienna, again following the lead of London, founded a special institute for childhood diseases. Around that same time Switzerland opened the first institute for orthopedics — whose very name embraces the concept of pedagogy. These pioneering endeavors, which opened the way for specialization in obstetrics, pediatrics, and orthopedics, promoted the interests of the princes through the professors of cameralism and medical policing, especially the previously mentioned J. P. Frank. Hygiene and curative and preventive health care for the working members of the population, especially the poor, became a crucial political factor in an increasingly production-oriented society, and at the same time apparently reflected the dictates of disinterested humanitarianism. It should be stressed that the state of medicine reflected a vital aspect of Germany's "belated nationhood" and her lagging economic development. In England and France, medicine set its sights on improving the health and sanitation of the poor in the service of the economic interests of an increasingly powerful bourgeoisie, while in Germany, even after the emergence of mercantilism, medicine continued to focus on the aggrandizement of the princes or the state. Thus Germany's medical undertakings must be understood within the framework of cameralist thinking as "medical policing" — a concept introduced by W. T. Rau in 1764 — and thus as a branch of administrative or "police science." That was why E. G. Baldinger, in 1782, referred to medicine as essentially a "political science."[30] To this day, medicine in Germany, especially in the social and administrative realm and social hygiene, has remained more paternalistic than elsewhere in the West. And it is still not clear whether the incipient German social psychiatry is cognizant of this overpowering tradition and able to break out of it — a movement this book would like to accelerate. Still, the same Frank who in 1788 saw the protection of the public against the insane as the primary goal later added an economic motive:

It was not so very long ago that the state did nothing more for the insane than lock them up to render them harmless to society. Now we know and practice another, a sacred duty: we return them as useful members to society, and this dual purpose, protecting mankind against the outbursts of the insane, and the healing of the latter, must guide us in the organization of an insane asylum.[31]

This characteristic shift shows that the new mental institutions, for all their surface similarities, differed from the old institutions of sequestration. They were no longer meant to isolate the insane from but return them — if useful — to society, whatever the term "society" may connote.

From the Enlightenment to "Sturm und Drang"

"The intellectual currents in Germany and the neighboring countries developed along more or less parallel lines, but the institutional changes came about later in Germany," for one thing because "the West European thinkers exerted a much greater influence on shaping political, social, and economic conditions than the contemporary German philosophers of the Enlightenment."[32] Eighteenth-century German medicine made important contributions to the theory of the nervous system which was widely discussed and exerted great influence in England and France. Among those was Friedrich Hoffmann's solidary-mechanistic doctrine of nerve tonicity and muscle reflexes. Another was G. E. Stahl's animism, which conversely saw the rational soul itself as the source of automatic movements, and which introduced the problem of an autonomous soul energy into medicine. And although this did not introduce the difference between primary-idiopathic and secondary-sympathetic disease, it did make them into permanent categories of medical philosophy.[33] And finally, there was A. von Haller, who through the concepts of sensibility and irritability believed to have proved the powers or capacity of all living matter. These theories were developed further during the second half of the century, thus, J. A. Unzer demonstrated that irritability was a characteristic of every part of a nerve, not just the muscle, and G. Prochaska generalized the concept of nervous energy in terms of natural philosophy.[34] But in general medicine and psychiatry the English clinicians from Whytt to Cullen and J. Brown lent *practical* significance to these theories, as did the vitalists at Montpellier, and from there they spread to the clinical school of Paris during the Revolutionary era.

Of course, eighteenth-century Germany also had its private practitioners who specialized in the treatment of hypochondria, hysteria, somnambulism, etc., and, believing the passions to be the causes of disease, recommended moral/mental cures and published their methods. Thus J. C. Bolten, in 1751, considered enlightening persuasion and soothing words useful even for physical complaints.[35] J. E. Zückert, in 1768, thought the passions were destructive, that the new sentimental generation had had extremely loose textural fibers in their mothers' wombs and was therefore too soft, but religion, philosophy, and diet were excellent precautionary measures.[36] And in the late eighteenth century, M. A. Weikard still found ample occasion to polemicize against possession and nervous spirits; he treated mental disorders by soothing the nerves and was the favorite practitioner of fashionable circles. Court physician in Fulda, he also practiced in Heilbronn and Pavia, and was summoned to St. Petersburg by Catherine the Great.[37]

All these doctors of the second half of the century hardly lagged behind their West European colleagues in theoretical knowledge. And most of them were men of the Enlightenment. Unzer, for example, published a freethinking medical journal; and his home in Altona was a social center, where his intellectual wife, Johanne Charlotte, performed her anacreontic songs. Weikard belonged to the illuminati. His irreligious pamphlet *The Philosophical Physician* was deemed dangerous enough to be banned. Yet their practical influence was minimal. Germany lacked the essential prerequisites which in early eighteenth-century England, and in mid-century France had become the literary and political sounding-board for "office hour psychiatrists." In Germany, where the middle-class elite was largely identical with the officialdom, health policies serving the interest of the state could thrive within the context of population politics and lead to corresponding institutions and/or medico-scientific disciplines. But for too long Germany lacked a free society with literary and political self-awareness; it lacked the medium of coherent public discussion. Wherever it did emerge, the development was slow or suppressed, or at best limited to local jurisdictions.

But as long as bourgeois society proved incapable of achieving self-awareness, of directing the advance of social processes or even influencing them, it could not develop the reflexive awareness that society itself creates not only its own growth but also its own ills. In England and France, on the other hand, that was a crucial premise for the fact that nervous disorders, hysteria, hypochondria, and suicide, the nervous system as a whole, and hence nervous energy and vitality — active life itself[38] — could become topics of public debate. Thus in Germany the demand for physicians of the nervous system and of the passions, for their therapeutic guidelines based upon a critical reassessment of contemporary culture and the resultant trends and institutions, was far smaller. German physicians were given little opportunity to develop sociosomatic theories of common sense, to philosophize about the sensibilities of the urban population, to confront self-induced moral disorders with the healing powers of nature, and to make nervous disorders the yardstick of civil, political, and economic freedom. Germany simply lacked the national market for this.

Of course, these themes did not disappear, but by the time they emerged — at first cautiously in *Sturm und Drang*, and later in Romanticism — the "market situation" had changed. The identical program carried out at different periods must perforce lead to different results. In general terms and in terms of cultural history, this delay, which also affected the institutionalization of psychiatry, has been described often enough, particularly since 1945. "The enlightenment [may be called] the political elementary school of the modern middle class, without which the part it has played in the cultural history of the last two centuries would be inconceivable. It was Germany's calamity that it missed attending this school at the time...and later on it was no longer so easy to overlook the limitations and prejudices of the movement." While the individual representatives of the Enlightenment remained isolated among the public, "the movement never completely penetrated public life, the social and political thinking of the broad masses, or the attitude to life of the middle classes.... The majority of the middle class and the intelligentsia were incapable of grasping the significance of the enlightenment in relation to their own class interests."[39] In addition to the economic and religious obstacles, countless other factors were held responsible for this weakness, including the decline of the cities, the enlightened views of some of the German princes themselves, and the fact that unlike in England (economically) and France (culturally and politically), there was no upward movement from the middle classes to the aristocracy.

The *Sturm und Drang* brought the first wave of Romanticism to Germany from England, whose Enlightenment had anyway never been one-sidedly rationalist since the days of Locke and Shaftesbury, and from Rousseauian France, a movement which Hauser sums up thus:

Whilst the middle class in France and England remained fully conscious of its own position in society and never entirely abandoned the achievement of the enlightenment, the German middle class came under the sway of romantic irrationalism before it had passed through the school of rationalism....As a form of emotionalism, the romantic movement still had a direct link with the revolutionary tendencies at work in the middle class....It is true that the starting point of German idealism was Kant's antimetaphysical theory of knowledge, with its roots in the enlightenment, but it developed the subjectivism of this doctrine into an absolute renunciation of objective reality, and reached a position of decided opposition to the realism of the enlightenment.[40]

Initially, however, this early romantic movement helped to create a literary public in Germany, as is attested to by the spectacular increase in the number of writers between 1773 and 1787, from three thousand to six thousand. Periodicals and literary circles sprang up everywhere as a veritable "reading craze" swept the country. These circles formed the core groups of informed private citizens who came together to exchange ideas and shape public opinion, although this term was not coined until the 1790s.[41] But *Sturm und Drang*, the literary attempt at a political breakthrough, also made manifest the failure of the middle class to come to terms with social reality, which was castigated for its lack of "magic." Individualism, the manifestations of "genius," were thought of as antihierarchic, the retreat to the idea of the *Volk*, the "people," and to history as antifeudal, and sentimentalism was looked on as antibureaucratic rather than antirational.

But it was precisely in the realm of praxis that the failure of the best intentions became most obvious. The front of the rulers and the privileged remained immutable and impenetrable....The success of Weimarian classicism and speculative philosophy was deeply rooted in that very constellation of political discouragement. Kant's philosophy mirrors the irreconcilable conflict between nature and law, the unchangeable antinomy between the existing absolutist feudal state and the intellectually essential legitimacy of bourgeois society.[42]

The absence of a practical political lever and link between the demand for economic freedom and for freedom of thought gave rise to the increasing dichotomy between the striving for external and inner freedom, between the economic and the educated middle class. The disappointment over the political failure of the turbulent 1770s was followed in the next decade by the growth of industrial society and — after Goethe's "escape to Italy" in 1786[43] — the, so to speak, psychophysically parallel flowering of an aesthetic-pessimistic classicism. And the same development took place in the two "specifically middle-class sciences that came into being in the eighteenth century":[44] economics and psychology. The two developed the doctrine of the external and internal "economy" of society largely independent of one another; the lessons of the English Enlightenment, mainly sensualism and common sense, offered no common material basis, either in social or in somatic terms.

Thus it was not the physicians but the philosophers, pedagogues, anthropologists, and poets who in *Sturm und Drang* began to reflect on their inner being and its irrationality, and that is why the later psychologists found their subject matter preformed by middle-class culture. Moreover, these cultured bourgeois, unlike the economic middle class, had no firsthand familiarity with the poor, and hence lacked the prerequisites for a realistic view of the insane. Rousseau was acclaimed not for his plebeian-revolutionary traits that had burst through the barriers of "good society," but for his sentimental ideal of education.[45] Finally, at a time when the political self-consciousness of the bourgeoisie was just beginning to develop and the power of the princes had not yet been broken, it was fatal to hold the individual responsible for emotional illness, irrationality, and misguided ideological concepts. This process, which had already taken root in the West, was in line with the bourgeoisie's renunciation of any claim to political power. Labeling the "misguided consciousness a flaw of the subject" at *this* stage narrowed the process "morally pejoratively, subjectivistically," turned it into an ahistorical perception of society,[46] and restricted social emancipation to individual inwardness through self-awareness. But this very individually moral self-limitation and self-accusation "caught on" with the public. There is no other explanation for the success of C. H. Spiess's tales of horror. In his *Biographien der Wahnsinnigen*, Spiess sets out to "prove that all of them were the authors of their own misfortune, and that consequently it is in our power to avoid a similar misfortune."[47] Pointing to the "sad events" of the French Revolution, he warns the people that great daring, passions, and the overstepping of norms and prohibitions is punished with insanity.

The unresponsiveness of the sense perceptive physicians (like Unzer) mirrors the weakness of the bourgeois impulses for social change as well as the lacking "politico-social content" of the sensus communis: "The concept of sensus communis was taken over, but in the removal of all political content it lost its real critical significance. Sensus communis was understood as a purely theoretical faculty, theoretical judgment, on a level with moral consciousness (conscience) and taste." In contrast to the common moral sense of the English, the most important thing for Kant was that "the character of moral law totally excludes any comparative reflection about others," and taste remains the arbiter of common sense.[48] In regard to the German cult of genius and the lack of a political public, Madame de Staël concluded: *"trop d'idées neuves, pas assez d'idées communes."*

Psychiatry as a medium of middle-class self-awareness in early nineteenth-century Germany was affected by the fact that it had not played that role in the eighteenth century and had only partially absorbed the Anglo-French tradition.[49] There is a lasting difference between the French view of English madness and suicide rates as a sign of decadence, which the English made part of their political self-consciousness, and the tendency of German psychiatrists and others of the middle class in search of national self-validation to look across the Western borders for evidence of cultural morbidity and decadence in sensualist thought.

Kant and "Empirical psychology"

Kant began his lectures in anthropology in 1772—73, and published his *Anthropology from a Pragmatic Point of View*, a more knowledgeable treatment of psychopathology than most contemporary medical works, in 1798. Moreover, Kant's systematization of psychiatric concepts has remained a factor in Germany; Germany's psychiatric model of the first half of the twentieth century, inexorably linked to the names of Kahlbaum, Schüle, Krafft-Ebing, and Kraepelin, was basically neo-Kantian, and German psychiatrists tend to make Kantian anthropology their point of reference.

Kant based both his anthropology and his psychopathology on three premises:
1. The "pragmatic point of view" of the knowledge of man (anthropology) aims at what man "as a freely acting being makes, can, or should make of himself." This specifically excludes the other possibility, physiological anthropology, "what Nature makes of man." Since one knows nothing about the physical foundations of behavior, one can only "speculatively theorize" about them.[50]
2. The basis for the approach is the traditional psychology of the innate, natural faculties in connection with the "unity of

consciousness" of the person who does not lose his identity throughout all the changes. All disorders and forms of irrationality are deduced from these faculties. This concept derived from the critique of sense perception, whose causal analysis proceeding from the outward to the inward, became secondary — not without profit psychologically, but somewhat of a loss from a somatologic and sociological vantage point. The same holds true, incidentally, for the development of psychology in Germany.[51]

3. On the question of method, the cognitive faculty makes Kant skeptical about observation, for it alters the object itself. Self-investigation can lead to the madhouse if the "creative imagination" overtakes the "rational elements," so that the "natural order of the cognitive powers" is reversed.[52] Here Kant attacks the pietists, "illuminism and terrorism," and the practice of keeping a journal that caused Pascal and von Haller such mental anguish. Travel and the enjoyment of literature, in particular the works of English writers, from Swift, Sterne, and Richardson to Johnson and Boswell, seem preferable.

Kant traces nearly all "weaknesses and illnesses of the soul" to the faculty of cognition. Given his cognitive psychological approach he begins with the weaknesses. He describes them as inabilities, abnormal states, congenital conditions that deviate from the rational norm of the individual faculties: the simpleton, the imprudent, the stupid, the coxcomb, the fool, the buffoon. It is fair to say that here lies the root of the German counterpart of the monomaniacs, the psychopaths of a later time.[53] As examples of the lack of intelligence Kant lists foolish, conceited, and deceptive behavior. In an excursus he includes the Jews in that last category: it is futile to try to "moralize" them with regard to their deceptive practices, he maintains, since they were merchants even before their expulsion, that is to say, always.[54] This elaboration is at odds with the views of the more emancipatory Councilor Dohm, who saw the external social situation as the cause of the corruption of the Jews and as the opportunity for their moralization. In contrast to the "concentration" of the pietists, the sufferer of the emotional disorder of "dispersal" is responsible for his failing,[55] because he "blindly follows the free play of his imagination without submitting it to reason," which, as for example through the excessive reading of novels leads to insanity.[56] This was the very form of mental weakness that Fichte at that time radicalized in his doctrine: "The principle of the dogmatists is faith in things for their own sake, that is, faith in their own dispersed self supported solely by objects.[57] This denies the independence of the self if that independence is mediated solely through objects, through nature. And one's personal philosophy, according to Fichte, depends on the type of person one is, not vice versa. This priority was to mark the idealist-characterological concepts of psychiatric unreason. The replacement of Holbach's ideological, false consciousness, which still lent itself to enlightenment through true knowledge of nature, by Fichte's dispersal is commented on by Habermas: "In German Idealism the prejudice of the French Encyclopaedists appears under the title 'dispersal,' a fixation of a weak ego or immature consciousness on the external props of existing things; what it means is the *reification* of the subject."[58]

For Kant, sound understanding with "weaknesses with regard to its exercise" is immature understanding. This holds true for children, women who talk too much, spendthrifts, who ought to be declared legally incompetent, and men everywhere insofar as rulers keep their subjects, and the clergy the laity, under virtual tutelage for their own good, since "a mechanical management of men under the regimen of others is everywhere the surest means of maintaining lawful order."[59]

Hypochondria (*Grillenkrankheit**) begins as a mild disorder, analogous to the chirping sounds made by a cricket, audible only to the victim. Here Kant could not even identify with Sterne's "hobbyhorses": they, too, were localized beyond the "borderline of sound understanding." As an illness of the mind hypochondria is the "disorder of the imagination," in which localized inner sensations gave rise to the fear of most dreadful diseases, whereas reason dictates that the general condition takes precedence over local manifestations. The hypochondriac is "capricious," and only the arbitrary deflection of attention from the painful sensation can help.[60] However, Kant, in *Von der Macht des Gemüts*, has made hypochondria the direct counterpart of that property: "One cannot demand of him who is stricken by that illness, and as long as he is, that he should master his morbid feelings. For were he able to do so he would not be hypochondriac."[61] This ambivalence encompasses the central problem of Kant's psychiatry. He sees melancholia in the same way: the special quality that marks its subjects is "gloomy self-torture," turning into a "frenzy of misery."

Kant sees actual unreason (emotional disturbance, mania) only as "raving" (delirium), as "essential and incurable disorder." Expressing an attitude typical for the prepsychiatric era about the

---

* Translator's note: "*Grille*" is the German word for "cricket."

futility of treating sequestered unreason, he concluded: "It is of little use to occupy oneself with it, because all methods of cure must be fruitless and fall short of their aim since the powers of the subject cannot cooperate (as is the case with bodily ailments) and yet the goal can only be attained through the person's own use of the understanding."[62] Kant includes all four forms of this incurable ranting under the charge of metaphysical dogmatism to symbolize something that he disputes; for here the subject produces something that it presents as objective although it is not subject to the laws of reason. Here, too, the fault lies in the deficient subordination of the imagination; a self-imposed, subjective law does not yield to objective law, hence the stress on the proximity to the likewise incurable creative poetic genius.[63] The madhouse, which Kant — rationally — sees as the substitution of external reason for an individual's lacking reason, should admit only those who are a danger to the community, not those who are merely self-centered, whose sole motive is self-preservation.[64] The most complete form of irrationality is lunacy (*vesania*), in which the victim, in systematic, closed speculation, fancies to "comprehend the incomprehensible." Here we are dealing not merely with disorder and departure from the laws of reason, but with "positive unreason, a different rule, a totally dissimilar standpoint, into which the soul is transported...and from the *sensorio commune* which is required for the unity of life (of the animal), it finds itself transported to a faraway place." Thus nature brings "a principle of unity into unreason, so that the thinking faculty does not remain idle, even though it is employed not objectively in the true cognition of things, but only subjectively for the continuation of animal functions."[65]

By emancipating the merely subjective and animal functions from the thinking faculty, Romantic medicine and philosophy were to claim insanity as their preserve, which Kant with critical intention had so stubbornly claimed for his philosophy. This is made quite obvious in the matter of forensics. Here Kant is willing to leave only ranting combined with fever as a physical disorder to the ministrations of doctors, while true insanity must remain in the realm of philosophy (which man, "as a freely acting being, makes, can, or should make of himself"). For on the question of responsibility, "the court of justice cannot refer him to the medical faculty, but must refer him to the philosophical faculty (because of the incompetence of the court regarding this question). The question of whether the accused at the time of his act was in full possession of his natural faculty of understanding and judgment is a wholly psychological question; and although physical derangement of the spirit perchance might now and then be the cause of an unnatural transgression of the moral law (which dwells in everybody), physicians and physiologists are generally still not advanced enough to see deeply into the mechanism inside a human being in order to determine whether the attack caused the atrocity, or whether it could have been predicted." If Kant were to leave irrationality to medicine, he would conversely have to question rationality and moral law, and hence the actual "jurisdiction" of philosophy. Reacting to a verdict in which an infanticide was declared insane and exempt from the penalty of death because she had drawn proper conclusions from false premises, Kant advanced a still widely held view: "On the basis of this argument it might easily be possible that all criminals be declared insane persons whom we should pity and cure, but never punish."[66]

Kant's jurisdictional claim for philosophers had practical consequences. Thus in 1804, a Hamburg teacher and theologian by name of Rüsau was condemned to death for having murdered his wife and five children in a fit of despair. It would appear that he was suffering from a psychotic fear of poverty. Two physicians testified in his defense, but public pressure and the findings of a university commission composed of professors of medicine, law, and of philosophy and theology, the last of whom were adamant in their insistence on the death sentence, tilted the balance against the defendant. The court found that Rüsau himself had created, fed, and given substance to his delusion since he had not allowed moral law to govern his actions even though possessing the free will to do so. Hence death was the deserved punishment and "a deterrent example to other similarly passionate men who, because of the cares of daily life, cravenly yield to despair."[67] Not only were the insane subject to moral law, whose philosophical rule did not allow for the possibility of physical impediment, but they also served as a warning example for the universality of its claim to validity — somewhat like the time when, as persons possessed, they were compelled to demonstrate the Church's claim to sovereignty.

Kant also enjoyed the complete support of his fellow discussant about the spiritual diet, the Royal Prussian Court Physician C. W. Hufeland, who suspected that the incipient natural philosophy threatened this position: He feared that the power of the mind over the body, which meets with the resistance of comfort-loving natural man, is threatened if, as has occurred in recent times, philosophy itself, the bearer of spiritual life, completely eradicates the distinction between mind and body in the identity system, and philosophers and physicians alike go so far in defending the independence of the mind from the body as even to excuse all crimes thereby and present unfreedom of the soul as their source, that soon things will reach such a pass that one will not be able to call any thing a crime anymore. But where does this view lead? — Is it not contrary to all law, divine and human, which, after all, is built upon that foundation? — Does it not lead to the grossest materialism? Does it not destroy all morality, all virtue, which resides in the life of the idea and its rule over the physical? — And hence all true freedom, independence, self-control, self-sacrifice, in short the most sublime thing that man can achieve: victory over himself?[68]

This natural philosophy, here perceived of as materialistic, was indeed the way in which the psychiatric physicians liberated the insane from Kant's rational rigorism and came to view them as sick and treatable.

Kant's impact on psychiatry is complex. His criticism of English philosophy enabled him to expose the defects in sense perceptive psychiatry. So, in one respect, he was skeptical about all external causes of insanity, at the time not a widely accepted position, but one reserved for a later scientific positivism. Love, pride, economic speculation, or "studying too hard" were "not the cause but the result of derangement." A man's unreason presupposes "a mental defect without which he would not have dared to make such demands in the first place." The merchant "who overextends himself," who "dissipates his powers in vast schemes...draws up his plan, like a fool, from the beginning." If unreason is something positive, it is also a "mere form," to which any "objects" can be adapted. Anything uttered by an insane person is random and indifferent to form.[69]

This formalism pushes Kant beyond criticism of the external causes of unreason and, disregarding the empirically observable, uncritically to the other extreme. As a pervasive etiological factor, Kant sees only the "inherited mental disorder." Since no external factor can be superior to reason, any sign of unreason is always a "breaking out of derangement." The germ of derangement develops together with the germ of reproduction, and is thus hereditary."[70] Ever since, every idealistic (and neo-Kantian) psychiatry has been burdened with the tendency to overestimate the intrinsic or unfolding innate or hereditary predisposition — particularly in Germany, but also in the degeneration theory adapted from France.[71] Among classical German anthropologists, Christoph Meiners is the strongest believer in heredity. He even considers the "faculty and mentality" of nations to be hereditary. The European peoples are superior to the Slavs and all non-European races, whereby the preeminent personality and economic specialization are based on the difference between inherited qualities. Meiners, whom Georg Forster refuted, and Gobineau built on, already maintained that the cross-breeding of superior groups, e.g. the Germanic, with inferior beings debases the nobler breed.[72]

The structural difficulty in Kant's psychiatry lies in the following. On the one hand, the irrationality of insanity is produced by the subject himself, whereby "the only general characteristic of insanity is the loss of sense for ideas that are common to all (*sensus communis*), and its replacement with a sense for ideas peculiar to ourselves (*sensus privatus*)."[73] For to that extent insanity offers the subjective as the objective, and it is therefore passive, heteronomous, mangled or obtuse reason, is presented in the form of prejudice, superstition, speculation, and dogmatism, and belongs, as an object of enlightenment, to "self-made immaturity."[74] On the other hand, the irrationality of insanity is also merely the effect of a "special nature," an inherited capacity, an eruptive disposition. Formally, insanity is no less originality — i.e. the cause of this effect is invisible — than genius, which follows the dictates of an innate talent. For the harmonious working of the mind produced by the imagination of the genius, like the disharmonious workings of the insane, "must take place through the nature of the subject."

Thus, for Kant, the irrationality of madness is both produced by the subject and given expression by his inborn nature; it is guiltless guilt, destiny — and it has not been able to get rid of this factor.[75] This reveals Kant's dilemma, which Lukács suspects to be the consequence of the critical cleansing of the formal awareness of all content-matter for the objects as for the subject itself. "For just as objective necessity, despite the rationality and regularity of its manifestations, yet persists in a state of immutable contingency because its material substratum remains transcendental, so too the freedom of the subject which this device is designed to rescue, is unable, being an empty freedom, to evade the abyss of fatalism.... The impossibility of comprehending and 'creating' the union of form and content concretely instead of as the basis for a purely formal calculus leads to the insoluble dilemma of freedom and necessity, of voluntarism and fatalism. The 'eternal, iron' regularity of the process of nature and the purely inward freedom of individual moral practice appear at the end of *The Critique of Practical Reason* as wholly irreconcilable and at the same time as the unalterable foundations of human existence."[76] Lukács sees this as the expression of bourgeois society, which smashes the old, "natural, irrational" bonds, and replaces them with an equally inexorable necessity (p. 128).

Indeed, Kant's theoretical-etiological contradiction of insanity is matched by its practical-therapeutic contradiction. On the one side, only the subject himself can cure his insanity, overcome his immaturity, "through sheer resolution master his morbid feelings." On the other, the innate, natural side, the irrationality of insanity is uncurable, effecting a change through therapy is impossible, for the physical manifestations that fall under the purview of the physician do not constitute the essence of insanity. Hence, Kant's anthropology can be only indirectly pragmatic here; it can only "dictate omissions," namely to refrain from irrational actions. In particular, it is dangerous to "marry into families where even a single such creature has been produced." And here (an ancient, deep-seated resentment), only the maternal side of the family is said to carry the seeds of irrationality and thus is dangerous.[77]

The same ambivalence becomes if possible even more concrete, if in Kant's treatment of the passions, the disorders of the appetites, which impede reason and are simultaneously a disease and moral evils. On the one hand, passion is always an "illness of the mind," a delusion, which, as "a motive of desire...is the internal practical deception of taking subjective reasons for objective ones...the mood of the inner sense for knowledge of the thing itself." On the other hand "passions are cancerous stores for pure practical reason," for they make one desire the absolute standard of all other; make "one's partial purpose the whole of one's purpose, which even in its formal principle smacks reason right in the face"; for in this way "passion surrenders freedom and self-control, and finds pleasure in a servile disposition." It turns into addiction. "Therefore passions are...without exception bad. Even the most well-intended desire if it aims (according to matter) at what belongs to virtue... is nevertheless (according to form), as soon as it changes to passion, not merely pragmatically pernicious, but also morally reprehensible."[78]

This relationship between the unreason of insanity and practical reason is reflected above all in the rigorism of moral therapy, to which nascent German psychiatry adhered far more rigidly than its English and French counterparts, but also in the later influence of legal-forensic interest in the development of psychiatric theory.

And finally, it was reflected in the permanent medical-moral conflicts of the debate about monomania and psychopathy.

Sturm und Drang meanwhile turned into a movement which, in dismay over the failure of politics, turned inward, to the *sensus privatus* of everyday experience, and dissatisfied with Kant's formalism, burst through the critical restriction of his method. This movement of individual psychology therefore employed the media of physiognomics and constitutional theory, of pedagogical arts, of pietistic self-observation and autobiography.

The writings of the pedagogue and aesthetician J. G. Sulzer and the theologians J. G. Herder and J. C. Lavater had made physiognomy (and mimicry) into a subject of general interest during the 1770s:[79] the belief in the harmony of man's external appearance and inner self was arrived at through the idea that "the body is nothing more than the soul made visible" (Sulzer). The symbolism of the individual parts of the body in Herder's *Plastik* (1778) demonstrates the moral condition of the functions of the soul. Ever since Lavater's *Physiognomische Fragmente zur Beförderung der Menschenkenntnis und Menschenliebe* (1775—78), this unteachable art of "human feelings" contributed essentially to a revival of Leibniz. Man, being a microcosm, is physically and spiritually created according to a coherent plan, which, through the internal-external identity determines the "infinite diversity" of mankind, and hence the uniqueness of the individual. The parts of the organism are in complete harmony, and "every part of an organic entity is an image of the entity, has the character of the entity." To be sure, Lavater, the "genius of the heart," is little concerned with verifiable method; he is satisfied with the "physiognomic feeling." That made him the target of G. C. Lichtenberg's satiric comment that one only saw in man what was already known about him; and moreover that our bodies tell "not only of our inclinations and abilities, but also of the whiplashes of destiny, climate, disease, nourishment, and myriad hardships." But here too the social conditions were not favorable to a consideration of social and somatic external circumstances. It is thus not surprising that toward the end of the century a medically founded constitutional theory originated in France (Hallé, Cabanis), whereas in Germany the line of psychosomatic symbolism was carried on in literature and natural philosophy.[80]

All the cited media of the quest for inwardness found their platform in a *Sturm und Drang* journal with the telling title: ΓΝΩΘΙ ΣΕΑΥΤΟΝ, or *Magazin zur Erfahrungsseelenkunde.*

For no matter how much its contributors tried to go beyond Kant, they too saw the Enlightenment, as the "revolution in the interior of man." Thus, J. H. G. Feder's psychological research was motivated by the desire to prevent "social conflict," as though the real revolution had already been accomplished.[81] This resembles the intention of Schiller, who in the 1790s wanted to prop the ongoing process of society's separation from the old natural state through aesthetics rather than psychology, a process that demanded the preservation of the state to prevent social anarchy: "The living clockwork of the state must be improved and made to strike, and here the turning wheel must be exchanged during its rotation."[82]

This periodical, which appeared in Berlin from 1783 to 1793, was founded and published by Carl Philipp Moritz, and subsequently Salomon Maimon became its co-publisher. Together with his book *Reisen eines Deutschen in England* (1783), the journal grew out of Moritz's trip to England in 1782. It became a repository for explorations of man's inner life, for the concrete rather than conceptual depiction of mental states, for the observation of one's own mental quirks and peculiarities and those of others, for therapeutic moral-pedagogical or religious recommendations based on such casuistry against internal or external social disorder. With unparalleled concentration, the journal met the needs of the public that was now beginning to take an interest in itself and to form a constituency. And it met those needs because its tone was not intellectually definitive, which was why the title page addressed itself to "scholars and laymen." The early issues still relied on English associative psychology (Hartley, Priestley) to enlighten its readers about religious superstition, but later on Leibniz's influence came to the fore. Phenomena that used to be explained in a physiological context began to attain psychological autonomy — for instance, vague ideas, dreams, vertigo, and sensibility itself. Kant struck these psychologists as too rigidly mechanical, too Newtonian. They connected all objects of experience to moods and the continuity of the self to help them learn more about "actual" life. In addition to Moritz and Maimon, the contributors included Lavater and Sulzer as well as K. F. von Irwing, Feder, the Jewish physician and philosopher Marcus Herz, and Oberreit, a theosopher and surgeon from Lindau. Herz even suggested that psychology had to take over the role of metaphysics in medicine.

The autobiographies of the two publishers created a sensation at the time. Moritz, in his *Anton Reiser, ein Psychologischer Roman* (1785—90), attributed his lack of inner equilibrium, his restlessness and his pervasive self-doubts to the psychic misery of his early childhood. Growing up in poor and unsettled circumstances, subject to mystical-pietistic influences, the badly reared child of bickering parents, he "had had too little independent existence from childhood on." Thus, he saw all external events as the inevitable consequence of his life, which thereby became one long process of self-searching via the pietistic technique of self-observation. In the preface, Moritz puts great stress on things "that initially seemed small and trivial," for they build up into "the inner history of a person." The book is intended to "sharpen the soul's observation of the inner self," and is justified in that "from a pedagogical standpoint it will never be futile for an individual to pay greater attention to himself and endow his individual existence with greater importance."[83] No one saw the difference between Moritz's sentimental psychology and Weimar's classicism more clearly than Goethe, who looked upon Moritz as a younger brother battered by fate. Commenting on the time they spent together in Rome during 1786, Goethe wrote: "Here, in the ambience of the loftiest art and loveliest nature, our companion Moritz never ceased to brood on man's inwardnesses, his faculties and developments."[84]

Maimon's *Geschichte des eigenen Lebens* (1792) created even more of a stir. For it described the rise of an uneducated Polish Jewish youth from poverty to renown, a philosopher who built a bridge from Kant and Fichte; and it proved, as Moritz put it, "that the mental powers can develop in the human mind even under the most oppressive circumstances."[85] Maimon became the living example of "man's leave-taking of his self-inflicted immaturity." Maimon's preface was similar to Moritz's. He, too, believed that "Nature makes no leaps. All great events are the consequences of much smaller ones," and these "seemingly minor occurrences in human life can be far more interesting and instructive" than the affairs of state and great political and military feats of history. Maimon wants to portray his life which "in itself is psychologically, pedagogically, and morally interesting and informative...from life." His life story is meant to take stock of "how much closer I have come to my destination" and "what might still be wanting" (pp. 206–10).

The approach of the articles in the magazine was no different: man has to be observed in his at-home clothes, not in his Sunday best. Since the editors believed that mental phenomena were most discernible in their aberrant state, the magazine's section on psychiatric medicine, filled with reports about wish-fulfillment dreams, passions, unconscious immoral desires, and even insanity, was the most popular. Maimon considered insanity merely a derangement of the lesser mental powers (imagination, memory), similar to alcoholic intoxication or dreams, and its therapy becomes an awakening. On the whole, the contributions were oriented toward therapy, whether in the sense of self-awareness, even the conscious recollection of childhood memories, or in the sense of ordering and harmonizing of individual or social disequilibriums, as a shock therapy against passions; or in pedagogic terms, like Moritz's demand for a moral physician to treat the psychological abuse at the orphan asylum of Halle; or else, by following Rousseau and extolling the curative powers of nature. Most of the contributors to the magazine based their psychology on a religious, and usually pietist, foundation. This too was seen as vanquishing the Enlightenment and at the same time its continuance by applying it to the inner man. And this vanquishing outweighed its object in terms of effort since the atheistic-materialistic component of the Enlightenment had anyway never really gained a foothold in Germany — not least because of the important role of the Protestant parish house.[86]

The sequestration of the insane and the incipient change in that movement in Germany had a counterpart in the role of the fool on stage and in literature. "With the buffoon on the stage [the rationalism of enlightened absolutism] had also averted the threat of being made a laughingstock." It had, "for the sake of sound reason, virtually spirited the stage buffoon off into the mad-house,"[87] in order to be *completely* rational — and this means: sociable. With the dissociation of the bourgeoisie into two strata — economic and cultural — at the end of the eighteenth century, this line of rationalism continued uninterrupted as pragmatic, economic reason on the part of the economic stratum: "The businessman has no sense of humor, because he despises this dangerous fiddle-faddle, for humor is an aberration or rather incivility of reason....He despises humor because it consumes reason, which he can turn to more useful purpose so as to be of use to his fellow man."[88] To that same extent, the cultured bourgeoisie of late rationalism, under which Promies also subsumes *Sturm und Drang*, discovered the fool within themselves, and in this new form brought him back into literature, and with his help began the game of reversing reason and unreason. But since emancipated bourgeois society did not form the backdrop for this game, the reason of the state remained taboo for them, and hence also for the "journal" psychologists, and they turned their energy toward protecting themselves against social disorder.

This justifies the observation "that rationalism with undertakings that investigated the irrational in order to be more cognizant of it, actually released the irrational."[89] For lack of a political *sensus communis* this "premonition of the Romantic soul,"[90] was concerned solely with protecting the now questionable private self of the bourgeoisie; it remained as remote from the will for political emancipation as from a medical approach to a practical change of the unreason of the insane. If psychiatry was to establish itself, it was not enough for the middle class to reveal their own psychological aberrations and disorders. What was needed was to give visibility to the irrationality of the insane *poor.*

2

Revolution from Above and the Obstructed Psychiatric Paradigm

The Medical and Romantic Impulse

The Treaty of Basel with Napoleon of 1795 reduced Prussia and the other north and central German territories to the role of spectator of Europe's political and social changes for ten years. It was during this time that most of the later reformers entered Prussian public service. They were, however, unable to institute the essential liberal reforms against the powerful cabinet regime of the Prussian state, which not only managed to hold on to its position in the face of the contagious revolutionary threat from France, but dug in its heels in defense of tradition. There was no social pressure "from below" to compel them to change their approach, and even the catastrophic economic situation, which in 1800 forced the government to distribute food stamps among the lower classes, could not make a dent. The government continued along its prerevolutionary, enlightened way, ruling not by but on behalf of the people.

However, the intellectual involvement of the autonomous literary community, the educated middle class excluded from political and social activity, was all the greater — so much so that even the attitudes toward the Revolution, the natural sciences, especially medicine, became the subject of literary and philosophical discussions. In this decade of seeming peace, in which Classicism yielded to Romanticism, and Kantian idealism to natural philosophy, writers and physicians alike were fascinated by disease, the dark side of the soul, by madness. It was a time in which physicians in literary and philosophical form began to focus on the disorders of the psyche, and writers sought to become the physicians of their feelings, their spiritual as well as physical ills — somewhat like the mid-eighteenth-century English writers. In Germany, the political revolution was perceived and emotionally experienced only by a literary public, but the political reality was one of reform by decree, not revolution. And likewise, the early physicians who made the irrationality of derangement their special concern were impelled by literary and philosophical considerations, without direct acquaintance with the subjects of their study. On both levels bourgeois society traversed tormented circuitous routes until it won the institutions adequate to its needs.

Yet it is equally true that the failure of the bourgeoisie in this predominantly agricultural country to see all of society, including the poor, in both social and political terms, gave the Romantic movement the opportunity to play an enlightening role both in the political area and in the field of psychiatric medicine. The first generation of both the Romantics and psychiatrists was born around 1770, and hence was far more exposed to the contradictions of the revolutionary epoch than the Classicists, most of whom came out of the eighteenth-century Enlightenment, and, after the *Sturm und Drang*, found their way to an effete aesthetic ideal of culture. Most of the younger generation not only had hailed the French Revolution, but soon thereafter had faced the difficult problem of deciding whether Napoleon was a liberator from feudal bondage or a foreign despot. None could foresee that Napoleon himself would soon help them reach the decision on behalf of the second alternative. This steered German Romanticism from its somewhat revolutionary beginnings onto a conservative and restorative track — in contrast to Western Europe, where Romanticism having begun as an antirevolutionary, legitimist movement, took a liberal, nonconformist turn with the victory of haute-bourgeois capitalism.[91]

At first, the "experience of the time," which did not seem to conform to rational maxims, led to a crisis-consciousness unknown to classicism, combined with a broadening of largely the inner experience of reality, both of these also being prerequisites for a psychiatric science. The experience of the Revolution in France with its contradictory, rapidly changing phases, liberated the play of the imagination between reality and possibility from Kantian laws, and suggested a transcendence into other possible realities. The longer the state of peace lasted, the more obvious its delaying function, its hollowness and unreality. The Romantics developed a sensitive nose for the reality of the rationally unreal, for the "reality of the nonvisible," of which the protest concept of "the German *Volk*" as a surrogate for the lacking nation-state unity of Western society, and at the same time more complete reality —

more complete because it had grown organically and was rooted
in mythology — was merely an expression.[92] Then too, those
writers were deeply aware of the overwhelming reality of their
own insecurity and instability, of the chaotic condition of the
world, and of the unpredictability of life. They accepted and
described the power of absurdity, irrationality, disease. They
were the first to perceive the depersonalizing effect of urban
life of which they were such a special part. For they found themselves at the mercy of disintegration and contradiction, not only
in the great world of politics, but also in their own professional
and personal lives: they were the first generation of writers to
earn their living mainly in the employ of industry or administration. Given the lack of an economically and politically self-aware
bourgeoisie, they found the objectivized functional rationality
demanded of and delivered by them even less patently rational
than their West European colleagues. That is why their protest
remained inner-directed, made them pit actual against imagined
reality and contributed in no small part to the central motif of
the doppelgänger.[93] As far as they were concerned, the question
of which of the contrasting realities would emerge victorious
was no longer an a priori decision. Unlike Classicism, they were
no longer able to bring order into the chaos, to assemble man's
sensual-empirical and intelligible character into a hierarchical
order of reason, to render irrationality harmless through rationality, or to harmonize rationally theory and practice, life and
death, health and disease. One-sided "pathological" distortions
in the graphic depiction of the negative, the darker side, seemed
less suspect than the celebration of predetermined equilibriums.

Liberal capitalism and its economic crises were accompanied
by waves of Romanticism, a testimony to the fact Romanticism
was no match for rational social reality. The antirational realities
were as much an expression of social refusal as of escapist movements, as much a realistic protest against all rational constriction
of bourgeois existence as an irrational cul-de-sac. That held true
for the evolutionary development of history, for the myth of the
Volk, and for emanational logic, as well as for the romanticization
of the sinister-mysterious, the imaginary and unconscious, the
dreams and utopian wish-fulfillments, of wandering, solitude, and
homelessness, of childhood and fairytales, of strangeness and
estrangement, of moods and drives, of physical and mental disease.

Particularly the last of these, indeed pathology in general, so
fascinated the Romantics that Goethe was driven to ridicule their
"hospital-poetry." For them disease represented the negation

of the ordinary, the normal, the reasonable, and contained the dualism of life and death, nature and non-nature, continuance and dissolution, which dominated their whole concept of life. It meant the depreciation of everything sharply defined and abiding, and it was in accordance with their hatred for all limitations, all solid and definite form."[94] Both the Romantics and the natural philosophers adopted this Friedrich Schlegel maxim: "If you wish to enter into the heart of physics, become an initiate of the mysteries of poetry!"[95] Novalis, Schelling, H. Steffrens, F. von Baader, L. Oken, J. von Görres came to their most challenging problems of medicine via the Romantic Scottish physician John Brown, who had already formulated their ideas of polarity and identity, and via the German advocates of Brownianism, the physicians A. F. Marcus and A. Röschlaub, who were teaching in Bamberg.

Brown exerted a particularly powerful influence on Novalis, that expert, highly meticulous mining engineer and mysterious inner-directed poet. Novalis polarized Brown's dual disease classifications of sthenia and asthenia and made them into physical concepts. The analogizing of sthenia and asthenia with strength and weakness, body and soul, outer and inner world, was a later development. This already implied the exaltation of the asthenic extreme: asthenic diseases, i.e. ailments of the sensibility and its organs, the nerves, make man sublime and spiritual. Man introduced both sensibility and nervous disease into nature, and with them, freedom and sin as an offense against nature, frailty, and, love, which is a disease in itself. The asthenic man — suffering, loving, finite — became the ennobled representative of Romanticism. Benightedness, too, is asthenic, as is its analogue, imprudence, and insanity is its more exalted form. In his *Fragmente*, Novalis noted: "Benightedness is twofold: indirect and direct asthenia. The first comes about through bedazzlement, excessive light, the second from a want of sufficient light. Thus there is imprudence due to a lack of self-stimulation and imprudence due to excessive self-stimulation — there, an excessively coarse, here, an excessively tender organ. The former is cured by diminishing light or self-stimulation, the latter, by increasing them or by weakening or strengthening the organ. Benightedness and imprudence due to lack are the most frequent. Imprudence due to excess is called insanity. The redirection of excessive self-stimulation modifies insanity."[96]

So madness as indirect asthenia was linked to an overly delicate nervous, organic constitution, the precondition for excessive self-stimulation: madness is imprudence due to excessive stimulation; benightedness due to bedazzlement. Even though here, as in Schelling — in contrast to the *Sturm und Drang* psychologists — the material organization and the physiology of stimulus were incorporated into the problem of insanity, openly and without idealistic prejudgment, this conceptual legacy of the Western and also German eighteenth century reached the German psychiatrists only within the framework of Romantic or natural philosophy. And, even more important, with few exceptions, this did not happen during the largely materialistic early phase of natural philosophy, one of sharp and abrupt contrasts of still rather liberal, prorevolutionary tendencies, but only after Schelling had laid the religious foundation of his philosophy (1804), Friedrich Schlegel had converted to Catholicism (1808), Görres had deserted republicanism and natural science for myth (1805) and nationalism (1806), and Jean Paul, E. T. A. Hoffmann, and Tieck had made insanity a literary theme. And rising above the social reality of the mentally defective poor and the material, somatic totality of insanity as a dread disease, they turned them into individual, traits of insanity, into a "higher state," to an anthropologic "borderline situation," so as to use these ultimate human possibilities to construct a metaphysical order for their own inner self, to bring meaning into chaos.[97]

At the same time, the galvanism that had already fascinated Herder remained valid. And mesmerism, coming from Paris, also found fruitful soil in Germany. Samuel Hahnemann, in developing his homeopathy, enlisted the Romantic notion of totality to polemicize against the medical theories of physical localization and inflammation, and questioned even the very purpose of medicine. In 1796, the Prince of Brunswick gave him money and land for a private sanatorium for the insane in Georgenthal Castle near Gotha. Although the *National-Zeitung* in 1798, lauded him as "the German Willis,"[98] his real success came only after 1806. Of course, self-treatment by laymen, championed by Hahnemann and widely practiced by philosophers and poets, had led to a public scandal in 1800. Schelling, when called to the bedside of Caroline von Schlegel's daughter, diagnosed her illness — dysentery — as nervous fever, and a physician was summoned only when the patient was dying, a mistake that put Schelling's professorship at Jena in jeopardy.[99]

All these influences confirmed and shaped the ideas of German psychiatrists, leaving little room for clinical positivism, somatic brain-research, and the social visibility of the insane poor within bourgeois society, which had been made possible in France by the Revolution. If such attempts were made, they usually came from outside or above, and were moreover stigmatized as divorcing theory from practice. The most important relative exception was Johann Christian Reil's *Rhapsodien über die Anwendung der psychischen Curmethode auf Geisteszerrüttungen* (1803), a work generally considered as the start of German psychiatry. The exceptional character which lifts this volume far above most later psychiatric writing derives from the fact that it was composed under the influence of the first liberal and near materialistic phase of Romanticism, whereas shortly thereafter Reil also resorted to Schelling's speculative system to smoothe over and resolve empirical contradictions. Hence, the Rhapsodien were called "Reil's last completely self-contained work."[100] Nevertheless, it is romantic through and through, as its poetic title implies.

This change in Reil's scientific orientation was paralleled by a political one as well.[101] Reil was born in 1759 in an East Frisian parish house. Studying medicine rather than theology, against his father's wishes, he had a private practice until 1788, when he was appointed professor of medicine at Halle. There he became one of the most sought-after physicians, and his wide-ranging scientific research activities brought him a chair at the new University of Berlin in 1810.[102] He specialized as an internist, surgeon, and opthalmologist and did research in anatomy, pathology, physiology, chemistry, and pharmocology. His notable contributions include the introduction of chemical reagents to study the structures of the eye and the brain, as important to brain anatomy as Gall's technique, and he recognized the importance of the pathological chemistry of the organism in the causes of disease. In 1796, he founded the *Archiv für Physiologie*, and remained its editor until his death. Reil was in contact with Fichte, Schleiermacher, Börne, Goethe, Steffens, Humboldt, Arndt, F. A. Wolf, and Gall. Like most of his friends, he started out as a Republican. As late as 1799, he dedicated the fourth volume of his major clinical study on fever to Napoleon. But by 1806 he had turned into a fervent patriot. Finally, in the wars of liberation, having long since become an enthusiastic disciple of Schelling, his hatred of the French surpassed even Fichte's. E. M. Arndt described him thus: "Fichte and Reil were to a certain degree the most tragic people in the capital because of the enormous ardor of their response to contemporary events and their burning hatred of the French, almost more intense in Reil than in Fichte."[103] In 1813, Reil, who had developed the first plan for the reform of insane asylums, was asked to supervise the reorganization of the Prussian military medical services. During the war, he was in charge of army hospitals on the left bank of the Elbe. It was here that he died of typhoid fever.

Reil's first significant work, *Von der Lebenskraft* (1795), made obvious that his theoretical interest would eventually lead him to the subject of insanity: his concern was always the relationship between matter and idea, body and soul. Reil's basic position was a kind of dynamic materialism,[104] which also influenced the young Schelling. This notion of matter evolved out of the enthusiastic response to the recent advances in thermal and oxygen chemistry and the theory of electricity. It has been said that this idea of matter might have led to concepts like Comte's and Gall's[105] had Germany's social conditions been as favorable for the natural and social sciences as France's. Reil followed in the footsteps of Glisson and Leibniz. Matter — according to the mixture of its elements and the forms of its aggregation — appears as a chain of increasing particularizations, whereby the beginnings of living nature are contained "in the womb" of dead nature. Life is a mixture of cruder and finer, less visible matter (e.g. light, heat, oxygen, electricity). Just as matter is energy, so organic matter is life energy or life: "Energy is thus inseparable from matter, a quality thereof, through which it brings forth phenomena."[106] An individual's temper (temperies) is his specific degree of that spontaneousness of matter, of vital energy. Disease never originates directly from the outside, but only by way of the unnatural mixture and form of vital energy, the deviation from one's specific temperature (*intemperies*, distemper).

Based on this theory Reil in 1799 in the fourth volume of his work on fever, incorporated mental diseases into his general pathology: they are in no wise superphysical, but rather a stimulus-induced disturbance of the mixture and form of the brain substance, an "abnormal vital process in the brain."[107] Like Pinel, Reil was sufficiently objective not to read any mysterious system into the "chaos" of mental disorders. He differentiated vaguely only between fixed delusion, rage, idiocy, and imbecility, and rigorously rejected Kant's (and Hoffbauer's) categorical-psychological deduction, because it transcended experience, as well as Gall's localizing approach.

1803, the year Reil published his major psychiatric work, *Rhapsodien*, has generally been considered the beginning of psychiatry in Germany. Certainly the intellectual situation was similar to that of the psychiatric beginnings in England and

France. One might speak of a union of enlightened and romantic thought when the Kantian Reil wrote this work, for decades the closest thing to a paradigm, shortly before his conversion to the systemic thinking of natural philosophy. And yet the contemporary political and socio-economic conditions of Germany left the subject of the exercise shrouded in invisibility. To be sure, the Reil of 1803, like Battie and Pinel, was both a successful medical scientist and a socially involved personage. And yet he never made an effort to acquaint himself firsthand with the deranged poor, to join their side, as it were, before making theoretical pronouncements about them. He had practically no experience with the mentally deranged when he wrote his basically poetic, literary anthropology. He did draw up a grandiose scheme for therapy, for the organization of asylums, and for the academic discipline of *"Psychiaterie"* — which, too, was his concept.[108] But Battie's and Pinel's public appeals were based on observation, practical organization, and liberating integration. Reil merely reminded the public, the rulers, and the state of their duty, expecting them to take action without however lending a hand to make this dream come true. Moreover, he started from the primacy of foreign and power politics: Only when the "body politic" learns to work in harmony like the bodies of nature, can princes, whose loftiest goal is the "well-being of the people," also be noble-minded toward the insane and show their "paternal concern" for the "socially immature."[109] And the only element of Reil's psychiatric paradigm that has been realized is also of a literary nature: he founded two psychiatric journals, both of a predominantly philosophical bent; however, public interest in the subject was not yet very widespread, and they soon ceased publication.[110] This, incidentally, was the only area in which Germany took the lead, and German psychiatry of the early nineteenth century can lay claim to being "literary." The flourishing cultural superstructure was the reverse side of Germany's controlled and belated economic development. That was why bourgeois society only gradually began to see the strata of sequestered unreason, including the insane poor, as an industrial reserve or as a social issue.

"An intrepid breed dares to approach the gigantic idea that makes ordinary man reel, the idea of extirpating one of the most devastating of epidemics from the face of the earth. And it truly seems as if we are approaching safe harbor and are about to dock."[111] The noble sentiment was not matched by deed. Reil's psychiatry was a postulative paradigm written largely in the conjunctive mode. As in Western Europe, there was a sequential connection with prison reform. Upon being asked by his friend, Reverend Wagnitz, the German protagonist of prison reform, to do an article for his journal on the dismal situation of the insane, Reil called their social position the "basement of our houses of correction." Reil's plaint about the condition of the outcast insane was even more poignant than that of the West European reformers, although or perhaps because he had scarcely had any firsthand dealings with the insane:

We lock up these unfortunate creatures like criminals in mad-boxes, isolated prisons, next to the nests of owls in bleak clefts above the town gates, or in the damp cellars of jails, hidden from the compassionate gaze of friendly eyes, and let them, chained in irons, rot in their own filth. Their fetters have chafed their flesh down to the bone, and their pallid, hollow faces await the nearby grave, which covers their woe and our shame. They are exposed to the curiosity of the rabble, and the mercenary keeper pulls them like exotic beasts for the amusement of the idle spectators....Epileptics, imbeciles, babblers, and somber misanthropes, all mixed up together in wild confusion ....The guards are usually unfeeling, cruel men neglectful of their duties who, in their control over madmen have seldom stepped outside the circle drawn by their whip.[112]

In Reil, the essential motive of Western psychiatry, in the reflexive self-consciousness of a bourgeois society producing its own sufferings, developed out of the contrast to the savage, to man in his natural state, still largely identical with his own body, still easily managing his life — i.e., the balancing of contradictions — and hence not suffering from mental ailments. Along with the external conditions, the inner conditions of human evolution also became more and more complicated: the "adjunct of the soul," which spread like a parasite, made the harmonizing of the contradictions more and more difficult, more and more psychological, and with it the chances of mental disease also continued to increase. "We draw closer to the madhouse step by step as we stride along the path of our sensual and intellectual culture."[113] The care of the mentally ill thus becomes not merely a matter of loving one's neighbor, but also a matter of necessary self-interest and "national happiness," especially since — beyond man's pathological acts — nature can burden anyone with a predisposition toward abnormality; and Reil actually ascribed even greater powers to nature than did Kant. Lukács interpreted the simultaneously aesthetic content of this "mood" as the Romantic-anthropological counterpart of Kant's natural-law thing-in-itself.

As "what was not created by man...the highpoint of interiorization of nature really implies the abandonment of any true understanding of it. To make moods (Stimmung) into the content presupposes the existence of unpenetrated and impenetrable objects (things-in-themselves) just as much as do the laws of nature."[114]

Reil shares the utopian concept of Romantic nature, that is to say — according to Lukács — "that aspect of human inwardness... which has remained natural, or at least tends to become, natural once more. 'They are what we once were,' says Schiller about the forms of nature, 'they are what we should once more become'" (p. 136). This is where Reil locates the physician, makes him into the healer, the mediator of the (good) physical nature not yet and no longer disharmonized by the soul and the social contradictions, the nature that we once were and should once more become. For medicine — both a natural science and an art — can expose man's spiritual material ambiguity, stimulate the desire for form amidst chaos, give nature back to man, nature in which man is no longer separated from man. Understanding and healing man means that the physician "re-creates" him "in terms of natural history." This holds true for somatic disease, insanity, and "moral disease," i.e. criminality, which is why Hufeland's attack on materialism as a force that canceled moral absolutes was directed against Reil as well. Reil, of course, believed that the physician molds the individual body just as the prince molds that of the body politic, and that the coordinated progress of the state and of science was already being guided by the "poetic eagle" of speculative natural philosophy.[115]

Reil's peculiar nature-, matter-, and somatically oriented "empirical psychology," for which he sought academic recognition, sees "plastic nature" as creating "the brain as an unformed mass (tabula rasa) out of animal matter," out of a predisposition that, through stimuli, particularly ideal stimuli, produces "the independent faculties." This secondary "authority" constitutes the historical character of the psyche, and also makes possible education and therapy through ideas: "Ideas establish the dynamic relationship of the brain."[116] Spontaneity is not permitted; "the soul evolves and changes constantly, just as the body evolves and changes and yet remains the same."[117] The basic mental energy is self-consciousness, the organ "of the coherence of our existence," of the personality, this, too, intertwined with the body, which Reil gleaned from manifestations of the split and alienation of self-consciousness (e.g. dreams, waking).[118] The three directions of the self-consciousness are mediated by three organs: the nervous system connects with the body (through coenesthesis); the sensory organs connect with the outer world; and the brain mediates the reflection of its own internal changes and the reproduction of concepts through the inner sense, the imagination. Consequently, mental disorders can arise only through these three routes.

But, then, how is insanity possible at all? The nervous system has its own centers (nodes, networks) that are linked to the brain: "but diseases can cause them to jump off and, as rebel chiefs, lead their own campaigns independent of the brain.... In this state, the synthesis in the consciousness becomes lost. The soul virtually moves away from its moorings; a stranger in its own home, where it finds everything to be topsy-turvy, the soul has lost its mast and rudder and is forced to swim on the waves of creative fancy toward alien worlds, times, and spaces."[119] Insanity has here become the want of coherence due to a rebellious, egotistical-parasitical separatism, an image favored by Romantic psychiatry as the political demand for national unity in the body politic became the common analogy, and science itself was seen as a patriotic act. On the other hand, Reil sought to process Condillac's sensualist marble statue aesthetically and romantically. Thus the brain becomes an organ, a series of sounding boards conducting a stimulus, which if disturbed "gives rise to dissonances, leaps, abnormal ideas, similar associations, fixed ideas, and corresponding drives and actions.... That is how the brains of insane persons are constituted...One fiber in the brain slackens and the divine spark within us turns into a fairy tale."[120]

Invoking the idea of the treason of the clergy, Reil, in the tradition of the Enlightenment, created a space for the material, organic explanation of the pathogenesis of mental diseases: "The priestlings in particular used them as their special weapon and mask to trick the rabble and force it into the yoke of their religious despotism."[121] Insanity can arise only via the three indicated organic paths. Here coenesthesis no longer has any relation to Kant's theoretical categories, and certainly not to a critical, political common sense. Its function is individual "private" self-preservation — through physical sensations and the concepts determined by the physical state, feelings of pleasure and displeasure, drives and sympathies, on which temperament, temper, passions, and habits build.[122] Constant physical stimuli thereby lead via coenesthesis to hysteria, hypochondria, abnormal drives, and delusive ideas about one's body (as, for example, the feeling that one's head is made of glass), while derangements of the extra-sensory organs produce false perceptions and derangements of the brain itself — as in Kant — cause the antirational dominance of the imagination and of the passions. Even though Reil sees insanity as a physical ailment, he yet believes that its manifestations differ with different people, for neither the soul nor its disorders are a single entity, but composites. Nor are the "rules of their construction" established, but "given by the individual in which they occur. Hence those who regard them as entities are bound to be confused."[123]

The true goal of the *Rhapsodies* was to adapt Western moral treatment as a "mental healing method" to German conditions. From now on, according to Reil's overall medical intention, mental treatment was to take its place alongside surgery and internal medicine in the treatment of all diseases, including somatic ones, for all methods have a material effect: "It is likely that the ultimate relative effects of all remedies, including the mental, consist in the transformation of the matter of the structure [of the organism]."[124] Unreason cannot, of course, be treated physically because it involves separations of very specific parts and disorders of the tenderest and most unstable substance. Therefore the mental healing method must be just as specific and selective in stirring or calming the soul and finding the specific methods of "rectifying the intemperance of the brain's vitality."[125]

Reil's description of these ways is both the height of unbridled Romantic fantasy as well as an example of "rationalist demonic nature."[126] And it can be downright ecstatic since this utopian blueprint remains free-floating and — in contrast to Western reformers — does not concern itself with the possibility of rectification by actual experience. Thus the lack of social prerequisites for coordinating reality and prior claims gave rise to a grotesque collection of assorted coercive measures against the alienated and mentally ill which were subsequently experimented with in institutions, and which led Neuburger to conclude that "the Germans seem to have excelled all other nations in the ingenuity of the torture which they sought to inflict upon their patients."[127]

The many approaches in mental therapy involved the coenesthesis and external sensations. "Thus we lead the patient from the lowest level of senselessness through a chain of mental stimuli to the full use of reason."[128] The pattern of this guidance prescribed that the patient first be broken, then brutalized and trained to absolute obedience, and having become abject, rewarded; first to involve him only passively and then actively. The commitment to an institution alone was designed to deprive the patient of all familiar supports, to confuse him, and make him a helpless tool in the hands of the doctors leading him to reason: a trip at night to a remote and unknown area; upon his arrival, sounds of drums and cannon to welcome him; keepers speaking in strange and sonorous tones. The appearance and character of the director are designed to make any resistance by the patient seem senseless: "Let his speech be terse, brief, and bright. The shape of his body should aid the soul and inspire fear and awe. He should be big, strong, muscular; his gait majestic, his mien stern, his voice stentorian." The therapeutic qualities of the physician or psychologist are like those of an artist: "Mostly he must extemporize the impressions to the patient's imagination and aspirations, depending on the situation and on his gift for forceful and surprising improvisation." Nonetheless, the therapy, to have the requisite forceful effect, usually requires "a few brutal passages through the nervous system." For instance: "Hoist the patient by a tackle block to a high vault so that he, like Absalom, may hover between heaven and earth; fire a cannon near him, approach him grimly with white-hot irons, hurl him into raging torrents, throw him in front of ferocious beasts...or let him sail through the air on fire-spewing dragons. A subterranean crypt, containing all the horrors ever seen in the realm of the ruler of hell, may be advisable, or perhaps a magical temple, in which, amid solemn music, the enchantment of a charming sorceress conjures up one glorious vision after another out of thin air."[129]

Special emphasis is put on torture. A selection from the repertoire: deprivation of food and drink, cold, the use of nauseants, emetics, and ptarmica, vesicants, setons, and scabies (because of the itching and inflammation), the application of white-hot iron to the neck vertebrae, or of hot sealing-wax to the palms, generally "the lower levels of torture," whipping with nettles or rods, submersion in a tub with live eels, corporal punishment, finally various fear-inducing and tormenting uses of water, such as walking across flimsy bridges or floating in leaky boats. But Reil also thinks of positive and pleasurable stimuli, especially after torture, as for instance good food, wine, perhaps even sexual access to a prostitute for the men, and for women, he believes that sexual intercourse and a possible pregnancy might be therapeutic — liberating the mind through the involvement of the polar opposite region of the body. Furthermore, Reil has a program of stimulation for every single sensory organ. He describes the effect of a piano constructed out of live cats, utilizes magnetism, and does not omit the theater: "The staff of the house should be well trained in acting so as to be able to play any role, depending on the needs of the individual patient, like the most expert illusionist," so that the physician can launch a frontal attack on the fixed ideas of the patient.[130] In sum, Reil's inventory of mental remedies was the fantastic-terroristic consequence of what was actually being done in England and France.

Reil's proposals for the reform of mental institutions were more practicable. He called for national public asylums to assure the absolute separation of the patients from their private sphere, to spread the small number of qualified physicians among a few large houses, and protect the patients from terrorization and citizens from wrongful commitment (e.g. in cases of inheritance disputes). Moreover, he recommended a strict division between therapeutic and custodial institutions. The therapeutic sanatorium should be located in a "pleasant setting" with all the features of a romantic "landscape." It should be somewhat like a dairy-farm and in no way be reminiscent of the previous institutions of confinement. Appropriate occupation is the uppermost principle. "Indolence and sloth disturb all order. Work makes well."[131] Since these were educational institutions, obstinacy was to be punished and malleability rewarded. The inmates were to be classified not according to station and disease, but rather according to individual peculiarities and the treatment plan. To assure the best chance of successful treatment, confinement in the earliest stages of the disease was advisable. The following is an integrative admission ticket into bourgeois society: "At first, every new aberrant patient is taught his lesson until he grows accustomed to obedience and is properly prepared for treatment,"[132] While during this relatively liberal and somatic phase the appeal to moral introspection remains in the background. The institutional board is composed of the chief supervisor, who is also responsible for the administration, the physician, and the "psychologist," who should be either a physician, philosopher, or preacher — proof that Reil does not quite know how to fit his new science or art into the classical faculties. The supervising personnel do not have to be government employees if they have the proper patriotic attitude. The staff, on the one hand, is merely the engine of the directors, but on the other hand, it also has representatives on the board of directors — a largely utopian democratic idea even today. Finally, Reil at least makes the demand that the institution should be a "nursery" for training young doctors: "The staff physicians would lecture on mental

diseases, mental treatment methods, and empirical psychology...
and would thereby have the opportunity of elucidating their
theoretical statements with examples."[133] Reil's psychiatry sheds
exemplary light on the consequences of the imbalance between
possible theory and impossible social practice.

Prussian Reform and French Influence

Reil's *Rhapsodies* created a stir — but more in a philosophical
than in an activating regard. Moreover, his appeal and his social
sanatorium utopia were still too liberal and emancipatory, not
sufficiently pedagogically integrative to satisfy the Prussian social
reformers. And without the protective cover of natural philosophy
his basic assumptions were too somatic-materialistic to be accepted by a medicine not yet oriented toward natural science. And
thus Germany found itself in the unique situation where professors of philosophy or medicine lectured about the insane and
mental therapeutics and wrote papers about them before the
subjects themselves — the mentally ill poor — gained social visibility, i.e. before they if not through revolution, then at least
through a series of social reforms, had expanded so greatly that
the layers of sequestered unreason became visible to bourgeois
society and their integration became a necessity. And in fact, the
Prussian reformers furnished the impetus for the practical reform
in the treatment of the insane, as did a minority of physicians
who, natural philosophy notwithstanding, were adherents of
idealist philosophy.

The characteristics that marked social reforms in Germany in
general also marked the insanity reform. The Prussian reform
movement had its beginning in the 1790s. Thus the serfs were
freed in 1805, and von Stein's abolition of internal tariffs in 1804
was a step toward economic progress. The proximity of revolutionary France and the economic blossoming of the French-
occupied territories on the left bank of the Rhine strengthened
the swelling demand for reform. However, radical measures
touching the very structure of society became possible only after
the Prussian defeat in 1806—07 showed up the weakness of the
feudal state. The resistance of the nobility was temporarily shaken,
and in pleading their cause the reformers appealed to the idea
of patriotism. The differences became evident in 1807, when
Hardenberg charged that the Universal Prussian Land Law of
1794, progressive in its intention, was designed "for a nation of

swindlers and criminals."[134] The reforms in the various social
areas — self-administration of towns, liberation of peasants,
choice of trade, equal rights for Jews, military and educational
reform — initiated in 1807—08 were marked and in part made
possible by the fact that the reformers succeeded in making
themselves, the administration, the actual sovereign,[135] to replace
the monarchic with "bureaucratic absolutism," thus largely
equating politics with administration.[136] This was the result of
the powerlessness of the citizenry demanding political and economic rights. This defense of bourgeois liberalism against the de
facto power of the aristocracy with its influence at court led B. G.
Niebuhr to the "insight that freedom rests disproportionately
more on the administration than on the constitution."[137] The
leadership claim of the bureaucrats sounded like a version of
Frederick the Great's "Everything for the people, nothing by the
people." Nevertheless, it was accepted by the citizenry, especially
since they were interested more in national liberation than in
political liberty and, later on, more in national unity than in the
constitution.

This situation gave the overall reform its basic character, and
the reformers, mostly Kantians, the conviction that society was
"malleable," that it could be steered without revolution toward
the fulfillment of an idealistic world plan. Whereas von Stein,
when catastrophe struck, was still committed to the idea of the
public weal, even if by way of established administrative channels,
Hardenberg, Schön, and Altenstein were swayed by the free-trade
interests of the East Prussian landowners, by the Königsberg
disciples of Adam Smith and Kant's pragmatic reason. The destruction of class institutions and the re-ordering of society along the
principles of free access to property and education, equality
before the law of parties to a labor contract, and freedom of competition paved the way for the sort of economic expansion enjoyed
by England and France. But this did not aim at granting political
rights to the bourgeoisie, but rather at preserving and strengthening
the authority of the government more effectively. The intention
was "an economically free society politically subservient to the
state."[138]

As in the Western countries, the initial impact of the reforms
spelled the ruin of countless small farmers and artisans. The ranks
of a "liberated," newly visible rabble, were further swelled by the
mass release of so-called cloister paupers in the wake of the mandated closing of numerous monasteries of cloisters. And the
traditional, mercantilist institutions of sequestration, the prisons,

and poor- and work-houses became engulfed in the crisis of social
reorganization. They accorded neither with the general liberal
principles nor with the needs of a nascent capitalist industry. So
they were disbanded or dismantled, and, according to the social
usefulness of their inmates, reconstituted as new differentiating
and practical institutions — a process that had begun in the 1780s,
but now gradually assumed quantitative importance. Particularly
within the framework of this constitutive process for liberal
economic society, the reformers, almost to a man, became interested in the reform in the problem of insanity. It should be noted
that the comprehensive reformist claim to social planning was
based on both the idealistic obligation of the state to educate
its citizens toward a freedom and reason as well as social responsibility — which went back to the welfare provisions of the
Universal Prussian Land Law. In 1817, Hardenberg and J. G.
Hoffmann, who was influenced by Owen, still feared that "the
training for factory labor" would be "at the expense of the
education toward decency and good citizenship." And they
postulated: "The constitution of the state unmistakably contains
the means of assuring youth the freedom that could protect it
against being spoiled early in life."[139] "The state," according to
Koselleck, "was virtually to serve as an institution for the prevention of alienation, which Hardenberg saw as the inevitable result
of the development of the world of technology."[140] But the
Restoration, and even more so the increasing power of industry,
thwarted the fulfillment of the reform demands. To the extent
that the state refused the social responsibility demanded by
economic liberalism, this problem, as a "social question" along
with that of the constitution, became the core issue of the political movement of a bourgeoisie alienated from or opposed to the
state. But that did not happen until the so-called *Vormärz*, the
prerevolutionary period between 1815 and the March Revolution
of 1848.

The educational reform faced similar difficulties. In reforming
the school system, the state maintained the direct means of
guiding the youth according to its precepts, replacing traditional
rote teaching with the free development of personal gifts, while
still demanding moral responsibility and reasonable conduct of
the citizens. The aims of the army reform were similar (instructive
particularly for the style of contemporary reform of institutionalized insanity). The purely mechanical punishments (e.g. lashings
and running the gauntlet) and drill for its own sake were to be
replaced by a sense of honor and duty, i.e. internalized restraint,

training in independent, rational action, education, and patriotism. All this showed the influence of Kant and the experience of the superiority of Napoleon's people's army.[141] However, the educational claim of the state also made the realization of morality the responsibility of the state — as not only Hegel had postulated. This hampered the development of the principle of Western societies of the "subordination of the state to the moral judgment of the citizens," the political public.[142] Beyond that the expansion of industry revealed that "the state's claim to universal education in fact stopped at the gates of factories and the shacks of home-workers."[143] This restricted the area of the bourgeoisie's critical moral and social common sense for independent public action. Education thus led merely to "an inner molding of the personality ...a pluralistic individual ethic, but not any true social ethic." The authoritarian power state was confronted by the educated, cultured state. "Since the duty of obedience to absolute, positive law was established from the very outset, no special problems of social ethics beyond that could exist.... Since the state was the highest embodiment of a social community, one could also expect from it the highest possible realization of welfare."[144] Nor were the churches able to activate political self-awareness and socio-ethical activity on the part of the citizenry, as happened in England. On the contrary: in most of the German states, the autonomous administrations of the Protestant churches in particular became mere appendages of the state ministries, and the political role of the churches became more and more limited, especially since the Restoration, to the propagation of monarchic state pietism and the unity of "throne and altar."[145] And even after Hardenberg's death (1822) after Prussian adminsitrative absolutism had ceased to be liberal, it took some time and involved the industrialization of the economy in the 1830s and hence the irrefutable evidence of the social question, before at least some segments of the citizenry were able to see through the myth of the identity of administration and politics, and looking beyond economic interests and idealistic or Romantic educational elitism, arrive at a social self-consciousness aimed at political change.

The practical insanity reform in Germany, that is to say, the emancipation of the unreason of insanity from rationalistic segregation and mechanical coercion, the differentiation of the insane according to curability and social utility, and their social integration began in Bayreuth in 1805. Diverse factors accounted for this situation. First and foremost, this reform was an integral component of Prussian reforms that adjusted society to the economic development. This is shown by the very fact that this reform was not based on Reil's Romantic theory but on the cooperation of Hardenberg and Langermann, a disciple of Kant and Fichte, although the way had been paved by the Romantic view of irrationality as an "internal experience" of the age.

Next, we must note that French approaches to insanity had already been tried on German soil even before the Prussian reforms. In the French-occupied territories on the left bank of the Rhine, the destruction of the feudal power structure allowed free economic activity to unfold. Later, the *Code Napoléon* was introduced there, and, in accordance with the French principle of regional administration, plans for universal health care, and for hospitals in Cologne, Neuss, Coblenz, Trier, and Mainz, were drawn up. "What basically distinguished the Napoleonic civic hospitals of the early nineteenth century was the distinct desire to reshape an entire area...in terms of the new welfare concept on the principles of equality and fraternity."[146] Thus in Cologne, "At the end of the eighteenth century, the care of sick and helpless people, of the insane and invalids, was still almost exclusively in the hands of charitable organizations. They were housed in convents; in 1790 Cologne still had 39. Most of them were disbanded when the city was occupied by French troops, and others were put under a hospital commission. Saint Cecilia's cloister and Saint Michael's were combined into the Cologne Civic Hospital, the first real hospital of the modern era."[147] The year was 1803. Here, as in the other Rhenish towns, all *citoyens* were entitled to care — a concept hitherto alien to Christian *Caritas*. A distinction was made between curable and incurable patients. Separate, albeit wretched accommodations were provided for the insane. In this way, the welfare commission had a pioneering effect on the administrative care of mental patients, though not yet on specifically psychiatric treatment. Shortly thereafter Munich instituted similar measures.

An imperial decree of 1803 had a similar salutary effect. Not only did it make those cast out as irrational more visible, it also made available to the local governments innumerable vacated monasteries, cloisters, and castles for conversion to factories and as separate, inexpensive quarters for the "liberated" insane. These "adapted" institutions on the one hand allowed the implementation of reform plans relating to insanity, while on the other, their thick walls and cells inhibited the development of individualized psychiatric therapy and encouraged the patriarchalism that marked German insane asylums. Nevertheless, it is remarkable that within three months after the decree of 1803, President von Stein seized the opportunity and instructed von Vincke, a regional official, to draw up plans for an insane asylum for the Prussian provinces on the other side of the Weser River.[148]

Finally, even in the early stages of the Prussian reform, admission to insane asylums was subject to legal restrictions by decree of September 29, 1803. To be sure, madmen and imbeciles — as they were designated — were still looked on as public dangers instead of as sick individuals amenable to treatment, as persons against whom the public had to be protected by the local police authorities. Only after official certification of madness or idiocy — after 1840 this could be done retroactively — could the respective local authorities order institutionalization. In 1825, the minister of justice made commitment subject to more stringent regulation by decreeing that in every instance a finding of idiocy had to be submitted without regard to person. It was only in 1839 that a decree by the minister of education allowed for the possibility that in the case of institutionalization for the purpose of treatment the certification of idiocy might be waived — because of the expenses and the damaging publicity.[149] Having found a sponsor at the Saxon court, J. G. Langermann (1768–1832), the son of a peasant, was able to study law and theology at Leipzig. When he sounded a call for university reforms there, the administration forced him out. He went to Jena in 1794, where he was introduced to philosophy by Fichte and to medicine by Hufeland. Novalis was among his students, and had personal contact with Goethe, Schiller, and Haydn. His dissertation (1797) on melancholia was his only psychiatric work. Hardenberg, impressed by him and his legal background recruited him for the medical board. He wrote a work on yellow fever which he dedicated to von Stein. After five years of work on behalf of insanity reform in Bayreuth, he became a State councillor in 1810, joined the Board of Censors in 1819, and drawn to veterinary medicine, became head of the Berlin School of Veterinary Medicine. Although not a psychiatrist, and regarding the reform in the area of insanity as merely one of many reform and administrative tasks, he became an advocate of ethical psychiatry. As a disciple of Kant, Fichte, and Windischmann, he opposed materialism in medicine, as well as magnetism and homeopathy, and said that his activities within the narrower circle of the Prussian reformers were pedagogically motivated.

Langermann's dissertation[150] also is not based on firsthand experience with "visible" mental defectives, but rather a theoretical treatment of the relevant literature from a Fichtian standpoint, an inquiry into the therapeutic possibilities in view of their irrationality. This and Fichte's "moral idea" induced him to take up Stahl's concept of insanity as an idiopathic disorder of the soul and to defend it polemically against the supernatural explanations of theologians and the somatic explanations of physicians (including Reil). Accordingly, the soul suffers from itself, from a conscious, misdirected striving, from a passion, which is why diagnosis — a Kantian conclusion — grows out of the qualities of the individual: his constitution, temperament, character, and "pathematology," the psychology of the passions. Langermann's subjective-idealistic conception of an "almost identical relationship between passions and insanity"[151] pushes him beyond both Stahl's and Kant's rationalistic belief in the incurability of insanity, to the renunciation of natural law. Thus he became the first to believe in the curability of self-produced and induced irrationality. For just as the insane must be held morally responsible for their irrationality, one can also call upon the remnant of their reason to exercise their moral duty of self-correction. That is the basis of the sublime profession of the psychiatrist, who, like an educator dealing with the misconduct and outbursts of children, has to gather and shape the souls of the "misguided" and the "dispersed" to the object-world, and to tame the passions. In this context corporal punishment, hot irons, and other methods of torture are advisable if the physical condition permits. Just as Reil arrived at the idea of torture in the treatment of insanity via natural philosophy and coenesthesis, so Langermann with pedagogical rigor arrives at a similar conclusion via reason as an ethical duty. As proof of the validity of this concept we are repeatedly told that stoic old-wives' tale that those who are sound of mind cannot become mentally ill.[152]

On May 28, 1804, Langermann submitted the plan "regarding the changes in the insane asylum of Bayreuth" Hardenberg had asked for. He took for granted that the plan was meant for the insane poor; the wealthy were to be housed separately. Since the asylum was supposed to serve a dual purpose — the treatment of inmates and the protection of the public — it was to admit all the poor thought to be curable, as well as all who were thought to be dangerous, even if incurable. Because of the public nature of the institution legal commitment was not necessary. The only distinction made was between rich and poor and by sex. In contrast to Reil's exclusively curative institution, Langermann's plan recommended the commitment of curable and incurable patients, if for no other reason than because an individual determination was frequently not possible. Of course, he said, we still lacked "an anthropology concerning the dynamics of the soul," but given the similarity between the mentally deranged and children, it is possible to arrive at the correct therapy by applying the pedagogic methods developed by Pestalozzi. Among the basic elements in the healing process are exercising the mind; physical activity even if senseless; strict authority, which can come from only one person, the physician; punishments — and equally rigorous disciplinary regulations for the attendants. Preachers do not make good therapists since they pursue different objectives; for insanity is not now equated with sin. Langermann rejects Willis and Pinel, and he believes that Reil's grottos and parks actually increase the "dispersal" of the insane, who can, after all, only "make themselves over" through physical work and free mental exercise, since reason, i.e. receptivity to moral law, educability, has not been completely extinguished in them.

Hardenburg's response, in the form of a decree to the Bayreuth chamber of February 1805, concurred with most of Langermann's positions and his "outstandingly fine and correct" treatment plan formed the basis for the reorganization of the Bayreuth asylum, the "first mental sanatorium in Germany." This was the first official recognition that insanity was a curable sickness. It demonstrated, said Hardenberg, the progress of psychology and medicine, and since the state was obligated to lend assistance to those unfortunates, and also to science, mental therapy would henceforth be the recommended method in the treatment of insanity — and moreover Langermann's, not Reil's. And Reil was found suspect by Prussian officialdom: his emphatic protests, his utopian irrationality, his democratic notions of organization, his joy-focused therapy, and his materialism, were seen as unpredictably Romantic, destructive tendencies that threatened the moral order. Langermann, who laid the blame for their disorders on the victims themselves and held them subject to moral law, posed no such threat. But Langermann's external order did not strike Hardenberg as secure enough, and so the physician's powers were restricted: supervision continued to rest with the Chamber, the legal commitment by the judiciary was retained, and a War and Dominion Councilor was appointed co-director with the physician. The employment of a salaried teacher underscored the pedagogical character of the plan. The physician's salary was small since he was expected to earn more from his rich, separately housed private patients. This financially practical arrangement did, of course, induce some medical directors to concentrate far more devotedly on the real source of their income and potential wealth than on the impecunious patients.

Of all psychiatrists, Langermann both personally and professionally best matched the bureaucratic and pedagogical absolutism of the Prussian reformers. Langermann's concept of the newly visible insane brought essential aspects of the image of man in their reforms into sharp focus. He identified the social integration of the insane with the extension of the claim to absoluteness of moral law and the responsibility of the rational personality to the irrational as well. He had no doubt that, given sufficient strength of will, even stupid individuals could become rational. Fools, the later psychopaths, were to be shown no mercy; they probably did not like the institution. Nor was he willing to exculpate completely those insane who committed crimes or suicide.[153] It was not a medical theory but rather his administratively and scientifically mediated philosophy that persuaded him in the name of moral law to sanction pedagogical instruction as well as military discipline and mechanical punishments, to help the insane poor find themselves and thus let them share in civic freedom.

Langermann's authority for a long time marked the idealistic efforts in Berlin to force reason on the insane. They eclipsed the approach at Bayreuth, for after the fire of 1798, the inmates were provisionally sent to the Charité Hospital (for budgetary reasons), i.e. under the control of physicians, and because Ernst Horn (1774–1848), a professor of practical medicine and, since 1806, the assistant medical director of the Charité, enthusiastically began to experiment with the new treatment methods of the mental patients. In his defense against his dismissal in 1818 he cited his emancipatory achievements: he was the first to separate the vegetating mental defectives from the syphilitics and scabies victims of both sexes; he had replaced chains with more liberal security devices, had rejected traditional medicaments as senseless, and had introduced a school curriculum (e.g. geography); and he had also delivered the first psychiatric lectures ever in Germany.[154]

But what was his regime like in other respects? His self-justification of 1818 is probably the best document on the expansion of the bourgeois rule of reason to the unreason of insanity within the context of the Prussian reform period. Although Horn maintained that his method was designed to affect the deranged patients physically in Reil's sense through coenesthesis, there was also the specifically Prussian idealistic excess of military harshness, forced obedience, and a sense of moral obligation that castigated all philanthropy as a Romantic weakness without parallel in the

West. All this made Horn, the disciple of Fichte a worthy successor of Langermann. The minutely planned daily routine began and closed with uplifting religious exercises. A variety of approaches and devices — therapy, education, discipline, and sadistic punishment — were used indiscriminately. If hundreds of pails of cold water were poured down from above or powerful jets of water were aimed at the sexual organ or the head was packed in ice or subjected to water torture, the explanation was: "It is conducive to the behavior, obedience, and discipline of the insane; it restores speech to mutes; it stills the drive of those who would take their own lives; it brings the quiet melancholic...back to self-consciousness; it...serves excellently in some cases to instill fear or as a punishment to maintain order and peace."[155] According to Horn's rationalization, the rotary machine, which could be operated by one attendant and could attain a speed of 120 revolutions per minute, made obstreperous patients compliant and indolent ones industrious. Appliances designed to keep a patient erect and immobilized for more than twelve hours, used both as therapy or punishment, were actually used by private practitioners. Sparing a patient "with effeminate sentimentality" was medically wrong and, moreover, sinful; total dedication to duty was the first principle which raises the question of the difference between the physician and the judge at the witch trials of old, who tortured the body to save the soul. Horn believed that work made people free, and since forced labor had proved economically ineffective, it became a moral end in itself, performed reluctantly and pointlessly. At the Charité ditches were dug and filled in again and patients were harnessed to a wagon and ordered to pull their fellow inmates across the grounds of the institution. Military drills were considered an effective method of winning compliance, which was equated with health. This therapeutic device, which soon reached other German institutions, was supervised by a military man, a former patient, and was also used with females. As in the army itself, disobedience and indolence were punished by drills with sand-filled backpacks. In the end, Horn became the victim of one of his therapeutic torture instruments — "Horn's Bag," in which maniacal patients were tied from head to foot to restrict their freedom of movement and kept in darkness. In 1818 he was charged with involuntary manslaughter in the death of a patient so confined, which put an end to his work at the Charité.

This Prussian therapy was thus not so much a question of medical skill as of a pedagogic-military, authoritarian imposition of reason and moral duty — with liberal intention. For the insane, the arbitrary coercion of absolutism was replaced by the legally sanctioned coercion of the people who, according to the liberal but ultimately unsuccessful hopes of the Prussian reformers, were to be administratively revolutionized "from above" into civil society. Yet, even though the chains fell, the mechanical and physically punitive coercion of the insane continued unabated — as it did throughout the West. Granted, exotic and painful coercive measures were invoked in France and England and some, not all, had even originated there. But, in those countries they were not developed with the perfectionism and claim to absoluteness or applied so assiduously and skillfully as in Germany.[156] This can only be understood in context. At the time of the proposed reform, England and France both in actuality and in self-consciousness, possessed something toward which society sought to raise the mentally ill, into which they sought to integrate them, and for which they wanted to make them economically useful: a bourgeois society created by them in a bourgeois revolution containing normatively obligating political public institutions that guaranteed individual elbowroom.

On the one hand, this created the social conditions for applying the natural sciences within the framework of a compatible philosophical tradition — medico-somatically and psychologically — to the unreason of insanity, particularly to the ideas on the treatment of the insane, which in this case and at this time, had a humanizing effect. On the other hand, bourgeois society and its conviction that it itself was the source of its disorders first created the premises for a socially oriented therapy for the insane. This set in motion the process we described as the internalization of coercion, in which mechanical-physical restraint increasingly turned into mental and moral-social restraint. Thus the question of humanitarian progress becomes idle, for the inner coercion imposed upon the insane through psychological means within the framework of moral management inflicted unnecessary suffering on them. What mattered was the fact that the insane were drawn into the dialectics of adjustment to the existing moral and social norms of established bourgeois society, and thereby into a social comparison with the other, "normal" citizens and their social demands. It thus became possible to assign a variety of factors a role in the treatment: the philosophy of common sense, of liberal-economic utilitarianism, romantic, religious, and other forms of the social movement; sensualist-positivist assumptions of the ideologues, and sociosomatic theories of the instincts. In this way, treatment was related to the tangible goal of the emancipatory integration of the insane, to the real (or desirable) conditions of bourgeois society. Nevertheless, in practice this made possible "Non-Restraint," and in theory, a mutually fruitful discussion of psychiatrists both with sociology and medicine, and through it, the most essential and irreplaceable elements of a scientific psychiatry.

These conditions did not exist in Germany for a Langermann, Horn, or Reil, in the face of widespread resistance, nor could the Prussian reforms institute them permanently and far-reachingly. That, so it seems, is the basic reason for the "Prussian approach" to insanity reform and for what is thought to be the paradox in the origin of German psychiatry: the discrepancy between the ethical idealism of its claim and the brutality of the means employed in its realization. Where the therapeutic internalization of restraint found no correspondence in the not yet functioning socio-moral norms of bourgeois society, where it could not be satisfied with social comparison and adjustment, where there were "no real social ethics" it could rely on, the practical desire to heal, hampered in its social realization, tends to become subjective and idealistic, "pure," and to invoke the absoluteness of the state and moral duty. Just as the cause of insanity was sought not so much in the physical or social environment but within the subject (from individual nature, predisposition, the idiopathic spiritual factor, conscious irrationality and immorality, to religious sin), and so the blame in whatever form is put on the subject, so the curability of insanity was founded more and more on the postulate that the subject, even in the state of insanity, must be made responsible to reason and to the absoluteness of moral law. It was ultimately this absoluteness that authorized, or even obligated the psychiatrist to restore the patient at virtually any price — save that of his life — to his own self, i.e. to his duty, to the rule of reason and of moral law. This "therapeutic idealism" therefore held it a duty to tax the patient physically and mentally with any conceivable means to the limits of his endurance, whether this meant the torture of all his faculties, the education of the mind, pedagogical activity devoid of all social utility, a religious appeal to self-examination, military drill, order and obedience as an administrative end in itself, and the entire spectrum of punishments of dependent persons going back to feudal times — and still widely accepted in Germany — and from the arsenal of punishments and tortures of criminal law.[157]

In those German states and provinces that had been exposed to Western ideas, whether through the revolutionary French rule change in the administrative and social structure in French-occupied territories; or through indirect French influence in the German territories, for instance the states of the Rhenish Confederation and the southwestern states which early on drafted a constitution, the reform of insanity soon overtook Prussia's. The territories in question were the Rhineland, Westphalia, Saxony, Baden, Württemberg, and Bavaria. True, their asylums were not as scientific as those of Prussia, but the idealism of the Prussian theoreticians was humanized by the French-materialistic practitioners of the "provinces" and adjusted it to the — still patriarchal — reality. And the specific mixture of these influences varied greatly from place to place. The desire to learn was overwhelming. When it turned out that the wars, the Continental blockade, and the patriotic movement prevented Prussian psychiatry from keeping abreast of Western progress, German physicians began to travel far more extensively than their Western colleagues. Study trips by psychiatrists, notably to France and England, became well-nigh obligatory after 1810, until the Franco-Prussian War put a temporary nationalistic stop to the flow of international scientific exchange. The "institutional tour" frequently was a prerequisite for appointment as medical director of an asylum. And scholarly literature in no small part consisted of comparative travel accounts. The plaque over the gate of the first asylum in Marsberg, Westphalia is characteristic of the emphasis on travel and for the new public nature of the insanity issue:

Every educated stranger, especially physicians passing through who wish to visit this insane asylum and hospital out of sympathy for their fellow men residing herein should register with the director, who will personally guide them through the house and, at their behest, show them those patients and inmates who can tolerate a visit by outsiders without harm to their mental condition. Experts are requested to tell the director frankly of any faults or defects they may discover, or any proposal they care to make toward improving the institution, or else set down their remarks in the conference room of the board of directors of the state hospital either open or sealed.

This cooperative relationship between institutional psychiatrists led to the development and independent practical as well as scientific self-confidence in their confrontation with the theoreticians of idealistic or natural philosophy, and later in the nineteenth century, these psychiatrists spearheaded a psychiatry based on experience, somatically oriented and influenced by the French experience.

The asylum at Sonnenstein-Pirna (Saxony), founded in 1811,

was representative of the emergence of German psychiatry outside Prussia. In the process of lifting the sequestration of the mentally ill, the typically mercantilistic prison dating back to 1716 was broken up and the inmates divided up: the criminals were sent to correctional institutions at Zwickau and Lichtenburg; the children to an orphan asylum at Langendorf; the incurably insane and other invalids remained at Waldheim, which was turned into a simple nursing home, while the curable mental patients were sent to the refurbished former fortress Sonnenstein, the first exclusively mental hospital in Germany.

As in Prussia, this reform likewise was imposed "from above." But unlike Hardenberg, Saxony's head of state, G. A. E. Von Nostitz und Jänkendorf, an anti-Romantic poet who had written an account of Sonnenstein,[158] in 1805—6 put C. A. F. Hayner and E. Pienitz, the physicians in charge of the reform, to study with Pinel and Esquirol. Hayner, a former theologian, disbanded Waldheim in 1807, drafted the plan for Sonnenstein, but stayed on as director at Waldheim with his incurable "brothers and sisters." Hayner, perhaps the most credible contemporary advocate of humanization, addressed countless petitions to the authorities protesting abuses, championing Pinel against Reil, and exposing the resort to old coercive methods under the pretext of new idealistic, pedagogical reforms: "Cursed be every stroke against a miserable creature of this pitiable class of sufferers: I cry woe to any man, be he of high station or low, who suffers people devoid of sense to be beaten!"[159] In the restraint of violent patients, Hayner allowed only the intermittent use of a strait-jacket under constant observation, and Autenrieth's padded "palisades chamber."[160] Yet Hayner also devised new machines, for instance the "hollow wheel," similar to the small wheels squirrels or birds run in to the point of exhaustion. The purpose, so he explained, was the then highly touted one of bringing the confused person back to his senses, of pulling the self-absorbed individual from his dream world to the real world,"[161] renewed proof that identity, the dominant theme of the time, was not merely an epistemological problem but increasingly motivated by the bourgeois quest for social identity. The humanitarian reformers gradually and surreptitiously became the instruments promoting the absorption of the insane who lacked social identity, and thus were an affront, into the discipline of the industrializing society and bring them into harmony with the requisite reason.

Pienetz (1777—1853), on the other hand, became the medical and administrative director of Sonnenstein, where he first applied the French *traitement moral*. His French wife — Esquirol had been a witness at their wedding — was fully involved in the treatment, in keeping with the idea of the institution as an extended family. The therapeutic approach also brought social differences to the fore. Pienitz distinguished between eminent, moderately eminent, and simple people. The funds for the last-named group were geared to the size of the community that was footing the costs, the degree of curability, and the perceived social danger. In addition there was a private home for melancholics. This economic gradation helped Pienitz amass a fair amount of wealth, though to be sure, some on the lowest level were treated free of charge.[162] Sonnenstein also introduced the important socio-psychiatric principle that an institution, if at all possible, should keep in touch with its released patients. Finally, Pienitz (1828) and Hayner (1833) managed to get rid of convict-attendants, a practice favored by Langermann for reasons of economy.

In Baden, too, the French influence played a part in the realization of social principles; the efforts for the emancipation of the insane were no doubt indicative of this process. In 1804, Baden appointed the first psychiatrist, J. C. Roller (the district medical officer in charge of insane asylums and hospitals for chronic diseases) to the Pforzheim asylum. From there, in 1826, the inmates were moved to the new asylum at Heidelberg, whose first director, F. Gross (1768–1852), a liberal supporter of the revolution, campaigned for legal reform and the right of mental patients, and mediated between idealistic and somatic psychiatry.

Baden was also the first German state to initiate the legal emancipation of the Jews with the constitutional edicts of 1807–1808. As everywhere in Germany, however — and unlike France — but no differently from Germany's emancipation of the insane — the emancipation of Jews was conceived as a protracted educational process with various coercive measures for testing the morality and rationality of the objects of liberation.[163] The fact of Württemberg's economic and political backwardness compared to Baden was borne out both by the later start of emancipation of the Jews (1828) and by the foot-dragging in the matter of an insane asylum. Before that was built all that was done was to move the inmates in 1812 from the overcrowded asylum of Ludwigsburg to the Zwiefalten Monastery, an institution sheltering a mixed clientele.[164]

In 1812 Hesse likewise opened a hospital for the chronically ill and the insane at Hofheim. In 1821, L. F. Amelung came to Hofheim to try to apply the experience gathered in his travels abroad, namely, to treat the insane as adults, and to abolish all mechanical restraints. His failure proved the futility of good will if — as the English Non-Restraint movement had demonstrated — the external and social conditions of the asylum (architecture, number and quality of attendants, etc.) are not first looked into and attuned to the emancipatory view of insanity. This in turn depended on how lively was the interest of society and the administration in the social question. Thus accidents occurred when Amelung tried to remove the bars from the three-story asylum to do away with all reminders of the time when the insane were confined in prisons. Amelung was killed by a violent patient (1849) — a not infrequent fate of psychiatrists, particularly the liberal champions of emancipation.

In 1814, in the Duchy of Westphalia, a Capucine monastery was turned into the mixed institution of Marsberg. The plans had been drawn up in 1811, during the reign of Jerôme Bonaparte. For this purpose, Dr. Stoll gathered the first statistics on the number of mentally ill in a German state. W. Ruer was appointed medical director of Marsberg. His treatment method tended toward the Reil/Horn rigor. But Marsberg also sparked movements that augmented the inventory of practices making up the institution of psychiatry. Thus Ruer launched a program of public enlightenment about insanity, and it began to dawn on people that the treatment of the insane must include the "treatment" of society itself. Ruer, like countless other psychiatrists who followed in his enlightened footsteps, was motivated by patriotism, the desire to improve the German nation and help bring about national unity. That was why he also edited the patriotic *Vaterländische Blätter* in the Duchy of Westphalia.

Furthermore, Ruer tackled the still unsolved problem of the staff, i.e. the people who have the closest and most frequent contact with the patients. The reformers did not want ex-jailers or ex-prisoners or ex-patients. But the only ones willing to take these jobs were people unable to make an honest living, who were therefore ready to attend lunatics and idiots, creatures on the lowest social level — surrounded as they were by an aura of menace and filth (Reil even thought that the insane gave off a special odor), all the things repugnant to religion, reason, and morality, that were either part of or ascribed to them. But what was needed for this job, which involved constant and unpredictable dangers to life and health and was miserably paid, were unbiased, enlightened, loving people, able to accept abuse and insult without thoughts of vengefulness or punishment. To deal with this problem, Ruer, in 1819, added a third pedagogical condition to his system. Not only the insane and society but the personnel as well had to be educated.[165] He introduced systematic training and qualifying examinations for his attendants, which were recognized by the government of Arnsberg.

French influence was also indirectly responsible for the first new mental institution on (later) German soil: in then Danish Schleswig, erected in 1817–20. Ever since the Rousseauian Struensee, state minister and physician, Denmark had been under the sway of French reformism. The Schleswig institution combined protection with treatment. Its architecture combined elements of Vienna's fools' tower, Bentham's Panopticon, and, above all, Esquirol's reformist building style. Its first medical director was P. W. Jessen (1793–1875). Having completed the compulsory institutional tour of Europe, he returned with skepticism about therapeutic rigorism. He found that the treatment of insanity in France and England involved less mental torment, but was just as effective as in Germany. On the theoretical plane he learned of Bell's discoveries about the sensory-motor nervous system which he tried to fit into analogous natural-philosophic categories and phenomena. However, he was among those natural philosophers who in the prerevolutionary natural-scientific era revised their ideas and tried to base their theories on provable medical findings. Accordingly, he arrived at more liberal ideas about social etiology and concluded that man "is inhibited, hampered, and oppressed in his free development only by the burden and care of life, through a want of education...."[166] As a prominent co-founder of the Association of German Alienists in 1806, Jessen, with reference to the Schleswig-Holstein question, emphasized the "national achievement" this founding represented.

Finally, the French occupation helped to improve the treatment of the mentally ill in Hanover. G. H. Bergmann (1781–1861), the physician responsible for this improvement, had studied in Paris under Broussais and Laennec (pathological anatomy). Differentiation among inmates had been tried in the old prison of Celle, in 1806, and a special section for the insane was set up. Bergmann joined this institution in 1810. His therapeutic method followed the French cerebral approach. In 1827, he combined two monasteries in Hildesheim to produce the type of institution that was to become prototypical for nineteenth-century Germany. This was the "combined mental home and hospital" after the mixed type and the absolute separation of a pure mental home had proved impractical. Commitment to a pure mental hospital had always seemed like a death verdict to the public, and psychiatrists, as they turned from theory to observation, had come to see how unreliable were their prognoses about curability or incurability. The solution was to bring all mentally ill, albeit differentiated, into one institutional complex.

In the theoretical area, Bergman brought phrenology to Germany. But as in the case of Jessen and others, it turned out that this "Germanization" was possible only in the guise of a mystifying natural philosophy. Bergman invoked the Schelling disciples G. H. Schubert and I. P. V. Troxler as well as Novalis and the Hegelian Rosenkranz. French cerebral psychiatry and German natural philosophy gave rise to the combination typical for the first somatically oriented German psychiatrists: the brain as the seat of insanity and faith in the immortal soul, unsullied by disease — the eternal spiritual principle — which appears as changeable only through the prism of life in the material organ. With the help of his investigations in brain anatomy, Bergmann modified Gall. If the cerebral cortex was the decisive organ for Gall, then for Bergmann it was the surface of the cerebral ventricles. Here he discovered tender marrow fibers, which he called "chords," and turned them into a sort of keyboard for the brain pneuma to play on. This connection was characteristic of the condition of German psychiatry: between empiricist discoveries and also the belief in their "progressiveness," and the effort to integrate their revolutionary effects by means of natural-philosophical systematization, even through a flight into the past, like Bergmann's recourse to the old spirit theory. This ambivalence between political, economic, and scientific ideas from the West and the German reaction to them also recurred in Bergmann's institutional practice. His hospital was attuned to physical influences and offered a variety of outdoor activities, including viniculture; he campaigned for public enlightenment, encouraged public and family participation, and introduced training courses for physicians. Yet he was autocratic, adopted the Prussian drill, and invented mystical explications for the curative powers of galvanism or organ music.[167]

This somewhat broad outline stresses the variety of the contemporaneous non-Prussian attempts as opposed to the spectacular Prussian example, the intensity and diversity of French influences, and, in connection with that, the countless practical elements of a possible psychiatric paradigm, found, or adapted, in the many small states that dotted the map of Germany. That these elements, nevertheless, were initially presented as concepts of philosophical-psychiatric theories, above all in Prussia, was primarily due to the fact that these theories represented the most distinguished and most universal national means of communication, especially after the Wars of Liberation. All in all, prerevolutionary German psychiatry was stamped by philosophical speculation rather than by the needs of the patients, despite the opposing trends from the lower level of institutional practitioners who were dealing with the palpable social situation. And it is enough of an indictment that the contrast that developed between philosophy and scientific and sociological research was more profound than it ever had been in English or French psychiatry — a situation that has perhaps become even more pronounced since the 1920s and 30s, especially since the inroads of existential philosophy.

To avoid creating a false impression of the effectiveness of the early reform activity and the scope of the task of a social integration embracing all manifestations of irrationality, let us cite the estimate of one F. Nasse, a disciple of Reil's, who said that in 1821 only one sixth of all mentally ill were being treated either by a doctor or in an asylum, whereas the vast majority were still in a state of exclusion — in prisons, jails, or in the streets. Furthermore, there existed a great lag between town and country, because the cities responded more sensitively to disturbances of order and also were better able to protect themselves. Therefore Nasse, discouraged by the limitations of medical services and the social interest of administrations, believed that the clergy should devote itself more systematically to the care of the indigent insane and that their theological studies should include psychological — that is to say psychiatric — training.[168] This, of course, was indicative of the neoreligious orientation of psychiatry during the Restoration. The inadequacy of dealing with the problem of the indigent insane was also pointed up in Horn's statistic, which showed that 75 per cent of all patients committed to the Charité in 1816 were quite clearly of the middle class.[169] Finally, it should be pointed out that as late as the mid-nineteenth century, psychiatrists still campaigned against putting the mentally ill in chains. A particularly dramatic, and typical account, even if perhaps embellished, tells of the seduction of an attractive girl by soldiers sent to the island of Borkum to quell a revolt. "The child [she bore] died, and the abandoned mother became melancholic. This was aggravated by the scorn of the community and the increasing watchful control of the church. In 1822 she became violent and was chained in the miserable cow barn of the poorhouse. And for forty-four years, until July 1866, she was kept in chains almost constantly, tugging, weeping, raging, ranting, whimpering. Because in her fury she tore anything she could lay her hands on, she was generally stripped of clothes throughout her ordeal."[170]

3

From the Restoration
to Bourgeois-Natural Scientific
Liberalism

Natural-Philosophical and Theological Psychiatry

The materialistic tendencies of Reil, at a time when the educated bourgeoisie of early Romanticism was also republican, were also manifest in Schelling's Jena period when, against Fichte's subjectivism, he sought to ascertain the idea of objectivity and the unity of contradictions through the observation of natural processes.[171] To be sure, his polemics against physiologists and chemists about the problem of life in his early writings on natural philosophy (1797—99), had already led him to reject or idealistically magnify their results, which he called mechanistic. Schelling was concerned primarily with reversing the polarities by appropriating all exogenous forces to turn them into endogenous forces, into drives or powers of the organism, just as the philosopher creates nature (which only produces semblance), turns it into active nature, and finds the identity of body and soul, nature and mind, on every level of life — not through mechanistic causal categories, but through intuitive, direct knowledge: "Nature should be the spirit made visible, and the spirit, invisible nature. Here, in the absolute identity of the spirit within us and nature outside us, the problem of how a nature outside of us is possible must be resolved."[172]

In his refutation of Western thought, Schelling called J. Brown's concept of "excitability" passive and mechanistic. "Yet the simply passive is an absurdity in nature." For always more advanced and more essential than that is the motive force, the drive, the instinct, whose higher level is genius, irritability as a positive thing, with sensibility as its negative. "In general, all knowledge is the negative of a (presumed) positive; man knows only what he has an instinct to know; it is a vain effort to try to make men understand what they have no urge to understand."[173] Schelling's "aristocracy of epistemology,"[174] mocks the pedagogical claim of the Enlightenment. Philosophy is not "learnable" by all (egalitarian) people, but as "intellectual contemplation," as immediate, feeling experience, accessible only to those who already possess this as instinct.[175] Schelling is trying to continue Kant's definitions – as in the *Critique of Judgment* and the *Anthropology*.[176] However, he wants to free them from their restrictions and endow them with the dignity of an immediate connection to, an identity with, the objective process of nature. This was the starting point of a tradition that still makes German theories of learning so inaccessible, or which makes German psychiatry ascribe an instinctual, naturally objective unassailability beyond all reflective philosophy or empirical verification to the brilliance or "endogeny" of psychoses.

Even in the question of disease, Schelling sees Brown as committing the ultimate sin of putting the "determination by exogenous factors" above permanence, whereas disease is in fact the discrepancy between irritability and sensibility, i.e. of the factors of excitability (so to speak Schelling's "thing in itself");[177] Both external stimuli and medical findings – thus Brown's sthenia-asthenia – presuppose the actual disease,[178] which indicates the logical place from which endogenous psychoses supposedly can be "triggered" exogenously; they "always already" exist. Schelling lent medicine a special philosophical aura. Medicine is that special science in the concrete series of nature, of natural science – like the ideal series of the mind, historical science – a special science aspiring to universality, to primal knowledge, to absolute identity, and thus with a special affinity to their science, the science of theology. And physicians indeed soon took ample advantage of that, just as the lofty position that Schelling assigned to medicine was in keeping with its social prestige, at least among the literary Romantics. It was thus not unusual to find a physician, C. A. Von Eschenmayer, occupying the chair of philosophy at Tübingen in 1818, and delivering the first psychiatric lectures (after Berlin and Leipzig).

Eschenmayer turned from the identity philosophy of his teacher Schelling to F. H. Jacobi, who sought to counter the discursive thought and atheism of the Enlightenment with intuitive "immediate knowledge" and supernatural religious experience. In these terms, Eschenmayer, in 1803, drew his conclusion from Schelling, blazing a trail for Schelling's "leap" into the beyond:

"Knowledge is extinguished only in the absolute, where it becomes identical with the known....Whatever lies beyond this point can thus no longer be knowledge, but rather a premonition or devotion."[179] In his reply of 1804, after his move from Jena to Würzburg, Schelling, despite his polemics, accepted Eschenmayer's dichotomy of philosophy, the mere negative of knowledge as opposed to the contemplation of the soul, of the divine within man, "which is one and the same as the absolute." However, Schelling tied this to the idea of corruption in the world, the consequence of man's fall from grace, which led him to the skeptical limitation of his own philosophy of identity: "In a word, there is no steady transition from the absolute to the real, the origin of the world of perception is conceivable only as a total break from absoluteness, through a leap....a falling away from the absolute."[180] According to Habermas, Schelling here forestalled Hegel's later criticism of his absolute identity in *The Phenomenology of the Mind*, in which he said that the philosophy of identity seemed to lack "the seriousness, pain, patience, and labor of the negative," and that it did not seem to him to be "serious about the otherness and alienation as well as about overcoming this alienation."[181] And in fact Schelling in 1804 took a step in that direction, which in some ways was more radical than Hegel's critique, but which since then has enjoyed the protection of not only idealistic systematization but also of God's providence. Since Schelling believed that the fall from grace had its origin in the absolute, and that it therefore presupposed freedom, fallen man himself represented the counter-absolute, the reverse of God, just as nature has come under the sway of matter, of the external.[182] This freedom of the fall from grace determines the radicalism of the separation from the absolute, of alienation, the "hardness and detachment of things," and the negative not merely as a deficiency, but itself as a positive — and that in twofold guise: the negative constitutes the positive (just as the power of evil is part virtue). But if the negative raises itself over the positive, then disorder will prevail over essential order, relative being over non-being, the external over the internal; the positive will emerge, and so will unity, namely "false unity" (again not merely a deficiency of truth, but itself a positive).

In this twofold guise, the state of nature and the state of man bear witness to, are evidence of, the falling away from the absolute and the absolute itself: natural catastrophes, the earth itself as a vast ruin, lamentation and utterance of the sorrow of animals, natural evil (everything poisonous, destructive, repugnant), generally all the power of the exogenous, of arbitrariness, chance, and irregularity; also everything feeble, finite, and transitory in life, pain, sickness, and death; finally, evil in the moral world — misfortune, want, and suffering, the vices created by the state, "poverty — evil in mass," the struggle of human beings for mere physical existence; as well as obstinacy, error, hatred, anger, melancholia, idiocy, and insanity.[183]

Thus disease, he wrote in 1809, testifies to the corruption of both man and nature, to "a life of its own, but a false life, a life of falsehood, a product of disquiet and corruption," to the dominance of the external, of disorder, of the periphery: "The most apt simile here is offered by disease, which, as the disarray brought into nature by the abuse of freedom, is the true counterpart of evil or sin."[184] This places disease and its former natural-philosophical, cosmic aspects in the context of divine providence. That was what made disease — as the "most apt simile" — so fascinating to the Romantics, and retarded the development of natural-scientific medicine, so dull by comparison.

In the *Stuttgarter Privat Vorlesungen* (1810), Schelling set the unreason of insanity into this framework, placing it prominently between the state and the spirit world. To prove that fallen man had returned to nature and was now condemned to the futile pursuit of his own, separate unity, Schelling adduces two factors: on the one hand, the social condition, which concerns the inorganic, "the preservation of the external basis of life"; on the other hand, the external, hence futile unity of the state: "The state, therefore, to say it outright, is a consequence of the curse on humanity." Because it resorts to physical coercion, the state cannot produce moral condition, and that is why the efforts of the French Revolution or of Kant to make the unity of the state compatible with the freedom of the citizens were futile. It is precisely the search for a just order that leads to despotism, as Fichte's closed commercial state demonstrates. Historically, the State became a tyranny to the extent that the church failed through its entanglement in the quest for power. Only Christ, who can again make man into a mediator between God and nature, can bring the human race true, inner unity. It then becomes possible to abolish the state, "the unity of nature, this second nature above the first," and if not "make the state dispensable or do away with it, at least help it free itself from blind power... and transfigure itself into intelligence."[185]

The superiority of man's inner unity over the ill-fated civic freedom, which from a professional vantage point could seem plausible to contemporary psychiatrists, was elaborated on by Schelling, who claimed that the individual might attain inner unity by developing his spirit (*Geist*) and thus anticipate the historical evolution of the human race. The powers that make up the individual spirit are mind (*Gemüt*), spirit (in the narrower sense), and soul (*Seele*), each of which in turn has three levels.

The mind is the unconscious, natural principle of the spirit. It appears as (a) desire, sympathy, sadness; (b) passion, lust, desire, irritability (expressing the yearning for being, from which man has cut himself off, which is why he never finds satisfaction); and (c) emotion and sensibility, the most exalted aspect of the mind.

The spirit is the ideal side, the personal, consciousness, conscious desire, i.e. will. Its lowest level is (a) willfulness, which is evil only when it controls; (b) the highest is the intellect; (c) and in the middle, at the point of indifference, is the will. The spirit cannot be man's highest power since it is capable of disease, error, and sin, i.e. the creation of non-being over being, which is why the following is valid: "It is not the spirit that is infected by the body, but conversely the body by the spirit, and "the highest corruption is precisely also the most spiritual."[186]

The soul is the third and highest potency. It is the divine spark in man. As being, it is the impersonal to which the personal, as non-being, should be subject. Therefore: the spirit knows, but the soul is knowledge; the spirit can be good, but the soul is goodness; the spirit can fall ill, but "there are no diseases of the soul." Soul is also rapport with God. "The health of the mind and the spirit depends on the constancy of the connection between the soul and the depths of the mind." Any disruption of this guidance and rapport spells illness — again in three forms: (a) as mental illness, melancholia, when yearning dominates feeling; (b) as idiocy, when willfulness dominates the intellect, which, as in Kant, merely aims at pleasure and is harmless; (c) but if the balance between the soul and the intellect is interrupted, "the most dreadful thing of all," insanity arises — "I should not have said 'it arises,' but rather, emerges." For here, with insanity, Schelling, once again on the highest level and at the threshold to the divine, develops the fall from grace and its consequent reversal of being and non-being, of basis and existence and of false unity.

Thus insanity is the corrupt and divine in man: "What is the spirit of man? Answer: a being, but out of the non-Being, i.e. understanding out of non-understanding. What then is the basis

of the human spirit in the sense in which we construe 'basis'?
Answer: non-understanding, and since the human spirit relates
as non-being to the soul, it also relates to it as non-understanding.
Hence the deepest essence of the human spirit, when contem-
plated apart from the soul and thus from God, is insanity. Insanity,
does not originate, it emerges when that which is actually non-
being, i.e. non-understanding, is actualized, when it wants to be
essence, being. Thus the basis of understanding itself is insanity.
That is why insanity is a necessary element, that must, however,
not emerge, not be actualized. What we call understanding, if it
is real, living, active understanding, is, in fact nothing but regulated insanity. Understanding can manifest itself, show itself
only in its opposite, in non-understanding. People who carry no
insanity within themselves are people with empty, sterile understanding. Hence the reverse saying: *Nullum ingenium sine quadam
dementia.* Hence divine insanity, of which Plato and the poets
speak. Namely, when insanity is ruled by the influence of the
soul, it is truly divine insanity, the basis of inspiration, of effectiveness." Thus insanity in obedience is creativity, but in
disobedient freedom, insanity is the foreboding of the fall. If,
for example, in bleak sorrow, the soul cannot guide the spirit and
the mind, then "the initially dark essence erupts, carrying along
reason as a relative to the soul non-being; insanity emerges as
the dreadful symbol of the will separated from God." For human
freedom stands above the mind, but below the soul. The action
of the will is evil when it remains "on its own basis," when it
follows the lower will, willfulness, when it alienates itself from
the soul. It is good when it alienates itself from willfulness and
submits to the soul, the "inner heaven of man."

Reason is indebted to a corresponding subjection: "Reason
is nothing but understanding in its submission to the higher, the
soul." Insanity, as unreason, here more uncompromisingly than
ever before is a rebellion, a want of submission. Just as the soul
is the active element in regard to reason as the passive, it is also
virtue in its active dominion over the will and desire. The imperative "let the soul act in you" obtains not only ethically, but also
aesthetically, when the work of art is to be freed from the personal-
subjective to the impersonal-objective, obtains for perfect health
and for the realization of the true inner unity in history instead
of the mere outer unity of the state. For only the soul as the
divine spark can create the divine; only the soul can create religion
and achieve the identity of being and non-being in love.

Finally, Schelling assigns insanity a role in relation to the demonic, to the world of spirits, to which he ascribes utmost reality to the extent that the spirit can affect the body, i.e. the body too carries the spiritual principle. The demonic is the — in rare cases — spiritually anticipated, albeit still separated, good or evil as absolutes. It appears on the one hand as clairvoyance, say, in soothsayers, and, on the other hand, by way of contrast, as insanity: "Insanity is thus the condition of hell."[187]

This system made it possible for physicians and naturalists to see the problems of life, health, and disease — especially insanity — as part of a universal framework, moreover one in which a privileged place was reserved for them, and which took all the possible relationships into account: the physical, chemical, and physiological, magnetism, galvanism, and the factors of excitability, sympathy, and demonism, as well as historical relations, aesthetics and physiognomy, ethics, epistemology, the state and, above all, religion; social relations, to be sure, only as theologically derived, and poverty only as "mass evil."

Schelling mirrors the exuberance of the literary public and the absence of a political public in Germany. Kant's basing of an "aesthetic judgment on the subjective a priori of our feeling of life...was in accord with the irrationalism and the cult of genius in the nineteenth century." But in the period between Schiller's aesthetic education and Schelling, an "educated society which is interested in art" had come into being. The freedom of the emotions as opposed to the intellect, the freedom of the spirit as opposed to the idea, "is freedom merely in an aesthetic state and not in reality.... It is the prose of alienated reality against which the poetry of aesthetic reconciliation must seek its own self-consciouness."[188] Going beyond aesthetics, Schelling, between 1804 and 1810, ascribed a meaning to this alienated reality — and precisely in its forms of error, evil, poverty, disease, insanity — which, although historically related to sublation, he understood (and increasingly so as he grew older) as an internal, religious, mystical renewal. During the restoration, this system of apostasy, of sinfulness, of a striving toward unity of the soul and freedom by subjugating nature and man, dominated those physicians devoting all or part of their time to psychiatric work who were responsible for the scientific systematization of psychiatry — or hampering it: i.e., the professors.

For the sake of a more detailed presentation of Schelling's original contribution we will refrain from a discussion of the systems of his epigones.[189] But, we should trace their effects on psychiatry, for they pointed the way until the mid-century.

Among the early psychiatrists, we drew a distinction between the materialistic early Romanticism of the younger Reil and the Prussian-administrative idealism of Langermann and Horn.[190] Similarly, we must distinguish between the early institutional psychiatrists whose Western orientation found expression in the linkage of their theories (overlaid of course with German ideas) and the concrete practice of the unsolved social problems on the one hand, and the early academic psychiatrists — from 1810 to the fifties — who celebrated psychiatry in terms of natural philosophy and more or less theologically. Schelling as well as Baader, Oken, and Görres left their imprint on contemporary medicine. Mention should also be made of Fr Jahn and his *Krankheiten als Afterorganisationen* and K. R. Hoffmann's *Idealpathologie* (1839), and above all, J. N. Ringseis, who until the late nineteenth century, saw diseases as self-motivating forces in the service of Satan, and revolutions as diseases of political life. The first step in his treatment was to purge the patient of sin, and armed with the Bible and Catholicism he battled against microscopes and dissections. Yet, despite, or possibly because of this, he was the attending physician to the great men of his time, of the theosophists Schelling and Baader and the atheist Feuerbach.[191]

But Schelling's influence was strongest on those medical professors who were fascinated by the "false unity," the unreason of the insane. And that influence continued throughout the 1830s and 1840s, after the breakthrough of the natural sciences in medicine, and even after he failed in his political mission in 1840 to extirpate seditious Hegelianism at the University of Berlin. Not coincidentally, his "psychiatrizing" disciples, among them Eschenmayer, H. Steffens, and G. H. Von Schubert, remained faithful to him even after his luster faded. Since the 1870s, when the neo-Kantian concept of experience, Dilthey, Nietzsche, the discovery of Schopenhauer, and the French theory of degeneration had restored the concept of unreason to psychiatry, nineteenth-century scientific positivism became a myth for psychiatry. In effect, its dominance in Germany was restricted to the 1860s, the decade in which both economic and political liberalism had its only and short-lived flowering in the history of German civil life.

At almost every German university, ideas on mental illness were expounded within systems of natural philosophy or religion, by physicians and/or philosophers including K. G. Neumann (Horn's successor in Berlin); H. Steffens in Breslau, whom insanity filled with "deep horror," not because of its victims, but because it was an expression of the "old chaos of disorder," and therefore could be treated only within the framework of a planetary cosmology; C. G. Carus in Dresden; J. C. A. Heinroth in Leipzig and D. G. Von Kieser in Jena, the greatest virtuoso of the polarization of man and nature, who placed them between a negative and a positive pole, called man's lower functions tellurian, and viewed health as a harmonious oscillation between the poles and disease as the domineering egotism of the negative pole, and consequently an "indecent form of life." Others were A. Haindorf in Münster; P. W. Jessen in Kiel; K. J. H. Windischmann in Bonn, a physician and professor of philosophy and history who sought to furnish the world-spirit with an empirical base in galvanism; Eschenmayer and Autenrieth in Tübingen; A. F. Marcus in Würzburg, who founded its first psychiatric university clinic in 1834; Reinseis in Munich; and J. M. Leupoldt in Erlangen, who believed purely scientific orientation to be "un-German."[192] And there also was Schelling's close friend Von Schubert, who, starting with dreams became increasingly concerned with mysticism and occultism, the "dark side of life," and J. Ennemoser, who favored exorcism, Justinus Kerner, a believer in and writer about spiritualism, whose book, *Die Seherin von Prevorst*, became a favorite target of the early somatic psychiatrists, who used this work — somewhat like the enlightened physicians of the Renaissance — to expose a woman said to be possessed by demons as mentally ill. And finally, a special group of professors deserves mention. Magnetism in Germany, unlike in France, had become an accepted part of the systems of natural philosophy. Under the influence of the popular magnetizer J. F. Koreff,[193] Von Hardenberg, overriding the protests of the faculties, set up chairs for animal magnetism at various universities. Among those appointed to professorships were K. C. Wolfart (Berlin), who may be said to have rediscovered Mesmer for Germany, C. F. Nasse (Bonn), an exception, insofar as he made the transition to somatic psychiatry, P. Krukenberg (Halle), Kieser (Jena), and J. B. Wilbrand (Giessen).[194] This field also produced one of the many short-lived periodicals so typical of the feeble link to reality, the *Archiv für den thierischen Magnetismus* (1817–24), edited by Nasse and Kieser.

These direct or indirect products of natural philosophy offer us a flood of literature concerned with the illness of the mind and the spirit, yet they failed to see the actual subjects, the insane, who after all were the source of the fascinating phenomena they described, without firsthand experience with them, without any serious consideration of the social reality of the indigent mentally ill, or without consideration of any practical steps to improve their physical and social situation. In other words, here an impressive segment of "educated society," which, aware of its exclusion from political and economic power, transformed the unreason of society into phenomena of the individual psyche, which, under academic auspices, might lend itself to treatment via inner renewal. The outer reality, chaotic and sick, and against which the ordinary citizen felt powerless, was no longer merely portrayed, as in early Romanticism, but deprived of its socially and somatically resistant externals, and internalized and individualized. And in this unrealized form of submission, compatible with the situation of "educated society," it could be made accessible to religious salvation.

We used the term "office-hour psychiatry" to describe the phase of preindustrial England and France, before the insane had gained social visibility, in which the middle class sought to interpret its inner and political self-consciousness via comparatively harmless manifestations of unreason — nervous disorders, hypochondria, hysteria, melancholia.[195] In Germany, this phase lingered on in the universities long after the onset of industrialization and the social effects of the existence of the indigent mentally ill had made themselves felt. The insistence of the academic "cultured" class on the pre-industrial approach linking the phenomena of insanity to the self mirrored the academic remoteness from social reality and increasingly began to look like escapism or camouflage.

The Schelling "immemorialities" natural-philosophical psychiatrists explored the dependence of merely passive, perceiving reason on the soul, instinct, genius, life, nature, the divine, being, which later also came under the governance of the irremovable and unfathomable state — in all conceivable directions — cosmological, ethical, theological, political, mystical, and magical.[196] Only the relationship to the social reality of bourgeois society remained ephemeral. This generation had barely experienced the wave of republican enthusiasm in Germany. Their youth was stamped by the wars of liberation — thus Steffens in Breslau during 1813, who like Reil in Berlin outdid everyone in patriotic fervor. Subsequently these natural philosophers, like Schelling himself, became increasingly legitimist, and finally downright reactionary. Although Oken and Carus played a leading role in the "national deed" of the scientists in 1822, the founding of the Association of German Naturalists and Physicians under the eyes of the censorship — a counterpart to the first "national deed" of the economic burghers, Friedrich List's League of German

Merchants and Manufacturers of 1819, the natural-philosophical psychiatrists did not. Their movement went in a different direction. In 1818, Heinroth saw psychiatric salvation in the Holy Alliance. During the revolutionary unrest of 1830, Kieser, as head of the Academic Guard, crushed the rebellion in Jena. Beginning in 1830, the majority of those mentioned above became involved in the struggle against the materialism of the emergent natural sciences and also turned to writing. And Görres, Ringseis, Heinroth, and Leupoldt also belonged to the mystical, reactionary Munich school which called itself "Christian-Germanic."[197]

Two other publications of this period deserve mention for different reasons. *Versuch einer Pathologie und Therapie der Geistes- und Gemütskrankheiten* (1811) by Alexander Haindorf (1782–1862) was the first German textbook on psychiatry laying claim to systematic comprehensiveness. Haindorf, a Westphalian physician of Jewish descent[198] became a Brownian in Bamberg, a natural philosopher in Würzburg, a Gall disciple in France. In 1816, at the University of Münster, he was one of the first to lecture on psychiatry, in addition to physiology and medicine. Although he did have some firsthand experience with the mentally ill he did not actually treat patients. But he was probably the only psychiatrist actively involved in the pedagogical tasks connected with the promised emancipation of the Jews: in 1826, in Münster, he founded and directed a school for the training of teachers and craftsmen of Jewish descent.

Haindorf's psychiatric textbook is really a comprehensive philosophy of nature. Nonetheless, with the help of case histories and understanding of the nervous system, he makes a sincere effort to base his speculations on empirical somatic findings. But in direct contradiction to his French authorities, his main concern is that medicine is not sufficiently grounded on philosophy. He therefore starts out with the idea of absolute life, making all physiological life finite, marred, broken, askew. "The general reason for this alteration or warped shape of life must be sought in a cosmic phenomenon, which affects every sphere of the world at least once in its lifetime, namely in the oblique position of its axis toward the sun." That is the source of climates, seasons, as well as work and disease. Individual life is a galvanic polarization (between positive and negative = creation and destruction = hydrogen and oxygen), coming from the whole, and after death returning to it through rebirth, which is why death is merely external, partial, momentary. Likewise, health and illness are merely two "relative notions of troubled life," the former subsumed under the whole, the latter a falling out of line of the individual, i.e. a disequilibrium through onesidedness and its struggle with the whole, which in a chronic case is construed as sickness. An innate condition is not the disease of an individual, but rather a "sick branch on the sound trunk of mankind."[199] And Haindorf's recommendation that "powerful nations" destroy such individuals at birth reveals the explosive potential that German idealism, in positing the constitution, predisposition, the nature of the subject, "temperament," the inner man, the mood as the "thing in itself," life itself as absolutes, brought into the twentieth century.

As in early Schelling, the definition of insanity starts off from the "idea of the soul in its loftiest and purest significance," the "world-soul," in which nature and spirit achieve divine unity. In the case of mental illness, the parallax in the definition of somatic illness is replaced by the singularly absolute historic view; mental illness is possible because the individual soul is out of step with the world-soul, it is finite, broken in time and in substance, has a history. Nor does it fall ill of its own accord; rather, the disturbance of its relation to the world is a spiritual disorder, and the disturbance of its relation to its sense of self is an emotional disorder, and the relationship of these two is akin to that of the ideal to the real, of male to female. Therefore woman, being less rational, cannot attain the highest level of irrationality, the disorder of reason and the imagination. The types of illness, from cretinism and idiocy to the most sublime irrationality, i.e. disordered reason, are made analogous to: (1) the hierarchy of faculties (from creature egotism to reason); (2) the development of emotions (from self-preservation to love of fellow-man, the "liberal" subordination to the Supreme Being, to the Godhead); (3) the progression from the realm of metals and plants to the kingdoms of animals and man; (4) specific chemical formulas; (5) the sections of the nervous system from the spinal cord to the cerebrum — as the somatic correlative under the earliest influence of Western thought. Finally, Haindorf's therapy limits itself in Brownian fashion to contrasting each instance of one-sidedness with its opposite, whereby in "spiritual therapy" the imposing, humbling attitude of the physician is crucial.

If Haindorf was not really influenced by the religious turn of natural philosophy — in fact, he championed the somatic aspect of his identities and in truly liberal fashion he opposed holding the mentally ill legally responsible. J. C. A. Heinroth's *Lehrbuch der Störungen des Seelenlebens* (1818), on the other hand, was the embodiment of theological psychiatry. If Haindorf eventually proved unable to satisfy the religious yearnings of his fellow Germans who felt cheated out of earthly political freedom and unity, Heinroth without a doubt was considered the leading representative of psychiatry during the Restoration. The son of a Leipzig surgeon, Heinroth (1773—1843) began his medical studies in Leipzig in 1791, and like many young physicians of his time, became the travel companion of a Russian nobleman. Next, he attended P. Frank's lectures at the University of Vienna, dabbled in theology at the University of Erlangen, and finally got his medical degree at Leipzig in 1805. After some postgraduate studies he lectured on anthropology, from time to time acted as a military physician for the French between 1806 and 1813, which afforded him firsthand experience with the insane, especially as a doctor at St. Georgen, a Leipzig orphanage and prison, a position he held for decades. From 1811 on, he taught psychiatric medicine. He wrote his doctoral dissertation (1817) on the problem of how to make the patient subservient to the doctor's will. In 1827, he became full professor. In his old age, his religious view of science, led him to the idea of "Christian Germanism."

Heinroth's textbook of 1818 was a so-called anthropological, religious synthesis of Schelling, Kant, Schiller, and Hegel, even though he rejected Hegel because of his theological extremism. Heinroth's book must be understood in terms of the concrete social situation, which at the same time shed light on the position of the insane and the discrepancy between theory and practice under the existing conditions in Germany. The same physician who was the first in Germany — and quite early even in relation to the West — to win academic recognition for psychiatry as an autonomous theory, gained his practical psychiatric experience primarily through his work at an old-fashioned multipurpose corrective institution for the sequestered insane, typical of enlightened absolutism, as though there had never been a revolution or even a reform from above. But this also supplied the momentum of his comparative progressiveness. For Heinroth was the first in Germany to discuss insanity in relation to socio-moral norms and to the social conditions in general, to make the identification between the mentally ill and "normal" people, and raise the question of social integration of the insane, granted the religious overtones of his approach. This purposeful aim at integration skipped the phase of the emphatically romantic demand for the emancipation of the mentally ill and of society. The theme of the guilt of unreason, the belief in reason, even if irrationally tinged and powered by the absolutes of life and disposition, and the preeminence of the restoration of a normative, interiorized social order derived from the period of enlightened absolutism and the nature of its institutions of sequestration. And they seemed to be all the more applicable to or representative of bourgeois society, since the Germany of 1818 showed no sign of a radical break in the social and governing continuity. For Heinroth — as for Hegel in his later years — the age of revolutions was past. Salvation rested with the state and the morality of the rulers. They alone were in a position to fight the unreason of liberal, acquisitive bourgeois society, the selfishness that was the cause of both insanity and criminality, and subjugate them to a reasonable — read Christian — order. Heinroth and people like him could hold these opinions at a time when liberalism had not yet developed in Germany because they believed they could simply continue along the lines laid down by absolutism, a tradition whose validity seemed obvious to the good professor. Thus Heinroth was justified in planning his textbook "from a rational standpoint," and the mercantilist state medicine of Frank's lectures evidently had also had an effect. So much now for this anticipatory, socially conditioned interpretation of the book.

Man and mankind, so Heinroth begins, are identical; they are consciousness that unfolds in stages — world-consciousness, self-consciousness, and conscience, or outside of, within, and above us. Conscience, the third stage, is the loftiest of the three. As self-surrender, it is that which is perceived, it is reason, the sole path to God, the source of physical and psychic well-being, an obstacle to "untrammeled vitality," allowing man to experience the bleak external/internal contrast. Conversely, the "human pathological condition" is "restrained vitality," namely "the consciousness not incorporated into conscience or reason." Insofar as this happens voluntarily — "for the capacity of free choice, arbitrariness, is after all man's original gift" — man transgresses not only against his own development, "revelation of life," but also against "the order and lawfulness of being and life itself."[200] Just as the inhibition and obstruction are rooted in the practices of bourgeois society, in the addictively futile quest for gain or loss, i.e. passion, and go from delusion to vice, so is disease rooted in the mind. Under the pressure of increasing compulsion and loss of freedom, turns into a sickness of the spirit, and ultimately of the will. All forms of unreason grow out of behavior that is sinful because it is in principle free and voluntary, insanity standing beyond reason and vice against reason. Heinroth does not exculpate criminals because of their physical or mental predisposition, since man's "predisposition" to free will is even "more basic," i.e. the fall from grace, guilt, is ever present. At best, a mentally ill defendant might be held unfit to serve a legally imposed sentence.

Rejecting Kant's theoretical reason as mechanical and as an elaboration of his practical Reason, Heinroth finds all theory inessential to therapy; for here, the action of the physician meets head on with the action of the patient. But that does not mean that Heinroth believes that moral treatment should be "subjectively moral." To that extent, the English, French, and the rather subjectively idealistic Langermann must be criticized. And even the Romantic-aesthetic analogy of the physician as artist is too mechanistic and subjective for Heinroth, since the artist puts his stamp only on a lifeless, passive object. In contrast, Heinroth tends to transfer the objective order of enlightened absolutism to bourgeois society: moral treatment must be "objectively moral," i.e., it is a retreat to an individuality that has broken through its barriers, since freedom is the preserve of hopeless cases; it is the forced imposition of form, order, law, "norm of reason" — in a word, "restriction," whereby the physician merely posits the conditions for the objective "generation of recovery," while the latter or the measure and order of nature, establish themselves through him.[201] This helps to explain why the non-restraint movement did not start in Germany, and why it was accepted there last, and then only fitfully.

The identification of man with mankind and the historicity of insanity — and not the actual condition of the insane — led Heinroth to draft a six-part monumental "evolutionary history of mental disorders": (1) Affects and passions correspond to the heroic age; (2) ecstasy, fantasy, eroticism, and therewith insanity and epileptic convulsions to the age of poetry; (3) the unendurability of "the loss of happiness, wealth, honor," i.e. melancholia and derangement to the "artificially intertwined society"; (4) fanaticism and religious melancholy to positive religion; (5) systematic derangement and frenzy to metaphysics turned literal; (6) foolishness and idiocy to the present degenerate, licentious, physically and morally enfeebled era.

The educated bourgeoisie of that time mirrored and indeed found their self-consciousness, identity, and reason in the medium of the unreason of insanity, the risks as well as the intensifications (cf. genius cult, clairvoyance), and in this genealogy now also their historical consciousness — whereby the perspective of Heinroth's construction, unlike Comte's three-stage law was obviously pessimistic. And considering that Haindorf, identified foolishness with the degenerate aristocracy and stupidity with the rabble,[202] it is remarkable that the bourgeoisie looked on the foolishness of the aristocracy tolerantly but was downright aggressive about the idiocy of the rabble, the lowest category of mental illness. As a result, morons and idiots were kept in isolation for a much longer time. Their social integration did not begin until classical liberalism had almost passed its peak. In the course of the development of psychiatry it became apparent that the more the rabble as proletariat strove toward the attainment of self-consciousness in the nineteenth century, the more its strength was felt as a threat to bourgeois order, the more a psychiatrically oriented society depicted them as physically, intellectually and morally weak and idiotic, and shoved them aside. Heinroth's pessimistic temporal diagnosis accorded with Hegel's predictions about the dangers that threatened bourgeois society.[203]

Heinroth was the first German to make a thorough study of English and French psychiatry, even though (or because) he had not traveled on the Continent and actually disliked the French because of their foreign rule. Lorry, being a Frenchman blinded by appearances, can explain man only from the outside. And Pinel "proves himself a French writer by holding on to nothing, letting go of the most important subjects as soon as he takes hold of them, and thus never exhausting any material."[204] However, Heinroth also treats German psychiatrists — Langermann, Horn, Reil, Hoffbauer — though somehwhat more gently, in the same stereotypical fashion. But instead of seeing man mechanistically as a thinking creature, and explaining him from the outside, and ascribing mental disorder to "causes," Heinroth maintains that only the "totality of conditions" can produce something; only the whole man, as freedom and will, can become ill, since the faculty for a moral and religious rational life (freedom and will) as their objective reference point predate the development of all life, even if the individual does not know it subjectively. In the subjugation to this objective reason lies the salvation of both therapy and therapeutic practice.[205]

Psychic disorder, like everything, according to Heinroth, is generated, i.e., it grows out of the union of the internal element (the mother, the psychic condition) and the external (procreator, determining stimulus, evil). Since, however, the body is merely the agent of the psyche, which in turn is subordinate to the conscience, the individual is responsible for his mood, his temperament, objectively and morally a literal interpretation of Kant's predisposition and Schelling's mood. If one's inner feeling has freely decided against reason and God, if in this state of falling from grace the external evil stimuli are given a chance, then the psyche is subject to the rule of unreason.[206] The available external stimuli of mechanistic physicians are thus helpless against the self-justified receptivity of the psychic condition, which for its part is the sum of one's past and — where not subject to reason — failed life. In 1822 Heinroth elaborated on this idea of all-embracing guilt: even a single display of anger is a psychic disorder; it reveals the individual's "failure to hold himself in check." To cure this failing, "one must undertake a thorough revolution of one's entire being," but people generally prefer to blame external factors for their failings. Just how literally re-storative was the reference to revolution was revealed by Heinroth's account: some time ago, he said, people were praising a "certain patriotic anger" (the Wartburg Festival), which in fact — as is so often the case — was nothing but common egotism.[207] Likewise, a sinful life of gluttony may lead to hemorrhoids, and these in turn can cause psychic illness. For all stimuli, including hereditary predisposition, affect the psychic condition only morally, and they can be resisted only morally. Here follows the critique of Heinroth, the cultivated bourgeois, of the economic bourgeoisie, who want to change the "world" to their liking. The "stimuli for evil" comes above all from the "world," i.e., from that which people have freely produced. The core of the "world" is selfishness. Money, power, property, enjoyment are not reprehensible in themselves, but if one allows oneself to be dominated by them, the result is the fall from grace, psychic illness, the subjugation of the soul to lower, mechanistic laws, the law of gravity, laws that turn man into an automaton, a machine living either only at the periphery or the center.

But, since Heinroth's universe does not recognize randomness, even disturbance is governed by objective order, namely by a morphology of the unreason of insanity whose strictly rational architectonics and reference to plant taxonomy implies a continuation and/or catching-up with eighteenth-century tradition. The consciousness stages of mind, spirit and will, as well as the types of psychic factors — exaltation/hypersthenia, depression/asthenia, and, for the sake of a normative threesome, a mixture of the two — constitute the categories of the morphology; each has three disorder syndromes. From them thirty-six forms are deduced, and they in turn are divided into countless subforms.

In Heinroth's anthropology, in which life is merely the hand-maiden of the spirit, the essence of the unreason of insanity is a consequence of a life in the service of evil,[208] an impediment in the development toward perfection, an inclination toward material things, toward non-being, i.e. the internal contractive or external expansive drift toward natural necessity, toward non-being — the two basic forms. Melancholia is thus a descent into one's own center, a drifting of the ego toward the object that depresses it; it is alienation, having become a "hollow, empty, self-consuming ego," with the "self-awareness of not belonging to oneself" and intensified reflection due to "disunion." In insanity, on the other hand, the ego is "virtually torn out of itself" with the object "and taken out of itself, wafted off into the dream shapes and airy figments of the imagination," here too, subject to the material law of gravity, since the imagination creates only what it must, linked to a reduction or sublation of the reflection in the "bliss of abandonment."[209]

These dense formulations, apparently the first examples in German psychiatry in which conceptualized factual observation permeated the nevertheless rationalist polarization, probably reflected Heinroth's actual, though not very intensive experience with the insane. This basis of mental disorders, which can be reduced to the formula of loss of ego, through egocentricity, also describes the state of society for Heinroth: "We are all physically sick, for we all live in this condition." Heinroth aims at a moral corrective for bourgeois economic society and a moral compensation for economic failure. For mental sickness is not simply due to egotism, manifesting itself subjectively as pain and discomfort, but also objectively as lack of success, inhibited activity, disarray in "business circles, in economic conditions, in personal relations." Dietetics, the "physical economy," becomes the guarantor of external economic activity: the former assures the success of the latter if it submits to the rule of "sacred reason," religion; if not, failure and unreason threaten.[210] The actual therapy, as already indicated, involves forcing irrationality back to the "norm of reason," described in a chemical-moral analogy as the "equation of opposing conditions," hence virtually a conflict of faculties between the doctor and the patient, whose outcome should not, for "objective moral reasons," be in doubt, for a healthy, religious personality must, after all, be stronger than an ailing, irreligious one. In his *Prophylactik*, Heinroth sees faith in God as the cure for all mental disorders, the solution to the inherent contradiction between the self and reason. Faith elevates the self to self-annihilation, reason to the idea; faith realizes the idea and brings about the unity of self and reason.

Nor do matters differ with states, which, like plants, are supposed to evolve into higher forms. In the past, according to Heinroth, they were only on the level of nature, established themselves as ends in themselves, and attempted improvement by means of revolution. But now, with the Holy Alliance, there exists for the first time a league of princes who put their states under the aegis of Christianity. Therefore the law of the state rather than the law of mere external existence can become an inner, divine law; that is to say, it can finally limit the free play of arbitrariness, a restriction necessary to inner human development. Up until then only the school and the church had enforced religious observance. However, the state as a moral entity must also impose that discipline in the state and in civil law. Until now, people have pursued money and profit. But once God becomes the ruling idea of the state, then all will believe, and the Jews will be nothing more than naughty children. That is the road that we, purged by revolution, must follow — the entire nation, but before that, the individuals; and at the same time this is the only effective road to prophylaxis, i.e. overcoming selfishness and thus "rooting out" psychic disorder.[211]

Goethe was critical of Heinroth's anthropology: "The author destroys the many unquestionable merits of this work by exceeding the limits set by God and nature."[212] These are the same limits that J. C. A. Grohmann, a Hamburg high-school teacher and Gall disciple, for a different but related reason, set for the state, that is, not in reference to the prophylactic rooting out of psychic disorders, but from the liberal position that denies the state the right to impose capital punishment. In a paper on various psychiatric and forensic issues, Grohmann wrote in 1827: "Life, just like religion, is beyond the power of the state. Religion is the beginning of rational life, which transcends civil laws. But physical life, lies outside and beyond the limits of the state....The state exceeds the legal sphere when it virtually takes life as a contribution or seeks to dispose of it.... The power of the state is coercive, not an annihilating force."[213]

The Prevolutionary Period. "Somatists" vs. "Psychists"

The 1830s were the era of the Industrial Revolution and the concomitant start of capitalist production and the political influence of the economic liberalism of the new middle class; it was the start of a civic social perception which changed the "rabble" into the "proletariat," a class that gradually began to look like a threat, of the acceptance of the natural sciences by the universities, even in the medical specialities, in literature and art the thirties are also said to mark the beginning of the "modern" era.[214] In psychiatry, the somatic approach initiated by the institutional doctors involved in the treatment of the insane (*all* mental patients, including the poor), won out over the academic natural philosophy and Idealism. And the first new institutional building on German soil, at Sachsenberg, near Schwerin (1830), perhaps symbolized the beginning of this movement. It was a process hampered and short-circuited on various levels by the considerable resistance and adverse reactions of powerful interest groups and intermediaries, yet in the 1840s, and especially during and immediately following the 1848 Revolution, it nonetheless turned out to be irreversible.

The July revolution of 1830 brought yet another impetus from France, although its impact was greater in Belgium,[215] Poland, and Italy. Nothing so typified the direction of this movement as the storming of the customs offices in Hesse.[216] With the establishment of the *Zollverein* the economic sector, like any bourgeois special-interest organization, not only achieved a measure of national unity, but more important, the customs union represented the last vital step toward industrialization, i.e., toward the first mass investment of fixed capital: the "free" labor contract introduced by bureaucratic reform had created "reserve armies," and the accumulation of capital between the mid-1830s and mid-1840s brought the first great wave of industrialization. Helped by the mediating role of the state this movement coincided with the initial surge of insane asylums in Germany, particularly during the early 1840s, whereas the corresponding development in England took place between 1810 and 1820, and in France between 1820 and 1830.[217] These time differences in the various countries were connected with their different pace of industrializations, with the concomitant continuing differentiation in the pool of the "irrational" according to their social utility, and, in the face of technological progress, with the increasing industrial need to rid production, and ultimately society itself, of interference from unpredictable, irrational behavior.

Given these concerns the economic sector found itself in complete agreement with the basic purpose of the Prussian administration: to educate the citizens to reason, regardless of the difference in the contemporary notion of reason. In any case, that constituted at least one of the Prussian government's motives in launching a program for the care of the aberrant members of society. Consequently in 1833 Altenstein commissioned two physicians, M. W. Von Mandt and J. N. Rust, to write a report on the state of mental institutions in England and France.[218] To be sure, economic expansion at that time was often impeded by the distrust of semi-absolute states toward this type of social undertaking, impediments that played no small part in the involvement of economic liberals in the Revolution of 1848. Even corporations were considered dangerous associations of private individuals subject to official licensing, a requirement in force until 1870.[219] Associations of scholars, scientists, and other educated citizens considered even more dangerous, faced grave difficulties, especially the Hambach Festival (1832), the controversy between right- and left-wing Hegelians, and "Young Germany" with its journalists and its "seditious intellectuals." And the enthusiastic support given the "Göttingen Seven"* showed that despite censorship and prosecution Germany's literary community was becoming increasingly political. During this phase, the progress of psychiatry and the impetus for its organizational unification emanated from the asylums rather than the universities, partly because of the government's patronizing attitude toward the academics and the reactionary policies in the hiring of teachers. Yet in other respects, the asylums were more dependent on the state than were the universities.

On the other hand, with regard to the proletariat, state and business initially cooperated far more readily. The workers, as a "free" class, had become a necessity for industry and thus an indispensable component of society as a whole. At the same time, the 1830s brought an awareness that the proletariat — a concept taken over from France — as an independent factor jeopardized and threatened to destroy bourgeois society in so far as it was still involved in fighting class restrictions. If the urban rabble stood so far outside of and beneath society that even its survival through procreation was questionable, the expanding proletariat gave rise to visions of a sinister, unleashed proliferation from below, together with a "loss of the feeling of law, legality, and honor," something already touched on by Hegel. He warned of the emergence of a two-class society, of the danger "...that despite the excess of wealth, civil society is not rich enough, i.e. its own

---

* Translators note: upon his ascension to the Hanoverian throne in 1837, Ernest Augustus, Duke of Cumberland, invalidated the constitution promulgated in 1833. Seven eminent professors at the University of Göttingen protested and lost their chairs; two who published a letter of protest were subsequently banished.

resources are insufficient to check the excessive poverty and the creation of a penurious rabble."[220]

This process pointed up the complicated situation the state found itself in as a result of its "belatedness." On the one hand, there was a willingness to accept laissez-faire, and for a long time even the poor laws[221] were rejected as interference with the balance of power. On the other hand, there was an attempt to master the situation by retaining or reinstituting the restrictive labor and social policies of mercantilism. In 1827, Dr. C. A. Weinhold, submitted a plan to check the spread of pauperism containing recommendations for restricting the freedom of movement and the procreative rights of all beggars and other "penurious persons living outside of wedlock," of those unfit to work and invalids dependent on public support, and of "all male servants, journeymen, and apprentices in the towns and in the country."[222] As late as 1835, the regulations for servants of Saxony, as part of the labor contract, granted the "master and mistress" the right of corporal punishment, or of "moderate violence."[223] The labor policies for railroad construction were typical of the position of the state. Although underwritten by the government, these were private undertakings. One of the reasons for their unqualified support was the fact that they seemed to offer a solution for dealing with the misery of the proletariat. The strikes that were breaking out throughout Prussia in protest against the wretched and arbitrarily fixed wages were being quelled by military force. In 1846 G. V. Vincke, a rather conservative regional government official from Hagen, spoke out in support of the social obligation of the state. He wanted railroad workers to have a say in negotiating wages, and he favored mediation boards to settle labor/management disputes. However, the regional government blocked his proposals, and through its support to the employers the railroad fiat demanded a "free labor contract" as the highest principle and called on the military to deal with any possible disruptions.[224]

Similarly, the insane asylums of this phase did not yet give up their more or less harsh mechanical restraint and moderate violence. Again and again anxiously insecure, cautious voices advised to build all asylums near garrisons, so that the military could intervene in case of revolts.[225] Architecturally, the first new asylums, such as Sachsenberg (1830) and Erlangen (1846), retained something of a prison character with their cell-lined corridors and their preoccupation with security and isolation.[226] And legislation continued to view the mentally ill primarily as dangerous. Thus in Silesia, a presidential decree of 1833 posited an inconsistent as well as far-reaching view of what type of behavior constituted a public danger: (1) raving mania; (2) extreme uncleanliness; (3) suicidal tendencies; (4) disturbance of public peace, order, and security.[227]

Psychiatry as institutional practice and scientific theory could be "liberal" only to the extent that liberalism succeeded in establishing itself as independent economic, political, socially responsible and literary activity by the citizens against the state — as the examples of England and France had shown. Yet this was still not possible in prerevolutionary Germany despite all the progress that had been made;[228] consequently the psychiatric beginnings were not yet able to break through the existing framework. The progress registered by Prussian psychiatry was in part still the product of the liberal reforms of Altenstein and Schoen. Altenstein in particular, the advocate of educating subjects to become individuals and citizens, waged a lifelong battle against officialdom and business to outlaw child labor, a practice that turned compulsory education into a chimera. He not only conducted the first inquiry into this problem and drafted the first, albeit unsuccessful bill to restrict child labor (1839), but he worked for improving the condition of the mentally ill, which meant fighting programs that were tantamount to revival of eighteenth-century sequestration. Thus, in 1832, the Prussian provincial administration decided to merge the poorhouses of Tapiau and Graudenz with insane asylums. Altenstein requested the Prussian chief of state, Von Schoen, to bar this plan, because such a merged institution was, he maintained, incompatible with the demands of humanity and science.[229] This contradictory period of transition also showed that progress was more likely in territories under French influence, e.g. Baden, Württemberg, Bavaria (the first state to establish psychiatric clinics at its universities), and Prussia, especially the Rhineland.

Although the somatically oriented institutional psychiatrists gradually prevailed during that period, once again a book by a professor became the representative work of the 1830s. K. W. Ideler, its author, who virtually secularized Heinroth, became the exponent of those who as "psychists" were pitted against the "somatists" — a simplified polarization of psychiatric historiography to describe the period from about 1805 to 1845. This concept might possibly be valid for that period when referring to the admittedly abstract facet of intellectual history: that Ideler and the other "psychists," departing from natural philosophy, sought to base psychiatry on an independent psychology, whereas the somatists fell away, as it were, on the other side of natural philosophy, and sought to furnish psychiatry with a purely somatic medical base. Yet under the given social conditions, both parties, each in its own way, remained wedded to an absolute. But more important, and largely overlooked is the fact that the "psychist" Ideler, via a theory of instinctual psychology, arrived at a sort of sociological psychiatry, the first and, in some respects, the only sociological psychiatry in Germany.

Ideler has often been called the German counterpart of Esquirol. And in fact, both attempted to incorporate insanity into actual "power play" of bourgeois society. The great difference however was that French civil society came to power under the Citizen King and Comte, whereas in prerevolutionary Germany it only began to take shape in its struggle against the semi-absolute state. Hence, Esquirol can represent civil society itself and the problem of the social integration of the unreason produced by that society. Ideler, by contrast, mirrors the ambivalence of his employer, the Prussian state, toward the economic liberalism of the bourgeoisie on the one hand, and its political liberalism on the other. His *Grundriss* of 1835 is dedicated to his friend, Von Altenstein. Ideler brought to psychiatry that abstract, endlessly polemical conflict between the idealists of the humanities — and in this context, the social sciences — who supported the more or less conservative state working toward social integration, and the natural-science materialists, primarily concerned with the emancipation of all social forces, with almost political liberalism. In Germany, this conflict prevented the sort of socio-somatic thinking — one is tempted to say still to this day — that eighteenth-century Enlightenment had made possible in England and France.[230]

Ideler (1795–1860), the son of a clergyman in Priegnitz, studied medicine in Berlin. He took part in the war against Napoleon, and in 1815, marched into Paris as a Prussian army doctor. In 1820, he went into general practice, until his friend Langermann helped get him appointed chief of the department of mental diseases at Berlin's Charité Hospital. There he was made professor of psychiatry in 1839, and from 1840 to 1860 he was the director of its new psychiatric clinic. The fascinating part in the career of this religious, introspective, depressive, music-loving hypochondriac was the relation between theory and practice, which he raised to a high level of abstraction. Ideler was filled with the missionary zeal of instructing and educating both his students and his patients; he was the author of numerous long works on the self-determination of man and the ethical renewal of the individual and society. But in practice, in the actual situation of the insane nothing was changed. The grotesque instruments of mechanical coercion going back to Horn remained in use throughout Ideler's regime, from 1828 to 1860. It has been reported that he would gather some fifty mental patients and preach to them to bring them to reason. And he felt a sense of accomplishment if even one of these would come to him to express remorse over past misdeeds. Obstinate patients were placed in the rotating chair or forced to stand for extended periods or subjected to similar disciplinary measures.[231] Ideler's behavior is usually described as paradoxical and incomprehensible, given his humanitarianism and profoundly ethical approach. But that is not so. Rather, what has been said about Langermann and Horn and what was one of the possible consequences of Kant's philosophy, is even more valid in his case: the unconditional nature of the morality demanded of the subject, legitimizes almost every means, every coercive measure, if morality is to emerge victorious and break through all external barriers and resistance and their internal correlatives, the passions. This approach marked both psychiatric practice and forensics. In the face of the internally necessary "rigorism of law," i.e. the premise of rational ethical freedom as an absolute principle, Ideler believed the sentencing or acquittal in individual cases to be a matter of "indifference."[232] Since in psychiatric therapy submission to the absolute moral principle and its implementing institutions is seen as an internal process, Ideler's theory led to the legitimation of the status quo, including the coercive instruments at the Charité. It is thus entirely consistent that for thirty-two years nothing changed in the situation of its mental patients. For the "pure thinker," which Ideler thought he was, is concerned with inner necessities, with ideas: a pure thinker does not rebel, does not want to reform the world.[233] The pointedness of these formulations virtually contained the seeds of Marx's reversals of them, especially since the materialistic physician, and also the Communist and the revolutionary "great mass," are in fact Ideler's adversaries, a point to which we will return.

In his *Grundriss der Seelenheilkunde*, Ideler rejects all previous psychology as being either too ontological or too logical, and for ignoring the role of passions and drives in spurring the will by "driving all opposing ideas from the consciousness."[234] Ideler's psychology by contrast is both empirical and ethical. It posits Kant's categorical imperative, the unconditional respect of moral law. But whereas Kant was still unable to close the split in the human organism, the dichotomy between thought and will, knowledge and morality, Ideler found their relative unity in the mind, for "morality is after all the uppermost concern of the mind." Therefore all striving of the mind, all drives, are aimed at freedom of action, and tend to become infinite, urgent, i.e. a passion, and out of inner necessity also tied to "painful self-denial," asceticism, to "discipline of the mind."[235] The same holds true for society, which spreads its powers liberally, but its discipline, asceticism, and harmony consist in the submission to its loftiest purpose: moral law and its institutions (state, family, education, law, religion).

Only within these moral boundaries does freedom of will exist, can pleasure be sanctioned, and can empirical psychology (and psychiatry) be possible. This involves the recognition of the "full dependence of reason on the impulses of the mind of the "dynamic" interrelation of the drives, one that is not logical and hence does not lend itself to direct verbal description. Consequently, the empirical psychologist is limited to "purely historical knowledge" and able to perform his diagnostic task solely by analyzing the motives between drives and actions. The historian who knows the "primal types of the powers of the mind," but who because of their unending, external modifiableness can engage only in "retrospective prophecy," finds himself in a similar situation as the psychologist. However, the latter's "practical genius" and "sure tact" enable him to understand the development of the impulses of the mind, to see in which of his dominating drives the individual remains true to himself — in terms of his character — has identity. But the materialistic physicians, putting organic results above moral findings, will exculpate a murderer, for example, "in order virtually to dismember the autocracy of the mind," they seek to build the moral forces from the lower organization of life, which Ideler tries to lead ad absurdum with the comment that, in its abstract and enveloping form, anticipates the breakthrough to psychoanalysis. For, so says Ideler, if that were true, then a "certain act" in the lower abdomen, as he dares to call it, would constitute a great moral activity.[236] What Ideler finds obvious is that only since Christianity's image of man have nations and individuals been relieved of the absolute necessity of moving toward one-sidedness and self-destruction. Rather, they can now be educated toward a harmonious development of all energy, so that work at the institutions is no longer a futile undertaking. Consequently Ideler coined the term "practical philosophy" for his discipline — i.e. the investigation of the empirical powers of the psyche and the conditions favoring moral education.

The psyche creates its own stimuli — self-causal — with no prompting from the body. Hence, there must exist "as many essential drives of the mind as originally different directions of the aspiring soul," whereby a drive is "essential" if it is active "before any civilization" and necessary "for the preservation of the social condition."[237] That is the basis for the similarities in individual character as it is of the phenomenon of history repeating itself. The institutions of property and class are essential to the preservation of the social condition, and this became even more clear-cut after the atrocities of the French Revolution. Egotism and the pursuit of money are necessary, since bourgeois society is founded on those principles, though within the boundaries and in service of morality. These opinions of Ideler are also representative of Prussia's ambivalence toward prerevolutionary German society. Work and industry as moral ends in themselves are socially stabilizing since they protect against the "wild desires of the great mass." Wealth per se teaches one the virtue of respect, just as the awareness of class differences — even in mental therapy — sharpens the mind.[238] Lastly, Ideler considers faith in goodness an irrefutable basic assumption, whereas materialistic skepticism about it will "simply remove [man] from the scene of activity."

Ideler's criticism of the "somatists", Jacobi, Friedrich, Gross as materialistic — although they of course would never have applied that term to themselves — is rooted in his positive interpretation of the "autonomy of the psyche." For the mind rules the bodily processes, pain is merely an inhibited drive, the physical character of the predispositions and temperaments is a "scientific void," and constitution, health, and disease can be considered in direct psychological terms and traced back historically to early childhood. Finally, organic life cannot sustain the infinite proliferation of a drive into a passion at the expense of all other drives, which constitutes their immorality.[239] In the eyes of Ideler, even Pinel, in addition to being somatic, is also too liberal, too indulgent in his ethical judgment, because he sees a disease automatism where unbridled passion is at work. He prefers Esquirol, the proponent of social integration, and adopts his moral-sociological etiology and monomania, i.e. passion as the root of insanity. Ideler agrees with Heinroth's excessive moral-pedagogical demand on the individual, but rejects his Schellingian thesis of the inherently evil nature of man for that absolves man of moral responsibility.

Ideler's authorities are ultimately Langermann and Stahl. In them he finds a reconciliation of idealism and materialism, which he sees as the victory of the former over the latter,[240] and, concretely, as the psychogenesis of insanity from passion: "In short, the insane man is the personification of passion, which permeates his every last fiber and manifests itself in all aspects of his spiritual and physical life."[241] This genetic connection allowed Ideler to view the unreason of the insane and the unreason of materialists and other political rebels as part of the same process. Consequently his psychiatry more clearly than ever before became the serviceable instrument of the ideological justification of the existing institutions. Thus, Ideler's "eronneous world view"[242] of the insane took on political overtones even before the beginning of the imperialist era. Just as insanity is the "unconcealed striving to destroy all order and coherence of the situation," one must realize that "today's world conquerors" and revolutionaries are the embodiment of passion and insanity, the only difference being that the insane isolate themselves while the literati interfere. On this new integrational level of the inner directed society, Ideler assigns the unreason of insanity the function of confirming the postulate from the negation that reason and morals demand the internalization of the prevailing ideas and institutions: "Insanity is thus simply any disturbance that conflicts with prevailing ideas and, unable to stand its ground against the latter, robs the mind of its composure and stands out more starkly in contrast to them." Since in liberal economic society the passions necessarily dominate, the majority of the people should by right be put away, but the psychiatrist Ideler fears for his livelihood, for in that event his livelihood would suffer.[243]

Just as in individual development the selfish drives are more powerful than ethical impulses, the Revolution was a time of satanic desecration and, since Robespierre, a "republic of cannibals." But then came forty years of moral progress, for the French realized the necessity of positive laws and absolute obedience, and found out that even despotism was preferable to mass violence and that mankind is served when, "with weapons in hand, the ruler's command to restore law and order" must be carried out "against the uncontrollable insurgents,"[244] just as in the treatment of the insane, the development of self-determination[245] and harmony of drives thwarts rebelliousness. While the enlightenment fought against medieval narrowness, now, conversely, untrammeled liberalism must be checked or else ennobled — through "restriction" — not economically, but morally. Just as the "genius of nature" manifests itself in the child, who needs discipline, not leniency, the aristocracy of the friends of truth, who know the "true needs," values censorship, and has little use for the parliaments and political (partisan) newspapers of France, England, and America.[246] Art and literature have also deviated from the moral purpose of the social compact: Voltaire is a subverter; Hugo, Dumas, and George Sand focus on the evil in man; and Rousseau, "who wanted to improvise a whole new world order on the ruins of the old, nay, destroy all law," is striking proof "that the idea, when it tears loose from its gradual developmental process and rushes toward its goal, must degenerate into insanity."[247] While the French, even after the Revolution, have failed to achieve moderation because of the activity of the masses, "the working class," Germany, where "wise rulers, celebrated heroes" rule, has achieved stability.[248]

The cooperation of "wise rulers" and economic expansion makes Ideler optimistic about Germany. Diseases are on the wane, the population is growing, and so the economy must be strengthened and colonies established. At the same time, life was becoming more natural, the "attitude toward life" more hopeful than in the revolutionary era, whereas "false liberalism" must be held responsible for the increase in mental illnesses.[249] Analogously, Ideler's moral-sociological "genetic explanation" makes the psychiatrist the "wise ruler" over the guilt-ridden life histories of his patients: "Insanity...always results from a complete and lasting suppression of reason by heightened passion whose development to that degree must be regarded as the sum total of all previous conditions of life and their relation to the outer world."[250] Thus, with Ideler, the intellectual-idealistic psychiatry of the "psychists" became part of those official, educational, and restrictive-oppressive institutions that, in order to legitimize and compensate for the economic expansion of social forces, threatened the individual with punishment for the abuse of the liberal development of their moral and political energies and interest — the punishment being the unreason of insanity.[251]

Nor, according to Ideler's forensic textbook, is the role of the psychiatrist any different before a court of law: moral freedom as the supreme positive legal principle, from which punishment is derived as a deterrent to assure "public order" also applies to the psychiatric expert, who develops his "objective pathology" from that supreme principle. That is to say, he psychologically places "the motive for the deed in a genetic context with the earlier life" of the defendant.[252] Against that, says Ideler, all the materialistic doctors have to offer is their subjective hypothesis that insanity is a brain disease. But they undermine the foundations not only of the state and civilization, but of science itself, and thus they provoke "the devastating censure of all well-meaning people."[253] Ideler demands the same internalization of discipline as self-discipline required by the economic needs of the industrializing society for science. For if one no longer wants a police in science, i.e. no longer wants psychiatry as a police science, "we therefore assume...the irrecusable obligation to fight relentlessly any doctrine that undermines welfare, whose poison, disseminated by cunning demagogues in times of general unrest, can send the undiscriminating populace into frenzied rage."[254] With inquisitorial-patriotic zeal Ideler compiled a blacklist of the positions that posed a threat to legal concepts and hence to society which even after his time made German psychiatry compartmentalize reason and unreason according to a predetermined political view:

Fatalism, which, denying all religious needs, declares the world to be the work of iron necessity whose mechanical law as determinism transforms human beings into automatons manipulated by hidden wires on the marionette stage of the world, produces the illusion of autonomous activity; sensualism, which, devoid of all creative spiritual power, ridicules the metaphysical concepts beyond its reach as mere self-deception and admits only palpably demonstrable truths; the chimera of a comparative psychology, which would seek to learn the secrets of the human soul from the life of animals which, after all, have no history or culture, and are mere clockwork....hollow skepticism, which, cognizant of its want of principles and presume the same lack in others, and thus incapable of any searching investigation of complicated constellations, dissolving the latter dialectically into sheer contradictions, thus serving egotism, which can find satisfaction only by violating morally valid principles; arrogance, which razes the intellectual achievements of millennia as outdated foolishness and extols its improvised wisdom as the proclamation of a new and better world order, communism, which would like to smash the lawful constitutions of nations in order to realize its mad notion of worldwide salvation and therefore writes the name of freedom on the banner of rebellion.[255]

While the idealist psychiatry of the "psychists" was plunged into crisis along with the state with which it identified,[256] and for a time after the Revolution of 1848 suffered a set-back, which is why Ideler's sociological approach was not accepted, the other reach for independence of the hitherto philosophical psychiatry started in the institutions. It produced the group of "somatists," who, no doubt far more energetically than the professors, strove to connect with the prerevolutionary tendencies of liberal bourgeois society. That is, they used the empirical data offered by their observations as institutional directors, leaning more strongly on French and English psychiatry, they sought to replace philosophy with positivist science, to follow the natural-scientific, materialist development of medicine in general, which, along with the physiology of J. Müller (from 1833 on) and Schwann and Schleiden's technological cell theory (1838—39), was beginning to gain a foothold in Germany. Furthermore, these "somatists" sought to liberalize and soften the pedagogical rigorism in the treatment of insanity. Their somatic approach also brought them awareness of the material situation of the patients. Finally, being more receptive to the aspirations of political liberalism than their academic counterparts, their following included psychiatrists who had been victims of political persecution.[257]

Among the "somatists" there were institutional directors and physicians: M. Jacobi, F. Bird, and W. Richartz in Siegburg; C. F. Flemming, who in 1830 succeeded in the then unheard-of idea of having his institution, Sachsenberg, built near a city (Schwerin) rather than in the traditional romantic rustic isolation; F. Nasse, who even though a professor at Bonn and director of a private asylum, nonetheless had practiced clinical psychiatry quite early, had based medical methodology on observation and systematized it, and was the first psychiatrist to adopt Herbart's associative psychology;[258] and C. F. W. Roller, the founder and director of the secluded asylum of Illenau, Baden (1842), a model example of the institution as "one big family," the dominant idea of the mid-century. In this, he referred to the work of French psychiatrists and to Lord Ashley, the conservative anti-capitalist champion of workers and the mentally deficient. He made the "insanity question" an integral part of the "social question." The medical association organized by him fought for social reforms, and he himself was instrumental in developing guidelines for the legal and governmental protection of the insane in Baden.[259] Finally, there was E. A. Zeller, like Roller the director of an institution. Put in charge of the asylum at Winnenthal, Württemberg in 1834, he modified the pedagogical restraint with somatic treatment as well as spiritual care. He got from Guislain the idea of "unitary psychosis" (*Einheitspsychose* — i.e. that the various forms of insanity are not independent but merely successive phases of a single disease process) and handed it down to his student Griesinger. He also demythologized Justin Kerner's *Seherin von Prevorst* as being mentally ill.[260]

Like most of his colleagues, he dabbled in music and poetry, and gained a measure of renown as the writer of Protestant hymn texts.

The "somatics," not coincidentally, also included forensic physicians like Friedrich and Blumröder. For Ideler's extreme forensic position would make it appear logical that many practicing physicians working for the courts sought the authority for their work in a natural science, in somatological theory rather than in the principle of moral freedom, and consequently they were favorably disposed toward the natural-science liberal opposition. And finally, there were some professors of medicine interested in psychiatry. One of them, K. F. Burdach, expressed "somatic" ideas, and delivered an address that played a role in the making of the 1848 Revolution. The occasion was the tricentennial celebration in 1844 of the old-liberal, free-trade University of Koenigsberg. In his official address as pro-vicechancellor, he accused the late-romantic, reactionary Minister of Education, Eichhorn, who was present, of being generally retrogressive.[261]

Like the political prerevolutionary era, the period of the "somatics" began around 1830. That was the year of not only the first new asylum, but also of Jacobi's important theoretical book. And 1831 saw the publication of the first work devoted solely to institutional practice in which its author, Roller, proclaimed a "new era" in the treatment of insanity, one in which psychiatrists would no longer look for the guilt or innocence of their mental charges, or seek to "pass judgment," but tender only "help and sympathy."[262] There was generally a unified stance against the idealist-philosophical and theological psychiatry of the Idelers and Heinroths. Just as Ideler had tried to connect with Kant's practical reason, now some of the "somatists" tried to connect with Kant's theoretical reason through the work of the philosopher Jakob Fries. In his *Psychologische Anthropologie* (1820–21), Fries had called on psychiatry to put an end to ethical-religious speculation and to turn to positivist realism as a basis of exact science.[263] Ideler was not the only one to have noted the dividing line between thought and will in Kant. The fact that both psychiatric trends, starting from different sociological premises (university vs. institution), attempted to link up with Kant, though at opposite ends, marked the point at which positivist science and philosophy also in this area threatened to diverge. Here, theory and practice as well as integration and emancipation were faced with the renunciation of either two things: (1) the mediation through reason as a critical yardstick of the claim to enlightenment, or (2) the equally critical acceptance of the seriousness of the empirical, though perhaps merely hypothetically experimental, controlled realization of theoretical and practical ideas. The confrontation of the two psychiatric schools under the abstract-alternate and abrupt formulation "somatists" vs. "psychists" symbolized this danger.

Of course, one could say that historically speaking the "somatists" were "right." This follows alone from the inability and lack of interest of the Heinroths and Idelers as well as the later reactionary-occult natural philosophers with respect to the "actual" mentally disturbed. In this context the parallel simultaneous development of physiology is of significance. Temkin[264] shows that the French physiologists, from Cabanis, Bichat, and Magendie to Claude Bernard, never quite lost touch with their philosophical tradition (Locke and Condillac as well as the school of Montpellier). That was why their materialism, despite its mechanism, never lost sight of the problems of the end/means relationship and of living organization and why it remained more or less a vitalist materialism. But in the Romantic era, the German physiologists were cut off from the eighteenth-century philosophical tradition. Idealist and natural philosophy represented a powerful enemy, one that furthermore forced them, as materialists, into political opposition when they tried to establish themselves in the late 1830s. The vitalist elements of natural philosophy also fell victim to this battle fought along absolutist lines. And so, says Temkin, a substantial number of German physiologists — Schwann, C. Vogt, Moleschott, Büchner, Dubois-Reymond, Freud's teacher Brücke, as well as the psycholgists Lotze and the left Hegelian L. Feuerbach — fell back not so much on biology as on biophysics and biochemistry as well as mathematical interpretations. Their materialism was unable to integrate vitalism. It was far more mechanistic than in France and in the terminology of Marxian critique, it ran the risk of turning into "vulgar materialism."

Psychiatry did not, of course, fully attain this level until the 1860s. The comparison, however, sheds light on the position of the "somatists" and their abstract-radical antithesis to the "psychists." And indeed, they were incapable of taking the decisive next step. Moreover, by and large they were still committed to the precepts of natural philosophy. Not coincidentally, Nasse was Reil's (only true) disciple, and Jacobi, the son of the philosopher F. H. Jacobi, the bridge from Kant to Schelling. The reason that most of the "somatists" believed insanity to be the result of a physical ailment lay in their refusal to admit that the soul, the divine spark within man in the view of natural philosophy, could fall victim to disease. Their analogies of the various bodily organs, especially the blood, to mental functions often differs little from the relationship craze of the genuine natural-philosophical psychiatrists. Basically speaking, the difference between them and the "psychists" was merely a formal one. Both camps engaged in a priori definitions, the only difference being that the one saw the pathogenesis of insanity as mental, the other as somatic. Yet there can be no doubt that the development of psychiatry into a science was made possible by the "somatists." The liberation of science from ontological, anthropological, and theological premises, and the liberation of the insane from religious guilt and pedagogically motivated mechanical restraint could only be achieved via the radical relativizing of all philosophical and institutional claims to absoluteness. And here the initiative came from the "somatists," although they could not make the breakthrough either theoretically or practically (most of them rejecting both the abolition of restraint and the clinical doctrine).

Maximilian Jacobi (1775–1858),[265] probably the most representative somatist, grew up in Düsseldorf. Through his famous father he met Goethe and Claudius. He studied medicine in Jena, Göttingen, and − most crucial − Edinburgh, and received his surgical training in London. Later, while in Munich, he helped reorganize the Bavarian public health service. After practicing medicine in Salzburg, he returned to Düsseldorf, and eventually rose to the position of government and medical councilor. In cooperation with Minister Von Altenstein he was instrumental in the founding of the Rhenish insane asylum in Siegburg. He headed this institution from its opening in 1825 until his death. His rule, to be sure, was patriarchal, marked, like that of his theoretical opponents, by pedagogical rigor. His merits and limitations can best be described by the fact that he accepted Tuke's work of 1813, and translated it into German in 1822,[266] although he rejected the non-restraint principle. He dismissed his most capable assistant, F. Bird, when the latter wanted to replace moral restraint in therapy with freedom of activity for patients. In later years, Jacobi became a prime target of theoretical and practical attacks by the two major forces of bourgeois liberalism: natural-scientific and economic materialism: based on his criticism of Jacobi's theory, Griesinger developed his own approach. And the authorities whom Jacobi had so faithfully served, in evaluating his institutional practice in terms alien to him, namely, economic efficiency, found costly waste out of all proportion to the rate of successful cures. It criticized his inefficiency, and, to effect savings, proposed to replace the attendants with nuns. Jacobi's humanitarian protest that cost should not be a factor in the treatment of the "mentally ill poor" was not listened to in the emerging capitalist society; what mattered now was the cost/success ratio.

Jacobi's theory was clearly outlined by 1821. At that time he said that if psychiatry was to be given solid foundation it must draw on the insights of the other medical specialities and on foreign experience and confine itself to "the most rigorous observation of nature and induction,"[267] even though prior to that time he himself had had few direct dealings with mental patients. The title of his major work of 1830, *Beobachtungen über die Pathologie und Therapie der mit Irresein verbundenen Krankheiten*, reflects his central theoretical thesis. He directs his polemics against Heinroth, whom he reverses as it were: the physical disorders are not the result of an original psycho-moral or sin-induced insanity, but rather bodily disease is invariably present first, and its secondary manifestations can include such mental phenomena as insanity. Insanity is simply a symptom of a somatic ailment. Hence one can speak only of "diseases linked to insanity." Jacobi's liberal-scientific, emancipatory intention aims to free insane from the basic postulate of the Christian-philosophical psychiatrists that the patients themselves are at fault. Hence, Jacobi denies that psychopathology can develop from normal psychology; and that is why he stresses the foreign and objectively inalienable nature of the disease process in the mentally ill. He thus asserts – for mankind in general as a possibility, and for the insane as a reality – that they are dominated, alienated, reified by something external, alien, and objective – the somatic disease – without any subjective guilt, objectively necessary, and without being able to defend themselves by anything they can do. This holds for ideas and feelings as for actions. Here was the point at which psychiatry attempted empirically, to preserve Schelling's "false unity," the reality and impenetrability of unreason. In contrast to the eighteenth-century Encyclopedists this was the beginning of a development that resembled the pattern of the, of course very dissimilar, problem of ideology that led to Marx, who, confronting idealism, insisted on the objective impenetrability of false consciousness, because and insofar as it was functionally contingent on the corresponding material conditions.[268] For Jacobi, Heinroth's philosophy represents nothing but the malicious indictment of people who cannot help their position as outsiders. He refuses to acknowledge that one can hold the insane responsible for their disorder, or for its cause, at the expense of their moral freedom, or that the psychiatrist, even if psychotherapeutically motivated, can make such a demand, one which can too easily become a claim to power.[269]

Jacobi's position was however integrated into a still largely natural-philosophical framework. Once physical disease, as the root of mental disease, became a postulate, in a number of case histories, even the slightest physical irregularities took on patho-genetic proportions. The necessity for the absolute difference between health and disease is based not on empirical but on loftier and simultaneously political premises, "since it forms the basis of faith in divine and human law, and without it neither ethics nor law can exist, both would become a chimera, and human life would lack the solid foundation needed to achieve morality, religion, and godliness through the implanted ideas of the good, the true, the beautiful."[270] Thus, there is still a goodly distance from Jacobi to the positivist division of labor between the physical and the "loftier" spiritual world. Yet the two have a factor in common: rhythm. Disease is arrhythmia, and restored health a return to rhythm, i.e. a development of the "sense of order, measure, and rhythm."[271] In general, the dominance of either organic or mental symptoms in a disease depends on the individual differences in temperament, and the importance of temperament derives from the fact that the entire human organism, not merely the brain or the nervous system, is the seat of the soul.[272] And history also shapes the temperament. Thus, their religious-political structure has helped the Jews preserve their physical-mental state; and even one's class or status leaves its mark on the body. But disease always originates in the body, through a revolution that shifts the harmony of the temperament. Consequently, any therapy, whether physical or mental, must follow that same route.[273]

While treating the chief forms of insanity in the traditional manner, Jacobi no longer claims the unity of a system growing out of a basic principle, as did the "psychist." Wyrsch[274] correctly points out that the factors eliminated from Jacobi's system — "the innate weaknesses and deficiencies...the degeneration of principle forms into secondary conditions, the ethical perversions and degradations" — were those that created the most problems in the late nineteenth century: feeble-mindedness and psycho-pathy, sexual perversions, and the chronic psychoses leading to mental deficiency.

Revolution, Medical Reform, and the Psychiatric Paradigm
(Griesinger)

In 1844, the same year that Jacobi published his thousand-page monograph on frenzy, witnessed an event that fairly institutionalized the victory of the institutional psychiatrists, i.e. the "somatists." The preceding decades had seen the appearance of countless psychiatric-anthropological "somatic" journals and their rapid disappearance. Now, with the help of institutional directors the first long-lived periodical, the *Allgemeine Zeitschrift für Psychiatrie und psychisch-gerichtliche Medicin*, was launched. Strange as this may seem, even though this journal proved its institutional strength (it continued to be published for more than a century), and even though it formed the basis for the association of German alienists, first as a section of the Association of Naturalists (1847), and later as an organization of their own (1865), it was nonetheless "belated." It marked an end, not a beginning, the end of a period of a psychiatry so philosophical as to be incapable of realizing crucial elements in the paradigm of a psychiatric science.[275] Thus Jacobi's *Tobsucht* at the time of its publication was already so "out-of-date" that he never published his projected works on the other chief forms of insanity. Instead, Griesinger's natural-scientific, materialistic major work of 1845 more and more came to be accepted as the starting point for all scientific discussion. Moreover, the Revolution of 1848 and the partial success of liberalism (despite the failure of the Revolution) wrought a change in the popular perception of the institutional directors who identified with the reform-bureaucratic tradition of the state, and of the contributors to the *Allgemeine Zeitschrift*. These men now appeared more and more anachronistic and "removed from life." Heinrich Damerow (1798–1866), the editor in chief of the *Zeitschrift* was the personification of this situation. The son of a clergyman, like many of his colleagues, he had studied psychiatry under Horn and philosophy under Schleiermacher, and more especially, Hegel. After several "institutional tours," he became professor at Greifswald, and then, as Altenstein's confidant, was put in charge of the department of mental diseases in the Berlin Ministry. In 1844, he became director of the Nietleben institution near Halle. All of Damerow's writings underscore the dubious nature of adherence to Hegelian thought after Hegel's death without having digested him. Damerow's political, philosophical, and psychiatric world consists of a collection of yet to be shaped idealistic syntheses — even after natural-scientific and economic criticism had concluded that "the Idea can be developed only out of real differences," and philosophy realized "only through the negation of existing philosophy."[276] This begins with his idea of the "relatively connected institutions for treatment and care-taking,"[277] which he sees as a higher synthesis of these previously separated types. In fact, the actual stimulus for this idea, which incidentally had already been realized in Hildesheim (1827) and Marsberg (1835) came from the dashing of the original optimistic hope that successful cures were more likely in large, imposing institutions devoted exclusively to treatment, as well as to an economy-minded bureaucracy that found the combination and joint administration of hospitals and care centers to be the cheaper solution.[278]

Similarly, Damerow projected countless other antitheses of which there was not exactly a shortage in his time. Thus, for him, psychiatry was the science of the future combining medicine and philosophy. And the soul was brought forth by the dialects of body and spirit, or, "out of the harmony of theory and experience of history emerged the soul, as the element of the future in history."[279] Nevertheless, his skillful idealistic mediation enabled him to bring together the various directions of psychiatry — the academic "psychists" and natural philosophers as well as the "somatists" of institutional practice — on the basis of his "universal" journal. Here, too, yearning for national unity proved to be a powerful motive, one that inspired him with the idea of a "German psychiatry."

Philosophy outweighed the natural-science approaches even for the "somatists." And nothing shows this more clearly than the fact that Damerow could commit the "somatists" to his idealistic program, which he formulated as an introduction to the first issue of his periodical whose co-publishers were "somatists" (Roller and Flemming), and which down to the last detail was an imitation of the year-old journal of the French psychiatrists.[280] This journal proved to Damerow that German psychiatry had reached "a higher factor of theoretical unity" in its development: that of anthropology, which represents the unity of man as body, soul, and spirit, and which is the root or background of all individual, peripheral, merely "artificial theories" of the tree of psychiatry. The fact that anthropology has brought unity to psychiatry is shown above all in the "practical, factual, concrete... objective nature of psychiatry," i.e., in the treatment of the insane and their public care. For it is there that psychiatry breaks away from the narrowness of individual theories of blood, brain,

passions, etc., taking the freer anthropological, i.e. the humane
position. The one-sided theories have objective, historical value
as "ends in themselves for science and as means to higher purposes
of life." Objective psychiatry, practice, life, i.e., the anthropological idea, continues to be the proper guide to theory. From this,
again in Hegelian fashion, he deduces that "German psychiatry,
applied in life, grown from word to deed" must be subordinated
not only to the idea, but also to the state: "The administrative
organism of the problem of insanity must be both subordinate
to and incorporated into the higher, broader authority of the
state." Applied, practical and official, objective psychiatry thus
becomes the mediator between physicians and government, theory
and practice, word and deed, idea and execution, method and
administration — as a mutual interpenetration and unification in
a third, independent, positive product, just as the soul grows
out of the body and spirit, the present out of the past and future.
In setting up these organismic categories, Damerow may have
done justice to the past, but hardly to the present, and certainly
not to the future. For Damerow, the state of public care of the
insane represents a valid yardstick of the spiritual culture and
the moral-intellectual freedom in a country. Yet this continues
to be a psychiatry "from above" in a dual sense: from the idea
and from the state. Thus he expresses admiration for the progress
in the handling of the problem of insanity in Austria: "Alone,
the decision from above to found a new large insane asylum has
become the spiritual level, bearer, and promoter of psychiatry
and the public treatment of the insane." He believes it is the
responsibility of the state to train medical "psychiatrists," and
that psychiatry develops to the extent that "it is the object of
special concern by the state," which explains Prussia's great strides
in this matter since Frederick William IV.[281] And therefore he
believed that his journal would not only serve to unify psychiatry
in its dealings with practical problems, not only facilitate unification through the application of the statistical method in all of
Germany, and not only help to bring nations closer together,
but that it would also serve the cause of Germany's national
unity.

Damerow was unaware that his enthusiastic, forward-looking
introduction to the journal was in nearly every respect an obituary
on the past:

1. In these final prerevolutionary years of growing social problems, the natural sciences, including psychiatry, despite a more
rigid censorship, were no longer agreeable to being pressed into

the framework of anthropological ideas and idealistic syntheses.

2. The same asylums that Damerow called "the finest humanitarian and charitable institutions" were beginning to be criticized
for operating along Romantic notions and isolating the mentally
deranged from the cities and society. They ought instead, it was
felt, to be turned into hospitals, since its inmates were merely
sick.

3. Damerow's Hegelian rejection of the non-restraint movement
as a mere negation of the past, as a hothouse fruit of England's
"unformed psychiatry," and his defense of mechanical restraint
as "intelligently applied overt restraint" were another instance
of "belatedness." This view dominated until other psychiatrists,
not affiliated with his journal, substituted its radical, unformed
negation for justification of the status quo.

4. Damerow was also rather helpless in the face of the impact
of capitalism on social processes and their effect on the position
of the mentally ill. Since there was less willingness to tolerate
special units isolated from the production process such as the
patriarchal insane asylums, the mentally ill were allowed closer
proximity to cities and society. The cost of institutionalization
was related to success of treatment, and therapy as far as possible
was oriented toward work. Damerow himself fell victim to this
economic thinking of the state, namely the remuneration for
his work in behalf of the mentally ill at the Berlin Ministry (1848),
despite his philosophically framed protest.

5. Damerow's subordination of psychiatry to the state and his
idealistic integration of Ideler's sociological approach continued
to obscure the connection between the "insanity question" and
the "social question." Support of the state was so much taken
for granted that political-philosophical emancipation was confined
to the realm of the neutral natural sciences. But in general medicine, Virchow, commissioned by the government to investigate
the Silesian typhus fever epidemic of 1847—48, blamed the
epidemic on the government and instead of medication or food,
he prescribed "total and unrestricted democracy," cooperatives,
and the slogan of the radical Struve: "Education, in conjunction
with freedom and prosperity."[282] He viewed his cell theory as
a model of the democratic state, medicine as "a social science,"
physicians as "the natural advocates of the poor, and the social
question...to a considerable extent as falling under their jurisdiction.[283] Hardly anything in psychiatry, much less anything
in Bismarck's government, could match this sort of self-confidence.
The man who came closest to this was R. Leubuscher, the only

doctor at the Berlin Workhouse (with an annual intake of 7,000 asocial mentally deranged individuals), and next to S. Neumann, a physician treating the poor, Virchow's closest friend in the fight for political democracy and medical reform during the 1848 Revolution. Leubuscher called on psychiatrists to come out of the isolated institutions and confront the social problems of "life." Historically-theoretically he distinguished between the "individual insanity" of the dispositions from the "social insanity" determined by a "law following the norms of society." Overtly visible insanity is the result of the "mutual interdependence of both series of phenomena."[284] This is the first reference to the social factor in what at one time was called the unreason of insanity.

6. While Damerow draws on Christianity for his anthropology, and perhaps uses a book review to have the German states arrive at a national religion[285] by way of therapy and psychiatry (incidentally, expelling the nonassimilable), and while religion was to play a part in asylums for some time to come, academic psychiatry, having become a secular natural science, renounced this approach. And the fact that natural-scientific − positivistic neutral research posed far less of a political danger than the science of the prerevolutionary era whose philosophical commitment also implied a political commitment − for or against the status quo − was no doubt connected with the liberalization of the universities in 1850s and 60s.

7. The attitude toward clinical instruction was skeptical or negative, less so Damerow's than that of most of his institutional colleagues, such as Leupoldt, Flemming, and Jacobi. They maintained that clinical demonstrations were harmful to patients. Behind this, however, was the justified fear of the institutional doctors that psychiatry would become even more strongly entrenched in the universities, that the mentally ill would be demythologized, from philosophically conceived irrational into somatically ailing individuals; that, deprived of the protective order of state and class they would be exposed to the disorder of society, the public, and the towns, and this in turn would deprive the classical asylum, as the self-sufficient microcosm of the world, of its romantic appeal and its moral-pedagogical claim. For clinic inevitably meant city. And this in fact was the appeal of the liberal, natural-science psychiatrists: to emancipate the mentally ill not from mechanical but from moral restraint, and to bring them as close as possible to civil society. Yet the new forms of emancipation were also followed by new forms of

integration; actual integration into the production process and, in the 1870s, a theoretical and philosophical integration into the doctrine of degeneration.

The emancipation of the Jews proceeded in an analogous fashion. Around 1860, their emancipation ceased to be seen from the pedagogical aspect of their obligation to prove their maturity, but as was the case from the very start in the French Revolution — from that of political liberalism and economic utility: "This line of reasoning revealed...a departure from the enlightened-absolutist conception of emancipation....The state was not there to educate ....all it had to do also for the Jews was to remove obstacles and create the conditions for the free development of the individual in civil society. The social integration of the Jews could no longer be the task of the state, but simply the task of society itself."[286] And here too — and just as emancipation was being realized — a new concept of integration was being posited: the concept of the "Jewish race."[287]

8. The failure of Damerow and his followers becomes most obvious in their Hegelian identification with the state and their effort to derive psychiatry from the state as well — despite the failed revolution and the reactionary 1850s. Damerow was on excellent terms with Kultusminister Eichhorn, the most hated man of the 1840s, and even his journal owed its existence to an initiative "from above." For only after Eichhorn, in 1843, announced that he would open his ministry's files to the journal and extend financial support by subscribing to forty copies, but only if Damerow were put in charge, could the journal be launched.[288] The title, incidentally, no longer — as often in the past — addressed the lay public; however, it did open its pages to the accounts of psychiatry's forensic services to the government. Thus it comes as no surprise that, after the 1848 Revolution, Damerow's journal frequently took a pro-state position against those doctors who championed the cause of the poor. Kieser read the signs of the times correctly. Writing in 1850, he equated the "unreasoning one-sidedness" of proletarian passions during the Revolution with the unreason of the insane, which in the past society had sought to fight or harmonize within the confines of institutions. Kieser reduces reason to the idea of order in which the pedagogical state and the power state converge. Like insanity, the "growing political mental confusion" is a mental disorder. Both are only mental and should be treated by strengthening reason and faith, i.e., humility. Hence, these are also the sole preventive means of "putting up a shield against the gathering

storm, and its consequences, that the proletariat proclaims."
A dike must be constructed against the "looming anarchy" of the
internal enemy and the growing danger from without, protective
armor for the imminent "days of decision" — under the eyes
of the "almighty everlasting wisdom from above."[289] A dissertation entitled *De morbo democratico* submitted to and accepted
by the medical faculty of the University of Berlin in that period,
i.e., in Ideler's days, is merely an extreme expression of that
view.

These eight aspects made it impossible for the younger psychiatrists to accept existing psychiatry any more than the existing
state, and steered them toward the natural sciences and liberalism.
Consequently, never before nor since in the history of German
medicine did so many psychiatrists — and doctors in general —
become politically involved as before and during the Revolution
of 1848. To be sure, a further factor entered into this, for this
revolution was marked by the spread of special socio-economic
interest groups — middle class, artisans, professions and trades,
and proletariat. The divisions and conflicts of these special interest
groups played no small part in the failure of the uncoordinated
and belated revolution, in which the workers demanded their
rights at a time when the bourgeoisie had not yet attained its
rights. The physicians concentrated their efforts on medical
reform[290] — long a subject of growing concern, and one that also
coincided with the revolution in France. Never before nor since
were doctors so closely tied to the state or so bureaucratic as in
those years. The medical schools enjoyed broad supervisory powers.
A Prussian edict of 1835 mandated the political clearance of medical students prior to their appearance before the official examining
board. The class ranking of doctors resulted in chaos. The low and
arbitrary remuneration of (young) doctors led to stiff competition
and to deficient care for the poor. Berlin, and Virchow's and
Leubuscher's journal *Medizinische Reform* — published from June
1848 to June 1849 — were the centers of the reform movement,
but their efforts failed in part because of their heterogeneity, the
orientation being now English, now French, now conservative, now
socialist. The movement was unified in its goals of independence
from the state and the academy of professional self-determination,
national unification, and also economic adaptation to the liberal
economic society in which "compulsory treatment" (for government employees as for the poor) was to be replaced by free choice
of treatment and of doctors. Yet this freedom also affected the
proletariat adversely, even though some employers in the 1840s —

even before Bismarck's time — experimented with social insurance in their enterprises. And though none of the demands was then realized, due to this revolutionary impulse, most of them materialized during the "liberal sixties." Thus the 1848 demand of Berlin medical students for abolishing the history and philosophy requirement was met in 1861, when physics replaced philosophy in the curriculum. Nothing could symbolize the new situation of medicine — and psychiatry — more tellingly. From a discipline integrated into political science and forensics, and reflected in philosophy and history, medicine was now, though only in terms of the subjective claim, liberated to a natural science. For objectively, allegedly discarded conditions remained — either as a political reality or an inherent task of science. But since that time, the positivistic approach of doctors and psychiatrists has lulled them into the belief that these conditions no longer have to be thought about. If medicine is now becoming aware of the consequences of this error, we tend to forget that the victory of natural science in medicine and psychiatry at that time was a great achievement, a liberation from theological, philosophical, and political restrictions on both theory and practice.[291]

This will explain why so many younger psychiatrists, unlike their elders, were politically active during the revolutionary period — even if in smaller numbers than their colleagues in general medicine. For even in the era of liberalism and natural science, psychiatry's economic and social role of defining and vouching for sanity did not change. We have already mentioned Leubuscher, and also Blumröder, a leftist councilman of Frankfurt. In 1848, Griesinger, a young associate professor at Tübingen, the same university that had expelled him for republican activities while a student in the thirties, belonged to the left.

E. von Feuchtersleben, like Kant and P. K. Hartmann a self-appointed psychosomatist, a prominent figure of Viennese society of the thirties and forties, and as dean of its medical school, the spokesman for Austria's medical reformers, was dismissed from his post in 1848. Like many contemporary psychiatrists, he was influenced by K. Rosenkranz, a Hegelian and a philosopher who lectured on psychiatry at Koenigsberg.

H. Neumann, the first of a long line of eminent Jewish psychiatrists in the late nineteenth century, was probably the only theoretical psychiatrist of the nineteenth century. His applied somatic and psychiatric "analytical method" was adopted by Wernicke and Freud. As assistant at the Leubus asylum in Silesia he sought during the revolutionary period to introduce a "constitutional administration" in which all employees would be given a voice, and he criticized the traditional psychiatrists as a "closed caste." These policies did not enhance his popularity at the institution, and in 1850, he left it, first serving as army doctor during the Polish uprising; subsequently, in 1852, he founded a private mental hospital near Breslau, which, significantly, he referred to as a "medical institution."

G. B. Heinrich, a young associate professor at Koenigsberg active in politics and medical reform in 1848 belonged to the Gagern-Dahlmann party, and for a while to East Prussia's democratic-constitutional party. The combination of a long-standing depression, and political disappointment drove him to suicide in April 1849. In a note written on New Year's Eve he said: "For weeks now I've been paralyzed and incapable of any activity whatsoever.... A new year stands before us. The idealistic dream of 1848 is over; now comes reality."[292]

K. Spurzheim, an Austrian reformer and nephew of the phrenologist, who headed an institution in Ybbs and later in Vienna, was a deputy in the Frankfurt Parliament in 1848.

While a student at Bonn, Ludwig Meyer was an active revolutionary, together with Schurz, Kinkel, and Spielhagen. Having taken part in an attack on an armory, he was charged with sedition and expelled from the university. During the reactionary period, he was protected by Virchow in Würzburg. In 1858, in Hamburg, he was the first German to accept Conolly and introduce the non-restraint principle. He was therefore predisposed toward working closely with Griesinger for a natural-science psychiatry and for the abolition of all mechanical restraint. Yet he was also typical of his time in that he ultimately became an enthusiastic Bismarck supporter and a National Liberal candidate for the Reichstag.

August Zinn, born in the Bavarian Palatinate, studied forestry before joining the 1848 Revolution. A civil commissioner in the provisional government, he was forced to flee to Switzerland in 1849. Here his friendship with the physiologist Ludwig, led him to the study of medicine. As a psychiatrist, he became involved in the reform of various Swiss and German asylums, the last one in Eberswalde/Brandenburg. He, too, remained politically active, and he too, as a Reichstag deputy, changed from the progressives to the "Löwe-Zinn" group and then to the National Liberals.

Finally, there was J. Spielmann of Bohemia, whose *Diagnostik der Geisteskranken* (1855) was almost forgotten, though it was scarcely inferior to Griesinger's theory.[293] In 1847 Spielmann joined the Prague asylum. He too was active as a revolutionary and he set an undoubtedly unique process in motion: he involved the inmates of his institution in the revolution. Since the revolution-aries had no printing presses, he had the patients copy the political leaflets by hand — a sort of mimeograph machine. Needless to say, he too was dismissed. As a result, as one of the first psychiatrists in private practice in Tetschen-Bodenbach, he became involved in numerous social-reform activities, and developed his noninstitu-tional psychiatric theory.

The above eight aspects outline the situation between 1840 and 1865. They also define the areas in which Griesinger arrived at his negation of existing psychiatry, which we believe, gave rise to the first comprehensive theoretical and practical paradigm of psychiatric science in Germany. That is to say, it completed that which Reil had begun, but which because of Germany's particular philosophical, socio-economic, and political development, could not materialize in the interim.

A comparative study of the social background of the psychia-trists based on their fathers' professions also testifies to the structural change that took place at mid-century. Available biogra-phical data show the following: 33 per cent of 67 psychiatrists who studied medicine between 1800 and 1845 were the sons of professionals, and the same held true for 42 per cent of 90 psychiatrists who studied medicine between 1846 and 1890. The increase occurred mainly in families of doctors, merchants, indus-trialists, and lawyers. However, as far as the sons of civil servants are concerned the difference between the early and later dates is imperceptible — a decrease from 56 to 54 per cent. This high proportion is yet another indication of the affinity between those from a "pillars of the state" milieu and psychiatry.[294] Both in the early and late century this civil-service contingent was made up in equal parts of higher administrative officials, clerics, and medical officers. Moreover, upward social mobility in the latter half of the century, in the liberal "free and equal" struggle for existence, was evidently much harder than in the bureaucratic, feudal closed society of the first half, when personal patronage extended even to scientific careers. Between the first and second half of the century, the proportion of those from the most modest social background possible for psychiatrists — petty officials, artisans, or small farmers — fell from 13 to 5.5 per cent.

Wilhelm Griesinger (1817—68) was the son of the administra-tor of the Stuttgart hospital who was killed by the family's mentally ill piano teacher.[295] In 1834, Griesinger began his medical training at Tübingen. He refused to attend the psychiatric lectures of the natural philosopher Eschenmayer, who was busy polemicizing against Hegel and D. F. Strauss. Instead Griesinger devoted himself to the study of Johannes Müller's physiology. The previously mentioned political university council forced him to leave and he went to Zurich. There he became a disciple of J. L. Schönlein, a naturalist-physician, even though later (1842) he opposed him as an ontologist. In 1838, after obtaining his doctorate, Griesinger spent a year in Paris, where he studied with Magendie. In 1839, he went into general practice at Lake Constance. In 1840, be began a two-year residency at the insane asylum of Winnenthal under the somatist Zeller. There he befriended one of the patients, the physician and naturalist Robert Mayer. This friendship led to their famous correspondence about the mechanical heat equivalent, the conversion of heat and motion, and the extension of the energy principle to all natural phenomena, including those of a physiological nature.[296] The two-year residency provided Griesinger with the basis for his major work of 1845, i.e., (a) the empirical material for observation, (b) his mentor Zeller's theoretical model of unitary psychosis, and (c) Mayer's ideas of the physical rather than organic sources of energy.

Nevertheless, for some time to come, Griesinger devoted himself almost exclusively to physiology, pathological anatomy, and general medicine. However, he never thought of this as antithetical to psychiatric medicine. In 1843, he became resident at Tübingen's university clinic under his childhood friend K. A. Wunderlich. Then, in 1847, he took over the editorship of Wunderlich's *Archiv für physiologische Heilkunde*. That same year he was made associate professor. 1848 was the beginning of a period of political activity that encompassed reforms in medicine and the field of insanity. In 1849, he became full professor at the Kiel university clinic, and in 1850, he accepted the offer of the Egyptian viceroy to head the Medical School of Cairo. Here he wrote major works on tropical diseases. In 1854, he became director of Tübingen's university clinic, and in 1859, he began his observations at the Mariaberg institution for feeble-minded children, which he incorporated into the second edition of his psychiatric book (1861). Since the government refused to see the importance of the outpatient clinic he wished to set up, he decided to accept a position at Zurich in 1860.

This was the beginning of Griesinger's second psychiatric phase, one of practical change. With the help of his friends Billroth and

Wesendonck, he converted the existing insane asylum into a clinic, i.e. he transformed institutional psychiatry into "university psychiatry," since he looked on insanity as a physical illness. At the same time, he introduced the non-restraint principle and planned for a new large insane asylum. Offered a chair at Berlin (1864), he agreed to accept it only on condition that in addition to his professorship he also be given a neurological clinic and an out-patient clinic, because he rejected the purely psychiatric specialization as lacking a somatic basis. He had traveled widely and continued to, mainly to familiarize himself with the freer handling of the mentally ill in Western countries. In England, he studied the non-restraint principle; in France, the "agricultural colonies," such as the farm founded by Fitz-James in 1847; and in Belgium, the settlement of mental patients at Gheel. In Berlin, he abolished all mechanical restraints, for which he was vehemently attacked, particularly since he had to succeed Ideler. Griesinger's combination of a "psychiatric and neurological clinic" which he instituted in Berlin remained the model for all "university psychiatry" for the next hundred years. In 1867, together with his friend L. Meyer and his pupil and successor J. C. Westphal, he founded the *Archiv für Psychiaterie und Nervenkrankheiten.* This was an attack on the institutional psychiatrists and their *Allgemeine Zeitschrift*; the liberal, natural-science university psychiatrists not only demanded free treatment for the mentally ill and the abolition of restraints, but they also ushered in an almost "imperialist" penetration by psychiatry of the (non-psychiatric) somatic brain and nervous diseases, and also — even more portentous — of society as a whole — i.e., those countless individuals whose "irrationality" could not previously become visible because they had never been in institutions, who had concealed their problems with society from that society, keeping them locked up within themselves. But now, as their "weakness" was becoming "conspicuous" to the pitiless diagnostic control agent of economic liberalism — efficiency — this army of the "irritable and weak," the "abnormal," the "sexual perverts," the psychopaths, compulsives, neurotics — the area in which the borderline between the "abnormal" and "normal" is indistinct — began to unburden themselves at least to the privately practicing neurologist or the clinical psychiatrist. Having hidden their "unreason" behind a "façade," they became visible to Griesinger, and prompted him to launch this psychiatric movement as well, or rather revive the tradition of "private practice psychiatry," integrating it in "clinical" psychiatry, particularly through the institution of the "out-patient clinic."[297]

On his deathbed — Griesinger died of appendicitis aged fifty-one — he learned that the association of the still powerful institutional psychiatrists had turned down his reform proposals, almost all of which were eventually realized. While his students, in keeping with the times, said that he had died "fighting for his beliefs,"[298] even his obituary was attacked. Although Griesinger helped shape both the institutional and the therapeutic practice of psychiatry, and despite his vital contribution to all subsequent theoretical directions — neuropathological, clinical, and psychoanalytical psychiatry — no comprehensive study of his achievements exists. The dominant institutional psychiatrists of his day (e.g., Damerow, Jacobi, and Flemming) whom he opposed, were naturally reserved or negative. And even though the subsequent period up to the turn of the century did accept him, the various schools extracted those portions that suited them (and hence soon became rigidified) from his paradigm; or else they soon found him too speculative and deductive. Griesinger's reputation suffered a serious setback in the late 1920s (and in the Nazi era), when medicine and psychiatry began to look backward toward philosophy, when the nineteenth century was castigated as positivistic and materialistic, and when, reacting neo-romantically, they turned to new or old ontologies and "totalities."[299] This response, which may not survive much longer, was manifested as early as 1932 by Gruhle, who claimed that all Griesinger had to offer was a classification of forms of insanity based on anatomy, that everything else was confused, and that he could not understand the reason for the many editions of his book.[300] According to L. Binswanger (1936), Griesinger established the "framework of clinical psychiatry" and probably also practiced "a psychology of understanding" (though, of course, Griesinger did not yet differentiate between "understanding" and "explanation," or set them against each other as separate entities), and both Kraepelin's clinical psychiatry and Freud's psychoanalysis derive from Griesinger's "framework." However, this insight supports a rejection of both Kraepelin and Freud in favor of Binswanger's anthropological, existential analytical psychiatry, which holds that "something" is added to life, to nature, before it becomes "humanness," hence his psychiatry starts out from "total being," which is why mental illness is not illness, but the "original possibility of humanness." With this, Griesinger is held responsible for psychiatry's fall from grace; since his time, constructive thought rather than anthropology has held sway; humanness has been depersonalized, and the phenomenological facts deformed.[301]

Ten years later, the same tune was being sung. J. Bodamer, in 1948, sees in Griesinger a classical, monistic, "absolutely mechanistic system," built up into a solid unit from the elements of reflex, association, and unitary psychosis, yet he concedes that Griesinger's concept of psychological disease and other matters do not perhaps fit into this scheme.[302] And eight years later, this reaction to nineteenth-century materialism continued on its course. J. Wyrsch misses the "person" quality of the "I" in Griesinger and feels "as though we had left the living world," since here the I is merely the abstraction of all that came before.[303]

The first more relevant interpretation of Griesinger seems to be that of Ackerknecht, who sums matters up thus: "Just as Marx claimed to have utilized Hegel's philosophy and at the same time to have 'put it on its feet,' i.e. interpreted it materialistically, so Griesinger could have claimed to have put romantic psychology 'on its feet.'"[304] In the United States, too, Griesinger has recently been rediscovered. 1965 saw the publication of a work that criticized the "official" psychoanalytic historian of psychiatry, Zilboorg, for his failure to recognize the psychological component in Griesinger. The authors, in contrast, in a remarkable feat, trace practically all basic concepts of psychoanalytical, dynamic psychiatry back to Griesinger.[305]

Finally, M. Schrenk, writing in late 1968, hints at a possible Griesinger renaissance and indicates that today's conflicts are very much a part of the developmental possibilities of Griesinger's paradigm: "Amazingly enough," he says, "Griesinger's thesis of the mental diseases as brain diseases — a thesis neither psychological let alone sociological but natural-scientific — wrought a decisive change in the realm of all the problems that we today call social psychiatric, that is to say...(1) in the position of the mentally ill within society; (2) in the problem of their hospitalization; (3) in the view of social influences on the causes of mental disturbances." Schrenk calls this "amazing" and "paradoxical" and believes that the only reason Griesinger was unable to give his social psychiatry today's accepted form was that his approach lacked the philosophical and medical "anthropological concept of the person."[306] It would appear that here we are still dealing with the unhappy German-idealist stereotype according to which a nonpersonal, materialistic natural science has to be mated with a "person" conceived "from above" or somewhere in order to comply with "reason." Griesinger's most legitimate student and follower, Karl Bonhoeffer, resisted the Nazi regime not only as part of the 20th of July group, but also as a dedicated natural-science psychiatrist and as a physician, much more readily than many of the psychiatrists whose approach included the idealistic, anthropological concept of the individual.

So much for an interpretation of Griesinger in terms of his biography. One of Griesinger's first scientific statements is an emphatic commitment (1842) to negation and against positivism (with which he is still charged today), to criticism and to the mediation of theory and practice. "Facts! Only facts! cries a positivism that has no inkling that at each point science must resort to negation at each new step, a positivism that does not want to see that every reconstruction of ideas must be preceded by their resolution." Thus begins the essay that shows Griesinger's double-faceted reflection, his two-front war against the speculation and ontology of the past and against the highly cumulative, many-faceted positivistic research of today. It is no longer the philosophers who ought to be the theoreticians, but those who themselves have "wrestled with the particulars of the material." And with those who consider themselves the "positive" ones, he pleads for the subjectivity, the "partisanship" of science, whose standpoints ought to be "something 'experienced,' a gradual result of study and the outlook on life of its owner," for "nature must be grasped with warmth and intimacy"; only then in negation something that "impels and furthers from the inside." At the same time, however, the subjective process is an objective one: "Research into natural history is itself nature, the necessary urge of the one side, the side seeking to know, toward the other, the perceivable; of which the subject feels himself to be the bearer, with pride and joy but not superciliousness." The "mutual interpenetration of practice and theory, of life and science" can succeed only to the extent that the individual balances the external and internal direction of his nature.[307]

With this basic aim, Griesinger tries to put philosophical medicine on its feet in terms of natural science. Thus he takes up the cudgels against the ontology of the "Christian-Germanic" Ringseis and the Prussian court physician Schönlein: against their "ontological concept of disease, which continues to dominate German medicine," against the systems by which disease "exemplars" are "shown under glass"; against the absoluteness of the distinction between sickness and health he posits the only means that appear to him as legitimate: "Physiology in the widest sense, pathological anatomy, and the criticism of the status quo."[308] Nothing else is possible but the negation and liquefaction of all that is final and all systems, the pursuit of all dysfunction and all the pathological details and stages of the disease process to its underlying material derangement, without predetermining the investigational process by means of an externally imposed absolute principle: "We do not yet understand the essence of any disease in these terms."[309] This essence, which is both "the entire history of the disease" and its material nature, thus becomes the utopia of Griesinger's natural-scientific medicine to which the theoretical mediation of the empirically observable via physiology must irrefutably refer, while never losing sight of the transitoriness, "the abstractness of all these attempts at explanation."[310] Griesinger thus reduces the method of physiology to the dialectical formula of the mutual interpenetration of the experimental-constructive and the historical-critical method.[311]

Pathology is also set on its feet. While Griesinger rejects the nosological system on which physicians base their practice, as "impractical," he regards theoretical pathology as "eminently practical, because it bridges and ties together practical medicine and physiology and anatomy, and thus provides a rational basis for medical judgment and procedure." At the same time, he finds pathology "philosophical" insofar as its universality is not super-imposed on it "aprioristically from the outside," from some world order, but in fact results from the configuration of the discrete components of that which has been empirically observed.[312] That is why Griesinger — like Marx — was rejected by the philo-sophers as a positivist and elementalist,[313] and by the positivists as a philosopher. Yet this also accounts for the concreteness, and durability of his paradigm. Griesinger's mediation of subject and object, negation and affirmation, theory and practice, construc-tion and historical critique, man and nature, characterizes the "seriousness" of the sustained and growing irreconcilability, the nonidentity of these circumstances.[314] Thus, Griesinger's neurophysiology (though less so that of his successors) is merely a "construction" open to its historical self-abrogation. And the psychiatry based on it is not a system, nor does it have a synthesis in an idealistic identity, however generously equipped it may be with a wide range of analogies. Hence, this psychiatry exposes mental diseases as actual disruptions and alienations of man's physiological activity without reintegrating them systematically or normatively; it is able to recognize real but previously invisible disorders, and in an unprecedently unreasonable manner opens society to the irrationality of derangement.

Griesinger's theoretical outline of psychiatry was presented in two articles in a physiological journal (1843 and 1844), in a review of Jacobi's *Tobsucht* (1844), and in his major comprehensive work (1845). The first article, *Über psychische Reflexactionen*, offers the "structure" of his theory. Since the spinal cord and the brain are anatomically connected, thus Griesinger begins, it seems appropriate to compare their "vital activities," i.e. "emphasize the parallels between the functions of the spinal cord and those of the brain insofar as it is the organ of the mental phenomena in a narrower sense."[315] With this — and this is crucial — Griesinger's paradigm links up with the tradition of eighteenth-century neurophysiological enlightenment psychiatry, with Whytt, Haller, Unzer, and even Reil, it is highly critical of German psychiatry, and ultimately bases itself on the more recent empirical neurophysiological results of primarily Western provenance, on Bell, M. Hall, J. Müller, J. Budge, B. Stilling, *et al.* Various experimental, comparative, and genetic findings persuaded Griesinger that there existed an "analogy," a parallel, harmony, between the spinal cord and the brain, i.e. between sensation/movement and imagination/aspiration. Accordingly, muscle tonus, as the purest reflex action, is the counterpart of the "mental tonus" of the brain, the consciousness — though even here, concepts ("psyche") can prompt "a corresponding temper in the spinal cord." On both levels he describes the tonus dialectically as a "state of seeming relaxation," namely as the outcome of two regulatory effects on the spinal cord or the brain: the "dispersal" of the impressions or concepts and their transformation into "motor stimulus" (pp. 11–13). In the brain, the more receptive part is called the mind; and the part that regulates the aspirations is called character. As in the spinal cord, the transition from concept to aspiration is based on an "organic need," on an "organic drive and urge." And as for intellectual action: "We feel it driving us, we feel how, in this final transition from concept to aspiration and action, we attain our conceived goal, the realization of our intellectual I, we feel that action is our destiny and liberation" (p. 25). For the intensity of this transition shifts it into the conscious and makes possible volition, and its freedom can be intensified through the exercise of the dispersing and combining functions of the brain. "Thinking makes free." It is impossible to draw a sharp distinction between reflex action and consciousness, volition, any more than between lower animals and man. "The beginning of conceptions...is extremely unclear and indefinite, their intensity increases through incomprehensible intermediary stages, and at a given point the quantitative difference in strength turns into a qualitative difference — namely into conscious awareness, at which point a concept first emerges into the foreground of the 'psyche.'" Just as the spinal cord is "charged" with an infinite number of impressions, of which only a few become conscious sensations, so the brain also is charged with ideas corresponding to its "specific energy," and the "infinite majority" of those ideas "remain buried." This "dark semiconsciousness" is the source of the movements between reflex action and volition, which cannot be called instincts only because they too are subject to experience, imitation, and habit formation, as for example, in language.[316]

To this outline, whose "transitions" admit no new (positive) principle "from outside" — consciousness, soul, person, I — Griesinger then added a reflection based on negation, on the theory of inhibitions. "The collective impact of other ideas on a nascent concept constitutes a psychological inhibition, which one may call reflectiveness...reflection" — the impelling and stimulating negative of all practical and theoretical vital activity.[317] This leads to two "basic forms" of disorder for both the spinal cord and the brain: too many and too few inhibitions, impediments, and easements for the dispersal and the motor stimulus, which manifests itself in the brain, as depressive or manic dis-temper of the mental tonus. This reversal of idealistic psychiatry turns mental alienation into a mere quantitative physiological change, yet it also takes it seriously as an "organic force," as a subjectively impervious objective disorder, perhaps somewhat similar to the difference between Fichte's "dispersal" and idealistic psychiatry and Griesinger. An analogous process takes place in the criticism of man's losing himself to social-material being through Marx's reversal of idealism: "Compared with its role in Fichte's philosophy, dogmatism in Marx's theory has become weightier, just as it was weightier in Fichte than in Holbach. It gains in the impenetrability of substance, in the naturally given character of objective deception."[318] Of course, the "dispersal" of Fichte and the idealistic psychiatrists had more in common than, say, the material being of Marx and Griesinger, not to mention their disciples. One of the consequences of putting idealism "on its feet" apart from its liberating aspect, was the failure of the natural-scientific and social-scientific "feet" to find a common rhythm within the medium of the liberal division of labor, and to this day they tend to march to their own drummer.

Griesinger draws an analogy to neuralgia, the physical pain conducted through the spinal cord, in positing the unassailable rule that all mental diseases are rooted in psychic pain, in the basic depression. Griesinger bases this concept of unitary psychosis on Zeller and Guislain, whom he quotes in his *Psychische Reflexactionen* (p. 36): "Originally, insanity is a state of indisposition, anxiety, suffering, pain, however moral, intellectual, cerebral pain."

The materialistic reversal, however, was also to fall heir to idealistic psychiatry, realize its psychological content by joining it to material being. Unlike the somatists, who believe that only individual organs not the psyche are subject to illness, Griesinger insists that the brain can suffer "primary" illness as well as illness caused by the "sympathetic irritation" of other organs, and also "by a wide variety of external factors."[319] This can lead to depression and − in regard to the concept/aspiration transition in particular − even to "sickness of the will." "We also believe we are not doing the 'soul' itself an injustice or ascribing anything unworthy to it when in the case of insanity we regard it as being sick to its core.[320] These somatological premises made it possible for psychology to gain a foothold in psychiatry.

In 1844, Griesinger broadening his basic analogy likened "irritation of the spinal cord" (accompanied by cramps, sensations of pain and cold, hyperemia, etc.) to insanity as an "irritation of the brain." Comparison of the discomforts of neuralgia to the conditions in which every impression and claim elicits a different mental response such as "psychic pain," "mental coldness," is evidence of the practice orientation of his "structure." In other words, he applied the comparison to the many people "whom one can find more frequently out in the world than in insane asylums, and which manifests itself in characteristic chronic ill temper and moodiness, suspicion, distrust, envy, and malice." Griesinger grants these people who later came to be called "psychopaths" or "sociopaths," terms of moral or political opprobrium, the same genetic explanation and the same "psychological process" of their disorder as the mental diseases − beyond any attribution of moral guilt. This leads him to the conclusion that "such individuals are also more to be pitied than hated."[321] But apart from that, the state of mental coldness" − like a limb that has fallen asleep is the result of diminished energy or inhibition that expresses itself in exhaustion, and particularly in indifference toward matters previously of great concern. Projecting outwardly, the patients experience their environment as "having become something quite different," reject it, replace it with hallucinations, and ultimately dream of or commit destructive or suicidal acts. The psyche simply does not remain untouched by the sufferings of the body, and Griesinger, who sees insanity as one of the possibilities "of the whole human being," insofar as man is constantly changing, physiologically "normalized" and theoretically emancipated from his basic isolation. For experience shows "at times sudden, at times more gradual changes in the cerebral conditions," are constantly at work, and "from this the unity of the 'I' is abstracted, and this possibility of change is the basis of the possibility of disease and improvement."[322] This biographical process of abstraction is simultaneously internalization of, and alienation from, the outer world. But because of the slowness of change, "we do not notice the speed of the progressive metamorphosis of our view of and response to the world and one's own self and the patient often is led to feel, and justifiably so, that he has become a different person with a completely different personality, and he is then not very far from suspecting a different *definite* personality within himself."[323]

These points cover essential aspects of Griesinger's major work. Mental diseases are brain diseases; for unlike the old body/soul dualism, this falls back on the simplest, the materialistic hypothesis, on structure, i.e. on the "explicable unity of soul and body," on the proposition that the soul is "the sum of all cerebral states," "the will as the function, the special energy of the brain."[324] Contrary to a "shallow materialism" however, self-determination and indeed all mental qualities remain untouched until — here again the natural-scientific utopia — they can be seen as a physiological problem. Until this comes to pass, however, and with its own nullification as the goal, the psychological procedure is adequate, though of course not that of dualistic, moral psychiatry, which is responsible for society's view of the mentally ill as immoral,[325] a view that Griesinger's materialistic construction wants to revise.

Within this framework, Griesinger proceeds along the lines of both instinctual and ego psychology. Just as in the model of reflex action, man's instinctual drives proceed in stages up to the point of "we *must* will," to renunciation, to conceptualization, so — applying Herbart's laws of the association of ideas — the ego is understood as a conflict of different conceptual entities. Ego strength is proportionate to the resolution and regulation of the conflict, the achievement of a sense of self, prudence, freedom. Of course, in accordance with human functions, the I presents different characters and, moreover, undergoes constant change, particularly during puberty,[326] a time of life that has remained the physiological model for the genesis of insanity. New feelings and drives develop, which initially confront the old I as an alien, unassimilated "thou." This "duplicity" of old and new conceptual entities triggers vehement affects, amazement and terror, which is why the first stage of insanity is nearly always marked by (melancholic) emotional disturbance. If the ego is weak, then there is a greater danger that it will be more readily subdued by the new abnormal perception than a strong I, and will then "be falsified and quite change its nature" or splinter into multiple egos.[327]

Besides puberty, Griesinger sees these other physiological states as phenomenologically comparable to insanity: affects, drugged states, intoxication, dreams, the transitional stages between wakefulness and sleep, febrile delirium.[328] Corresponding to the fight against the "ontology insanity" and the energetistic dialectic quantity-quality, there are infinitely many transitions and indeterminate intermediate areas between these states. If the psychiatrist does not admit that before a court, he alienates himself from the ethical-normative standards of lawyers. The metasocial natural-scientific position bars Griesinger from thinking in terms of "morality and proper civil order in the world."[329] The "essential change" in a man, the "alienation" from his former self, remains the criterion of insanity, concepts that thus come to occupy a central place in psychiatry.[330] Of course, the relations between this and Marx's contemporaneous idea of social alienation, which also is arrived at by a reversal of existing philosophy is merely formal. To this day, no one has succeeded in establishing a substantive relationship between the two forms — except at the price of an ontological-anthropological, unhistorical short circuit. Something of the sort took place in the false unity of the first objectification of neo-Romanticism reimported from France, Morel's theory of degeneration, which rigidified Griesinger's enlightened, open, and unconciliatory "alienation" into religious-biological "degeneration." The fact that in the late 1860s, Griesinger himself gradually came to accept Morel shows that the paradigmatic aspect of his psychiatry was due not so much to his "person" as to his "time," Germany's socio-economic and philosophic-scientific liberal period of transition. Perhaps we can simply ascribe it to his early death.

The main topic under the heading of general predisposition was the social situation. Economic liberalism became topical in Germany too. And Griesinger's support of economic liberalism brought him awareness of the social question. To be sure, he did see worrisome phenomena in civilization (the increase in brain work; liberal education; driving ambition that unduly taxes some individuals; economic, social, and political dishonesty; the pursuit of success; enjoyment instead of closeness to nature; general discussion), but these things, at worst, lead to a "frenzied irritation of the brain," and the revolution certainly will not have any pathogenic effect. Prosperity, education, and hygiene, as well as the insane asylums are evidence that the progress of civilization enhances life and health. Far more important, for Griesinger, is the experience that the socially inferior (by class and trade), the uneducated and the poor, are more likely to become insane. From this he concludes — following Virchow — that hunger, poverty, the plight of the urban masses and the consequent alcoholism, as well as defective formation of intelligence, of the inhibitory and critical faculties (i.e. of the faculty for negation),[331] predispose to insanity.

Along with the economic society's interest in the poor masses the relationship between the irrationality of the poor and of the insane took on importance in Germany — indispensable for a psychiatric paradigm. But now irrationality already appeared as morally demythologized, industrially technologized, "cerebralized": as a flaw in the intelligence that controls the instincts and as alienation in the sense of functional, so to speak role-theoretic, differentness. Because of that, and because with the increase in asylums the number of observable indigent insane also increased, Griesinger was the first to "see" clearly the symptoms of schizophrenia which "existed" conceptually only since the turn of the century, i.e., the "dichotomy of the soul," the schism or "split in the ego," and the permanent mental deficiency. The same holds true for feeblemindedness and idiocy, which were just becoming socially visible in Germany. This led Griesinger to the justified observation that the insane asylums were the place to get to know the insane, and by the same token the institutions for the feeble-minded would bring firsthand insight into this type of mental defect.[332] And as a counterpart to this, Griesinger discovered a new ailment specific to the good bourgeois, to "the educated class": neurosis. This disorder, in fact but not in concept had much in common with the hypochondria and hysteria of the eighteenth-century upper class. But now — in view of the socio-economic situation — it generally took the form of "compulsion."[333] And Griesinger's discovery that young female teachers and governesses were particularly prone to mental disease sheds light on the emancipation of women and their integration into the labor process. Of the previously socially excluded groups, beggars and vagabonds were the only ones who managed to escape the risks and perils of the competitive society. According to Griesinger they rarely fall victim to mental illness because they are indifferent to and uninterested in the rewards society has to offer.[334]

Among the individual factors Griesinger stressed hereditary predisposition, which he linked to upbringing, before both became "rigidified" by weltanschauung and clashed abstractly as race vs. class, heredity vs. environment. In specific cases the problem is often not an inherited mental disease but simply a broken family imitation, and "psychical continuation of peculiarities of character."[335] In the second edition of his book, Griesinger approaches the theory of degeneration positively, though he integrates it into his model and arrives at the staunchly liberal conclusion that every individual, according to his life history, has within him a potential organic or mental breeding ground for nurturing a "gap in the ego," insanity.[336] Etiologically, he pays special attention to sexuality. On the one hand, masturbation and immoderation still are seen as major culprits, but on the other hand, he also mentions sexual deprivation. Thus he agrees with a French account about an ailing wife who recovered her health after running off with her lover, i.e. no longer suppressing her desire,[337] a notion that hitherto only Reil had dared to advance.

The forms of mental disease are described psychologically within a natural-scientific structure, and hence Griesinger has no qualms about interpreting the transitions between the individual symptoms and stages both dynamically and teleologically. The duality of the approach is kept open as unreconciled. On the one side, the subject, by acting, is responsible for the transition from one stage of insanity to the next. On the other side, we are dealing with merely the progress of the objective, organic disease process, in regard to which the actions of the subject are not willed.[338] The *one* disease process begins almost always with the basic depression, the psychic pain, as the first stage. This can manifest itself as melancholia (lack of focus, emotional pain, change or loss of the world and the self, hallucination as a substitute for the loss) or as hypochondria (each sense experiences its own sensations, does not reach the objects it touches, is cut off from satisfaction, with emptiness as the result). Here, Griesinger — as well as several French scientists — for the first time recognized the cyclical alternation of depression and mania, which subsequently led to the concept of manic-depressive insanity.

The transition from depression to mania or frenzy is psychologically the attempt by the subject to compensate for the inhibition of depression, to overcome a poor self-image and the feeling of grief through the intensification of self-regard and the externalization of instinctual energy in a wide range of activities. Both mania and depression give rise to secondary disorders, hallucination, and delusion. They represent the effort of the subject to explain to himself, through projection, the inhibition or intensification, the fear of becoming different, the alienation. Delusion is the attempt at explanation, rationalization, passive or active objectification of the frustration or satisfaction of personal emotional needs.[339] Yet this is an unconscious or barely conscious process. The will may have been made to serve the extravagant fixed delirious conception, and the excited mind soothed, but that calm is deceptive, covering a state of far deeper irrationality, for now the ego itself has become alienated and undergone a change.[340]

That is the transition to the residues of insanity, to the "consecutive states of mental debility." While the affects have calmed down and the activity of the organic process and of the subject have subsided, now the basic disorder is the defect of intelligence itself. The subject is no longer able to form the propelling internal contradiction between the mental images. But not all activity is gone; Griesinger made the crucial observation that these individuals too become more defective only to the extent that they are left to their own devices and no demands are made on them. These are the states of debility: partial insanity (Griesinger also includes moral insanity), general insanity, moronism, idiocy, and cretinism.

Therapeutic practice requires the utilitarian critique of the pre-existing situation, in which the insane were merely the objects of a self-complacent humanitarianism and of the state, but not of medical science:

For this reason, also, we must acknowledge these humanitarian principles as rules of treatment only in so far as they further our aims; we must remember that that humane treatment is not always the most humane which best accords with the particular sentiments of the physician, or is most agreeable to the feelings of the patient, *but that which works a cure.* Psychiatry then should never degenerate from the gravity of a practical science into a system of sentimentality, such as even a layman could scarcely be found to defend.[341]

Thus the old psychiatry was not so much for the indigent mentally ill as for the psychiatric community, its moral law and

its confirmation of the absolute state. Not until later did psychiatry show that it could exist on its own as a positivist science.
Griesinger believed that like theory, therapy too had to be both
physical and mental. The old ego and its residual faculties had
to be engaged. Keeping occupied was crucial. In the second
edition, unlike the first, Griesinger admitted to having been
won over to Conolly's non-restraint principle. In contrast to
the traditional treatment in Germany — a mixture of coercion
and "pleasing descriptions of Christmas presents" — Griesinger
now sees restraint of any kind as neglect, and demands the absolute removal of all mechanical restraints and their replacement
by active treatment methods.[342]

Griesinger presented the practical (therapeutic and institutional)
aspect of his paradigm programatically in a series of articles in
the first volume of his *Archivs*. This reform program upset the
ruling institutional psychiatrists much more than his theoretical
construct. "Practical need" was to be the sole criterion. That
made the existing distinction between curable and incurable too
normative and impractical. He proposed a division into acute
and chronic cases, and the creation of both short- and long-term
mental institutions, and the installation of temporary "municipal
asylums" in every town, the very opposite of the existing institutions. This temporary facility would be located not in a romantic
rural setting, but on the outskirts of the town, geared to the
"floating population." Its doors should be open to all acute
mental cases, as well as to victims of brain and nervous diseases.
In contrast to the previous legally complicated and difficult
process of commitment, immediate admission should be possible.
This would prevent suicides and accidents and be crucial to the
chances of cure. Whereas the rich have private asylums, the public
asylum is meant primarily for the poor, at lower costs, and should
provide free care. The social decline of the educated middle class
in the new economic-bourgeois society was symbolized by the
fact that the poor were no longer seen as just the lower classes
but also as "the class of the population that, with good education
and careful intellectual formation and no other means, is dependent on the steady returns of its sole capital, its intellectual
powers, and whose income stops in case of illness, making acceptance in a private asylum generally impossible."[343] The social
marginality of proletarians and intellectuals unites them in the
insane asylum, which does provide a few private rooms for the
intellectuals, but only one class of care.

The other therapeutically active features of the asylum are in part still social-psychiatric wishful thinking, especially in Germany. Before a patient is committed, a doctor from the asylum should visit him at his home in order to get to know him in his "former environment." The confinement should not exceed one year. The patient knows his family to be nearby, which facilitates the "readjustment to the old." Trial leaves, work outside the institution, and ambulatory aftercare are made possible.[344] Altogether, Griesinger's concept of a "temporary stay" anticipates the end of his own clinical approach: he entertains the possibility of today's social-psychiatric ideal of halfway houses, round-the-clock ambulatory clinics, follow-up treatment, work-release programs, and clinical and ambulatory treatment. Of course, Griesinger still sees the insane only as sick. Hence, architecturally the urban asylums were to look like hospitals, with no resemblance whatever to the traditional insane asylums with their "little spires, and similar foolish curlicues," with a church, bowling alley, etc. Instead, an "observation ward" with round-the-clock supervision would insure the accurate diagnosis of all new patients.[345] Finally, the municipal asylums in university cities should also be used for clinical instruction and therefore should be located near the other university clinics.

The asylum is the objectification of Griesinger's theoretical insight that the insane are sick people among other sick people, that the era of their isolation and their special position as a whole is past, and with it the "guild-like seclusion of psychiatry." The "unity of so-called mental diseases with the other brain and nervous diseases" is the integration of psychiatry in medicine as one speciality among others.[346]

One more group is to be taken out of the old, overcrowded institutions: Griesinger recommends that the peaceful feeble minded and morons, paralytics, and epileptics (here, too his economic orientation puts him in the position of anticipating the future: he speaks of "social and intellectual nonentities") be cared for together with physical invalids in large treatment facilities by religious fellowships whose other therapeutic activities he rejects.[347] Likewise, distinctions should be made among the chronic insane remaining in asylums according to economic utility and freedom of movement. The "barrack-like mass care of chronic mental patients still capable of humane existence" must be terminated.[348] Griesinger castigates the principle of protecting and safeguarding society. Because of this, all mentally disturbed individuals are judged by the rare instances of truly dangerous cases and senselessly and destructively robbed of their freedom. "It is also certain that individual dangerous acts, like individual accidents in the world, cannot possibly be prevented, whatever precautions are taken, even if all patients were tied and locked up all the time."[349] This is the first documented relativization of a socio-economically motivated and philosophically confirmed perfectionism.

Further decentralization was to eliminate the economic inefficiency of the existing asylums. The institution should provide for a secure, closed-off area for the truly threatened or dangerous inmates, and also physically separate though jointly administered Western-type "open care facilities." The first level of these is the "agricultural colony," where patients and attendants live and work together, and a still more open facility is "family care": "It provides something that even the most splendid and best run institution in the world can never provide: a full life among healthy people, the return from an artificial, monotonous medium to a natural social one, the boon of family life."[350] That is to say, the mental patients are to be sent to live with farmers or workers in the surrounding villages, or else settled in a colony modelled on the cheap company housing for workers, going up everywhere (such as the *cité ouvrière* in Mulhouse), a more economical solution than the erection of new asylums. These open facilities have the advantage that they "can be endlessly expanded at far lower costs and are in part themselves so advantageous economically that under good direction they may almost pay for themselves." This approach to the treatment of the insane can be summed up thus: "Each should be given that measure of freedom appropriate to him. Experimentation relating to this measure should be continuous."[351]

The degree of emancipation of the insane conceived of by Griesinger and his contemporaries coincided with their integration into urban life and especially into the production process. Thus Griesinger motivates his championing of non-restraint:

All this, especially the most crucial of all, a good staff of attendants, requires means and the question of Non Restraint and of free treatment is therefore mainly a question of money. But any money used for such purposes is well spent, in that creating such conditions will make more patients fit to work, i.e. productive, and make more patients ready to be released (as cured or improved).[352]

Thus, Griesinger is credited with the first complete German paradigm of psychiatry as a science, after Reil, whom Griesinger repeatedly cites, who made a pioneering attempt, got bogged down in writing and became the victim of Germany's "belatedness." Like Battie and Pinel, Griesinger in Germany was the first — after Reil — to dedicate himself to psychiatry after being successful in another medical discipline and enjoying social prestige. All three men could establish their paradigm only in that specific transitional period in which the industrial-capitalist economic expansion and the at least partial political emancipation of the bourgeoisie made the unreason of the poor and the insane and also the inherent unreason of man irrefutably visible to bourgeois society and which gave rise to the social question. This comparison, of course, encompasses great differences in content since the three societies did not develop at the same pace. Battie, Pinel, and Griesinger each supplied a complete paradigm: a new way of seeing the insane within the framework of a specific social relationship of rationality and irrationality, with institutional changes in the demarcation between the insane and society, with a comprehensive and expanding theorization of insanity, and with a change in therapeutic practice. All three — but not Reil — gathered experience in asylums before positing any theories, though Griesinger's practical experience was limited to two years, and he arrived at a theoretical construct before conceiving and carrying out any practical institutional changes. Finally, it may be said of all three that emancipation was their primary goal, whereas their successors — Tuke, Esquirol, Kraepelin — were concerned primarily with moral or social integration.

The special character of Griesinger's psychiatric practice was partly the result of its place in time, mainly the 1860s, that brief span which saw the unfolding not only of economic liberalism but of a political liberal public spirit in Germany. Thus, Griesinger concluded his work on non-restraint with the vow that in case the state decreed the abolition of mechanical restraint in asylums, he would oppose it "with utmost determination," even though it would be consistent with his goals. "But if at some point public opinion would become interested…to learn which asylums have adopted the principle of free treatment and which had not, I would then not regard this as harmful, and I cannot see how one could justifiably oppose such a request."[353] And Ludwig Meyer, Griesinger's friend, made the public the forum for the liberation of the mentally ill from isolation and mechanical restraint: in 1858, when he became chief physician for the insane in Hamburg, he publicly auctioned off in one day the instruments of restraint still in use.[354]

Concluding Remarks

We hope we have given at least some impression of how developing industrial-capitalist bourgeois society learned to deal with those who, by its gauge of rationality, it deems irrational, using as examples the mentally suffering or mentally ill. Psychiatry, as science and as institution, developed as the most effective tool in these dealings. We have traced its genesis and have tried not to omit any of its complex relationships, whether philosophical, literary, political-economic, or natural-scientific. In the century since the close of its formative phase, psychiatry has not proved particularly reluctant nor thought too deeply about carrying out the tasks assigned to it by the state and society. Its dependencies have remained the same to this day, whether it has unhesitatingly widened its jurisdiction or made itself the compliant instrument of the National Socialist annihilation machinery, whether it has expanded its diagnostic and therapeutic possibilities in terms of natural science or remembered its emancipatory claim in psychoanalysis, or now in social psychiatry. Hence the question still remains whether psychiatry is more of an emancipatory or integrative science, i.e. whether it aims more at the liberation of the mentally suffering or the disciplining of bourgeois society, whereby Foucault's answer — the "dominion of silence" is unhistorical, one-sided, and unsatisfactory. At any rate, since 1945 at the latest, no psychiatrist has the right to that designation if in his dealings with himself and with those under his care he has not reflected on that question.

Appendix:
Criteria for a Historiography
of Psychiatry

Around 1900, psychiatry looked on itself with uncritical matter-of-factness as natural-scientific enlightenment, as a fight *against* demonologic and other social superstitions and for the human rights of the mentally ill, a fight that was waged now against, now in league with the state authorities, and especially against religious attitudes and institutions. Within this framework the medical historian Haeser in 1881 simply presented the development of psychiatry as parallel to the various phases of general medical pathology, distinguishing only between a purely theoretical founding phase in the eighteenth century and a descriptive, a pathological-anatomical and finally a physiological period.[1] Kirchhoff's *Geschichte der deutschen Irrenpflege* of 1890 follows a similar pattern. Aggressive against theological dogmas, Kirchhoff advances the thesis that only in a nation where common sense has won out over fantasy can the victory of fantasy over reason — his definition of mental illness — receive adequate (medical) treatment. His basic attitude is one of trust that civilization holds the key to dealing with the disorders that it (in part) has caused. Here we find a view that gained currency at the start of the twentieth century, namely that the history of psychiatry sheds "light on the cultural history of humanity."[2]

The same Kirchhoff, in his history of psychiatry of 1912, goes a step further when he puts psychiatry among the "humanities" rather than among the natural sciences — although in combination with medical "art" which must offer treatment and restore both mental and physical equilibrium. That very same medical art paved the way for the negation of the enlightened natural-science nineteenth century: psychiatry, having received the gift of anatomy from medicine, once more is developing toward an art, i.e. toward treating not the defective organ but the person as a whole.[3] Kraepelin's retrospective *Hundert Jahre Psychiatrie* (1917) was a virtual swan song for the nineteenth century – a partisan plea for the monopoly of natural-scientific observation and for the fight against the prejudicial notion that mental disease was an emanation of personal folly or baseness, hence a stigma on the family, and that it was incurable.[4]

Since the 1920s, other concepts of psychiatric history and of psychiatry itself have emerged into the spotlight. What had been once vaguely referred to as a "humane discipline", was in 1928, more specifically called an "exposition in terms of a history of ideas" by Birnbaum, who was concerned with the inner connection, the intellectual bond, between intellectual positions, with mental guidelines and principles. This method was meant to justify some selective criteria: the stress is on things of contemporary importance; practical psychiatry is omitted, because psychiatrists are of interest only as representatives of mental orientations; and a distinction is drawn between the scientific ("a continuous, closed, systematic research movement") and the prescientific period, in which viewpoints were contingent on temporal and cultural factors.[5] Gruhle's exposition of 1932 moves more or less within this framework. It is noteworthy that the post-1840 period, which up to then had been celebrated as the founding era of the actual (natural-) scientific psychiatry, held no interest for him because of its excessively materialistic orientation and one-sided preoccupation with institutional practice and etiological brain hypotheses. Instead, the ideas of Romantic psychiatry are now again seen as more important for the present age.[6] Hence, Leibbrand's *Romantic Medicine* (1937) also struck a responsive chord for psychiatry.[7]

The post-World War II period is marked by a wealth of historical examinations unrivaled since the 1820–50 period. However, none of them deals with the National Socialist era, for that would raise the problem of incorporating the "destruction of worthless life" into the historical continuity.[8] Instead, there is a major effort to process the ideas of phenomenology and existential philosophy, which L. Binswanger and others introduced into psychiatry in 1922. The prevailing trend now is to see psychiatry as a humane discipline. Its scientific elements are ignored, relegated to prefaces, limited to a problem of the not discussed practical psychiatry, or "raised" to the phenomenological or anthropological plane and thus formally made compatible with the mind. Common to these efforts is a casual dismissal of the materialistic nineteenth century.

Thus, in 1948, Bodamer embarked on his *Ideengeschichte der Psychiatrie*, following N. Hartmann's methodology of a phenomenologic analysis of the objective mind.[9] Bodamer's contribution of a conceptual typology is tainted by intellectually broad and ideologically one-sided value judgments. For instance, in his view system formations conceal problems by their over-emphasis of reality; universal creations, i.e. putting an epoch on a metaphysical or religious basis, are the monopoly of the Germanic nations; the Latin countries (among which he includes England) are guilty of the "destruction of the soul," whereas the Germanic nations assure a steady opposite movement; finally, the manifestations of the objective mind attain their timeless continuity through "archetypal problems," e.g. the body/soul problem.

Bodamer's work (1953) on the origins of psychiatry is more concrete. It is the first to imply various sociological and political "conditions" for the origin of the science, but neutralizes them in the "framework of intellectual history," the "zeitgeist." Methodologically Bodamer connects to Dilthey, and he sees the intellectual history of psychiatry as merely "a transfiguration of the great, periodically surfacing historic changes of the human spirit which with the aid of unknown forces propel the process of history toward a goal hidden from us. Each discrete epoch of this process can, according to Dilthey, be grasped only as a specific attitude of human consciousness toward reality."[10]

Spoerri in 1955 inquired into the cognitive value of historical contemplation.[11] For him, history has shown that in the question of endogenous psychoses (especially schizophrenia) there has been no cognitive progress. This proves to him that psychiatry is a humane discipline rather than a natural science. Whereas all empirical sciences have some irrational content, the body/soul relationship stands at the center of psychiatry, and although its coincidence can be experienced, it cannot be explained scientifically, and is therefore metaphysical (according to N. Hartmann). In this sense, schizophrenia too is an insoluble, metaphysical problem. Analogous to the phenomenon of love, the essence of schizophrenia lies in the totality of its manifestations. For the model for the genesis of schizophrenia, according to Spoerri, we must turn to the humanities, just as for a work of art one can marshal only conditions, not reasons.

Wyrsch based his history of endogenous psychoses (1956), which he believes to be largely identical with psychiatry, on the contrast between his era and the nineteenth century. True, back then psychiatry had arrived at diagnoses and the concept of disease, but because, as a science, it "was compelled to remain detached and 'objectify,'" it closed itself off from the life situation of the stricken person. Binswanger contrasts Wyrsch's existential analysis to this — but also spoken language, art, and literature. Here, the conditions for their existence can be made clear, since the precondition here is involvement rather than detachment, although less can be learned about the causes and conditions of psychoses.[12] Wyrsch elaborated on these ideas in a second work (1960): by understanding phenomena, psychiatry becomes an open discipline, while, as a natural science, it merely masters its material. This approach reinterprets even the age of witchhunts: whereas the enlightened nineteenth century presented the burning of helpless mentally ill persons as witches, as textbook examples of religious superstition, Wyrsch sees them as the consequence of causal, natural-scientific thinking, since here internal diseases were seen as having external causes.[13]

From Spoerri's psychiatry-metaphysics and Wyrsch's "interpretation of the intrinsically ungraspable,"[14] it is but a short distance to Schöne's work (1951) on the literary depiction of insanity, which, according to him, is a motif in the 150-year-old countermovement to the Age of Reason. He attributes a "metaphysical comprehension" to literature, an essential reevaluation transcending the facts, an ascription of meaning to madness by the entrance of the writer into this "counterworld" through the valid uniqueness of intuitive knowledge." From unreason the writer at least brings the mentally ill back into a "metaphysically ordered space," thus "he ensures the further existence of the world." Of course, "the writer excludes" the most profound mental derangement, absolute loss of sensateness "the final darkness."[15]

Tellenbach (1958) sees the role of the humanities in psychiatry as a question of the anthropology that underlies a given conception. His basis obviously is a scale of values that measures according to the degree of topicality. Thus, natural-scientific psychiatry is based on Cartesian anthropology, whose ideal of objectification, quantification, and causal relationship demands that every psychosis have an organic substratum. This conformity to the law of nature is expanded and replaced in a psychiatry of understanding by the conformity to the laws of reason of the Diltheyan historical and experiential subject. Psychoanalysis wants to understand Dilthey's incomprehensible, no longer immediately evident motivational connections, and toward this end declares Goethe's *homo natura* to be a physical apparatus. And its sole achievement according to Binswanger's formula — is an understanding of what has been explained (by natural science). Binswanger's "phenomenological-anthropological ontology" (1922) enabled Tellenbach to see the possibility of a "unified conceptualization in psychiatry," i.e. psychiatry as a science. Heidegger's being-in-the-world here becomes a "processual unity of self and world," and, as phenomenological anthropology, is provided "with the claim of an empirical science." This approach limits, accounts for, and transcends all the earlier ones: only man's existential condition makes psychiatric symptoms possible as a "human potential," and only to this extent can they have a (natural-scientific) cause and can psychiatry be a "science of understanding" (von Baeyer). Thus, medical action leads not to an objectification but to a new world of encounter, since the psychotic phenomena are seen as a failure or denaturing of encounter. As an anthropological ontology, the orientation toward the humanities becomes the all-encompassing, constitutive approach for all modes of psychiatric thinking.[16] Since Tellenbach views this insight as the crucial achievement of the present era, he contradicts himself when in 1961, he attacked the historical view that extends the present backwards into the past.[17]

Leibbrand and Wettley's *Geschichte der abendländischen Psychopathologie* (1961), is the first basic, overwhelmingly detailed history of psychopathology, even though their approach follows that of the above-mentioned authors. The "not unconditional premise" consists in accepting the concept of "insanity" in a programmatic sense as "a given totality," construed as a "universal existential possibility of the being which is at the mercy of the gods and intertwined with them." This determines the method, which is not meant to be a "tinker-toy construction" of analytical psychology. Instead, "the internal intellectual context" is found in history rather than in the change in thinking, in the "universally recurring thoughts." "Value connections" make the conflicts stirred up largely by simplifying partisans, insubstantial. Contrary to the natural-scientific thinking prevalent especially in Germany, the ahistoricity (in the sense of N. Hartmann), Leibbrand and Wettley claim that concepts of disease are phenomena of the mind, the zeitgeist. This humanities-oriented, "historical-conceptual process," seeks the "concrete, existential connection," which — in line with Dilthey — is "individual, hence subjective"; it strives to "raise 'man's role in society above the confines of time and place.'" In their linkage of value structures the authors display partisanship for present-day existential analysis as against "outdated" psychoanalysis. This work, too, omits practical psychiatry.[18]

Only few works step outside the framework of this uniform postwar trend, which without a doubt indicates a new, independent "German approach" in psychiatry and its history. In 1957, Ackerknecht methodologically attacked a "history of the giants," and chose to present history in its totality, i.e. not follow the practice of extracting whatever happens to be in fashion. The vehement antipsychoanalytic affect joins him to the aforementioned authors: the neglect of the philosophical psychiatrists, because practical psychiatry is not indebted to them, separates him from them. He gauges their social conditioning by the changing expansion of the area of mental disorders in the various societies and historical eras, but does not carry this theme through. Instead, this generally sober presentation views the history of psychiatry as a constant struggle between mentally and somatically oriented approaches.[19]

Panse's *Geschichte des psychiatrischen Krankenhauses* (1964)[20] is almost the only recent historical presentation of practical psychiatry to demonstrate the gap between theory and practice. It also offers the enlightened ideal of human dignity, respectively the needs of the mentally ill as the main focus. Practical psychiatry is elevated to the rank of social science without critical reflection: for the community, "the mentally ill, being its socially most endangered children, should actually be the crown witnesses for how far it has in fact been able to realize those ideals." The achievement of humanitarian progress in history is credited to the somatic psychiatrists. At the same time, the paternalistic, sociopolitical complaint is raised that social psychiatry's ideals of progress (consumption, production, technology) are detrimental to the political task of a "new order of public health."[21]

However, the most important works in France, England, and the United States show that history — beyond the relatively uniform picture in Germany — has to be seen from other vantage points as well. In 1941, Zilboorg published the first representative history of psychiatry from a psychoanalytic — psychodynamic point of view.[22] The revision of history from this approach was so one-sided, however, as to diminish the scientific value of the work. Moreover, Zilboorg practically equates the history of psychiatry with the history of growing humanitarian concerns: after people learn to overcome fear and prejudice, they can psychologically understand their fellow men. Here the idea of enlightenment is handled with outstanding naïveté; particularly after 1945, this could scarcely be plausible. Zilboorg's book ideally lends itself to Foucault's structuralist criticism.

For Henri Ey (1948) — as for Ackerknecht — the history of psychiatry is a dialectical development based on the constant mutual opposition of the dynamistic and the mechanistic viewpoints.[23] The dynamistic view is functional-hierarchical, final humoral, total, synthetic, sees pathology as endogenous, constitutional, and disease as disequilibrium, degeneration, or reaction. The mechanistic viewpoint — correlative to it — is morphological-additive, causal, solidaristic, atomistic, analytical, sees pathology as exogenous and disease as an exogenous traumatism, parasitical, accidental. Through a universal synthesis Ey attempts to bring this dialectical history into his own theory: *"la conception organo-dynamiste."* Of course, this synthesis is in fact a victory of one side over the other and once again a victory of the twentieth century over the nineteenth: the integration of the organic-mechanistic view by the dynamistic view. Behind it stands a commitment to the hierarchical *natura naturans*, which makes no leaps, unfolds in the higher form of *"psychisme"* into a *"causalité interne,"* *"selon un élan propre, celui de la liberté,"* with the faculty of adaptation. Hence, in contrast to physical disease as life-threatening Ey sees mental disease and hence psychiatry as *"la pathologie de la liberté."*

D. Leigh, in his history of British psychiatry (1961), seeks to enhance the plausibility of his presentation of the individual epochs by making the detailed biographies of "the giants," combined with analysis of the relative social conditions, the main thread of his work.[24] The other recent British history is that of Hunter and Macalpine (1963) written from a justifiably skeptical point of view.[25] Psychiatry, in comparison to medicine, still has no solid scientific base; the indvidual case is interpreted subjectively in line with a given school, etiology is speculative, pathogenesis obscure, classification symptomatic, i.e. arbitrary, somatic therapy purely empirical and dependent on fashion, and psychotherapy still in its infancy and quite doctrinaire. Above all, no one can say to what extent psychiatry belongs among the sciences or the humanities. One reason for this is the fact that psychiatry must be practiced not according to the given scientific possibilities, but under the pressure of social, humanitarian, economic, theological, and legal necessities. Consequently a history of psychiatry cannot yet be written. Instead, the authors rely on documentation: they present more than eleven hundred pages of tersely annotated texts by psychiatrists and non-psychiatrists from three centuries. This may well be one of the best books in this field.

1961 saw the publication of *Madness and Civilization* by the French structuralist Foucault.[26] He transposes the history of psychiatry to a single structure: to the dialogue between the "world" of madness and the normal "world." This dialogue, which Foucault pursues on the plane of art, science, scholarship, bourgeois morality, social and economic conditions, was still open during the Renaissance, became in the Enlightenment a monologue of reason about madness, and ended in absolute speechlessness, in the silence of the insane asylum, at the very instant that is traditionally celebrated as the "liberation of the insane" by Pinel and Tuke (c. 1790) and as the birth of psychiatry as a medical science. Here the dialectic of the Enlightenment becomes thematic, yet at the same time it is unilaterally resolved in terms of its destructive aspect. Of course, this was possibly only on the basis of the limiting structuring of reality. Nevertheless, this represents the first important approach to a scientific sociology of psychiatry.

The first, almost complete and critical survey of the attempts at psychiatric history is that of Mora in the United States (1966).[27] Nearly all these attempts are judged inadequate. However, the five reasons given for this poor showing are only partially valid, since Mora himself unhistorically takes the psychodynamic standpoint for granted:

1. For the most part the historiography is the work of prominent psychiatrists, unfamiliar with historical methods.

2. Most works are somatically oriented and demonstrate a humanitarian philosophy only as a balancing attempt of unconscious guilt feelings to compensate for a mechanistic, impersonal orientation.

3. The studies are mainly inductive and aimed at contemporary utility and at the significance of great men, because everyday clinical day-to-day work, the historical-genetic analysis of personality, leaves its mark on scientific work.

4. Because the psychoanalysts have not yet realized that theirs is a mature discipline, and they neglect history.

5. Freud himself almost totally ignored the history of his field. Instead of the inductive method, Mora somewhat naively recommends a progressive theory of continuity, according to which the present always sees itself in the guilt of the past, and the

— relative — truth always results from a continual, albeit cyclical progress. Historiography need merely put up the signposts for this evolution, concentrate on pioneers instead of heroes, and consider the sociocultural factors purely as background.

Notes

Introduction

1   Rainer Spehlmann, *Sigmund Freuds neurologische Schriften* (Berlin, 1953).

2   Jürgen Habermas, "Zur Logik der Sozialwissenschaften," *Philosophische Rundschau*, 1967, especially pp. 185 ff.

3   Klaus Doerner, *Die Hochschulpsychiatrie* (Stuttgart, 1967), pp. 85–88.

4   If, in the recent past hospitals and other psychiatric institutions have nonetheless shown a willingness to embark on new paths, two factors account for this: (1) a scientific one — the advances in psychopharmacological research; and (2) a sociological one — the emergence of a sociopsychiatric societally oriented view and the corresponding establishment of half-way houses. It is the "pragmatic" purpose of this study to present these two essentially ambivalent conditions and their complex interrelationship in a historical framework and thereby create the basis for a psychiatric approach consistent both in theory and practice.

5   August B. Hollingshead and Fredrick C. Redlich, *Social Class and Mental Illness* (New York, 1958).

6   Reimann, *Die Mental Health Bewegung* (Tübingen, 1967), esp. pp. 93–99.

7   Max Horkheimer and Theodor W. Adorno, *Dialectic of Enlightenment* (New York, 1972), pp. xvi, 12–39 *passim*.

8   *Ibid.*, xv.

9   *Ibid.*, 41.

10   Habermas, *Theorie und Praxis* (Neuwied, 1963), p. 229.

11   H. J. Lieber, *Philosophie, Soziologie und Gesellschaft* (Berlin, 1965), pp. 3f.

12   On the ideological repercussions of the partnership idea inherent in such formulations, cf. Doerner, "Die sexuelle Partnerschaft in der Industriegesellschaft," *Soziale Welt*, 17, 1966.

13   In psychoanalysis, which in all these relationships holds the dual position

of both a natural science and a humane discipline, such a control is impossible on empirical grounds, not for reasons of principle.

14   "I regard it as an enormous danger in German thinking, and this danger is merely the obverse of one of the great virtues of that thinking, that its interpretative inclination leads it to interpret that which is merely explicable ...to 'deepen' and turn into a problem of interpretation also that which can be grasped only through the 'making,' the 'mechanism'.... This methodological discrepancy, of interpreting instead of explaining, is nothing but a reiterated methodological expression of an unpolitical psychological stance which has been found often enough in life." Mannheim, *Wissenssoziologie*, p. 61.

15   W. Leibbrand and A. Wettley, *Der Wahnsinn* (Freiburg, 1961), p. 4.

16   See H. H. Wehler (ed.), *Moderne deutsche Sozialgeschichte* (Cologne, 1966).

17   "Obviously the burden of my argument is that this quality of being determined by effective-history still dominates the modern, historical, and scientific consciousness...that our whole being, achieved in the totality of our destiny, inevitably transcends its knowledge of itself." (Hans-Georg Gadamer, *Truth and Method*, p. xxii). In contrast, Habermas (*Logik der Sozialwissenschaften*, p. 175), "Yet the substance of the historical allegation of being absorbed into reflexion is not untouched by this...authority and knowledge do not converge.... Reflexion does not work itself off on the facticity of the handed-down norms without leaving a trace."

18   K. Lenk (ed.), *Ideologie* (Neuwied, 1961), pp. 13–57.

19   H. Plessner, in *ibid.*, 218–35.

20   Kurt H. Wolff (ed.), *From Karl Mannheim* (New York, 1971), pp. i–cxxx.

21   Lieber, *op. cit.*, pp. 1–105.

22   W. Hofmann, *Gesellschaftslehre as Ordnungsmacht* (Berlin, 1961).

23   Habermas, "Logik...," pp. 149–92.

24   The fact that important psychiatric studies increasingly are being published in the glossy handouts of pharmaceutical firms instead of in professional journals, and are then passed out to psychiatrists as a scientifically noncommittal yet attention-getting "cultural superstructure" is indicative of psychiatry's alienation from its history, its unhistoricity.

25   "In fact history does not belong to us, but we belong to it.... The focus of subjectivity is a distorting mirror.... That is why the prejudices of the individual, far more than his judgments, constitute the historical reality of his being." (H. G. Gadamer, *Truth and Method*, p. 245).

26   Lieber, *op. cit.*, p. 11.

27   *Immer noch philosophische Anthropologie?*, p. 72.

28   Habermas, "Analytische Wissenschaftstheorie," in *Zeugnisse* (Frankfurt, 1963), p. 480.

29   *Idem, Theorie und Praxis*, p. 229.

30   The bearers of such a revolution, according to Kuhn, must concentrate on crisis-provoking problems, be young, or new to the crisis-ridden field, and thus less deeply committed to the world view and rules set by the old paradigm and have previously worked successfully in some other science (for which the principal *raison d'être* is an external social need.) Thomas S. Kuhn, *The Structure of Scientific Revolutions* (Chicago, 1962), p. 143.

31   *Ibid.*, 19, 163.

32   Richard Hunter and Ida Macalpine, *Three Hundred Years of Psychiatry, 1535–1860*, (London, 1963), p. ix.

33   W. Bromberg, "Some Social Aspects of the History of Psychiatry," *Bull. Hist. Med.* II, 1942, p. 132.

34   Habermas, *Analytische Wissenschaftstheorie*, pp. 473 f.

35   *Idem, Theorie und Praxis*, p. 177.

36   *Idem, Strukturwandel der Öffentlichkeit* (Neuwied, 1962), pp. 7 f.

37   W. Conze and H. Mommsen, "Sozialgeschichte," in H. U. Wehler (ed.), *Moderne deutsche Sozialgeschichte* (Cologne, 1966), pp. 16–26, 27–34.

38   H. Plessner, *Die verspätete Nation* (Stuttgart, 1962).

39   Michel Foucault, *Madness and Civilization*, trans. Richard Howard (New York, 1973). Foucault was the first to point out the significance of the movement toward the sequestration of irrationality. It figures in his book (pp. 38–64) under the title of *The Great Confinement*. However, his structuralist approach makes him lose sight of the historical differences between the various European countries, which results in frequent distortions and false generalizations. On the whole, Foucault's work was and is based on the French situation. Like its predecessors, it proves that only a few efforts in psychiatric historiography have gone beyond recording the "national standpoint," and are able to see the development of psychiatry within the framework of the development of bourgeois society and thus perceive the historical differences between the developmental stages of individual countries.

40   W. Hofmann, *Ideengeschichte der sozialen Bewegung* (Berlin, 1962), pp. 22 f.

41   Foucault, *op. cit.* p. 51.

42   This imputed closeness to nature gave rise to the long-held belief that the insane are able to endure hunger, cold, and pain. In a reversal of practice and theory, the insane first were subjected to hunger, cold, and abuse, and it was then concluded that they possessed unique characteristics of insensitivity. Typologies such as those of "the worker" developed in similar fashion. The observations of alienists about the alternation of insanity and specific physical ailments in an individual are of a different order. Even today, this empirical, unexplored fact is accepted as central evidence for the physical "profundity" of insanity. The early alienists held to the belief that their derangement protected the insane against other illnesses. This was yet another

way of reassuring oneself of the special position of the insane as opposed to "normal" people.

PART I: *Great Britain*

1   Colloquial speech still pins the tag of "poor madman" on all those whom we, out of a mixture of disdain, rejection, pity, and a benign refusal to take them seriously, seek to set apart. This book hopes to examine the historical reality underlying this key concept. The "poor madman" was at first a concept of administrative reason which sought to categorize the varieties of unreason. Later, it designated the incorporation of the problem of insanity into the "social question," as well as the sentimental-harmonizing component of philanthropic efforts still with us. Finally, this concept makes clear that psychiatry as a science could not have come into being if limited to the treatment of the well-to-do mentally ill; it needed the social visibility of the insane as a mass, i.e., as "pauper lunatics": as a problem of public order, as an object of emancipation, and, in connection with that, through the comparison of the variety of individual cases, as an opportunity for developing a generic terminology and systematic concepts. This too makes clear that psychiatry, from its very beginnings, was a science of both emancipation and integration. Kisker, though harmonizing the contradictions, points to this connection (cf. K. P. Kisker, "Die Verrücktheit, die Armut und wir," *Nervenarzt*, 38, 1967).

2   Richard Hunter and Ida Macalpine (London, 1963), *Three Hundred Years of Psychiatry*, pp. 299 f.

3   R. Koselleck, *Kritik und Krise* (Freiburg, 1959), p. 11.

4   Arnold Hauser, *The Social History of Art*, 2 vols. (New York, 1951) II, p. 542.

5   Jürgen Habermas, *Strukturwandel*, p. 71.

6   *Ibid.*, 72 f.

7   *Ibid.*, 74 and 78.

8   *Ibid.*, 106.

9   *Idem*, *Theory and Practice*, p. 47.

10   *Idem*, *Strukturwandel*, p. 69. (Thus, under the concept of "property" Locke subsumes life, liberty, and estate.)

11   *Ibid.*, 70.

12   Gadamer, *Truth and Method*, p. 24.

13   F. Meinecke, *Die Entstehung des Historismus*, *Works* vol. III (Munich 1965), pp. 19–26.

14   T. Willis, *An Essay on the Pathology of the Brain and Nervous Stock*, in Hunter and Macalpine, *op. cit.*, pp. 191 f. This contrasts sharply with the rather loving therapy for melancholics. But historiography, disregarding

practice and social conditions, has tended to confine itself to Willis' theoretical elaborations on the closeness of melancholy and mania.

15   F. Glisson in 1677 ascribed an intrinsic power to the body, the ability to move in response to stimuli, i.e. irritability or excitability – independent of the nervous system. This endowed the physical-internal, the unconscious life, with a spontaneity that virtually reduced Willis' rationally guided nerve spirit to a secondary superstructure of the conscious. However, Glisson's *natura energetica* furnished Shaftesbury's "inward sentiment" with medical, somatic underpinnings. Cf. Glaser, *Das Denken in der Medizin* (Berlin, 1967), p. 54.

16   T. Sydenham, *Dissertation*, pp. 367 f.

17   *Ibid.*, 376.

18   Michel Foucault, *Madness and Civilization*, p. 149.

19   Sydenham, *op. cit.*, p. 376.

20   *Ibid.*, 401.

21   Hunter and Macalpine, *op. cit.*, pp. 223 f.

22   Hysteria is more or less identical with hypochondria, melancholia, spleen, vapors, lowness of spirits, etc.

23   This term is employed by Ackerknecht. Cf. Ackerknecht, *Kurze Geschichte*, p. 28.

24   T. H. Peardon (ed.), *Locke's Second Treatise of Government*, (New York, 1952), p. ix.

25   Blackmore, *A Treatise of the Spleen and Vapours*, pp. 261 f.

26   Cheyne, *The English Malady*, pp. i–ii, 262.

27   Mead, *Medical Precepts and Cautions*, pp. 88 f.

28   Robinson, *A New System of the Spleen*, pp. 399 ff.

29   Locke, *An Essay Concerning Human Understanding*, vol. II, ch. 11, par. 12–13.

30   *Ibid.*, ch. 33, par. 1–13.

31   Daniel Defoe, *An Essay upon Projects*. Moreover, he proposes "to maintain Fools out of our own Folly," namely by holding a lottery for the equal profit of the poor and fools. His projected Fool-House was to be free of all class distinction; all the inmates should be considered poor, mad shows should be forbidden, and those who would make sport with the inmates should be punished by the head of the institution.

32   Defoe, *Augusta triumphans*, in Hunter and Macalpine, *op. cit.*, p. 267.

33   The social criticism and satire of writers employing psychiatric concepts is often interpreted as a schizophrenic emotional impoverishment. Gabel seems to have done so in his treatment of Swift, particularly when he takes Swift's ironic account of medical views on consumptive diseases through as a schizophrenic speech disorder (Gabel, *Formen der Entfremdung*, p. 33). Gabel's witty false conslusion has Bergsonian overtones, as the context reveals (p. 34).

34   Quoted in Norman O. Brown, *Eros and Civilization*. Brown's psychoanalytic interpretation of Swift's scatological visions turns them

into the polar opposite of Defoe's optimistic enthusiasm for the exploitation of nature.

35   Such a section had previously been set up (1728) in the London hospital named after Thomas Guy, its founder, on his instruction.

36   Hofmann, *Ideengeschichte der sozialen Bewegung*, pp. 22 f.

37   Mottek, *Wirtschaftsgeschichte*, II, 72.

38   *Ibid.*, 67–77.

39   Hofmann, *op. cit.*, p. 15.

40   Habermas, *Theorie und Praxis*, p. 47.

41   *Ibid.*, 217 f.

42   Hunter and Macalpine, *op. cit.*, p. 357.

43   *Ibid.*, 300.

44   One of the few medical works to come from the private madhouses of that time was a book entitled *The Best Method for the Cure of Lunaticks*, by Thomas Fallowes, a quack and owner of a madhouse. In it he praises "the incomparable Oleum Cephalicum" as a panacaea for madmen, one of the many substances which, by causing an inflammation of the scalp, was to drive out madness.

45   Hans Holborn, "Der deutsche Idealismus in sozialgeschichtlicher Bedeutung," in Wheler (ed), *Moderne deutsche Sozialgeschichte*, p. 101.

46   André Maurois, *The Miracle of England* (New York, 1937), p. 398.

47   John Wesley, *The Desideratum*.

48   Quoted in Hunter and Macalpine, *op. cit.* p. 424.

49   *Ibid.*, 404.

50   William Battie, *A Treatise on Madness* (London, 1758), p. 7.

51   *Ibid., passim.*

52   Leibbrand and Wettley, *op. cit.*, p. 339.

53   As did Shakespeare, whose revival was sparked by Johnson: "The lunatic, the lover, and the poet are of imagination all compact" (*Midsummer-night's Dream*, V, 1).

54   Battie, *op. cit.*, pp. 27–32.

55   *Ibid.*, 33–38.

56   *Ibid.*, 41–58.

57   *Ibid.*, 59–67.

58   *Ibid.*, 68–86.

59   *Ibid.*, 4.

60   *Ibid.*, 2.

61   *Ibid.*, 93.

62   *Ibid.*, 94–99.

63   Bedlam Hospital was ruled for four generations by one family, the Monro dynasty — approximately contemporaneous with the Hanoverian dynasty of the British royal house. In their care and treatment of the insane the physicians of that family merely followed tradition. Their real important

role was as patrons of London painters and writers.

64   Quoted in Leigh, *The Historical Development of British Psychiatry*, vol. I (Oxford, 1961), pp. 50 f.

65   Quoted in Hunter and Macalpine, *op. cit.*, p. 413.

66   Smollet's novel was first serialized in *The British Magazine*, a monthly, in 1760–61.

67   Cf. Leigh, *op. cit.*, p. 9 and Hunter and Macalpine, *op. cit.*, pp. 451–56.

68   Leigh, *op. cit.*, pp. 11–14.

69   The term "neurosis," introduced by Cullen, retained its meaning as a disorder of the nerve function without any significant structural damage for over a hundred years, until psychologically internalized, it lost its reference to the nerves. This trend was accelerated in the late nineteenth century by the development of neurology as a speciality and came to fruition not with Freud, but, ironically, when psychiatry was forced to the conclusion that the trembling and other "neurotic" responses of many soldiers to the technologizing process of World War I were due to psychological factors, not to organic causes. In Germany but also in other countries fighting wars, this was a scientific judgment, but it was also seen as a contribution to military morale and to the economy, since it offered a handy tool for fighting the pension claims of veterans. This is one of the most revealing examples of the interweaving of social and political factors in the cognitional process in psychiatry.

70   William Cullen, *First Lines of the Practice of Physic*. The first detailed description of the straitjacket, i.e., the instrument that best symbolizes the change from physical coercion as protection against the unreason of the insane to physical coercion as a therapeutic device, was given by MacBride in *A Methodical Introduction to the Theory and Practice of Physick*. The use of this instrument in England goes back to the late 1730s. It is also to be found in Romantic fiction, in Richardson's *History of Sir Charles Grandison* (1754) and Smollett's *Sir Launcelot Greaves* (1762). Cf. Hunter and Macalpine, *op. cit.*, p. 449.

71   Cullen, *op. cit.*

72   Regarding Brown's influence on psychiatry, see Leibbrand, *Romantische Medizin*, particularly pp. 50–56.

73   Thomas Arnold, *Observations on the Nature, Kinds, Causes, and Prevention, of Insanity*, I (London, 1806), 10, 11.

74   *Ibid.*, 20–22.

75   At the turning point of the phase dealt with in this section, Hartley wrote *Observations on Man, his Frame, his Duty, and His Expectations*. In it madness is likewise no longer simply a disorder of reason, but stands within the more comprehensive framework of man's relationship to himself. Theoretically he combines Locke and Newton, i.e., he sees a correlation between idea associations and the vibrations of the nerves (via corpuscles or fluids).

76   Arnold, *op. cit.*, pp. 60–61. According to Arnold, madness is linked to

nostalgia only where it is infrequent: in the less civilized, i.e. "unpolished" parts of Europe, whereas the polished societies "make of rude and zealous patriots benevolent, though less ardent, citizens of the world" (p. 208). Of course, Arnold, like all others, misconstrues the true cause for the infrequency of madness in "unpolished" areas: The emergence into visibility of the insane members of society is proportionate to its politico-economic development. This explains a phenomenon that has continued to bother psychiatrists and filled them with pessimism about society, namely that with the number of insane asylums the number of insane seems to increase endlessly.

77   *Ibid.*, 242.

78   Arnold, *Observations on the Management of the Insane*, quoted in Hunter and Macalpine, *op. cit.*, p. 469.

79   For a summary of Whytt's neurological discoveries, see Ritter, *Zur Entwicklungsgeschichte der neurologischen Semiologie*, p. 510.

80   Robert Whytt, *An Essay on the Vital and Other Involuntary Motions of Animals*, p. 290.

81   Whytt, *Observations on the Nature...*, p. 111.

82   Foucault, *op. cit.*, p. 157.

83   "The bourgeois ideal of naturalness intends not amorphous nature, but the virtuous mean. Promiscuity and asceticism, excess and hunger, are directly identical, despite the antagonism, as powers of disintegration." Horkheimer and Adorno, *op. cit.*, p. 31.

84   Maurois, *op. cit.*, p. 401.

85   Hauser, *op. cit.*, pp. 551 f.

86   *Ibid.*, 557.

87   Somatic nerve theory categorized "sympathy" as the objective capacity to share the feelings and sensations of others. With the passage of time this changed, became internalized, into the subjective feeling of finding others sympathetic or unsympathetic.

88   Vere, J. *A Physical and Moral Enquiry....*, pp. 32–34.

89   If we recall the throng of institutions of bourgeois private life, which, although generally industrialized today, owe their emergence to that attitude, then one can dilate what Hauser says about the art of English Romanticism: " 'Good taste' is not merely an historically and sociologically relative concept, but it has also only limited significance as a category of aesthetic valuation. The tears which are shed in the eighteenth century over novels, plays, musical compositions, are not only the sign of a change in taste and of the shift of aesthetic values from the exquisite and the reserved to the drastic and the importunate, they mark, at the same time, the beginning of a new phase in the development of that European sensibility of which the Gothic was the first triumph and of which the nineteenth century was to be the climax. This turning point signifies a much more radical break with the past than

the enlightenment itself, which, in fact, represents merely the continuation and completion of a development that had been in progress since the end of the Middle Ages. The criterion of mere taste breaks down in face of a phenomenon like the beginning of this new emotional culture, which leads us to a wholly new concept of poetry." (p. 567).

90   N. Robinson was among the first to revive the use of music therapy on a neurotheoretical basis. His book *A New System of the Spleen* contains a chapter entitled: "Powers of Musick in Soothing the Passions, and allaying the Tempests of the Soul, under the Spleen, Vapours, and Hypochondriack Melancholy."

91   Cf. J. Starobinski, *Geschichte der Melancholie behandlung* (Basel, 1960), pp. 75–78.

92   "Country News," in *The Gentleman's Magazine*, LVII, pt 1, 1787, 268.

93   Habermas, *Theorie und Praxis*, p. 218.

94   Thomas Reid, *The Philosophical Works*, II, ed. Hamilton (London, 1895), 774 ff.

95   R. Spaemann, *Ursprung der Soziologie* (Munich, 1959), pp. 54 f.

96   F. Hutcheson, *An Essay on the Nature and Conduct of the Passions and Affections with Illustrations on the Moral Sense* (London, 1728), p. 63.

97   Reid, *An Inquiry into the Human Mind on the Principles of Common Sense* (Edinburgh, 1764), p. 12.

98   J. Gregory, *A Comparative View of the State and Faculties of Man with Those of the Animal World* (London, 1765), pp. 13–15.

99   Gregory, *Observations on Duties and Offices of a Physician*, in Hunter and Macalpine, *op. cit.*, p. 438.

100   W. Hofmann, *Ideengeschichte der sozialen Bewegung* (Berlin, 1962), pp. 7–12.

101   H. Mottek, *Wirtschaftsgeschichte Deutschlands*, II (Berlin, 1964), p. 75.

102   For an early, and historically seen, theoretical approach to a sociology of illness produced by society itself see H. P. Drietzel, *Die gesellschaftlichen Leiden und das Leiden an der Gesellschaft* (Stuttgart, 1968).

103   Hofmann, *op. cit.*, pp. 23–38.

104   Hauser, *op. cit.*, 703 ff.

105   *Ibid.*, 815.

106   *Ibid.*, 815–16

107   According to Leigh's generally comprehensive psychiatric bibliography of eighteenth-century England, (*op. cit.*, pp. 84–93), there were two striking exceptions to the generally gradual increase of publications, more or less contemporaneous with the two qualitative changes in the development of psychiatry referred to by us. Between the 1840s and the 1850s, the number of publications increased from six to seventeen, and between the 1870s and

the 1880s, from eleven to twenty-seven.

108   Thus the telling title of a work by John Bell is: *The General and Particular Principles of Animal Electricity and Magnetism, Showing How to Magnetise and Cure Different Diseases, to Produce Crises, as well as Somnambulism, or Sleep-walking* (London, 1792).

109   J. Aikin, *Thoughts on Hospitals* (London, 1771), pp. 65 ff.

110   J. Currie, "Two Letters on the Establishment of a Lunatic Asylum at Liverpool," in *The Liverpool Advertiser*, August 29, and November 12, 1789. Quoted from Hunter and Macalpine, *op. cit.*, pp. 518 f. Here we see the trend of neutralizing insanity not only as a disease process but also with regard to class. The latter still has not been accomplished. Thus Hollingshead and Redlich, in *Social Class and Mental Illness*, impressively demonstrate the difference in diagnosis and therapy according to class. Currie notwithstanding, the reality of the class society is still with us.

111   The significance attached to the harmfulness of bad air, or rather to the curative powers of fresh air led — also within the framework of the Reform Movement — to the establishment of separate sections for contagious diseases in hospitals. On this point and the panoptic idea in general, see D. Jetter, "Ursprung und Gestalt panoptischer Irrenhäuser in England und Schottland," *Sudhoffs Archiv* 46: 27—44, 1962.

112   This method as the moral power of man over others was thus being practiced in England even before Mesmer's magnetism arrived there. The first English work on this subject was the previously cited John Bell (cf. note 108). Not until the Victorian era did England become so romantic as to nurture the spread of magnetism.

113   From an anonymous report, "Détails sur l'établissement du docteur Willis, pour la guérison des Aliénés," in *Bibliothèque Britannique, Littérature* (Geneva, 1796), quoted from Hunter and Macalpine, p. 538. There is no doubt that Francis Willis was the first perfect example of the image of a psychiatrist endowed with special, mysterious personal powers and able to establish contact or rapport where others had failed, an image that with ever new motivations has persisted. Not coincidentally, it arose first in private asylums, as in Willis' institution and Tuke's Retreat. For here the pressure of private economic competition played a major role, which is why, like other enterprises, they advertised their special achievements in newspapers and magazines. Such imputed power over others had a special aura since these enterprises were often run by clergymen.

114   D. Leigh, *The Historical Development of British Psychiatry*, I, (Oxford, 1961), 71 f.

115   William Perfect, *Methods of Cure in Some Particular Cases of Insanity and Nervous Disorders* (Rochester, n.d.). Perfect was among those physicians relying heavily on Battie.

116   To this day, some laymen as well as physicians tend to diagnose

"shifty-eyed" individuals as insane. This follows the tradition of seeking to gain control over the patient through "eye-to-eye" contact.

117   William Pargeter, *Observations on Maniacal Disorders* (Reading, 1802), pp. 50–51.

118   J. Ferriar, *Medical Histories and Reflections*, in Hunter and Macalpine, *op. cit.*, pp. 543–46. Ferriar also introduced the term "hysterical conversion" to signify a change in symptoms.

119   J. M. Cox, *Practical Observations on Insanity*. The idea of the mutual replaceability of qualitatively different diseases in the psychiatric realm goes back to R. Mead, *Medical Precepts and Cautions*. Observations of synchronous, alternating, or mutually exclusive diseases concern an empirical area that has always attracted pragmatic therapeutic experimentation. The greatest success was achieved at the turn of the century when malaria was enlisted in the treatment of progressive paralysis.

120   Foucault, *op. cit.*, pp. 249 f., castigates the submission of patients to a regimen of constant objectifying observation. But in fact this presumption of natural science, medical knowledge was practically abandoned here and the distancing attitude rejected.

121   We must bear in mind that at this time there existed no scientific possibilities for separating today's endogenous psychoses (manic-depressive syndrome, schizophrenia) from psychopathological syndromes of a different origin: e.g. from cerebro-sclerotic, senile, endocrinologic, toxic-infectious, epileptic, or syphilitic psychoses. Likewise, later psychopathic states, reactions based on idiocy, psychogenic reactions, behavioral disorders, etc. were to a large extent classed as insanity, especially since with the foundings of institutions, the interest in hysteria and its equivalents diminished. The Retreat refused admission only to congenital idiots.

122   Hunter and Macalpine, *op. cit.*, pp. 685 ff.

123   M. Jacobi, *Sammlungen für die Heilkunde der Gemütskrankheiten*, I (Elberfeld, 1822), 30.

124   Foucault, *op. cit.*, pp. 252–54.

125   *Ibid.*, 245.

126   H. Laehr, *Gedenktage der Psychiatrie* (Berlin, 1889), p. 95. The first special asylums exclusively for "criminal lunatics" were opened in Dundrum, Dublin (1851), and Broadmoor (1863).

127   Quoted from Hunter and Macalpine, *op. cit.*, p. 703.

128   For Haslam's biography, cf. Leigh, *op. cit.*, pp. 94–114 and 121.

129   Thomas Bakewell, "A Letter, addressed to the chairman of the Select Committee of the House of Commons," Stafford, Chester, 1815 (quoted from Hunter and Macalpine, *op. cit.*, p. 707).

130   George M. Burrows, *An Inquiry into Certain Errors Relative to Insanity; and Their Consequences* (London, 1820), *passim*.

131   Hofmann, *op. cit.*, p. 33 and 37 f.

132   Burrows, *op. cit., passim.*

133   Marshal emphasized the role of defective cerebral blood vessels as a cause of madness.

134   C. T. Thackrah, *The Effects of Arts, Trades and Professions, and of Civic States and Habits of Living on Health and Longevity* (London, 1831), Introduction. Thackrah was a physician to the poor of Leeds, and his book was the first medical voice to be raised against industrial capitalism, though, more from a romantic approach to the natural life. Two years later, the first more stringent factory laws were passed.

135   John Reid, *Essays on Insanity, Hypochondriasis, and other Nervous Affections* (London, 1816), pp. 58ff.

136   H. Holland, "On the Pellagra," *Medico-Chirurgical Transactions*, London, 1817.

137   T. Sutton, *Tracts on Delirium Tremens* (London, 1813).

138   Burrows, *Commentaries on the Causes, Forms, Symptoms, and Treatment, Moral and Medical, of Insanity* (London, 1828). To be sure, the apothecary John Haslam had at least approximately described progressive paralysis in terms of psychopathology. Haslam anticipated an approach that was adopted by psychiatry only a hundred years later: a combination of continuous, daily experience with mental patients and detached, objective observation. This was the basis of his unparalleled virtuosity in the description and differentiation of psychopathological states and processes. Along with progressive paralysis, he also described manic-depressive insanity, compulsion, childhood psychoses, and, above all, the symptomotology of schizophrenia, which the psychiatric community "saw" only in the late nineteenth century. At the same time, he introduced cerebral dissection as a diagnostic tool. His definition of insanity deals with a factor that continues to plague psychiatry to this day. He calls insanity "an incorrect association of familiar ideas, which is independent of the prejudices of education, and is always accompanied with implicit belief, and generally with either violent or depressing passions" (*Observations on Insanity*, p. 10). He stresses that in diagnosis only "familiar ideas" should be considered, and that these are to be sharply distinguished from the prejudices that are rooted in the patient's particular social milieu. That is to say, he recognizes the difference between pathological notions and those that seem strange to the diagnostician only because of social class differences. Haslam continues the tradition of the intellectual insanity concept; passions are merely secondary symptoms. Although he rejects punishment as absurd, since insanity is a brain disease, he has no qualms about restraints, including chains, as "protecting and salutary restraint" (p. 126). That is why contemporary psychiatrists inclined to think in terms of emotional problems, of restraint as an inner moral force, and enthusiastic about emancipation, considered him reactionary.

139   W. Lawrence, *Lectures on Physiology, Zoology, and the Natural History of Man* (London, 1819), pp. 111 ff.

140   W. E. Mühlmann, *Geschichte der Anthropologie* (Bonn, 1948), p. 80.

141   G. Rosen, "Social Attitudes to Irrationality and Madness," *Journal of the History of Medicine*, 18: 240, 1953.

142   A. Combe, *Observations on Mental Derangement* (Edinburgh, 1831). Phrenology is treated in detail in connection with France.

143   M. Neuburger, "British and German Psychiatry in the Second Half of the 18th and Early 19th Century," *Bull. Hist. Med.*, 18: 139 ff., 1945.

144   N. Dain and E. T. Carlson, "Social Class and Psychological Medicine in the United States, 1789–1824," *Bull. Hist. Med.* 18: 139 ff., 1945.

145   The increasing "nationalization" of the insane in public institutions was evidenced in legislation. The law of 1808 at first only allowed the counties to build public asylums. When this was not enough to meet the social need, a new bill of 1845 mandated that the counties build institutions. This law was the work of A. Ashley Cooper, the Earl of Shaftesbury, who represented the late-romantic, anticapitalist commitment of conservatives to the underprivileged in mid-nineteenth-century England.

146   S. C. Ellis, *A Treatise on the Nature, Symptoms, Causes and Treatment of Insanity* (London, 1838). Ellis and other directors of the "pauper lunatic asylums" succeeded in getting as many as three-quarters of their poor inmates to do regular work. And despite their rejection of the former punishments for moral insubordination, patients who refused to work were subjected to treatment by instruments – the rotary machine or the electric machine. This characterized the social character of psychiatric progress: the individual was not pressed into any administrative or moral order. Rather, the road from unreason to reason now led through submission to the work order of an efficient society.

147   Hill, *A Concise History of the Entire Abolition of Mechanical Restraint and of the Non-Restraint System* (London, 1857), pp. 57–58.

148   R. G. Hill, *Total Abolition of Personal Restraint in the Treatment of the Insane* (London, 1839), pp. 37–38.

149   Hill, *A Concise History of the Entire Abolition of Mechanical Restraint and of the Non-Restraint System* pp. 58 ff. Battie and Haslam were also "premature" and hence at first ignored. This too would indicate that English psychiatry was "premature" as far as the Continent and especially Germany was concerned, which is why psychiatric historiography tends to ignore the first paradigm of psychiatry, namely the British.

150   For biographical data on Conolly, see Leigh, *op. cit.*, pp. 210–67 and Hunter and Macalpine, *op. cit.*, pp. 805–9, 1,030–38. Conolly's two most important works are entitled *On the Construction and Government of Lunatic Asylums* (1847), and *The Treatment for the Insane without Mechanical Restraints* (1856).

151   Conolly, *On the Construction*, p. 143.

PART II: *France*

1   A. Wettley, "Die Stellung des Geisteskranken in der Gesellschaft des 19. Jahrhunderts," in W. Artelt and N. Rüegg (eds.), *Der Arzt und der Kranke in der Gesellschaft des 19. Jahrhunderts* (Stuttgart, 1967). The author was the first in Germany to take Foucault into consideration. However, she hardly deals with the thesis of seeing in the emancipation of the insane, generally treated as an act of philanthropy, as a form of coercion attuned to the conditions of bourgeois society. Furthermore, it does not seem very convincing to explain the exceptionally rigorous work ethos of institutions of isolation in France of all places – à la Max Weber – in terms of Protestantism. (cf. p. 53).

2   Michel Foucault, *Madness and Civilization*, p. 59.

3   Jürgen Habermas, *Strukturwandel*, pp. 81 f.

4   *Ibid.*, 83.

5   J. Bodamer, "Zur Phänomenologie des geschichtlichen Geistes in der Psychiatrie, *Nervenarzt*, 19: 303, and K. E. Rothschuh, "Vom Spiritus animalis zum Nervenaktionsstrom," *Ciba Zeitschrift*, No. 58.

6   O. Temkin, "Materialism in French and German Physiology of the Early Nineteenth Century," *Bull. Hist. Med.*, 20: 320 ff., 1946.

7   In Whytt, we saw a similar trend toward making the psyche a part of medical theory. But he limited himself more to the analysis of the nervous system, and thus promoted a neurological model of medicine such as Cullen later carried out. Montpellier, on the other hand, introduced the analysis of all bodily organs and tissues, thereby broadening the anatomical-physiological basis of nineteenth-century medicine.

8   G. Rosen, "The Philosophy of Ideology and the Emergence of Modern Medicine in France," *Bull. Hist. Med.* 20: 328–31, 1946. Our description of Condillac's method, which Diderot called "Locke *perfecté*," is based on E. B. de Condillac, "Essai sur l'origine des connaissances humaines," 2 vol. 1746–54, in, Lewis White Beck (ed.), *18th-Century Philosophy* (New York, 1966), pp. 165–170.

9   P. H. D. Holbach, "Systeme de la nature ou des lois du monde physique et du monde moral," in K. Lenk, *Ideologie*, pp. 69–73.

10   Quoted in Foucault, pp. 104 f.

11   Jürgen Habermas, *Theory and Practice*, tr. John Viertel, (Boston, 1973) p. 257. Also cf. Lieber, pp. 6 f. and 60–62.

12   *Op. cit.*, p. 258.

13   Marx, *Thesen über Feuerbach*, p. 593.

14   Rousseau therefore was one of the most popular objects of the psychiatric (and often resentful) genre of "pathography" of important personalities that reached its highpoint in the late nineteenth century.

15   Arnold Hauser, *The Social History of Art*, II, 571.

16   R. Koselleck, *Kritik und Krise*, p. 133.

17   Hauser, *op. cit.*, p. 568.

18   Koselleck, *op. cit.*, p. 143.

19   This concept of nature is interpreted by Lukács in *History and Class Consciousness* (Cambridge, Mass., MIT Press, 1971) as follows: "'Nature' here refers to authentic humanity, the true essence of man liberated from the false, mechanizing forms of society: man as perfected whole who has inwardly overcome or is in the process of overcoming, the dichotomy of theory and practice, reason and senses, form and content; man whose tendency to create his own forms does not imply an abstract rationalism which ignores concrete content...." (p. 137).

20   Hence: "The *volonté générale* is a consensus of hearts rather than of arguments" (Habermas, *Strukturwandel*, p. 113).

21   Rousseau, "Discours sur les sciences et les arts," in Beck (ed.), *Eighteenth-Century Philosophy*, pp. 151–63.

22   "Before Rousseau, except in certain forms of lyric poetry, a writer had spoken only indirectly about himself, but after him writers spoke of hardly anything else, and in the most free and easy manner. It is since that time that the idea of a literature of experience and confession first arose which was uppermost in Goethe's mind when he declared that all his works were only 'fragments of a great confession'" (Hauser, *op. cit.*, p. 570).

23   J. Starobinsky, *Geschichte der Melancholiebehandlung* (Basel, 1960), pp. 86 and 60. At the same time, Rousseau brought to light the multiple contradictions of this view of psychiatry: if it is a rational science, it arrives at the first contradiction when it talks about the "laws of the heart," which, according to Rousseau, are inaccessible to any rational notion of laws. Furthermore, the theme of psychiatry is the deviation from the irrational laws of the heart, i.e. the irrationality of the irrational. Finally, psychiatry as practice is subject to a third contradiction insofar as Rousseau's concept is immanent to it. Not only does the social need make it a medical obligation to find rational means even against the rationally totally unknown; with Rousseau, rational science acknowledged that a major portion of the causes of derangement lay in rational science itself, in too much rationality. No wonder that a science that is so often urged simultaneously to be an anti-science frequently resorts to using irrational-direct means to fit accord with the idea of the irrational-immediate "natural man," generally in combination with both anticapitalist and antiliberal social criticism, while English psychiatry never lost its historical phase, in which it positively identified the liberal, capitalist social structure and mental disorders.

24   P. J. Buchoz, "Mémoire sur la manière de güerir la melancholie par la musique," in F. N. Marquet, *Nouvelle methode facile et curieuse, pour connoitre le pouls par les notes de la musique*, 2nd ed. (Amsterdam, 1769). Quoted in Starobinsky, *op. cit.*, pp. 85 f.

25   On this, and similar interpretations by Tissot, cf. Foucault, *op. cit.*, pp. 151, 155 f., 186.

26   B. de Saint-Pierre, *Oeuvres*, III (Paris, 1818), pp. 11 f., quoted in Foucault, *op. cit.*, pp. 192 f.

27   For Mesmer, see R. Kaech, "Der Mesmerismus," in *Ciba Zschr.* No. 105 (1947), and W. Leibbrand, *Romantische Medizin*, pp. 126–33.

28   Psychiatry has experienced three fundamental emigrations, which, not coincidentally, have a series of common features: all were in the direction from Germany to Western countries; all were forced and involved, among other things, the charge of materialism, with the result that the incriminating theories reached their full development in the Western countries; and all subsequently were brought back to Germany, where, however, the relationship to them has remained uncertain. The theories are those of Mesmer, Gall, and Freud.

29   The physician, and later Jacobinic "friend of the people," J. P. Marat in 1784 wrote an essay, *Mémoire sur l'electricité medicale*, on this theme.

30   Swedenborg is one demonstration of the general nature of the phenomenon of Mesmerism. He too arrived at spiritualism via the body/soul problem. That this met a need of the upper-class public is shown by the success the spiritualist Cagliostro (Balsamo) enjoyed at European courts. In 1785, his involvement in a fraud helped to point up the declining authority of the French monarchy. Finally, there is the case of the priest J. J. Gasner, who scored considerable success at that time with his exorcisms of demons.

31   It is idle to argue whether the revival of spiritualism should be credited to the Enlightenment, as the anti-Enlightenment forces claimed, or whether it was the countereffect of restorative forces, as the proponents of the Enlightenment maintained, for instance Voltaire: "The more reason advances, the more fanaticism gnashes its teeth" (Kaech, *op. cit.*, p. 3,819). The natural scientist Berthollet, who doubted the powers in magnetism, was almost strangled by Mesmer supporters (*ibid.*, p. 3,833). The controversy can be discussed only within the framework of the movement of the unfolding bourgeois society.

32   Cf. e.g. W. Glassner, *Reality Therapy, a New Approach to Psychotherapy* (New York, 1965), and O. H. Mowrer, "The Basis of Psychopathology: Malconditioning or Misbehavior?," *J. Ass. Women, Deans and Couns.* 29: 51–8, 1966.

33   Plessner, *Die verspätete Nation*, p. 74.

34   "Beggary is the fruit of poverty, which in turn has numerous causes: the state of agriculture, the production of manufactories, the rise in prices, the growth of the population, etc." (Brissot de Warville, *Théorie des lois criminelles*).

35   Habermas, *Strukturwandel*, pp. 110 f.

36   G. Eckert, *Der Merkantilismus* (Brunswick, 1949), p. 45.

37 Mirabeau, H., *Observations d'un voyageur anglais*, p. 4.

38 On De Sade, see Foucault, *op. cit.*, pp. 210 and 227 f.

39 *Ibid.*, 204.

40 Foucault's view of this (pp. 204 ff.) as a regression to the role of the medieval leprosarium ignores the — economically and scientifically — totally different situation. The "progress" of the medical attention given the insane and other interned groups is — no matter how problematic the implications — attested to both by the subjective intention and the objective success, and cannot simply be written off as a "strange regression."

41 R. de Saussure, "French Psychiatry of the 18th Century," *Ciba-Symp.*, II, 5 (1950), p. 1,226.

42 Mirabeau, *Des Lettres de Cachet*, vol. I, p. 267.

43 Abbé de Récalde, *Traité sur les abus qui subsistent dans les hôpitaux* (Paris, 1786), p. III.

44 Habermas, *Strukturwandel*, p. 110.

45 Hofmann, *Ideengeschichte*, p. 38.

46 R. Jones, *An Inquiry into the Nature, Causes, and Termination of Nervous Fevers*, Salisbury, 1789. Quoted in Leigh, pp. 73 f.

47 Koselleck, "Staat und Gesellschaft in Preussen," in Wehler (ed.), *Moderne deutsche Sozialgeschichte*, pp. 55 f.

48 E. Kraepelin, "Hundert Jahre Psychiatrie," *Zeitschrift für ges. Neurol. und Psychiat.*, pp. 161 ff.; H. Gruhle, "Geschichtliches," in O. Bumke (ed.), *Handbuch der Geisteskrankheiten*, IX (Berlin, 1932).

49 E. Ackerknecht, *Kurze Geschichte der Psychiatrie* (Stuttgart, 1947); H. Ey, *Etudes Psychiatriques*, I (Paris, 1948).

50 See Leibbrand and Wettley, *op. cit.*, p. 657, whose emendations are based on a dissertation by W. Lechler (Munich, 1960).

51 Ey, *op. cit.*, p. 30.

52 Saussure, "Philippe Pinel," in H. Kolle (ed.), *Grosse Nervenärzte* (Stuttgart, 1956), I, p. 220; Foucault, *op. cit.*, pp. 236 ff.

53 Foucault, *ibid.*, 237 ff.

54 For instance, the Maison de St. Lazare in Paris, founded by St. Vincent de Paul in 1632.

55 H. Laehr, *Gedenktage der Psychiatrie* (Berlin, 1889), p. 102.

56 See H. Rosen, "The Philosophy of Ideology and the Emergence of Modern Medicine in France," *Bull. Hist. Med.*, 20 (1946), and Leibbrand and Wettley, *op. cit.*, pp. 658 ff,

57 Rosen, *ibid.*

58 K. Sudhoff, *Kurzes Handbuch der Geschichte der Medizin* (Berlin, 1922), p. 334. Bichat's failure to refer to Cabanis is due to the fact that his clinical positivism was emphatically antirevolutionary, whereas Cabanis always regarded himself as related to the Revolution.

59 See Ackerknecht, *op. cit.*, p. 35; Leibbrand and Wettley, *op. cit.*,

pp. 403–410; Ey, *op. cit.*, pp. 44 f.

60   P. J. G. Cabanis, *Rapports du Physique et Moral de l'Homme* (Paris, 1802), I, 6 f.

61   At this point, Adorno's *Negative Dialectics* continues the criticism beyond the *Dialectics of Enlightenment*.

62   Heine called Destutt de Tracy, the other leader of the school of Ideologues, the Fichte of Materialism. Cf. Temkin, "The Philosophical Background of Magendie's Physiology," *Bull. Hist. Med.* 20 (1946), p. 15.

63   See K. E. Rothschuh, "Vom Spiritus animalis zum Nervenaktionsstrom," *Ciba-Zeitschrift*, No. 89 (1958) p. 2,970. It goes without saying that in the controversy over Galvanism, Cabanis enthusiastically sided with Galvani's (1791) and Alexander von Humboldt's (1797) "identity theory," which essentially inspired the ideas of polarity and identity in German Romanticism: by looking on the muscle as a kind of Leyden jar with positive and negative electricity, people believed in an identity between electricity and nervous fluid, nervous energy and ultimately life itself.

64   Cabanis, *op. cit.*, II, 593 ff. Schopenhauer relied on Cabanis in order to present gravity as a primordial form of the human will (Temkin, "The Philosophical Background...," p. 15).

65   Cabanis, *ibid.*, 513 f.

66   *Ibid.*, 491–92; here translated from Starobinski, *op. cit.*, p. 86.

67   On the naturalization of the utopian in Destutt de Tracy, see Lieber, *op. cit.*, p. 63.

68   *Soziologische Exkurse*, p. 167.

69   See Leibbrand and Wettley, *op. cit.*, pp. 656 ff.; Saussure, "French Psychiatry," p. 1,222; *ibid.*, "Philippe Pinel," in Kolle (ed.), *op. cit.*, pp. 216 ff.

70   See Rosen, "The Evolution of Social Medicine," pp. 17 ff.

71   Philippe Pinel, *A Treatise on Insanity* (London, 1806) Trans. D. D. Davis. With an Introduction by P. F. Cranefield, pp. 45–47.

72   *Ibid.*, 288.

73   Rosen, "The Philosophy of Ideology," p. 332.

74   E. Lesky, "Die Spezialisierung ärztliches Problem gestern und heute," *Münch. Med. Wschr.*, 18 (1967), p. 1,019. Citing a number of examples, the author shows that the evolution of the medical specialities depended more on these sociological premises than on technical inventions. Thus, around 1841, in a small German town, the principle of the otoscope was discovered and described. But only with its rediscovery by A. Politzer during the 1860s in Vienna, was the specialty of otology developed through the treatment of the available pool of poor patients. Unfortunately, Lesky also refers to "philanthropy" as the "mood of the times," isolated from the economic and social situation. Thus she remains committed to the customary abstract scheme of socio-economic/cultural dualism, which detracts from

the explanation for the emergence of psychiatry.

75 Pinel, *op. cit.*, pp. 3–50.

76 The fact that Pinel approached insanity from the perspective of mania rather than from the simpler and more closely related forms of melancholia and nervous disorders is symptomatic of the break with everything that came before him.

77 Even today, academic psychiatry takes a similar view of the susceptibility of certain professions to mental disorders, which, of course, tells us nothing about the factors that determine this "fact."

78 At first Pinel — like Locke and Condillac — refused to believe that the outburst of such an irrational spontaneity was possible. But evidently the visible lessons of the Revolution and the many impulsive, rationally incomprehensible acts of violence worked to change his mind and thus, with "manie sans délire," created the theoretical nucleus of the paradigm of French psychiatry. Among the many proofs for the existence of this form of disease we find Pinel's description of a characteristic scene: in the time of the prison massacres, a revolutionary troop broke into Bicêtre under pretense of freeing certain victims of the old tyranny who might have been hidden among the inmates. And in fact they did find one inmate who appeared to be rational, and complained bitterly about his unjust confinement in chains. The revolutionaries triumphantly freed him and were about to arrest, or perhaps even attack the suspect director of the institution, evidently an enemy of the people. The unshackled inmate, however, excited by the tumult, grabbed a saber and gave free rein to his sudden thirst for blood until he was disarmed and again put in chains. Pinel, not without satisfaction, relishes the victory of scientific authority over what seemed to him a dangerously naive absoluteness of the rational desire for liberation.

79 Only if, like Foucault (*op. cit.*, pp. 255 ff.), one were to set aside Pinel's root problem of *manie sans délire* — can one arrive at the thesis that bourgeois society perfected the rule of silence over the insane. It goes without saying that Schopenhauer cited this form of illness to illustrate his voluntaristic philosophy (*Welt als Wille und Vorstellung*, II, ch. 32).

80 Panse, *op. cit.*, p. 20.

81 Thus in E. Haisch, "Irrenpflege in unserer Zeit," *Ciba*, No. 95, p. 3,149.

82 Habermas, *Theory and Practice*, pp. 101–5.

83 K. W. Ideler, *Grundriss der Seelenheilkunde* (Berlin, 1838), II, 99.

84 Pinel derived these emphatically presented wishful thoughts largely from reports about the Spanish Hospital in Saragossa, where a similar system had been employed since the time of the Arabs.

85 Starobinsky, *op. cit.*, p. 65: some of the therapeutic examples are not from Pinel's major work cited here, but from his article "Mélancolie" in the *Encyclopédie méthodique*.

86   This was frequently forgotten by Pinel's successors and was interpreted as a special gift of the physician as Foucault correctly points out (*op. cit.*, p. 275).

87   Starobinsky, *op. cit.*, p. 70.

88   Comte, "Sommaire appréciation de l'ensemble du passé moderne" in: appendix to *Système de politique positive*, vol. 4, p. 41.

89   Rosen, "Evolution of Social Medicine."

90   This contrasts particularly with Germany, where most eighteenth- and nineteenth-century psychiatrists were the children of public officials. Theirs was an unbroken tradition showing no signs of increasing social mobility.

91   For an account of Esquirol's life, see e.g. Ey, *op. cit.*, II, pp. 87–97.

92   Quoted from Haisch, "Irrenpflege," p. 3,148.

93   Laehr, *Gedenktage*, pp. 88 f.

94   On this law, see Wettley, "Die Stellung des Geisteskranken," in, Artelt and Rüegg (eds.), *Der Arzt und der Kranke*, p. 64; Panse, *op. cit.*, pp. 145–148 and 620 f. Ey, *op. cit.*, (p. 14) comments critically that with this law bourgeois society wanted to remove a source of trouble and safeguard itself, i.e. it soothed its conscience; in fact, however, it merely camouflaged the true needs of the insane.

95   Comte, *Discourse sur l'esprit positif*, pp. 24–27.

96   See Comte's concurrence with De Maistre's politically meant adage; that "Everything that is necessary persists" (Comte, *Sociologie*, vol. I).

97   Esquirol, vol. I, pp. 9–12 and 30, similarly, Comte's emphasis on the supremacy of the feeling faculties and passions in human nature (*Sociologie*).

98   Esquirol, vol. I, pp. 31–34.

99   We must bear in mind that postrevolutionary France had, for instance, the first higher institutes of technology, a major instrument of social advancement.

100   In support of this and other claims, Esquirol almost always could marshal statistical proof, and since that time, such proof has served as the criterion for the scientific claims of psychiatry. However, statistics soon became an instrument of psychiatrists in their institutional politics: the one who could offer numerical proof of the best cure ratios had the best chances in the competition, not only for private patients but also for public funds (Panse, *op. cit.*, p. 25).

101   Esquirol, vol. I, pp. 21–31.

102   Comte, *Discours*, p. 29.

103   *Idem, Sociologie*, vol. I.

104   Esquirol, *op. cit.*, vol. I, pp. 281–300.

105   *Ibid.*, II, 158.

106   *Ibid.*, I, 112–122.

107   Ey, *op. cit.*, pp. 35–38. This, however, reveals the sterility of Ey's Bergsonian polarity between mechanicism and dynamicism, for Esquirol explains his concept of hallucination essentially dynamically, as an excess of energy.

108   Esquirol, *op. cit.*, I, 238 ff.

109   *Ibid.*, I, 238 ff; II, 2 ff.

110   *Ibid.*, II, 379. On homicidal monomania, see *ibid.*, 50–56 and 349–379. For a historical overview of the problem of monomania and moral insanity from the legal perspective, see Berthold, *Die Entwicklung der moral insanity*.

111   Quoted from Leibbrand and Wettley, *op. cit.*, p. 433.

112   The both reifying and humanizing movement of seeing the insane not as personally guilty but as somatically ill was symbolically concentrated in the bedside treatment instituted by the Belgian reformer J. Guislain (1797–1860). In 1829, he introduced reforms at the asylum of Gent, delivering lectures on psychology, hygiene, and beginning in 1850, psychiatry. It was Guislain who introduced the concept of the unitary psychosis (i.e., that all forms of illness are merely phases of a single process) into the European discussion.

113   This happened, for instance, in the case of the leaders of the Munich Soviet republic. Those who weren't killed were examined and written about by men like Kraepelin or E. Kahn, in "Psychopathen als revolutionäre Führer."

114   Comte, *Sociologie*, vol. III.

115   Hauser, *op. cit.*, p. 754.

116   *Ibid.*, 755.

117   Esquirol, vol. II, p. 15.

118   On Gall, see Kirchoff, *Deutsche Irrenärzte*, I, 22–24; Hunter and Macalpine, *op. cit.*, pp. 711–16; Leibbrand and Wettley, *op. cit.*, pp. 456–61.

119   Gall, *Philosophisch-medicinische Untersuchungen über Natur und Kunst*, I, 673. That this laid the basis for what came later is also shown by this: "It is, after all, an everlasting truth that no beast and no man has ever learned or otherwise acquired anything for which he did not possess an innate gift, a natural aptitude" (p. 128).

120   *Probleme und Ergebnisse der Psychologie*, pp. 34–39. Gall had already referred to his work of 1791 as "medical psychology."

121   Broussais, *De l'irritation et de la folie*.

122   The phrenologists took it for granted that their theory was not merely a natural science but also a practical social science. This assumption can be seen in Broussais' proposal to the July monarchy to the effect that every candidate for the new bureaucracy be given a craniological test designed to weed out all the unfit — a both fascinating and questionable step in the direction of technocratic social planning. (Wettley, *Die Trieblehre Comtes*, pp. 37 f.)

123   A. L. J. Bayle, *Recherches sur les maladies mentales* (Paris, 1822). The synopsis of hitherto heterogeneous phenomena necessary for this discovery could occur at this time only in the anatomically oriented Charenton, at which Bayle worked. At the same time, at Salpêtrière work on this problem was also being done but no solution was arrived at since here, under Esquirol's directorship, the preformed hypotheses were too rigidly psychological. (Leibbrand and Wettley, *op. cit.*, pp. 447 f.)

124   The discovery of a psychopathologic syndrome for a specific external cause had already occurred in England for pellagra and delirium tremens. And Haslam, in 1798, had also described the connection between dementia and paralysis.

125   Comte, *Sociologie*, vol. I.

126   *Ibid.*, 353–57 *passim.*

127   Georget, *De la Folie.*

128   Voisin, *De causes morales and physiques des maladies mentales.*

129   See Pinel, *Physiologie de l'homme aliéné, appliqué à l'analyse de l'homme social*, pp. 229 f. The annihilation of the insane became one of the possible consequences of sociosomatic positivism.

130   Ten years later, Voisin summed up his experiences in this area, which is primarily of pedagogical relevance, in *De l'idiotie chez les enfants.*

131   Leuret, *Du traitement moral de la folie.* In Germany, on the other hand, Leuret in particular found agreement at this time.

132   Mehring, *Geschichte der Sozialdemokratie*, p. 678; on Buchez, see Leibbrand and Wettley, *op. cit.*, pp. 523 f. and 669.

133   Cerise, *Des fonctions et des maladies nerveuses*, pp. 1–2.

134   *Ibid.*, 169.

PART III: *Germany*

1   Karl Marx called this stratum the "light infantry of capital…thrown by it, according to its needs, now to this point, now to that", (*Capital*, pt. VII, ch. 24, sec. 5). For the numerical significance, cf. Lütge, *Deutsche Sozial- und Wirtschaftsgeschichte*, pp. 273–78 and 244 ff. "In the ecclesiastic lands of eighteenth-century Germany, about fifty out of a thousand inhabitants were clerics, and two hundred and sixty, beggars. In Cologne, the authorities estimated the number of beggars as between twelve and twenty thousand, out of a total population of fifty thousand. And their number was large in Bavaria too. It was lower in the Protestant areas, but still frighteningly high by modern standards" (p. 274).

2   Kirchhoff, "Grundriss einer Geschichte der deutschen Irrenpflege," pp. 127 and 140.

3   Haisch, "Irrenpflege in alter Zeit," p. 3,146.

4   *Ibid.*, 3,145.

5   Kirchhoff, *op. cit.*, p. 216.

6   Sombart, *Der moderne Kapitalismus*, vol. I, p. 815.

7   *Ibid.*, 820.

8   Hanna Arendt, *Vita Activa* (Stuttgart, 1960), p. 47. This also describes the basis for the transition of the irrationality of insanity from a derangement of the mind to a disorder of the feelings, of the vital energy, of life.

9   Hofmann, *Gesellschaftslehre als Ordnungsmacht*, pp. 29 and 33: "The labor of unfree people (whether bondsmen, serfs, slaves, prisoners, or however restricted in their freedom whether temporarily or permanently) is ...inefficient."

10   Mottek, *Wirtschaftsgeschichte*, vol. II, pp. 76 and 78 f.

11   Plessner, *Die verspätete Nation*, p. 41.

12   Lütge, *op. cit.*, p. 275.

13   Kirchoff, "Grundriss," pp. 112 f.

14   *Ibid.*, 126 f.

15   *Ibid.*, 138.

16   *Ibid.*, 147 f.

17   Wagnitz, *Historische Nachrichten und Bemerkungen über die merkwürdigsten Zuchthäuser in Deutschland*, quoted in Kirchoff, "Grundriss," pp. 115 f. Wagnitz's major reform suggestions are contained in *Ideen und Pläne zur Verbesserung der Polizei- und Kriminalanstalten.*

18   Panse, *op. cit.*, pp. 15 f.

19   Thus an article in the regulations of 1580 for the attendants stated: "To learn as much as possible about each individual's peculiarities, for they roll, rant and rage, and for no cause bite back and are incited to greater anger" (Rieger, *Über die Psychiatrie in Würzburg*).

20   Kirchhoff, "Grundriss," p. 108.

21   Laehr, "Gedenktage," p. 66.

22   Kirchhoff, "Grundriss," pp. 142 f. and 152 f. Germany still had joint penal and insane institutions as late as 1850, e.g., the Berlin Workhouse, in Gera, and in Strelitz.

23   Haisch, *Irrenpflege*, p. 3,146.

24   Panse, *op. cit.*, p. 17.

25   Jetter, "Zur Planung der Schleswiger Irrenanstalt," p. 136.

26   Frank, *System einer vollständigen medicinischen Polizey*, vol. IV, p. 146. This, like the other Josephinean reforms, hardly brought any overall changes. Vienna's Mad Tower remained a source of derelictions and later a profitable target for criticism of medical psychiatry; for, despite everything, it was not replaced by better quarters for the insane until 1869. Now (1969) it serves as housing for nurses.

27   Rürup, "Die Judenemanzipation in Baden," p. 247.

28   On the relationship between Jews and the insane as objects of the

Nazi extermination actions, cf. Doerner, *Nationalsozialismus und Lebens-vernichtung*, pp. 121 ff.

29   Lesky, *Spezialisierung*, pp. 1017 ff.

30   Rosen, *The Evolution of Social Medicine*, pp. 17 ff.

31   Frank, *Supplement-Bände zur medicinischen Polizey*, vol. 3, p. 223.

32   Lütge, *op. cit.*, p. 297.

33   Professor Stahl must be credited with helping to perfect the sequestration of irrationality. Among other things, he was instrumental in the promulgation of a Prussian edict of 1716, prohibiting "hawkers, actors, jugglers, tightrope-walkers, lottery-sellers, prestidigitators, puppeteers, marionette players...and so-called Quacks" from participating in county fairs. An important reason for this was the irritation of professional and enlightened medical men with the successful itinerant medico Johann Andreas Eisenbarth (Promies, *Der Bürger und der Narr*, pp. 81 f.).

34   Rothschuh, *Vom Spiritus animalis zum Nervenaktionsstrom*, pp. 2967 f.

35   Bolten, *Gedanken über psychologische Kuren*.

36   For Zückert, see Leibbrand and Wettley, *op. cit.*, p. 302.

37   Kirchoff, in *Deutsche Irrenärzte*, vol. I, pp. 17–19.

38   In the sense of footnote 8 in this part. On the continuation of rationalist segregation: "Whereas the fool on the stage remained a foreign body within the natural, regular practice of art demanded by common sense, the born fool − the bourgeoisie had established itself as the yardstick of what was human − became the counterpart of the bourgeois norm: either inhuman, or all too human, but always humanly contemptible" (Promies, *Der Bürger und der Narr*, p. 72).

39   Hauser, *op. cit.*, pp. 593, 594.

40   *Ibid.*, 509, 605.

41   Habermas, *Strukturwandel*, pp. 86 f.

42   Krauss, *Studien zur deutschen und französischen Aufklärung*, p. 388.

43   *Ibid.*, 388 f.

44   Habermas, *Strukturwandel*, p. 42.

45   Holborn, "Der deutsche Idealismus," in Wehler (ed.), *Moderne deutsche Sozialgeschichte*, p. 91.

46   Lieber, p. 60.

47   Spiess, *Biographien der Wahnsinnigen*, p. IV f.

48   Gadamer, *op. cit.*, pp. 6, 31.

49   In the eighteenth century, there was no German physician who would have a scientific conclusion about the insane after extensive observation. A relative exception was J. E. Greding, who, after 1758, as doctor at the Waldheim poorhouse (Saxony), strove to improve the conditions of the insane, although his scientific interest focused mainly on the deceased. In this pathological-anatomical area, he did however attract much attention abroad.

50   Kant, *Anthropologie in pragmatischer Hinsicht*, pp. 1 f. Schleiermacher's crushing and ironical critique, published in *Athenaeum*, vol. 2, 1799 (reprinted in *Klassiker der Literatur*, vol. 29 (Rowohlt, 1969), pp. 118–122) deals with this very point: Kant, says Schleiermacher, merely wanted to show that one cannot arrive at an anthropology on the basis of his assumptions, and thus provided the "negation of all anthropology," whereas true anthropology can only be both pragmatic *and* physiological: "physiological and pragmatic is one and the same thing, only in different directions." This foreshadowed the dissatisfaction of later philosophy and science with Kant.

51   Flugel, *Probleme und Ergebnisse der Psychologie*, pp. 13 f.

52   Kant, *op. cit.*, pp. 15 and 3.

53   Leibbrand and Wettley, *op. cit.*, pp. 362 ff.

54   Kant, *op. cit.*, pp. 108 f.

55   Leibbrand and Wettley, *op. cit.*, p. 653.

56   Kant, *op. cit.*, pp. 109 and 111.

57   Fichte, *Werke*, vol. III, p. 17.

58   Habermas, *Theory and Practice*, p. 259.

59   Kant, *op. cit.*, pp. 112 f.

60   *Ibid.*, 117. If today, the mentally ill still torment themselves or are tormented by others that their suffering is "mere imagination," this is undoubtedly connected to the strong suggestion of Kant's demand for reason in this area.

61   Kant, *Von der Macht des Gemüts durch den blossen Vorsatz seiner krankhaften Gefühle Meister zu werden*, p. 25.

62   Kant, *Anthropologie*, p. 119. It is also a sign of pre-psychiatric thinking that hypochondria is ranked above mania, to whose segregated status there was little direct access.

63   Kant's *Wahnwitz*, the impairment of judgment, is interpreted by Leibbrand and Wettley (*op. cit.*, p. 367) as mania, and by Kisker (*Kant's psychiatrische Systematik*, p. 24) as schizophrenia. This merely underscores the unreliability of such retrospective interpretations if the types of disease (as in Kant) are deduced solely from the various impairments of the individual capacities.

64   "Self-preservation," having become a bourgeois absolute, could prevent sequestration even in the presence of the irrationality of insanity.

65   Kant, *Anthropologie*, pp. 121 f.

66   *Ibid.*, 119.

67   Brachmann, *Der Fall Rüsau*, p. 25.

68   Kant, *Von der Macht des Gemüts*, from the preface by C. W. Hufeland, pp. 5 f.

69   Kant, *Anthropologie*, pp. 123 f. Kant's skepticism about all external (somatic or social) causes makes it impossible to charge him with psychophysical "empirical dualism," as Kisker attempts to do ("Kants psychiatrische

Systematik," pp. 25 f.). Rather, it really clarifies the as-if dualism of German Idealist psychiatry still, in the twentieth century.

70   Kant, *Anthropologie*, p. 123.

71   Leibbrand and Wettley, *op. cit.*, pp. 519 ff; Doerner, "Zür Geschichte der endogen Psychosen."

72   Mühlmann, *Geschichte der Anthropologie*, pp. 63–65.

73   Kant, *Anthropologie*, p. 125. When Kisker says (*Kants psychiatrische Systematik*, p. 25) that *sensus communis* here anticipates the existential-analytic category of interpersonal communication, he forgets that *sensus communis* as a touchstone for the correctness of judgment represented merely a theoretical capacity.

74   Kant, *Anthropologie*, pp. 125 f. and 137, and *Kritik der Urteilskraft*, § 40.

75   Kant, *Anthropologie*, pp. 133.

76   Lukács, *Geschichte und Klassenbewusstsein*, pp. 147 f.

77   Kant, *Anthropologie*, p. 123. Schleiermacher in his review accused Kant of "treating the female sex as a subspecies."

78   Kant, *Anthropologie*, pp. 166 and 195 f.

79   Kloos, *Die Konstitutionslehre von C. G. Carus*, pp. 26–29.

80   *Ibid.*, 30 f. At that time, the Scottish neurophysiologist Charles Bell (*Essays on the Anatomy of Expression in Painting*, 1806) based his physiognomy as an "anatomy of expression purely empirically" on a precise description of the mimetic muscles. He also describes the physiognomy of the "raving Bedlamites," but ascribes it to the external conditions, to the mechanical restraint in that hospital.

81   On this periodical, see Leibbrand, *K. P. Moritz und die Erfahrungs-seelenkunde* (p. 399).

82   Quoted after Krauss, *Studien zur deutschen und französischen Aufklärung*, pp. 390 f.

83   Moritz, *Anton Reiser, ein psychologischer Roman*, p. 312, p. 5.

84   Quoted from the epilogue to *ibid.*, p. 379.

85   Maimon, *Geschichte des eigenen Lebens* (Berlin, 1935 [1]), from the foreword to the first edition (1792) by K. P. Moritz, p. ix.

86   "The German bourgeoisie owes its extended intellectual rule over large connected areas to the many bases in the Protestant vicarage. These origins explain the major effect of the theological dowry, which vitiated any consistent movement of German Enlightenment toward materialism and atheism. It is significant that the great villains Don Giovanni and Franz Moor are the literary and musical embodiment of philosophical materialism and atheism" (Krauss, *op. cit.*, p. 428).

87   Promies, *op. cit.*, pp. 56 and 272.

88   Bernhardi-Tieck, *Bambocciaden*, 3 vols., (Berlin, 1797–1800), quoted in Promies, *op. cit.*, p. 97.

89   Promies, *op. cit.*, p. 261.

90   Leibbrand, *K. P. Moritz*, p. 412.

91   Hauser, *op. cit.*, 673 f.

92   Plessner, *Die verspätete Nation*, p. 48.

93   Cf. Arno Schmidt, *Die Ritter vom Geist*, pp. 213—62.

94   Hauser, *op. cit.*, p. 671.

95   Quoted in Leibbrand, *Romantische Medizin*, p. 49.

96   Novalis, *Fragmente*, IV, § 326.

97   Schöne, *Interpretationen zur dichterischen Gestaltung des Wahnsinns.*

98   Laehr, *Gedenktage*, pp. 42 f. and 69.

99   Jaspers, *Schelling*, p. 16, and also Leibbrand, *Romantische Medizin*, pp. 164 f. A further example for the medical enthusiasm of poets is supplied by Jean Paul, who tried to rid Platen of pains with magnetic strokes.

100   Boldt, *Über die Stellung und Bedeutung der "Rhapsodien,"* p. 64.

101   For a biography of Reil, see Neuburger, *J. C. Reil*, and Donalies, *J. C. Reil.*

102   According to Lenz, *Geschichte der Königlichen Friedrich Wilhelm Universität zu Berlin* (vol. I, pp. 46 f, 102 ff, 202) Reil, not C. W. Hufeland played the leading role at Berlin's medical faculty.

103   Neuburger, *op. cit.*, p. 92.

104   This concept may mediate in the controversy between Boldt, who calls Reil a materialist, and Leibbrand and Wettley (*op. cit.*, p. 654), who reject this.

105   Leibbrand and Wettley, *op. cit.*, pp. 388 and 393.

106   Reil, *Von der Lebenskraft*, p. 23.

107   *Idem, Über die Erkenntnis und Cur der Fieber*, vol. IV, p. 45.

108   Mechler, *Das Wort "Psychiatrie,"* pp. 405 f.

109   Reil, *op. cit.*, pp. 479 f.

110   In 1805, Reil and A. B. Kaissler started the *Magazin für die psychische Heilkunde* to which Kaissler was almost the sole contributor of essays on natural philosophy, and in 1806 the journal folded. From 1808 to 1810, Reil and J. C. Hoffbauer, a philosopher, put out *Beyträge zur Beförderung einer Curmethode auf psychischem Wege.* It was Reil's pupil F. Nasse, who, in 1818, launched the first medically oriented psychiatric periodical.

111   Reil, *Rhapsodien*, p. 52.

112   *Ibid.*, 14 f. The reference to their housing "above the town gates" shows that in Germany the medieval tradition of localizing the insane, who religiously-ontologically were seen as having overstepped the border, within the town walls, the borderline between town and non-town.

113   *Ibid.*, § I, pp. 7—18.

114   Georg Lukács, *History and Class Consciousness: Studies in Marxist Dialectics*, trans. Rodney Livingstone (Cambridge, Mass., 1971), p. 214.

115   Reil, *Rhapsodien*, pp. 481—88 and 52 f.

116   Ibid., 47.

117   Ibid., 115.

118   Ibid., 54 f.

119   Ibid., 62 ff.

120   Ibid., 46 and 8 f.

121   Idem, Fieberlehre, vol. IV, p. 43.

122   Idem, Rhapsodien, pp. 133 ff.

123   Ibid., 123 f.

124   Ibid., 26.

125   Ibid., 49 f.

126   O. Rommel, "Rationalistische Dämonie," in Deutsche Viertel jahres-schrift, 17, 1939.

127   Neuburger, "British and German Psychiatry," p. 329.

128   Reil, Rhapsodien, p. 253.

129   Ibid., 476, 33, 236.

130   Ibid., 209 f.

131   Ibid., 468.

132   Ibid., 472.

133   Ibid., 479.

134   Koselleck, "Staat und Gesellschaft in Preussen," in Wehler (ed.), op. cit., p. 61.

135   Ibid., 63.

136   Kehr, "Zur Genesis der preussischen Bürokratie," in ibid., pp. 40 and 42.

137   Quoted after Koselleck, op. cit., p. 83.

138   Ibid., 61.

139   Quoted ibid., p. 79. In this context "spoiling" is not yet meant as cultural criticism, but rather as an expression of concern about the potential of harm to the personality by industrial labor at an early age.

140   Ibid., 79.

141   Braubach, Stein und die inneren Reformen in Preussen, pp. 67 f.

142   Holborn, "Der deutsche Idealismus," in Wehler (ed.), op. cit., pp. 95 and 102.

143   Koselleck, in ibid., 80.

144   Holborn, op. cit., p. 103.

145   Ibid., 97.

146   Jetter, "Das Krankenhaus des 19. Jahrhunderts," in Artelt and Rüegg, op. cit., p. 71.

147   Hundertfünfzig Jahre Regierungsbezirk Köln, pp. 238 f.

148   Laehr, op. cit., p. 49.

149   Ibid., 116. Elements of this legislative attitude, which sets a standard for all the mentally ill based on the handful of insane who are indeed dangerous, and thus gives priority to the protection of the public over treatment

of the sick still persist. Cf. Panse, *op. cit.*, pp. 208 ff., as well as Wettley, "Die Stellung des Geisteskranken," in Artelt and Rüegg, *op. cit.*, pp. 66 f.

150 Langermann, *Dissertatio de methodo cognoscendi curandique animi morbos stabilienda* (Jena, 1797), quoted from Ideler, *Grundriss der Seelenheilkunde* (1835), whose introduction, "Langermann und Stahl als Begründer der Seelenheilkunde" (pp. 3–94), made extensive reference to Stahl's theory and Langermann's dissertation.

151 Leibbrand and Wettley, *op. cit.*, p. 500.

152 One of these old-wives' tales is still used to rationalize the exclusion of mentally disturbed students, "neurotic worriers," from the universities, e.g. W. Thiele, "Neurosen bei Studenten," in *Die Berliner Ärztekammer*, 4: 221–25, 1967.

153 Cf. H. Laehr in Kirchhoff (ed.), *Deutsche Irrenärzte*, vol. I, p. 42.

154 Horn also won equality of treatment for the insane and the physically ill and also introduced numerous technological devices (for instance, Cox's rotary machine) from England, akin to the import of models of mechanical looms and steam engines from England, which German entrepreneurs often managed only by illegal means, through partially government-financed industrial espionage. (Motteck, *op. cit.*, pp. 114 f.)

155 Horn, *Öffentliche Rechenschaft über meine zwölfjährige Dienstführung als 2. Arzt des königlichen Charité-Krankenhauses nebst Erfahrungen über Krankenhäuser und Irrenanstalten*, pp. 222 f.

156 For a comprehensive listing of the coercive and torture instruments used on the insane see Schneider, *Entwurf zu einer Heilmittellehre gegen psychische Krankheiten* (1824).

157 Regardless of the questionable practice of tracing elements of National Socialism back to Prussianism, it remains a fact that this "therapeutic idealism" can be found in most of the psychiatrists instrumental in the extermination of the mentally ill and other "irrationals" under Hitler. This "stance," moreover, is far more demonstrable than another frequently adduced cause, the objectifying spirit of natural science, an accusation that — one is tempted to say — springs from a typically German antiscientific resentment. To be sure, it was literally a matter of "cure at any price," i.e. the affirmation of murder if other means proved ineffective. In addition, there was the underlying postulate of the achievability of ideal, perfect health — if not in the individual, then certainly in the "national body." And this too was an analogy which the politically unreflective and belated nation (and psychiatry) embraced more unrestrainedly than the bourgeois society of the West (cf. Doerner, *Nationalsozialismus und Lebensvernichtung*).

158 Nostitz and Jänkendorf, *Beschreibung der Königlichen Sächsischen Heil- und Verpflegungsanstalt Sonnenstein*.

159 Dehio, in Kirchhoff (ed.), *Deutsche Irrenärzte*, vol. I, p. 97.

160 F. Autenrieth (1772–1835) was Professor of Medicine in Tübingen.

An authoritarian politician and organizer, he turned his position as university chancellor during the Restoration (1822—32) into a kind of dictatorship. which made him such enemies as R. Von Mohl. As a friend of Reil's, he nursed natural-philosophic ideas about the insane, for whose pedagogical punishment — besides the relatively humane palisades chamber — he lovingly devised torturous instruments of restraint, such as the facial mask, which stifled the screams of the raving maniacs, to protect the sensibilities of the physician. Autenrieth, incidentally, was also spared extensive personal contact with the mentally ill. (Cf. R. Gaupp, in Kirchhoff (ed.), *ibid.*, 55—57.).

161   Hayner, "Über einige mechanische Vorrichtungen, welche in Irrenanstalten mit Nutzen gebraucht werden können," *Zschn. f. psych. Ärzte* (1818), p. 339.

162   Cf. G. Ilberg, in Kirchhoff (ed.), *op. cit.*, I, pp. 99—101.

163   Rürup, *Die Judenemanzipation in Baden*, pp. 255 ff.

164   Panse, *op. cit.*, p. 27.

165   Because his duties were so demanding, the administration required the following of Ruer: an imposing figure, physical strength, health, a fearless appearance, powerful voice, knowledge of empirical psychology, knowledge of human nature, and love of his fellow man; i.e. he had to be a "personage." The situation of the "staff", almost as critical today as then, is illuminated by the research and findings of R. D. Hemprich and K. P. Kisker, "Die 'Herren der Klinik' und die Patienten," in *Nervenarzt*, 39: 433—41, 1968.

166   Quoted from Kirchhoff (ed.), *op. cit.*, p. 146.

167   Leibbrand and Wettley, *op. cit.*, p. 676, and O. Mönkemöller, in Kirchhoff (ed.), *op. cit.*, pp. 123 ff.

168   Wettley, "Die Stellung des Geisteskranken," in Artelt and Rüegg, *op. cit.*, p. 58.

169   Based on documentation in Burrows, *Untersuchungen über gewisse die Geisteszerrüttung betreffende Irrtümer*, pp. 136 f.

170   F. O. Funcke, *Reisebilder und Heimathklänge*, 3rd series (Bremen, 1873), quoted in Haisch, "Irrenpflege," p. 3,150.

171   Lukács, *Die Zerstörung der Vernunft*, pp. 112 ff., and Habermas, *Theorie und Praxis*, pp. 108 ff.

172   Schelling, *Ideen zu einer Philosophie der Natur* (1797), *Werke*, vol. I, p. 706.

173   *Idem, Von der Weltseele* (1798), vol. I, p. 574.

174   Lukács, *Die Zerstörung der Vernunft*, pp. 118 f.

175   Thus Schelling, unlike Brown, is out to find the "ground that placed excitability before all   real excitement" (*Werke*, vol. IV, p. 196). And his view of the relationship between education and educability is no different.

176   Cf. Kant's *Anthropology*, especially § 55. Kant, like Schelling, speaks about the "animating principle." But for Kant that principle is the mind — and for Schelling, the soul, which, as a drive, as instinct, like genius, is

anchored all the more in the objective natural process. While Schelling looks on genius as a pure creative faculty of the imagination, Kant sees it as an aspect of the subjective faculty, the "nature of the subject," not divorced from the acquisition of "certain basic mechanical rules," which is why nature itself does not "originally produce it," but merely "sets the rules for art."

177   Leibbrand, *Romantische Medizin*, p. 59 f.

178   Schelling, *Werke*, vol. IV, pp. 195 and 211.

179   Eschenmayer, *Die Philosophie in ihrem Übergang zur Nichtphilosophie*, p. 25.

180   Schelling, *Philosophie und Religion* (1804): *Werke*, vol. IV, pp. 20 f., 13, 28.

181   Habermas, *Theorie und Praxis*, p. 113. (The section in which this passage appears does not appear in the English-language edition.)

182   "The counterpart, as an absolute having all qualities in common with the first, would not be true in itself and absolute were it not able to understand itself in its selfness so as to be true as the other absolute" (Schelling, *Werke*, vol. IV, p. 29).

183   This compilation of Schelling's ideas is from Habermas, *Theorie und Praxis*, pp. 122 f., with some elaboration by this author.

184   Schelling, *Philosophische Untersuchungen über das Wesen der menschlichen Freiheit* (1809); *Werke*, vol. IV, pp. 258 and 263. It goes without saying that defending the legal incompetence of the insane in their interest would constitute a challenge to Schelling's entire system.

185   Schelling, *Stuttgarter Privatvorlesungen* (1810), *Werke*, vol. IV, pp. 352 f.

186   Whereas, for Schelling, the body is merely the blossom that is the source of the honey or the poison, he says: "Anyone at all familiar with the mysteries of evil knows that the highest corruption is also the most spiritual, that in it all that is natural, and hence even sensuality, even lust, are overpowered by such corruption, that it turns into cruelty, and that the demonic-diabolic evil is far more alienated from enjoyment than the good. Thus, if both error and evil are spiritual and derive from the spirit, the spirit cannot possibly be supreme" (*ibid.*, 360).

187   *Ibid.*, 370.

188   Gadamer, *op. cit.*, pp. 55, 74.

189   The historiography of psychiatry usually does the opposite. Leibbrand and Wettley, for instance, comment on Schelling's definition of insanity only with the adjective "curious," but quite properly point to the survival of his ideas to the present, as in V. von Weizsäcker's *Pathosophie*.

190   We are ignoring a third, mediating line of development, that starts with J. C. Hoffbauer, a philosopher and pupil of Kant's, who despite an equally limited experience, published three books between 1802 and 1807, in which

he insists, against Reil, on the autonomy of mental processes and disorders, but attacks Langermann's ethical subjectivism. As a Kantian, he derives insanity from the faculties, but defines it above all as a deepening (fixation) or dispersion of attention. Only the genius can find his way back from profound dispersion to the purpose of nature and reason and self, whereas the average person goes mad — in the stage of passions still voluntarily, i.e., culpably, but after the habituation of deviation from the self as a disease (*Untersuchungen über die Krankheiten der Seele*, vol. I, pp. 23 ff. and 274). His efforts at keeping psychology remote from spiritualism and materialism by observing "positive" phenomena (vol. III, p. iv), were not particularly appreciated by the speculative social situation in Germany. His approach was subsequently integrated by J. F. Herbart and F. E. Beneke in terms of natural science and physiology, whereas interest in the scope of "pure" psychological observation did not develop until the latter part of the nineteenth century, perhaps not until F. W. Hagen's *Studien auf dem Gebiete der ärztlichen Seelenkunde* (1870).

191   Leibbrand, *Romantische Medizin*, pp. 103 ff.

192   *Ibid.*, 163.

193   Koreff was a physician, a student of Steffens' and one of E. T. A. Hoffmann's Serapion Brothers. Among others he treated A. W. Schlegel, K. Von Humboldt, and, in Paris, the Lady of the Camelias, with magnetism.

194   Haisch, *Irrenpflege*, p. 3,841.

195   This also seems to be demonstrable today in that patients with phasic psychoses measured by intellectual self-involvement (according to education and profession) tend to show hypochondriacal symptoms (Doerner and Winzenried, *Wahninhalte phasischer Psychosen*, pp. 40 ff.).

196   Schelling, *Philosophische Einleitung in die Philosophie der Mythologie oder Darstellung der rein rationalen Philosophie*, in *Werke*, vol. V, pp. 715 and 732.

197   Schelling's impact on German psychiatry has scarcely been examined. Yet he is partly responsible for the (more irrational, anti-spiritual) coinage *Geisteskrankheit* (spiritual illness), the German term for insanity. Schelling postulated that the soul, the "divine spark in man," cannot fall ill, in contrast to Hegel, who said, "The spirit is free and thus per se not capable of this disease" (*Encyclopädie der philosophischen Wissenschaften*, p. 354). Existential-analytic psychiatry has thus far refrained from reflecting on Schelling's questionable legacy handed down by Heidegger. An especially important and barely recognized relationship (except by Leibbrand and Wettley, *op. cit.*, pp. 518 ff.) exists between German natural philosophy and later French romanticism, to the extent that it developed into the theory of degeneration. Its author, B. A. Morel (1857), like Schelling based his ideas of degeneration running through several generations of a family to the point of idiocy on the fall from grace. His theory, within the framework

of French tradition, was, of course, a social one from the very outset. Prior to Heine, Gall had already ridiculed the French and tried to show that for all their enlightenment they had been taken in by German romanticism (Leibbrand and Wettley, p. 669). G. Meiners' anthropology, like Carus' memorial essay on Goethe's 100th anniversary, "Über ungleiche Befähigung der verschiedenen Menschheitsstämme für höhere geistige Entwicklung," anticipated Gobineau. Nor has there been much investigating of how these theories of degeneration and ethnology, as worked out in France, came back to Germany in the 1870s—1890s. These ideas played a significant part in the development of German imperialism shifted "into the inner individual soul" (Arendt, *Origins of Totalitarianism.*)

198   Haindorf was probably the first Jewish psychiatrist in Germany. According to H. Spatz, B. Stilling (1810—79), a physician in Kassel, was the first Jewish neurologist. In terms of the sociology of knowledge, the contribution of Jewish doctors to German neurology is a significant but unexplored chapter. Here is a sketchy overview: In the first half of the nineteenth century, Jewish physicians were largely shut out from any meaningful positions in psychiatry. In addition to Haindorf, we can mention K. F. Stahl, the younger brother of the conservative Prussian political scientist, who headed an institution in Bayreuth, and later the Franconian asylum of Karthaus-Prüll. Not until the 1870s were German Jews granted the at least formal right to social and professional advancement. The anti-Semitism of the imperialist era set in shortly thereafter. At this time, German psychiatry was already largely professionalized and socially integrated. At the same time, neurology, which, hovering between internal medicine and psychiatry occupied the position of outsider, especially with regard to established psychiatry began its fight for recognition as a separate academic discipline. As a result of all these factors, Jewish doctors, themselves still social outsiders, were able to work successfully in neurology much more readily than in the then increasingly national-liberal-statist psychiatry. Consequently Jewish doctors made a substantial contribution to the genesis of neurology. For the very same reasons, Jewish neurologists depended largely on their private practice — because of the persistence of social barriers against Jewish physicians at universities. Neurological therapy in private practice, which was bound to be unsatisfactory, therefore focused on hysteria and other neurotic disorders. These sociological conditions constituted an essential part of the factors that led up to psychoanalysis They explain why psychoanalysis was founded and developed largely by Jewish physicians who had started as neurologists. Freud was one such doctor among many. Later times found it suitable to discover the "Jewish materialist" component in the neurological and instinct theory of Jewish neurologists. Finally, these dynamics help explain the apparently permanent rejection of psychoanalytic psychiatry by the other German psychiatrists.

199   Haindorf, *Versuch einer Pathologie und Therapie der Geistes- und Gemütskrankheiten, passim.* The term *Wahnsinn* (insanity) contains both the meaning "poor" and "askew" (*wahnschaffen*). Something that is "askew" is rationally harder to attack than what runs "counter" — and hence is more threatening (F. Kluge, *Etymologisches Wörterbuch*, Berlin 1967, p. 832).

200   Heinroth, *Lehrbuch der Störungen des Seelenlebens vom rationalen Standpunkt aus entworfen*, part I, pp. 21–25.

201   *Ibid.*, 51–57 and part II, pp. 3 ff.

202   Haindorf, *Versuch*, pp. 82 f.

203   Heinroth, *Lehrbuch*, part I, pp. 67 f. Cf. Hegel, *Grundlinien der Philosophie des Rechts*, § 241–46. The establishment of the disease form dementia praecox (later schizophrenia) at the end of the century is probably connected to this pessimistic bourgeois sense of being threatened: Abstractly-theoretically, this form could, after all, have been "seen" earlier.

204   Heinroth, *ibid.*, 117.

205   *Ibid.*, 147.

206   *Ibid.*, 200.

207   Heinroth, "Abhandlung über die Seelengesundheit," in Burrows, *Untersuchungen über gewisse die Geisteszerrütung betreffende Irrtümer,* (translated into German by Heinroth), p. 203.

208   Schelling's origin of evil, of the negative in the absolute itself, is here no longer taken seriously to make room for the integration of evil into the moral rational order.

209   Heinroth, *Lehrbuch*, part I, pp. 383 ff.

210   Heinroth, *Abhandlung*, p. 197, 203 f.

211   Heinroth, *Lehrbuch*, part 2, pp. 377–83. The numerous affinities between Heinroth and Hegel (cf. *Encyclopädie* pp. 353 ff.) are easily demonstrated, whereas the differences are to be sought primarily in Heinroth's theological determination.

212   Quoted by Leibbrand, *Romantische Medizin*, p. 48.

213   Quoted by Leibbrand and Wettley, *op. cit.*, p. 437.

214   Hauser, p. 239.

215   Belgium offers a further example for the connection between the bourgeois political and economic revolution and the visibility of the insane. Here, after the revolution of August 1830, the monarchy was installed and limited by a constitution that served as a model for all liberal framers of constitutions throughout Europe. The same revolution sparked the reforms, on behalf of the insane, and which were realized during the next few years by H. Guislain, starting with Ghent, in practical treatment, research, and teaching as well as in theory.

216   For this and the following, cf. Mottek, *Wirtschaftsgeschichte*, pp. 119–134.

217   According to data in Laehr, *Gedenktage*, 9th ed. (1937), revised by the author.

218   *Acta betr. den Reisebericht des Prof. Dr. Mandt und des prakt. Arztes Dr. Rust in specie über die Irrenanstalten in Frankreich, England* (Greifswald-Berlin, May 20, 1883), from the former Berlin Secret State Archive, in Leibbrand and Wettley, *op. cit.*, p. 661.

219   Mottek, *op. cit.*, p. 128, Lüttge (*op. cit.*, p. 355) observes that in Germany the idea of "national economy" won out over liberal free trade. In support of his thesis, he points out that the notions of a mercantilist national-political economic control persisted throughout the nineteenth century and gained in strength thereafter.

220   Hegel, *Philosophy of Right* trans. T. M. Knox (Oxford, 1942), p. 150.

221   That the rejection of the legal right of the poor to assistance was a matter of tradition was evidenced by the explanation of the provincial estates of 1835: "In the opinion of the assembly, poverty cannot become a legal condition....Legitimized poverty will destroy the shame and the religion of the poor, for it would dissolve the bond of charity between religion and the poor" (cited by Koselleck, 'Staat und Gesellschaft in Preussen 1815–1848," in Wehler (ed.), *Moderne deutsche Sozialgeschichte*, p. 480). Similar motives most likely played a part in the obligatory legal discrimination against the mentally ill.

222   Weinhold, *Von der Überbevölkerung*, pp. 45 f.

223   Mottek, *op. cit.*, p. 39.

224   Koselleck, in Wehler (ed.), *op. cit.*, pp. 77 f. The railroads and their social consequences also bore on the development of medicine and psychiatry. Initially, many doctors were skeptical about this innovation. Analogous to some monarchs who saw the railroads as a threat to their privileged rapid transportation and consequently rejected them as democratically egalitarian and corrupt, medical commissions spoke of the harmful effects of the railroads on the riders and mere bystanders (Lüttge, *op. cit.*, p. 364). For another thing, in 1836 the railroad shares set off the first wave of speculation. This enabled German psychiatrists to do what their English colleagues had been able to do back in the eighteenth century: reflect systematically on the socio-economic pathogenesis of mental disorders resulting from speculation and other expressions of economic egotism. Finally, beginning in the 60s and 70s the railroad district played an exemplary part in bringing the previously hidden to public attention. It is no coincidence that during that same time, homosexuality, transvestism, exhibitionism, and other (sexual) deviations first became visible to psychiatry and systematically became the object of its investigation even though they had always existed. For the earliest scientific accounts of such individuals invariably are set in railroads, terminals, or in their vicinity, and the persons involved frequently are in commerce, circumstances that are still operative today. This is an impressive example of

the significance of social conditions whose development constitutes the object of a discipline and thus also decisively of the discipline itself. It is likewise an impressive example of the problem-creating, expository character of technological efficiency in the development of bourgeois society, especially as it was only since that time that homosexuality, etc. much more so than previously, have been "made" a penal problem.

225   Haisch, *Irrenpflege*, p. 3,160.

226   Panse, *op. cit.*, p. 28. Only a short time later, liberal psychiatrists like Griesinger would criticize these brand-new installations as "barracks."

227   Laehr, *Gedenktage*, p. 33.

228   Unlike England or France, before 1848 industrialization in Germany in part still had to assert itself against the state. Hence, the misery of the poor was due more to the limited capacity of business than to early-liberal exploitation under the system. A political public in the sense of parliamentarianism existed at best in the southwestern German states. The bourgeoisie did not seriously confront the "social question" until the 1840s, whether through attempts at pragmatic solutions, Christian reform proposals, social utopias, revolutionary movements, or the rudiments of a social science. The natural sciences were still learning from the West, still occupied a defensive position vis-à-vis the officially sanctioned natural philosophy. And the literary form of established bourgeois society, the modern novel, had not yet achieved viability in Germany. There was nothing comparable to Balzac's and Stendahl's social and naturalistic novels, nor those in-between integrating psychiatry.

229   Laehr, *Gedenktage*, pp. 85 f.

230   Of course, the allegiance to Bismarck's state, in which nearly all psychiatrists joined after 1870, brought the two camps together. This was the period in which German psychiatry — and all psychiatric historiography is in agreement on this — "caught up" and became "leading" in Europe. The unity which politically this time too came "from above" and which theoretically, was not based on coming to terms with the demands of the Enlightenment, inspired not only the most comprehensive synthesis of psychiatry, the concept of schizophrenia (E. Kraepelin and E. Bleuler), but also several "philosophically" and ideologically endangered, abstract connections, such as idealistic monism, idealistic racial concepts and motivations for the euthanasia problem, socio-biological theories or the mythologizing of the "endogenous" as opposed to the "exogenous."

231   Kirchhoff, *Grundriss*, pp. 154 f.; Leibbrand and Wettley, *op. cit.*, p. 501.

232   Ideler, *Lehrbuch der gerichtlichen Psychologie*, p. 8.

233   Ideler, *Grundriss der Seelenheilkunde*, vol. II, pp. 495 ff.

234   *Ibid.*, vol. I, p. 130. Ideler was the first to legitimize the efforts of recent, especially American theory to find psychoanalytic elements

throughout psychiatric history. Conversely, a hitherto historically largely unreflected psychoanalysis cannot be indifferent to the theoretical and ideological context in which the sublimating power of passions, the theory of drives, the dynamics of the mind, the significance of childhood, etc. appear in Ideler.

235   *Ibid.*, 123–27.

236   *Ibid.*, 141–44.

237   *Ibid.*, 238.

238   *Ibid.*, 281–90.

239   *Ibid.*, 522.

240   Ideler, *Grundriss*, vol. II, pp. 61 and 138. This position, with its repeatedly idealistic synthesis between the contradictions of body and soul, of materialism and idealism, finds its complement in today's conciliatory concept of the psychosomatic element in medicine, a notion that generally hides the fact that it actually means "psychogenetic." What was at issue then, and still is today, is how to settle the argument over the unreconcilableness of "the seriousness, the pain of the negative," and the harshness and objectivity of alienation, in society as in nature, rather than using the medium of theory to arrive at a short-sighted harmonization and meaning.

241   *Ibid.*, 227.

242   *Ibid.*, 59.

243   *Ibid.*, 249–51.

244   *Ibid.*, 284.

245   The connection between the now interiorized notion of self-determination and the eighteenth-century theories of nerves, of the tension and tuning of the nerve fibers has been referred to earlier.

246   Ideler, *Grundriss*, pp. 5 f.

247   *Ibid.*, 328–34, and also *Der Wahnsinn in seiner psychologischen und sozialen Bedeutung*, p. 155.

248   Ideler, *Grundriss*, vol. II, pp. 335 f.

249   *Ibid.*, 402 f.

250   *Ibid.*, 355.

251   Ideler's theory of disease encompasses two important aspects. Melancholia is a depression of the mind, but not a negation, inactivity, but rather negative activity, utmost tension, "rigidification of the mind." This paradoxical observation which correctly describes the depressive inhibition, also becomes the conceptual basis of the catatonic form of schizophrenia. But in Ideler, it means that melancholia too is a subjective activity of the psyche that does not break the thread of psychological meaning (*ibid.*, vol. II, pp. 601 f.). Correspondingly, Ideler can accept *manie sans délire*, even homicidal monomania, but not the assumption of a purely physical, automatic compulsion to kill. In his idealistic framework, Ideler must demand a psychogenetic connection here too: at some point in the subject's life, a "secret

contradiction" must have existed in his mind which later manifested itself in insanity or murder. The Idealistic claim demands control not only over the surface life of the individual, but also over his inner guilt, "the secret story of his heart" (*ibid.*, vol. II, pp. 596 f.).

252   Ideler, *Lehrbuch der gerichtlichen Psychologie*, pp. 12 f., 17 f., 236–39.

253   *Ibid.*, 4.

254   *Ibid.*, 9.

255   *Ibid.*, 9 f.

256   Compared to highest legal principles of moral freedom the material-somatic and material-economic conditions embodied in the state are negligible: the state can legitimately punish persons victimized by education or their environment "only on the principle of self-preservation, of the imperative self-defense against those who rebel against its law," for if in a war, in case of attack from the outside, the state has the right to sacrifice good citizens, it has the even greater right "to persecute ruthlessly" those harmed by society itself, "its internal foes, who through crime, seek to subvert the necessary legal order (*ibid.*, 28 f.). The indigent and mentally ill, devoid of reason, are also coupled here, where reason is presumed as the power of objective ethical discrimination. Making the internal social compulsions (from capital punishment to killing the mentally ill) the norm for the war against external foes also did not become more generally legitimate until the 1890s.

257   J. B. Friedreich lost his medical chair at Würzburg in 1832 because he had stirred up the students. He became a court physician in Weissenberg, and it was only here, that is, through forensics and from a 'somatic' standpoint, that he came to psychiatric theory.

C. F. Flemming resigned as director of the Sachsenberg asylum in 1852 when the authorities, during the post-1848 reaction, installed a clergyman in official quarters in the asylum against Flemming's wishes.

G. Blumröder, a former theologian and novelist, came to psychiatry through his friendship with Gall and his work as a doctor for the poor and at the courts. In 1848, he was a leftist district deputy in Frankfurt, went to Stuttgart with the rump parliament, and there was arrested. Having contracted tuberculosis in prison, he was released in 1850, and died of the disease in 1853.

258   Cf. H. Schipperges, "Leitlinien und Grenzen der Psychosomatik bei F. Nasse," in *Confin. Psychiat.* 2:19–37, 1959. At any rate, Johannes Müller, the founder of the German physiologic paradigm, came out of this so-called "Nasse schooling."

259   It is therefore not surprising that this practitioner, though in conservative-integrative terms, recognized the reality of the "insanity question" as the question of the insane poor. His statute provided for six-months'

free treatment of indigent mental patients provided that application for admission was made within six months of the onset of illness. He also established a free out-patient clinic for the treatment of the poor. At the same time, in his "Illenau community" Roller typified the omnipotent "asylum patriarch" who rejected the non-restraint principle. He was criticized by liberals for making his asylum into a permanent retreat for the insane from society (with its own music teacher, spiritual adviser, gymnastics, lectures, and dances), and not heeding the need for their soonest possible reintegration into the production process.

260   In the often politically motivated discussions between idealists and materialists, Kerner's *Seherin* was not the only proof adduced for the existence of the supernatural, but also Kaspar Hauser, for example. This fourteen-year-old boy who appeared in 1828 in Nuremberg, was put in the care of a high-school teacher by name of Daumer, a medical layman with a fanatic belief in therapy and education. He subjected Hauser, who evidently suffered from temporal lobe epilepsy and mild feeblemindedness, to painful experiments and insane, excessive pedagogic demands, with no chance of success, merely to demonstrate a higher reality, the presence of "positive faith" as opposed to "common materialistic sense." (G. Hesse, "Die Krankheit Kaspar Hausers," in *Münch. Med. Woschr.* 109: 156–163, 1967).

261   H. Von Gagern saw this speech as an encouraging sign that the "pre-revolutionary movement" was reawakening (Wentzke and Klötzer, *Deutscher Liberalismus im Vormärz*, p. 288).

262   Roller, *Die Irrenanstalten nach allen ihren Beziehungen*, 1831.

263   In 1817, Fries lost his chair at Jena because of student fraternity intrigues. In line with his political liberalism, he subsequently became a spokesman for the anti-Semitic "Hepp! Hepp! movement" in Heidelberg, while the Baden government strove to protect its Jewish subjects and therefore confiscated Fries's *Über die Gefährdung des Wohlstandes und des Charakters der Deutschen durch die Juden* (Heidelberg, 1816) (Rürup, *op. cit.*, pp. 262 f.). These events may help to explain why in Baden, it was not a Liberal, but the "state-medicine" conservative Roller in cooperation with the government who tried to improve the situation of the insane, and the poor in general. Later, Roller too became an enthusiastic admirer of Bismarck.

264   Temkin, *Materialism in French and German Physiology*, pp. 322 f.

265   For Jacobi's biography, see Herting, in Kirchhoff (ed.), *Deutsche Irrenärzte*, vol. I, pp. 83–93. As pointed out before, the geographical distribution of the above list of prominent "somatists" shows that nearly all of them worked in areas influenced by France in the time of the Revolution.

266   Jacobi took as the epigraph for his translation a sentence by his father intended for Fichte, and it characterizes the son as well: "And truly only his heart, the veritable faculty of ideas, elevates man above himself."

267   Jacobi, *Sammlung für die Heilkunde der Gemütskrankheiten*, vol. I, pp. viii f. and 35 f.

268   In regard to Marx in this context, see Lieber, *op. cit.*, pp. 64 f., as well as Habermas, *Theory and Practice*, pp. 263 f.

269   Cf. Leibbrand and Wettley, *op. cit.*, pp. 496 f. Still today, this natural-scientific-liberal nucleus of somatically oriented psychiatry is too easily ignored by its psychoanalytic existential-analytic critics and sacrificed to the claim of comprehensive, unmarred understanding of meaning even when the incursion rather than eruption of something objectively impenetrable, alien, would suggest the breach of pursuable continuity of meaning and a ctitical reserve vis-à-vis the possibilities of a subjective hermeneutics.

270   Jacobi, *Die Hauptformer der Seelenstörungen*, vol. I: *Die Tobsucht*, p. 527.

271   Jacobi, *Sammlungen*, vol. I, pp. 114 f.

272   *Ibid.*, vol. II, *Über die psychischen Erscheinungen und ihre Beziehung zum Organismus im gesunden und kranken Zustande* (1825), pp. 156 ff.

273   *Ibid.*, 185–90, 377 ff.

274   Wyrsch, *Zur Geschichte und Deutung der endogen Psychosen*, p. 17.

275   On the history of the founding of the *Allgemeine Zeitschrift*, see Bodamer, *Zur Entstehung der Psychiatrie als Wissenschaft im 19. Jahrhundert*, pp. 511 ff.

276   Marx, *Kritik des Hegelschen Staatsrechts*, p. 210 and *Kritik der Hegelschen Rechtsphilosophie*, introduction, p. 384.

277   Damerow, *Über die relative Verbindung der Irren-, Heil-, und Pflegeanstalten* (1840).

278   Panse, *op. cit.*, p. 30.

279   Damerow, *Die Elemente der nächsten Zukunft der Medizin*, quoted in Leibbrand, *Romantische Medizin*, p. 174.

280   Interestingly enough, the literary cooperation of German psychiatrists launched their professional union. For Damerow, his journal was the first, essential intellectual precondition "the intellectual bond" for all further steps (Damerow, *op. cit.*, Introduction to vol. I, p. xxvi).

281   *Ibid., passim.*

282   Ackerknecht, *Rudolf Virchow*, p. 11. Unlike Ackerknecht, Jacobi, in *Medizinische Anthropologie* (1967), is more concerned with Virchow's concordance with the idealistic tradition of German medicine.

283   Ackerknecht, *op. cit.*, p. 36. Of this impassioned appeal a critical-social foundation of medicine, nothing formally remained in the course of the progressive division of labor, except for a few "composite" disciplines like social medicine or social hygiene while the actual medical specialties positivistically "liberated" themselves from it completely. At the same time, the conceivable content of the critical-sociological self-reflection of medicine was dissipated along the inconspicuous and incoherent edge of its academic

teaching enterprise, e.g., labor-, social-, state-, insurance-, forensic medicine, hygiene, history of medicine, and something like philosophy of medicine. Furthermore, most of these fields in various ways were put in the service of work efficiency and productivity. Of course, one cannot speak of an independent social psychiatry in Germany, even as a splinter product of the division of labor.

Virchow, in contrast, saw the liberation of the proletariat as one of the goals of the 1848 Revolution: "Thus, Christianity emancipated the slaves, the Reformation the burghers, the revolution the peasants; and now we are concerned with bringing the workers, the propertyless classes, into the great cultural movement. That is the long struggle of mankind against inhumanity, of nature against the unnatural, of human rights against privilege" (*op. cit.*, p. 139).

284   Leubuscher, Introduction to Calmeil: *Der Wahnsinn*, pp. 1–21.

285   Damerow, review of Stürmer's *Zur Vermittlung der Extreme im Staatsleben durch die Heilkunde* (Leipzig, 1845), in *Allgemeine Zeitschrift der Psychiatrie*, vol. 2, 1845, pp. 159 f.

286   Rürup, *Die Judenemanzipation in Baden*, p. 296.

287   As in the person of the liberal historian, L. Häusser in the parliamentary discussion on the definitive realization of the emancipation of the Jews in Baden (*ibid.*, 297).

288   H. Laehr reports on this in connection with the fiftieth anniversary of the periodical (*Allgem. Zschr. Psychiat.*, 50:21, 1894) and adds: "Meanwhile, Germany had achieved unity with its blood in the political area too — a unity that the journal advocated in a literary way in the scholarly-scientific area and also achieved within a narrower circle."

289   Kieser, "Von den Leidenschaften," in *Allgem. Zschr. Psychiat.*, 7:251, 1850.

290   See Ackerknecht, *Beiträge zur Geschichte der Medizinalreform von 1848*, and also Diepgen, *Die Revolution von 1848–49 und der deutsche Ärztestand*.

291   Instead of sounding the battle cry "Back to ontology!" the present-day dilemma might be more readily resolved if we bore in mind that medicine could have emerged as a social science after the events of 1848, if the failure of the revolution had not sparked an almost total retreat into the neutralizing ivory tower of the natural sciences on the part of doctors. This development delineates the possibilities and objective tasks of the present.

292   From the eulogy in the *Allgem. Zschr. Psychiat.*, 6:445–56, 1849.

The other form of resignation, the rechanneling of political energy into the area of natural science, which played a vital role in the development of German science, was expressed most authentically in the diary entry of 9/25/1849 of the bacteriologist F. Cohn: "Germany dead, France dead, Italy dead, Hungary dead — Liberty, Equality, Unity dead, Love, Faith, and

Hope dead — cholera and the court-martials immortal. I have withdrawn into myself from the unfriendly world out there, I am buried in my books and studies; seeing few people, learning a great deal, inspired only by Nature" (quoted in Leikind, *Bull. Hist. Med.*, 7:51, 1939).

293   To be sure, K. L. Kahlbaum, the later founder of clinical psychiatry in Germany, continued along the lines of both Spielmann and H. Neumann.

294   Even though the available data may be inconclusive, it seems as if far fewer French and English psychiatrists came from a civil-service background, and many more from the economic bourgeoisie and the lower social classes.

295   For biographical data on Griesinger *et al.* see Leibbrand and Wettley, *op. cit.*, pp. 509 f.; R. Thiele, in Kolle (ed.), *Grosse Nervenärzte*, vol. II, pp. 1–14; K. Bonhoeffer, "Die Geschichte der Psychiatrie in der Charité im 19. Jahrhundert," in *Zschr. Neur. u. Psychol.*, 168:37, 1940.

296   Preyer, *R. V. Mayer....Briefe an W. Griesinger*, (1889).

297   Griesinger, "Über einen wenig bekannten psychopathischen Zustand," *Gesammelte Abhandlungen*, vol. I, pp. 180–91.

298   See Eulogy in *Arch. Psychiat. Nervenkr.*, 1:760 f., 1869/70.

299   The medical historian Diepgen for example knows only of a "materialistic pseudo-philosophy" in the post-Romantic nineteenth century (Diepgen, *op. cit.*, p. 57). On the other hand, for his times he senses a *weltanschauung* behind every microscope that must encompass all one-sidednesses: "A good physician has to operate with such a universalism. This is the total view of medicine that German National Socialism demands of him" (p. 60).

300   Gruhle, *Geschichtliches*, pp. 16 f.

301   Binswanger, *Freud und die Verfassung der klinischen Psychiatrie*, pp. 180 ff.

302   Bodamer, *Zur Entstehung*, p. 527 and *Zur Phänomenologie*, p. 308.

303   Wyrsch, *Zur Geschichte und Deutung*, p. 47 f.

304   Ackerknecht, *Kurze Geschichte*, p. 67. Unfortunately, Ackerknecht does not carry through the (altogether feasible) documentation for his analogy, and we too have to limit ourselves to hints or suggestions in this direction.

305   Dietze and Voegele, "Griesinger's Contributions to Dynamic Psychiatry," pp. 579–82. Recently, Griesinger has also been claimed for the Pavlovian psychiatry of the East European block (cf. A. Mette, "W. Griesinger als materialistischer Neuropathologe," in *Forschen und Wirken*, vol. I, Berlin, 1960; also, K. Fichtel, "W. Griesinger — ein Vorläufer der materialistischen Reflextheorie," in *Zschr. ärztl. Fortbild.*, 18:1032, 1965). Alone this universality justifies the view of Greisinger as "paradigmatic."

306   Schrenk, *Griesingers neuropsychiatrische Thesen und ihre sozialpsychiatrischen Konsequenzen*, pp. 445 and 450.

307   "Theorien und Thatsachen," in *Abhandlungen*, vol. II, pp. 3, 5 f., 6 and 8.

308   "Herr Ringseis und die naturhistorische Schule," in *Abhandlungen*,

vol. II, pp. 64 f. and 67.

309   *Ibid.*, 65.

310   "Über den Schmerz und über die Hyperamie," in *ibid.*, 177.

311   "Bemerkungen zur neuesten Entwicklung der allgemeinen Pathologie," in *ibid.*, 106 f.

312   *Ibid.*, 98 and 101 f.

313   "Elementalism" is one of the favorite charges leveled against Griesinger; cf., e.g., G. Bally, "Grundfragen der Psychoanalyse und verwandter Richtungen," in Gruhle (ed.), *Psychiatrie der Gegenwart*, vol I/2, *Grundlagen und Methoden der klinischen Psychiatrie*, Berlin, 1963. In Mühlmann's anthropology (*Geschichte der Anthropologie*, p. 92) we find the same criticism applied to the same period.

314   Alfred Schmidt (*Der Begriff der Natur in der Lehre von Marx*) similarly interprets these relationships in Marx, e.g. p. 22. Our interpretation is also influenced by Adorno's *Negative Dialectics*.

315   "Über psychische Reflexactionen" (1843), in *Abhandlungen*, vol. I, p. 4.

316   *Ibid.*, 16–17. Leibbrand and Wettley (*op. cit.*, p. 511) assume, no doubt correctly, that Griesinger's model of a quantitative intensification and its reversal into a qualitative change was at some point influenced by R. Mayer. Psychology is constituted here through physical rather than biological analogy, which makes the model more rational, shows its structural character more openly, and reduces the temptation of an uncritical-immediate confusion with reality. At the same time, this sketches the scenarium of the psychoanalytical unconscious, though by rejecting the quasi-ontological independent development of individual faculties, which actually remain in flux between organic state, social influence (habit), semiconsciousness, and consciousness; no different — if you wish — to the agencies of bourgeois society in the 1840s, which were still disorganized and scarcely differentiated from one another.

317   "Über psychische Reflexactionen," p. 30.

318   Habermas, *Theory and Practice*, p. 261.

319   "Über psychische Reflexactionen," p. 37.

320   *Ibid.*, 42 f. It is therefore not at all paradoxical that Griesinger's critique was kindled by the "somatists" rather than the "psychicists."

321   "Neue Beiträge zur Physiologie und Pathologie des Gehirns" (1844), in *Abhandlungen*, vol. I, p. 53. Today   1969 — in contrast, "sociopaths" has been equated with "enemies of society," and under the generic term "psychopathic failures" as another subgroup, "parasites: prostitutes, vagabonds, hippies, Oblomovists, loafers, idlers," and as yet a third subgroup, "eccentrics: anarchists, dreamers, adventurers, outsiders, confidence men" (H. Dietrich, *Psychiatrie in Stichworten*, Stuttgart, 1969, pp. 53 f.). There is hardly anything better designed to convince this author of the validity of

his investigation.

322 "Neue Beiträge," pp. 77–78.

323 *Ibid.*, 78.

324 *Mental Pathology and Therapeutics.* With an Introduction by Erwin H. Ackerknecht (New York and London, 1965, reprinted from 1867 English-language edition) p. 5, as well as a review of M. Jacobi's *Tobsucht* (1844), in *Abhandlungen*, p. 105.

325 It is not possible here to present systematic evidence that the general social stereotype of insanity at a given time depends on the theoretical views and practice of those psychiatrists who one or two generations earlier gave credence to that particular view — i.e., is the product of psychiatry itself.

326 Griesinger, *Mental Pathology and Therapeutics*, pp. 43–49.

327 *Ibid.*, 50 f.

328 *Ibid.*, 115 f.

329 Review of Jacobi, pp. 90 f., as well as the lecture at the opening of the Berlin University psychiatric clinic (1868), in *Abhandlungen*, vol. I, pp. 192 ff.

330 *Mental Pathology and Therapeutics*, p. 117.

331 *Ibid.*, 146 ff.

332 *Ibid.*, 352–75.

333 "Über einen wenig bekannten psychopathischen Zustand" (1868), in *Abhandlungen*, vol. I, pp. 180–91.

334 *Mental Pathology and Therapeutics*, pp. 147 f.

335 *Ibid.*, 157.

336 *Ibid.*, 166.

337 *Ibid.*, 219–20.

338 *Ibid.*, 206, 273 f.

339 *Ibid.*, 70, 273, 304, and 311. Ackerknecht (*Kurze Geschichte*, p. 62), observes that Griesinger's "*Beeinträchtigung*" was rendered as "frustration" in the English translation.

340 *Mental Pathology and Therapeutics*, pp. 273 and 303 f.

341 *Ibid.*, 460.

342 *Ibid.*, 491–95.

343 "Über Irrenanstalten und deren Weiterentwicklung in Deutschland," in *Abhandlungen*, vol. I, p. 273.

344 *Ibid.*, 276. Griesinger recognised the connection between essential elements that were not realized until the 1920s in the ambulatory clinics of the Soviet Union and later in England and Canada.

345 *Ibid.*, 276 f.

346 *Ibid.*, 285.

347 *Ibid.*, 285.

348 *Ibid.*, 290.

349 *Ibid.*, 293.

350   *Ibid.*, 301.
351   *Ibid.*, 306, and 308.
352   "Die freie Behandlung," in *Abhandlungen*, vol. I, p. 327.
353   *Ibid.*, 330 f.
354   See O. Mönkemüller in Kirchoff (ed.), *Deutsche Irrenarzte*, vol. II, p. 77.

Appendix

1   Haeser, *Lehrbuch der Geschichte der Medizin*, vol. II, p. 1,028. The earlier reflections on the history of psychiatry are not considered here, since they are part of the period being investigated.
2   Kirchhoff, *Grundriss einer Geschichte der deutschen Irrenpflege*, pp. 1–3.
3   *Idem, Geschichte der Psychiatrie*, pp. 1–10.
4   Kraepelin, *Hundert Jahre Psychiatrie,* pp. 173–75.
5   Birnbaum, *Geschichte der psychiatrischen Wissenschaft,"* pp. 10–15.
6   Gruhle, *Geschichtliches*, pp. 1–4 and 15–17.
7   Leibbrand, *Romantische Medizin.*
8   J. Wyrsch hints at this task in "Klinik der Schizophrenie," in Gruhle (ed.), *Psychiatrie der Gegenwart*, vol. II, Berlin 1960, pp. 1–26; also, Doerner, "Nationalsozialismus und Lebensvernichtung."
9   Bodamer, *Zur Phänomenologie des geschichtlichen Geistes in der Psychiatrie.*
10   *Idem,* "Zur Entstehung der Psychiatrie als Wissenschaft im 19. Jahrhundert," pp. 511 f. and 517–19.
11   Spoerri, "Besitzt die historische Betrachtung über das Wesen der Schizophrenie aktuellen Erkenntniswert?"
12   Wyrsch, *Zur Geschichte und Deutung der endogenen Psychosen*, pp. 1–8.
13   *Idem, Gesellschaft, Kultur und psychische Störung*, pp. 92–94 and 113 f.
14   *Ibid.*, p. 114.
15   Schöne, *Interpretationen zur dichterischen Gestaltung des Wahnsinns in der deutschen Literatur*, pp. 23–25 and 199 f.
16   Tellenbach, "Die Rolle der Geisteswissenschaften in der modernen Psychiatrie."
17   *Idem, Melancholie*, p. 3.
18   Leibbrand and Wettley, *Der Wahnsinn*, pp. 1–4.
19   Ackerknecht, *Kurze Geschichte der Psychiatrie*, pp. 1–9.
20   Panse, *Das psychiatrische Krankenhauswesen.* This work begins with a "History of the Psychiatric Hospital," a term that replaced the old term

"Irrenanstalt" (insane asylum) in Germany after 1945. The term *Irrenanstalt* was popularized by Jean Paul in 1807 (F. Kluge: *Etymologisches Wörterbuch* Berlin, 1967, p. 329).

21　Panse, *op. cit.*, pp. iv and 1—3.

22　Zilboorg, *A History of Medical Psychology*, p. 525.

23　Ey, *Etudes psychiatriques*, vol. I, pp. 21 ff. and 55 ff.

24　Leigh, *The Historical Development of British Psychiatry*, vol. I.

25　Hunter and Macalpine, *Three Hundred Years of Psychiatry*, pp. i—viii.

26　Foucault, *Madness and Civilization: A History of Insanity in the Age of Reason.*

27　Mora, *The History of Psychiatry: A Cultural and Bibliographical Survey.* Evidently, Americans have recently shifted to a social-historical treatment of individual issues, i.e., to the process whose results create the prerequisites for an examination of knowledge, i.e. inquiries like ours. These investigations will be considered in context.

Index

absolutism, 14, 17
  France, 98–100, 116–17
  Germany, 164, 208
Ackerknecht, E., 119, 276, 297, 305, 340, 342, 344
Acts of Parliament, 20, 22, 37–8, 46, 68, 82, 85
Addison, Joseph, 28
  Spectator, 21
Adorno, Theodor W., 308, 343
  Dialectics of Enlightenment, 5, 301, 318
Agrarian Socialists, 67
Aikin, John, 69–71
  Thoughts on Hospitals, 69
alcoholism, 65, 87, 284
d'Alembert, J. L. R., 122
alienation
  French, 109, 128, 131, 134, 139, 144
  German, 229, 244, 280, 283, 284, 286
Allgemeine Zeitschrift für Psychiatrie und psychisch-gerichtliche Medizin, 263, 274
Altenstein, K. von, 208, 247, 249, 250, 260, 263
Amelung, L. F., 221, 222
Ancien Régime, 98–118
Andree, John, 54
animism, 42, 100, 175
Annales médico-psychologiques, 160
anthropology, 3, 180, 243, 264, 295, 325

arachnoiditis, 156
architecture, of institutions
  English, 72
  French, 118, 143
  German, 172, 248, 288
Archiv für den thierischen Magnetismus, 235
Archiv für Physiologie, 198
Archiv für physiologische Heilkunde, 273
Archiv für Psychiatrie und Nervenkrankheiten, 274
Arendt, Hanna, 323, 333
Arndt, Ernst Moritz, 198
Arnold, Thomas, 49, 50–4, 55, 102, 307
  On the Management of the Insane, 54
Artelt, W., 314, 320
Ashley, Lord (Shaftesbury, 7th Earl of), 69, 257
Assembly, French Revolutionary, 119, 120
Association of German Alienists, 223, 263
Association of German Naturalists and Physicians, 236, 263
Association of Medical Officers of Asylums and Hospitals for the Insane, 87
associative psychology, 88, 189, 257
Asylum Journal of Mental Science, 87
asylums, insane, 3, 70
  attendants, 40, 92–3, 135, 221, 222–3, 289, 323
  English, 51, 69–72, 83–4, 87, (reform) 80, 94

French, 118, 142—3, 145
German reform 199, 211, 246—8, 266, 267, 287—9
private, 20, 32, 44, 116
see also hôpitaux généraux
Austria, 265
Autenrieth, F., 220, 235, 329—30

Baader, F. von, 196, 234
Baden
Illenau Asylum 257, 339
Pforzheim Asylum, 221
Baeyer, W. von, 296
Bailly, Jean Sylvain, 110, 113, 120
Bakewell, Thomas, 73, 83, 311
Baldinger, E. G., 174
Bally, G., 343
Balzac, Honoré de, 152, 336
Bank of England, 22
Baquet, 112
Barthez, P. J., 100, 127
Bath, 60
Battie, William, 39—45, 47
influence, 53, 64, 74
Treatise on Madness, 40—1, 306
Bavaria, 249, 322
Bayle, A. L. J., 144, 156, 157, 322
Bayreuth, 210, 212, 213, 214
Beckford, W., 61
Beddoes, Thomas, 73
Bedford Asylum, 82—3
Bedlam Hospital, 20—1, 33, 40, 82, 83, 306
behaviorism, 3
Belgium, 246, 334
Belhomme, J., 128
Bell, Charles, 88, 223, 279, 326
Bell, John, 310
Beneke, F. E., 332
Bentham, Jeremy, 67, 72, 91
Panopticon..., 72, 223
A Table of the Springs of Action, 72
Bergmann, G. H., 223, 224
Bergson, H., 321
Berlin, 174, 270
Charité Hospital, 171, 215
Friedrichstadt, 171
Workhouse, 250, 267, 323
Bernard, Claude, 259
Bernhardi, A. F., 326
Berthold, F., 321

Berthollet, C. L., 316
Beyträge zur Beförderung einer Cur-methode auf psychischem Wege, 327
Bicêtre, 115, 117, 120, 122, 128, 133, 158, 319
Bichat, François Xavier, 100, 123, 156, 259
Anatomie générale, 101
Traité des membranes, 123
Bildungsbürgertum, 164—92, 241
Billroth, Theodor, 273
Binswanger, L., 275, 293, 295, 296, 342
Bird, F., 257, 260
Birnbaum, K., 9, 293, 345
Bismarck, Otto von, 266, 270, 271, 336, 339
Blackmore, R.
Treatise of the Spleen and Vapours..., 29, 305
Bleuler, E., 336
Blumröder, G., 258, 270, 338
Bodamer, J., 276, 314, 340, 342, 345
Ideengeschichte der Psychiatrie, 294
Boldt, A., 327
Bolingbroke, Henry, 23, 100
Bolten, J. C., 176, 324
Bonald, L. G. A. de, 140
Bonaparte, Jerôme, 222
Bonhoeffer, Karl, 276, 342
Bordeu, Théophile, 100, 107, 111, 127
Borkum, 225—6
Börne, L., 198
Boswell, J., 61
bourgeoisie, 1, 16, 324
English, 18th C, 26—8, 35, 51, 57—9, 63; 19th C, 68, 79—81
French, 18th C, 99—103, 113—14; 19th C, 124, 319
German 18th C, 168, 169, 176, 326; 19th C, 193, 201, 269, 290, 336
threats to, 242, 245—6, 247, 334
see also Bildungsbürgertum; self-awareness
Boyle, Robert, 24
Brachmann, R., 325
Braubach, M., 328
Brissot de Warville, J. P., 316
British Medical Association, 93
Broca, Paul, 155
Bromberg, W., 303

Broussais, François Joseph Victor, 140, 141, 152, 155, 156, 223, 321
Brousse, P., 141
Brown, John ('Brownianism'), 49–50, 196, 227, 228
Elementa medicinae, 49
Brown, N. O., 305
Brown, Thomas, 73
Brücke, E., 259
Brunswick prison, 170
Buchez, Philippe Benjamin Joseph, 107, 140, 159–60, 322
Studien zur Entwicklung des Irreseins, 159
Büchner, G., 259
Budge, J., 279
Burdach, K. F., 258
Burke, Edmund, 74
Burrows, George M., 84–6, 90, 311, 330, 334
Byron, G. G. N., 67

Cabanis, Pierre J. G., 122, 123–7, 128, 156, 157, 188, 259, 318
Rapports du physique et du moral de l'homme, 124, 128
Cagliostro, 316
Calmeil, J. L., 341
Calonne, Charles Alexandre de, 100
Campagne, 151
Capucine monks, 171
Carlson, E. T., 313
Carlyle, Thomas, 69
Carus, C. G., 235, 236, 333
case histories, 73, 75
Catherine the Great, 176
Cerise, L., 141, 159, 160, 322
certification, 82, 212, 287–8
chains, 83, 133, 166, 225
chair, confining, 171
Charenton, 137, 142, 143, 150, 322
Charlesworth, Edward P., 92
chartist movement, 66
Chateaubriand, François René de, 152
Cheyne, G.
The English Malady…, 29–30, 305
Chiarugi, V., 49, 119
Christian-Germanic school, 237, 239
Christianity, 158, 230, 245, 252, 267
churches, 37, 38, 102, 166
classicism, 178, 193, 194

Claudius, Matthias, 260
clinical school
English, 175
French, 123, 142, 144, 147
German, 274
Code Napoléon, 121, 142, 211
coffee-houses, 22, 24, 28, 100, 110
Cohn, F., 341
Colbert, Jean Baptiste, 98
Coleridge, S. T., 68
Cologne, 211, 322
Colombier, J.
Instructions sur la manière de gouverner les insensés, 118
Combe, Andrew, 89, 313
common sense, 23–4, 62
Commons, House of, 82, 83, 85
Comte, Auguste, 140, 142, 151–2, 153, 155, 320, 321
law of observation, 139, 145, 147, 156, 157
Condillac, Étienne Bonnot de, 101, 103, 122, 123, 131, 203
influence, 259, 314
Condorcet, Marquis de, 122, 128
Conolly, John, 64, 87, 90, 93–5
influence, 271, 287, 313
conservatism, 64–77
Conze, W., 13, 303
Corvisart, G. N., 153
Cousin, Victor, 122
Couthon, Georges, 133
Cox, J. M., 76, 311
craniology, 154
Crichton, A., 49, 129
An Inquiry into the Nature and Origin of Mental Derangements, 73
criminal lunatics, 82
Critical Review, The, 46
Cullen, William, 48–9, 128, 129, 307
'cultural school' (US), 3
Currie, J., 71, 310

Dahlmann, F. C., 271
Dain, N., 313
Damerow, Heinrich, 263–9, 275, 340, 341
Darwin, Charles, 73
Darwin, Erasmus, 73, 76
Daumer, 339
Daumier, H., 152

De morbo democratico, 269
Declaration of Human and Civil Rights, 119, 125, 133
Defoe, Daniel, 20, 31–2, 33, 305
   Robinson Crusoe, 23
degeneration, theory of, 141, 159, 185, 234, 283, 285, 332–3
Dehio, 329
De La Rive, G. C.
   Letters to the Editors of the Bibliothèque Britannique, 77
delirium, 87–8, 322
delusion, 42, 53, 286
demonomania, 147–8
Denmark, 223
depression, 281, 286
Descartes, René, 100, 101, 295
Destutt de Tracy, A. L. C., 131, 318
Diderot, Denis, 122, 314
   Le Neveu de Rameau, 104
Diepgen, P., 341, 342
Dietrich, H., 343
Deitze, H. J., 342
Dijon, 105
Dilthey, Wilhelm, 9, 234, 294, 295, 296
disease, concepts of, 25, 49, 50, 53, 230, 337
dispersal, 181, 182, 280
display, of lunatics, 16–17, 21, 167
Disraeli, Benjamin, 69
dissenters, religious, 67
Doerner, Klaus, 301, 324, 326, 345
Dohm, C. W., 173, 181
Dollkasten, 166, 171
Donalies, G., 327
Doppelgänger motif, 195
Doublet, F.
   Instructions sur la manière de gouverner les insensés, 118
Dreitzel, H. P., 309
Dubois-Reymond, E., 259
Dumas, Alexandre, 255
Durkheim, E., 3

Earle, P., 73
Earlswood asylum, 90, 93
Eckert, G., 316
Edinburgh, 87, 260
education
   and democracy, 266
   English, 73, 85, 94

French, 105–6, 125, 135, 140, 146, 147, 159
German, 172, 209–10
Eichhorn, J. A. F., 258, 268
Einheitspsychose, 133, 257, 281, 321
Eisenbarth, J. A., 324
electricity, *see* galvanism
Ellis, S. C., 313
Ellis, William, 91–2
emancipation, of insane
   English, 95
   French, 119–38, 299
   German, 210–18, 267, 289
   goal, 1, 5, 6, 290, 291
   see also integration
emigration, 113, 316
Encyclopedists, 100, 102, 122, 127, 261
'English malady' (spleen), 24, 99
Enlightenment, 1, 5, 299
   claims, 6, 8, 14
   English, 65
   French, 100–4
   German, 175–80
Ennemoser, J., 235
Epictetus, 51
epilepsy, 54, 90
Erlangen asylum, 248
Erskine, Thomas, 82
Eschenmayer, C. A. von, 228, 234, 235, 273, 331
d'Eslon, 127
Esquirol, Jean-Etienne-Dominique, 118, 137, 141–3, 144–53, 320
   Des maladies mentales, 144
   influence, 223, 253, 290
Ethnological Society of London, 88, 93
ethnology, 88
excitability, 50
existentialism, 3, 275, 293
extermination, of insane, 164, 322
Ey, Henri, 119, 298, 320, 321, 346

Fallowes, Thomas, 306
family, 67, 70, 71, 80, 109, 165
Fawcett, B., 73
fear, 74, 76, 159, 205
Feder, J. H. G., 189
Ferriar, J., 49, 73, 76, 129, 311
Ferrus, G., 141, 158, 159, 161
Feuchtersleben, E. von, 270
Feuerbach, Ludwig Andreas, 103, 234, 259

Fichte, Johann Gottlieb, 198, 212, 213, 227, 230, 325
  dispersal, 181, 182, 280
Fichtel, K., 342
Fitz-James, 274
Flemming, C. F., 257, 264, 267, 275, 338
Flugel, J. C., 325
Fodéré, E., 141
forensics, 47, 183–4, 251, 258, 268
Forster, Georg, 186
Foucault, Michel, 14, 26, 56, 70, 80, 119, 291
  Madness and Civilization, 299, 303, 305, 314, 346
Fourcroy, 122
Fowler, Thomas, 77, 129
Fox, Henry, 46
France, 15, 52, 207–26
  abolition of *Ancien Régime*, 98–118
  Positivism, 139–61
  Revolution and emancipation of insane, 119–38
Frank, Johann Peter, 174, 239
  System einer vollständigen medicinischen Polizey, 172, 323, 324
Frankfurt Madhouse, 171
Franklin, Benjamin, 28, 38, 110, 122, 127
Frederick the Great, 167, 208
Frederick William IV, 265
Freud, Sigmund, 2, 270, 275, 299, 333
Friedrich, J. B., 253, 258, 338
Fries, Jakob, 339
  Psychologische Anthropologie, 258
Fromm, E., 3
Funcke, F. O., 330

Gabel, J., 305
Gadamer, Hans-Georg, 9, 302, 304
Gagern, H. von, 271, 339
Galen, 101
Gall, Franz Joseph, 89, 140, 141, 153–6, 157, 321, 333
  influence, 198, 224
  Sur les fonctions du cerveau, 153
Galvani, Luigi, 111, 318
galvanism, 38, 55, 61, 197, 318
Garat, 122
Gasner, J. J., 316
Gaupp, R., 330
Gay, J., 22

Gazette de Santé, 128
genius, 180, 183, 186, 331
Gentleman's Magazine, The, 309
George III, 69, 74
Georgenthal Castle, 197
Georget, E., 141, 157, 322
Germany, 3
  mercantilism and *Bildungsbürgertum*, 164–92
  from Restoration to liberalism, 227–91
  revolution and psychiatry, 193–226
Gheel, 109, 274
Ghent, 321, 334
Glaser, H., 305
Glasser, W., 316
Glisson, F., 26, 100, 199, 305
Gobineau, A., 186, 333
Godwin, William, 67
Goethe, Johann Wolfgang von, 178, 190, 195, 245, 315
  influence, 198, 212, 260, 296
Goldsmith, Oliver, 61
Görres, J. von, 196, 197, 234, 237
Göttingen, 174, 247
Graudenz, 249
Great Britain, 15, 20–95
  Industrial Revolution, Romanticism and psychiatry, 34–63
  Reform Movement and restraint, 64–95
  sequestration and the public, 20–33
Greding, J. E., 324
Green, M., 61
Gregory, J., 62, 63, 309
Griesinger, W., 257, 260, 263, 270–90, 336
  Archivs, 287
  Über psychische Reflexactionen, 279, 281
Grohmann, J. C. A., 245
Gross, F., 221, 253
Gruhle, H., 119, 275, 293, 342, 345
Guillotin, Joseph Ignace, 110, 122
guillotining, 110, 113
Guislain, J., 281, 321, 334
Guy, Thomas, 306

Habermas, Jürgen, 9, 12, 22, 182, 229, 301, 304f, 306f
Hadfield, 82
Haeser, H., 292
Hagen, F. W., 332

Hahnemann, Samuel 197
Haindorf, Alexander, 235, 237—8, 333—4
    Versuch einer Pathologie und Therapie
        der Geistes- und Gemütskrank-
        heiten, 237
Haisch, E., 319f
Hall, M., 279
Hallaran, W. S., 49, 76, 91
Hallé, N. J., 126, 188
Haller, Albrecht von, 48, 55, 100, 101,
    175, 181, 279
hallucinations, 42, 53, 148—9
Hambach Festival, 247
Hamburg, 15, 170, 171
Hanover, 223
Hanwell asylum, 87, 91, 93, 95
Hardenberg, Friedrich von, *see* Novalis
Hardenberg, Karl August von, 207—8,
    209—11, 212, 213—14, 235
Hartley, David, 53, 189, 307
Hartmann, N., 294, 296
Hartmann, P. K., 270
Haslam, John, 83, 86, 129, 311, 312, 322
Hauser, Arnold, 21, 166, 304, 314
Hauser, Kaspar, 339
Häusser, L., 341
Haydn, Franz Joseph, 212
Hayner, C. A. F., 220, 221, 330
Hegel, Georg Wilhelm Friedrich, 11, 210,
    247—8, 263, 334, 335
    The Phenomenology of the Mind, 229
Heidegger, Martin, 3, 296, 332
Heidelberg, 221
Heine, H., 318
Heinrich, G. B., 271
Heinroth, J. C. A., 90, 235, 237, 238—45
    influence, 253, 261
    Lehrbuch der Störungen des Seelen-
        lebens, 238—9, 334
    Prophylactik, 244
Helvétius, Claude Adrien, 101
Helvétius, Madame, 122, 123, 127
Hemprich, R. D., 330
Herbart, J. F., 257, 282, 332
Herder, Johann Gottfried, 188, 197
    Plastik, 188
Herting, 339
Herz, Marcus, 189
Hesse, 246
Hesse, G., 221, 339
Hildesheim, 264

Hill, Robert Gardiner, 92—3, 313
Hippocrates, 129
historiography, of psychiatry, 9, 249,
    292—300
Hobbes, Thomas
    Leviathan, 17
Hoffbauer, J. C., 199, 327, 331—2
Hoffmann, E. T. A., 197, 332
Hoffmann, Friedrich, 48, 175
Hoffmann, J. G., 209
Hoffmann, K. R.
    Idealpathologie, 234
Hofheim, 221
Hofmann, W., 9, 302, 303f, 323
Hogarth, William, 40
Holbach, Paul Heinrich Dietrich, 102,
    122, 182, 280, 314
Holborn, Hans, 306, 324, 328
Holland, H., 312
Hollingshead, August B., 301, 310
hollow wheel, 220
Holy Alliance, 237, 245
homeopathy, 197
homotonie theory, 107
Hooke, Robert, 24
Hôpital général, Paris, 15, 21
hôpitaux généraux, 15, 98—9, 114—18,
    119—23, 144
Horkheimer, Max, 308
    Dialectics of Enlightenment, 5, 301
Horn, Ernst, 215—16, 234, 263, 329
'Horn's Bag', 216
Horney, K., 3
Howard, John, 71, 117
    An Account of the Principal Lazarettos
        in Europe, 71
Hufeland, C. W., 184, 202, 212, 325
Hugo, Victor, 255
Humboldt, Alexander von, 152, 198, 318
Humboldt, K. von, 332
Hume, D., 52
Hunter, A., 77
Hunter, Richard, 56, 298, 303f
Husserl, E., 3
Hutcheson, F., 62, 309
hygiene, 139, 143, 174
hypochondria, 26, 56, 107, 182, 284—5,
    325
hysteria, 25—30, 38, 51, 107, 284,
    305
    functionalization, 52, 54—63

idealism, 182, 185, 193, 238, 280, 326
Ideler, K. W., 134, 249–56, 258, 329
   Grundriss der Seelenheilkunde, 249–50,
     251, 319, 336
identity theory, 5, 220, 318
Ideologues, 123–7, 144
idiocy, 31, 42, 59, 90, 148–9
Ilberg, G., 330
individualism, 58–9, 104–6, 178
Industrial Revolution, 34–5, 65, 169
industrialization, 168, 169, 246, 336
Insane Offenders Bill (1800), 82
insanity, 5, 24, 157–8, 196–7, 266
   England, 31–3, 89, 94
   France, 101, 102, 109, 130, 131,
     145–8
   Germany, 182–3, 186, 191, 203,
     231–3, 238, 243–4, 254–5, 261,
     281, 332, 334
   law (1838), 158
   see also pauper lunatics
Institution of St. Anne, 159
institutions, 13, 17
   England, 20–2, 70
   Germany, 164, 166, 168, 175, 205,
     206, 211
   see also asylums, lunatic; *hôpitaux
     généraux*; prisons; workhouses
integration, social, of insane
   England, 91, 95
   France, 158, 160, 268
   Germany, 239, 242, 268, 289
   goal of psychiatry, 1, 5, 6, 288, 290,
     291
   see also emancipation
Ireland, 32, 76
irrationality, *see* insanity
Irwing, K. F. von, 189
Italy, 246
Ivry, 142

Jacobi, F. H., 228, 259
Jacobi, Maximilian, 80, 257–9, 260–2,
   267, 275, 311, 339
   *Beobachtungen über die Pathologie
     und Therapie der mit Irresein
     verbundenen Krankheiten*, 261
   Tobsucht, 263, 279, 344
Jahn, F.
   Krankheiten als Afterorganisationen,
     234

Jänkendorf, 220, 329
Jaspers, K., 327
Jean Paul (Johann Paul Friedrich Richter),
   197, 327, 346
Jefferson, Thomas, 122
Jessen, P. W., 223, 235
Jetter, D., 91, 310, 323, 328
Jews, 181, 262, 268
   emancipation, 13, 171, 172–3, 221,
     237, 341
   German contribution, 208, 268, 333
   persecution, 323–4, 339
Johnson, Samuel, 42, 306
   Rasselas, 58, 60
Joly, 119
Jones, Robert, 117, 317
Joseph II, 171, 172
*Journal of Psychological Medicine and
   Mental Pathology*, 87
Julius Hospital, 171

Kaech, R., 316
Kahlbaum, K. L., 180, 342
Kahn, E., 321
Kaissler, A. B., 327
Kant, Immanuel, 178, 180–7, 201–2,
   270
   *Anthropology from a Pragmatic Point
     of View*, 180, 228, 325, 330
   Critique of Judgment, 228
   Critique of Practical Reason, 187
   influence, 208, 251, 258
   Von der Macht des Gemuts, 182
Kehr, E., 328
Kerner, Justinus
   Die Seherin von Prevorst, 235, 257,
     339
Kiel, 167
Kieser, D. G. von, 235, 237, 268, 341
Kinkel, J. G., 271
Kirchhoff, T., 9, 321, 322, 336
   Geschichte der deutschen Irrenpflege,
     292, 345
Kisker, K. P., 304, 325, 326, 330
Kloos, G., 326
Klötzer, W., 339
Kluge, F., 334
Kolle, K., 318
Königsberg, 208
Koreff, J. F., 235, 332

Koselleck, R., 21, 22, 117, 209, 304, 315, 328
Kraepelin, Emil, 119, 180, 275, 290, 321, 336
  Hundert Jahre Psychiatrie, 293, 345
Krafft-Ebing, R. von, 180
Krauss, W., 324, 326
Krukenberg, P., 235
Kuhn, Thomas S., 12, 303
  Structure of Scientific Revolutions, 11

labor
  England, 35, 37, 64—5
  Germany, 165, 167, 168, 249
Laehr, H., 311, 320, 323, 327, 335, 341
Laënnec, R. T. H., 223
Lafayette, J. de, 110
Lamennais, Robert de, 141
Lamettrie, Julien Offray de, 101
Langermann, J. G., 211, 212—15, 234, 250, 329
  influence, 254
Larrey, J. D., 153
Lassalle, Ferdinand, 159
Lavater, J. C., 188, 189
  Physiognomische Fragmente zur Beförderung der Menschenkenntnis und Menschenliebe, 188
Lavoisier, Antoine Laurent, 110, 122
Lawrence, W., 88, 313
Lechler, W., 317
legislation
  England, 68, 313
  France, 120, 121, 143—5, 150
  Germany, 165, 248—9, 328—9
  see also Acts of Parliament; *Code Napoléon*
Leibbrand, W., 8, 42, 119, 326
  Geschichte der abendländischen Psychopathologie, 296
  Romantische Medizin, 293, 307, 316, 331, 345
  Der Wahnsinn, 302
Leibniz, Gottfried Wilhelm, 188, 189, 199
Leicester, 50, 51
Leigh, D., 298, 307, 310, 346
Leikind, 342
Lenk, K., 9
Lenz, M., 327
Lesky, E., 130, 318, 324

lettres de cachet, 98, 117, 120
Leubuscher, R., 266, 267, 269, 270, 341
Leupoldt, J. M., 235, 237, 267
Leuret, F., 141, 159, 322
liberalism
  England, 64—77
  Germany, 227—91
Licensing Act, 22
Lichtenberg, G. C., 188
Lieber, H. J., 9, 301
Lincoln Asylum, 92
Linnaeus
  Genera morborum, 48
List, Friedrich, 236—7
literature and psychiatry
  England, 57—61, 67, 68
  France, 104
  Germany, 191, 200, 315, 336, 340
Liverpool asylum, 47, 71
Locke, John, 23, 24, 101, 259
  Essay Concerning Human Understanding, 31, 305
London, 54, 87, 174
Lorry, Anne-Charles, 242
  De melancholia et morbis melancholicis, 107
Lotze, H. J., 259
Löwe-Zinngroup, 271
Lübeck, 170
Lucipia, L., 141
Ludwig, 271
Ludwigsburg, 171, 221
Lukács, Georg, 186, 187, 201, 315, 326, 330
lunatics, poor, *see* pauper lunatics
Lüttge, F., 322, 335
Lyons, 15

Macalpine, Ida, 56, 298, 303f
MacBride, D., 307
Macpherson, J., 58
madness, 41—2, 43, 45, 53, 71, 86
  see also insanity
Magazin für die psychische Heilkunde, 327
Magazin für Erfahrungsseelenkunde, 73, 188, 189
Magendie, François, 259, 273
magnetism, 110, 111, 112, 235, 332
Maimon, Salomon, 189

Geschichte des eigenen Lebens, 190, 326
Maistre, J. de, 320
Malesherbes, C. G. de, 100, 116, 117
Malthus, Thomas Robert, 65
Manchester, 47, 70
Mandeville, Bernard, 24, 28, 76
 Fable of the Bees, 23
 Treatise of the Hypochondriack and Hysterick Passion, 28
Mandt, M. W. von, 247
manic-depressive insanity, 285
manie sans délire, 132, 149, 319
Mannheim, K., 3, 9
Marat, J. P., 316
Marcus, A. F., 196, 235
Mariaberg, 273
Marquet, F. N., 315
Marsberg, 219, 222, 264
Marshal, A. D., 86, 312
Marx, Karl, 103, 159, 261, 314, 322
 social alienation, 283, 340, 343
masturbation, 137, 285
materialism, 103, 199, 202, 212, 259
Matthey, 108
Maurois, André, 306
Mayer, Robert, 273, 343
Mead, R., 305, 311
Mechler, A., 327
medicine
 English, 28, 87–8
 French, 115, 119, 121–3, 139
 German, 171, 174, 175, 263–91
Medico-Chirurgical Review, 93
Medico-Psychological Association, 93
Medizinische Reform, 269
Mehring, F., 322
Meinecke, F., 23, 304
Meiners, Christoph, 185, 186, 333
melancholia
 England, 25, 26, 50
 France, 106–7, 132, 149
 Germany, 182, 244, 285, 337
Mendelssohn, Moses, 173
mental health movement, 3, 4
mercantilism, 14, 114, 164–92, 248
Mercier, L. S., 115
 Tableau de Paris, 114
Mesmer, Anton, 110–13, 235
 De planetarum influxu, 110
 Mesmerism or the System of Reciprocal Effects, 111
mesmerism, 110–13, 197, 316
Methodism, 38, 68, 73
Mette, A., 342
Meyer, Ludwig, 271, 274, 290
Mill, John Stuart, 67
Mirabeau, Honoré de, 115, 122
 Lettres de Cachet, 116
Mirabeau, Victor de, 116
Mohl, R. von, 330
Moleschott, J., 259
Mommsen, Heinrich, 13, 37, 303
Mönkemöller, O., 330, 345
monomania, 148–53, 188, 321
Monro, John, 44, 45–6, 47, 306
 Remarks on Dr. Battie's Treatise on Madness, 45
Monro, Thomas, 83
Montesquieu, Charles de Secondat, 30, 99
Montpellier, 100, 101, 106, 127, 175, 259, 314
Moore, W., 73
Mora, G., 9, 299–300, 346
moral management movement, 43–4, 74–5, 91
moral philosophy, 23, 34, 36, 61–3, 68, 73
Morel, B. A., 141, 283, 332
Morgagni, Giovanni Battista, 54
Morison, Sir Alexander, 87
Moritz, Carl Philipp, 191
 Anton Reiser, ein Psychologischer Roman, 189–90, 326
 Reisen eines Deutschen in England, 189
Mottek, H., 306, 309, 323, 334
Mowrer, O. H., 316
Mozart, Wolfgang Amadeus
 Bastien und Bastienne, 110
Mühlmann, W. E., 313, 326, 343
Mulhouse, 289
Müller, Johannes, 257, 273, 279, 338
music therapy, 60, 106, 107, 110, 111, 112, 126

Napoleon, 123, 127, 128, 153, 193, 194, 198
 Code, 121, 142, 211
Nasse, F., 225, 235, 257, 259, 327, 338
National Association for the Promotion of Social Sciences, 93

National Liberals, 271
National Socialists, 3, 276, 291, 293, 323–4, 342
National-Zeitung, 197
natural philosophy, 193, 197, 224, 225, 227, 234, 235
Necker, Jacques, 100, 115
nerves, theory of, 48–50
nervous system, 25, 88, 106, 107, 125–6, 175
Neuburger, M., 204, 313, 327, 328
Neumann, H., 270
Neumann, K. G., 234
Neumann, S., 267
Neumünster, 167, 170
neurology, 55, 333
neurosis, 2, 48, 284, 307
Newcastle-upon-Tyne, 47
Newton, I., 307
Niebuhr, B. G., 208
Nietzsche, Friedrich Wilhelm, 234
Non-Restraint system, 64, 90–5, 143, 218
in Germany, 271, 274, 287, 289
Nostitz, G. A. E. von, 220, 329
Novalis (pseud.), 196, 212, 224
Fragmente, 196, 327

Oberreit, 189
Oken, L., 196, 234, 236
Order of Harmony, 113
otology, 318
outcasts, 164–75
out-patient clinics, 274, 339
Owen, Robert, 85, 209
Oxford Movement, 69

padded cells, 91, 112, 220, 330
Panse, B., 319
Geschichte des psychiatrischen Krankenhauses, 297, 345
Das Psychiatrische Krankenhauswesen, 119
paralysis, 88, 322
progressive, 156
paranoia, 42
Pargeter, William, 73, 75, 311
Paris
Academy of Science, 118
epidemic (1780), 115

Hôpital général, 98–9
Mesmer blesses tree in, 113
Peace of, 34
Pascal, Blaise, 181
patent of toleration, 171
pathography, 314
pathology, 73, 278
patriotism, 207, 222, 236, 243, 264
Paul, Jean, *see* Jean Paul
pauper lunatics, 1, 16, 20, 31, 304
England, 37–8, 40, 46, 47, 50, 63, 83
France, 98, 116, 119–23; 19th C, 133–4, 135, 143, 146
Germany, 164, 170; 19th C, 200, 207, 208, 213, 225, 284
Pavlov, Ivan Petrovich, 342
Peardon, T. P., 305
pellagra, 87, 322
Perfect, William, 73, 75, 310
Pestalozzi, Johann Heinrich, 172, 214
Peterloo Massacre, 65
phenomenology, 293
Philosophes, 100–4
philosophy, 8
German, 264
natural, 193, 197, 224, 225, 227, 234, 235
practical, 252–3
Scottish moral, 23, 34, 36, 61–3, 68, 73
Phrenological Society of Warwick, 93
phrenology, 89, 153, 154–5, 156, 321
German, 224
Physiocrats, 100, 113–18, 169
physiognomy, 188, 326
physiology, 124, 259, 278
Pienitz, E., 220–1
Pinel, Philippe, 49, 109, 117, 118, 119, 122, 127, 142
De la certitude…, 127
influence, 139, 141, 148, 242, 299
Nosographie philosophique ou la méthode de l'analyse appliquée à la médecine, 123
Traité médico-philosophique sur l'aliénation mentale ou la manie, 128
Pinel, Scipion, 157–8
Physiologie de l'homme aliéné appliquée à l'analyse de l'homme social, 157
Pitt, William, 46, 64

Plato, 232
Plessner, H., 9, 10, 302, 303f
Poland, 246
political economy, 36
Politzer, A., 318
Pomme, Pierre
    Traité des Affections Vaporeuses, 107
poor laws, 65, 248
Pope, Alexander, 22
population politics, 164–75
Positivism, 127
    France, 139–61
    Germany, 185, 234, 277, 322
poverty, 65, 335
    see also pauper lunatics
Pressavin, J. B.
    Nouveau Traité des Vapeurs, 109
Preyer, W., 342
Priestley, J. B., 189
prisons
    England, 67, 72
    France, 114–18, 121
    German reform, 170, 201, 208–9
Pritchard, James C., 89
    Physical History of Mankind, 88
    Treatise on Insanity, 89
Prochaska, G., 175
projection, 73
proletariat, 242, 245–6, 247, 341
Promies, W., 191, 324
Protestantism, 169, 191, 210, 258, 314,
    326
Prussia, 193, 207–26, 246–7, 324
psychiatry, 6–11, 11–14, 41
    England, 34–9, 61, 85–95; reform,
        69–84
    France, 106, 128, 130, 140–1, 153–61;
        reform, 141–53
    Germany, 180, 193–226, 227–45,
        259–60; reform, 249, 263–91
    historiography, 9, 249, 292–30
    and sociology, 1–6, 250, 276, 291
psychists, 245–62
psychoanalysis, 2, 252, 275, 333, 337
psychodynamics, 72–3
psychology, 25, 202, 276
    associative, 88, 189, 257
psychopathology, 8, 73
psychopathy, 4, 90, 188, 296
psychoses, 2
    endogenous, 119, 294–5, 311

unitary (Einheitspsychose), 133, 257,
    281, 321
public concepts, see visibility of insanity
Pussin, J. B., 134

Quakers, 73, 77, 84
Quesnay, François, 116

railroads, 335
Rau, W. T., 174
Récalde, A. de, 317
Redlich, F. C., 301, 310
reflexes, 55
Reform Movement, 64–95
reforms
    France, medical, 115, 119, 121–3,
        141–53
    German, medical, 171, 174, 193–226,
        263–91; social, 168, 169, 172
Reid, John, 87, 312
Reid, Thomas, 62, 309
Reil, Johann Christian, 117, 198–207,
    214, 327
    influence, 227, 234, 279
    Rhapsodien über die Anwendung der
        psychischen Curmethode auf Geis-
        teszerrüttungen, 198, 328
    Von der Lebenskraft, 199
Reimann, H., 301
repression, 73
Restoration
    France, 141–53,
    Germany, 209, 227–91
restraint, 64–95
    abolition, 90–5, 271
    instruments auctioned, 290
    mechanical, 91, 166, 222, 248, 266
    moral, 74–6, 216–17
    physical, 49, 74, 76, 83, 216–17
    see also therapy
Retreat (Tuke's), 64, 73, 77–82, 119
Revolution
    and emancipation of insane, 119–38
    French, 64–5, 104, 117, 139–40,
        142, 319
    in Germany, 193–226, 246, 258,
        263–91, 341
    Industrial (English), 34–5, 65, 169
Ricardo, David, 65
Richardson, Samuel, 60, 104, 307
    Pamela, 59

Richartz, W., 257
Richter, Johann Paul Friedrich, *see* Jean
    Paul
Rieger, C., 323
Ringseis, J. N., 234, 235, 237, 277
Ritter, G., 308
Robespierre, M. de, 137
Robinson, N., 305, 309
Rochefoucauld, François de la, 119
Roller, C. F. W., 257, 258, 264, 339
Roller, J. C., 221
Romanticism, 6, 81
    England, 36–7, 57–61, 67, 308
    Germany, 73, 168, 177, 193–207
Rommel, O., 328
Röschlaub, A., 196
Rosen, G., 89, 313, 314, 318f
Rosenkranz, Karl, 224, 270
rotatory machine, 76, 91, 216, 251, 329
Rothschuh, K. E., 318, 324
Rousseau, Jean Jacques, 104–6
    Discours sur les sciences et les arts,
        105, 315
    influence, 106–9, 179, 255
Roussel, 122
Royal College of Physicians, 39, 46
Royal Society of London, 24
Royer-Collard, P. P., 137, 140
Rüegg, N., 314, 320
Ruer, W., 222, 223, 330
Rürup, R., 323, 330, 341
Rüsau, 184
Rush, Benjamin, 49
Ruskin, John, 69
Rust, J. N., 247

Sachsenberg, 246, 248
Sade, Marquis de, 98, 115, 137
St. Clare, W., 61
St. Luke's Hospital, 40, 41, 87
Saint-Pierre, Jacques Henri Bernardin de,
    109, 316
Saint-Simon, Claude Henri, Comte de,
    140, 159
Salpêtrière, 115, 120, 122, 133, 142,
    322
Sand, George, 255
Saragossa, 319
Saussure, R. de, 318
Sauvages, F., 101, 127

Saxony, 248
Schelling, Friedrich Wilhelm Joseph, 50,
    196, 197, 199, 227–34, 330, 331,
    334
    influence, 234, 236, 332
    Stuttgarter Privat Vorlesungen, 230
Schiller, Johann Christoph Friedrich von,
    189, 202, 212, 233
Schipperges, H., 338
schizophrenia, 284, 294, 336
Schlegel, August Wilhelm von, 332
Schlegel, Caroline von, 197
Schlegel, Karl Wilhelm Friedrich von,
    196, 197
Schleiden, M. J., 257
Schleiermacher, F., 198, 263, 325, 326
Schleswig, 170, 223
Schmidt, Alfred, 343
Schmidt, Arno, 327
Schneider, P. J., 329
Schön, H. T. von, 208, 249
Schöne, A., 8, 295, 327, 345
Schönlein, J. L., 273, 277
Schopenhauer, Artur, 234, 318, 319
Schrenk, M., 276, 342
Schubert, G. H. von, 224, 234, 235
Schüle, H., 180
Schurz, C., 271
Schwann, Theodor, 257, 259
Scotland, 15, 48
    moral philosophy, 23, 34, 36, 61–3,
        68, 73
Scott, Sir Walter, 67
segregation, of insane, 20, 90, 164–75,
    324
self-awareness, of bourgeoisie, 28, 35, 60,
    99, 168, 176, 201–2, 325
sensibility, 56, 57, 66, 101, 108
sensus communis, 24, 179, 186, 326
sensus privatus, 186, 188
sequestration, of unreason, 14–17
    England, 20–33, 36
    France, 98–100, 114–18
    Germany, 164, 191, 324
    see also institutions
Shaftesbury, Anthony Ashley Cooper,
    7th Earl, (Lord Ashley), 69, 257
Shaftesbury, Anthony Ashley Cooper,
    3rd Earl, 23–4, 62, 313
Shakespeare, William, 306
Shelley, P. B., 67, 68

Sheridan, Richard Brinsley, 75
Siegburg, 260
Sieyès, Abbé E., 125
Silesia, 249, 266
    Leubus asylum, 270
Smith, Adam, 36, 208
Smith, J. C., 76
Smollett, Tobias, 57, 307
    Sir Launcelot Greaves, 46
social background of psychiatrists, 141, 272, 319, 320, 342
Société médicale d'émulation, 123
Société médico-psychologique, 161
Société phrènologique, 156
Society for the Diffusion of Useful Knowledge, 93
Society for the Protection of Aborigines, 88
sociology, 157
    of knowledge, 6–11
    and psychiatry, 1–6, 14
sociopaths, 343
somatism
    France, 153–61
    Germany, 131, 245–62, 263, 339
Sombart, 223
Sonnenfels, J. von, 167
Sonnenstein-Pirna asylum, 219–20, 221
South Sea Bubble, 22, 30
Spa, 108
Spaemann, R., 309
Spatz, H., 333
Spehlmann, Rainer, 301
Spielhagen, F., 271
Spielmann, J., 271–2
    Diagnostik der Geisteskranken, 271
Spiess, C. H.
    Biographien der Wahnsinnigen, 179, 324
spiritualism, 112, 316
spleen, 29, 32, 38, 51, 54
Spoerri, T., 8, 294, 345
Spurzheim, Johann Caspar, 89, 153
Spurzheim, K., 271
Staël, Madame de, 180
Stahl, G. E., 42, 43, 100, 175, 213, 324
    influence, 254
Stahl, K. F., 333
Starobinski, J., 309, 315
state, role of
    England, 64, 83–4, 85

France, 116
Germany, 169, 189, 209, 230, 245, 265, 268, 338
statistics, 320
Steele, Richard
    Tatler, 21
Steffens, H., 196, 198, 234, 236, 332
Stein, Heinrich Friedrich Karl von, 207, 208, 212
Stendhal, 336
Sterne, Lawrence
    Sentimental Journey, 61
    Tristram Shandy, 58
Stilling, B., 279, 333
Stoll, 222
straitjackets, 91, 134, 142, 220
Strasbourg, 174
strikes, 65, 248
Struensee, J. F. von, 223
Struve, G. von, 266
Sturm und Drang, 175–80, 188
Stürmer, von, 341
Sudhoff, K., 317
suggestion, 111
suicide, 30, 145–6, 147
Sullivan, H. S., 3
Sulzer, J. G., 188, 189
Sutton, T., 312
Swedenborg, E., 316
Swieten, G. van, 171
Swift, Jonathan, 24, 32, 305
    Gulliver's Travels, 23, 32
    A Serious and Useful Scheme to Make a Hospital for Incurables, 33
    A Tale of a Tub, 33
Switzerland, 174
Sydenham, Thomas, 26–7, 305
syphilis, 156

Tapiau asylum, 249
Tellenbach, H., 8, 295, 296, 345
Temkin, O., 259, 314, 318, 339
Tenon, J., 118
Tetschen-Bodenbach, 272
Thackrah, Charles T., 87, 312
therapeutic idealism, 218, 329
therapy, 50
    English, 74–9, 80
    French, 106, 108, 135–8, 152–3

German, 187, 191, 200, 204–6, 213, 214, 216–17, 251, 286–9
milieu, 159, 274
nature, 80, 108, 136
water, 60, 109
work, 80, 91, 108, 135, 160, 206
see also moral management; music therapy; restraint; traitement moral; travel
Thiele, R., 342
Thiele, W., 329
Thirty Years War, 15
Thompson, C., 3
Thomson, James, 58
Thouret, 122, 123
Tieck, Johann Ludwig, 197
Tissot, Simon-André, 316
    Traité des nerfs et de leurs maladies, 108
Tocqueville, A. de, 117
torture, 204, 205, 213, 216, 329, 330
trade unions, 65
traitement moral, 127–38, 204, 221
travel, as therapy, 27, 61, 181, 219
Treaty of Basel, 193
Trélat, U., 140, 159
Trotter, Thomas, 73
Troxler, J. P. V., 224
Tuke, Samuel, 64, 299
    Description of the Retreat, 78, 260, 290
Tuke, William, 77, 117
Turgot, Anne Robert Jacques, 100, 115, 120, 122, 123

United States, 3, 144, 276, 299
Universal Prussian Land Law, 207, 209
universities, 267, 273–4
unreason, see insanity
Unzer, J. A., 175, 176, 279
Unzer, Johanne Charlotte, 176, 179

Vaterländische Blätter, 222
Vere, James, 60, 308
Vienna, 110, 171, 174
    Mad Tower, 172, 223, 323
Vincent de Paul, 317
Vincke, G. V., 248
Vincke, L. von, 212
Virchow, Rudolf, 266, 267, 269, 271, 340–1

visibility, of insanity
    Belgium, 334
    England, 20–5, 37, 38, 51, 58, 64, 69, 70–1, 95, 308
    France, 99, 113–14, 116, 140
    Germany, 164, 165, 192; 19th C, 207, 211, 219, 267, 274, 284, 290, 335
vitalism, 100–4, 114, 123, 127, 175
Voegele, G. E., 342
Vogt, C., 259
Voisin, F., 157, 158, 322
Volk, 178, 194, 195
Voltaire, François Marie Arouet de, 255, 316

Wagnitz, H. B., 117, 170, 171, 201, 323
Waldheim, 220, 324
Walker, S., 73
Walpole, Robert, 22
wars of liberation, 198, 236
Wartburg Festival, 243
Washington, George, 110
watering places, 60, 107–8
Weber, Max, 3
Wehler, H. H., 302, 324, 335
Weikard, M. A.
    The Philosophical Physician, 176
Weinhold, C. A., 248, 335
Weizsäcker, V. von, 331
Wentzke, P., 339
Wernicke, K., 270
Wesendonck, O., 274
Wesley, John, 38, 61
    The Desideratum: or, Electricity Made Plain and Useful.., 38, 306
Westphal, J. C., 274
Wettley, A., 42, 119, 314, 320, 330
    Geschichte der abendländischen Psychopathologie, 296
    Der Wahnsinn, 302
Whytt, Robert, 48, 55–7, 100, 279, 308, 314
Wilbrand, J. B., 235
will, 72, 74, 75, 112, 158, 231
Willis, Francais, 73, 74–5, 129, 310
Willis, Thomas, 24–5, 42, 304
Windischmann, K. J. H., 212, 235
Winkelmann, J. J., 131
Winnenthal asylum, 273
Winslow, Forbes B., 87

Winzenried, F. J. M., 332
Wolf, F. A., 198
Wolfart, K. C., 235
Wolff, Kurt H., 9, 302
women, 26−7, 32, 37, 238, 284
Wordsworth, William, 68
workhouses, 15, 20, 167, 209
Wunderlich, K. A., 273
Württemberg, 221
    Winnenthal asylum, 257
Wyrsch, J., 8, 262, 276, 294−5
    Zur Geschichte und Deutung der endogenen Psychosen, 119, 340, 342, 345

York asylum, 47, 82, 83
York Society of Friends, 77
Young, Edward
    Conjectures on Original Composition, 57
'Young Germany', 247

Zeller, E. A., 257, 273, 281
Zilboorg, G., 276, 297−8, 346
Zinn, August, 271
Zollverein, 246
Zückert, J. E., 176, 324
Zwiefalten Monastery, 221